Yoga, the Body, and Embodied Social Change

Yoga, the Body, and Embodied Social Change

An Intersectional Feminist Analysis

Edited by Beth Berila, Melanie Klein, and Chelsea Jackson Roberts

LEXINGTON BOOKS
Lanham • Boulder • New York • London

Published by Lexington Books
An imprint of The Rowman & Littlefield Publishing Group, Inc.
4501 Forbes Boulevard, Suite 200, Lanham, Maryland 20706
www.rowman.com

Unit A, Whitacre Mews, 26-34 Stannary Street, London SE11 4AB

British Library Cataloguing in Publication Information Available

Library of Congress Cataloging-in-Publication Data Available

ISBN 978-1-4985-2802-3 (cloth : alk. paper)
ISBN 978-1-4985-2803-0 (electronic)

∞™ The paper used in this publication meets the minimum requirements of American National Standard for Information Sciences Permanence of Paper for Printed Library Materials, ANSI/NISO Z39.48-1992.

Printed in the United States of America

Contents

Acknowledgments

We'd like to thank all of our contributors for sharing their research, expertise, and experience. We're grateful to all of you for your wise words and fierce commitment to raising consciousness and creating social change.

We want to acknowledge all of our teachers, mentors, students, and allies for their inspiration, support, and camaraderie over the years. We are grateful for the wisdom you've shared with us as well as the invaluable lessons, opportunities for growth, and community you've provided.

Finally, we want to express our deep love and appreciation to our family and friends that sustain us as we do this work. Your love and care sustain us.

Introduction

What's the Link Between Feminism and Yoga?

Beth Berila

Yoga in the West is now a $27 billion dollar industry.[1] Studios litter street corners like Starbucks franchises and are often as commercial. Yoga is used to sell everything from cars to clothing to food. The prevalence of yoga throughout Western culture makes it a hotbed of contradictions that reveal a great deal about power dynamics and body politics in contemporary U.S. culture. A look at who is included and who is excluded in this picture of yoga indicates that yoga has become a prime vehicle for the broader racial, gender, cultural, economic, and sexual politics that manifest throughout U.S. society and Western society more broadly. The rising popularity of yoga and mindfulness has turned both into silver bullets that are invoked to solve a variety of social ills, all the while often reinscribing them. However, yoga as a practice also holds deep potential for radical individual and collective transformation.

This anthology brings a feminist intersectional analysis to bear on an analysis of those contradictions, offering deep insights into cultural location and community relations. *Yoga, the Body, and Embodied Social Change: An Intersectional Feminist Analysis* is the first academic book of its kind to collect the growing area of feminist scholarship on yoga, body politics, mindfulness, and social change. While much academic work has been done on feminist theory and the body, and a growing body of work is being done on yoga and social justice, no academic collection has yet brought together these fields to specifically examine what yoga has to offer embodied feminist social change. These issues are increasingly saturating the broader public sphere, as several organizations are utilizing yogic principles for social transformations (including the Yoga and Body Image Coalition. All three editors are affiliated with the latter organization, as are many of the book's contributors). The recently published anthology *Yoga and Body Image: 25 Personal Stories about Beauty, Bravery, and Body Image* and a previous collection, *21st Century Yoga: Culture, Politics, and Practice,* helped catalyze discussions about the exclusionary nature of many yoga spaces but also the empowering nature of yoga as a practice.[2] Fortunately, these efforts are beginning to make their way into academic scholarship.

This collection brings together interdisciplinary feminist scholars to consider contemporary manifestations of yoga in the United States as well as the liberatory potential yoga as a practice can offer marginalized groups. The authors challenge many of the prominent myths of yoga, including the reduction of yoga to physical weight loss and exercise rather than as a spiritual practice of self and community empowerment. They also challenge other myths around yoga, such as the dominant media perception that only thin, bendy, "pretty" people can do yoga. As our authors point out, the "face" of yoga has become a white, hyperflexible, able-bodied, upper class, heterosexual, thin, and traditionally beautiful cisgender woman, which makes many Western yoga spaces deeply exclusionary. Anyone who does not fit the stereotype of a thin, white, able-bodied, hyperflexible, middle- to upper-class, heternormative, cisgender woman becomes "Othered," both through erasure from media representation but also through exclusionary practices in yoga studios. Growing conversations on social media point to the ways that many yoga teachers teach to that stereotypical body, leading practices that are inaccessible to many people who do not fit that image and to many people living with dis/abilities. Gendered language, such as saying that "men's bodies are x" while "women's bodies are y" exclude anyone who does not adhere to heteronormative and cisgender binaries. In addition, yoga classes and trainings are often cost-prohibitive, while the culture of expensive yoga clothing often turns a yoga studio into a class-based fashion show. Moreover the South Asian, Indigenous, and African roots of yoga are too often erased and/or appropriated.[3] Western yoga, then, has become a site through which we can see contemporary manifestations of age-old systems of oppression. Many of the articles in this collection trace the insights gained from looking at how they play out in the phenomena of yoga as it has been taken up in the West.

Recent conversations about the lack of diversity in mainstream yoga has exploded the blogosphere, led by groups such as South Asian American Perspectives on Yoga in America (SAAPYA), the Yoga and Body Image Coalition, the Yoga Service Council, and the Accessible Yoga and the Race and Yoga conferences. Yoga teacher trainings that focus on making yoga accessible to different marginalized communities have abounded in recent years, including Yoga for All, Curvy Yoga, Yoga for Round Bodies, Accessible Yoga, and Mind Body Solutions (which works with communities living with dis/abilities), while other trainings have enhanced their social justice component. Organizations such as Red Clay Yoga, the Holistic Life Foundation, Off the Mat, Into the World, Third Root Community Health Center, The People's Yoga, Spiritual Essence Yoga, Green Tree Yoga and Meditation, EBYoga, and Afro Flow Yoga, among many others, strive to challenge dominant power dynamics in the mainstream Western yoga world in order to make yoga both accessible and empowering for marginalized groups. The trend at the writing of this book appears to be a public outcry to address how systems of oppression such as racism, classism, heterosexism, homophobia and transphobia, ableism, sexism, size discrimination, and other systems of oppression show up in yoga spaces.

However, as often happens when the status quo is challenged, a backlash has also emerged. Case in point: in 2015, controversy erupted when a Seattle yoga studio offering a class for people of color received threats and public backlash from whites in the community who were offended at the respectful request in the class' promotional blurb that white students not attend the class.[4] Despite the fact that the class had been offered for the previous five years and fact that no one was actually turned away from the class, the backlash forced a temporary cancellation of the class; when the class resumed, it did so with a police presence to protect the students. This incident highlights the very need to have such a class in the first place. Classes such as curvy yoga, LGBTQ+ yoga, or yoga for people of color exist in an effort to create safer spaces for marginalized groups. Often those communities do not feel welcome in other yoga classes, because systems of oppression do not stop at the door of the studio. In fact, as many of the essays in this collection discuss, mainstream yoga in the West is often infused with discrimination, becoming yet another tool for oppression. It can be difficult if not impossible to do deep self-study and reach some level of liberation through a yoga practice when the practice itself has been inscribed with oppression.

In the face of what some have called the yoga industrial complex, many yogis have reasserted the spiritual roots of yoga, calling out the Western emphasis on *asana*. While many yoga classes exclusively feature challenging, bendy, physical postures or promote yoga as a way to lose weight, this other dimension of yoga strives to ground the practice in its spiritual and cultural roots. The latter style of yoga invokes meditation, pranayama, philosophical classics, and a spiritual self-study that can lead to both internal and external transformation. This direction often tries to resist the commodification and Westernization of yoga, but it can also lead to a competition around authenticity. Since many practitioners of yoga in the West—particularly the ones who have become the "face" of yoga in mainstream media—are white people, cultural appropriation is rampant. Statues of Ganesh and Lord Shiva decorate studios alongside decorative pillows from Ikea, while white yoga teachers drop Sanskrit words (sometimes mispronounced) and wear mala beads like fashion. On the one hand, the attempt to maintain yoga's roots in its tradition is an important counter to the earlier trend to turn it into a Western fitness craze. However, too often the two strands merge, until the markers of South Asian Indigenous or African tradition become commodified and appropriated by white yogis. When one looks around a yoga studio and sees few people of color, we have to critically interrogate the line between honoring yoga's roots and appropriating them.

However, yoga, in its truest form, offers a deeply empowering practice of self-awareness, self-care, resilience, and unlearning oppression. It can enable a process of liberation, both on the individual and collective levels. It can inform social justice efforts in empowering ways. In the words of the great feminist poet, activist, and cancer survivor Audre Lorde, "Caring for myself is not an act of self-indulgence. It is self-preservation, and that is an act of political warfare."[5] Many yoga practitioners are exploring how yoga can both empower marginalized groups and offer critical tools for the dismantling of oppression. The essays in this collection explore some of those ways, offering insights into why the practice of yoga can be integral to creating a more socially just world. Yoga itself can create *embodied empowerment*, making it a potentially invaluable tool for feminist liberation. For that potential to be achieved, however, we need to better understand the feminist analysis of contemporary body politics that provide the foundation for this book.

FEMINISM AND THE BODY

Feminist theorists have long featured the body in their study of sociopolitical analysis.[6] The body, we have argued, is a critical site for both the inscription and the resistance of sociopolitical power dynamics. While much feminist theory has featured discussion of the body, it has nevertheless often privileged discourse over material embodiment. Much feminist theory remains highly cerebral when talking about the body rather than leaning toward more corporeal experiences. As such, it has sometimes reinforced the Cartesian Mind/Body split even while challenging the patriarchal roots of privileging that Eurocentric model over other forms of knowledges. While this theory offers useful insight, it is important to also turn to the feminist insights offered by community-based work, which tends less toward the highly cerebral, and to the work of many feminists of color who have challenged the elitism inherent in what counts as theory.[7] Much of this work, both inside and outside the academy, creates an important blend of embodied social change that, directly or indirectly, can be seen in some of the exciting contemporary yoga and social change initiatives.

Issues such as body image, sexual assault, the racialization of different bodies, constructions of health and disability, and heternormative and gender queer performance have informed feminist theory about the body over the past decade. Bodies become markers of power dynamics, as some bodies are situated differently within power hierarchies and become targets for violence and oppression. Women of color, queer folks, people living with dis/abilities, people with larger bodies, and working class communities have all been marginalized in power dynamics, which is why we bring an intersectional feminist analysis to this project: different bodies are inscribed with oppression in different ways.

The term intersectionality was first officially "coined" by Kimberlé Crenshaw, though it has deep roots in several previous iterations, all of which help us see how race, class, gender, sexuality, ability, and nation work together to create myriad combinations of identities that position us in complex power dynamics with one another.[8] Women of color activists, from Sojourner Truth to Ida B. Wells to the Combahee River Collective to the writers in the groundbreaking book *This Bridge Called My Back*, to bell hooks to Daisy Hernandez have long spoken to how critical it is to understand gender in its relations to other axes of identity, including race, class, sexuality, dis/ability, and national location.[9] Much of this analysis comes out of both their lived experiences and their extensive community organizing. Rather than assuming monolithic groups (e.g., women are this, men are that), intersectionality helps us nuance our understanding to see that, for instance, a working class transgender woman of color will have a different experience of oppression than will a heterosexual, cisgender white man living with a dis/ability. The essays in this collection bring an intersectional lens to our understanding of yoga, body politics, and feminist embodied liberation, which is important when we start to look at the role of contemporary U.S. yoga as both sites of oppression and social change. Indeed, as feminist scholars Patricia Hill Collins and bell hooks note when they talk of the matrix of domination, institutions—or in this case, yoga—can be both sites of oppression and venues for social change.[10] Many of the essays in this book speak to this tension, offering both a critique of yoga and inspiring examples of how it becomes a vehicle for both individual and collective embodied social transformation.

One of the insights all these multiracial and queer feminists offer is that in order to shift the dominant oppressive paradigm, the voices of those on the margin need to provide the lens—either by centering them or by disrupting the entire center/margin paradigm. Indeed, as hooks has noted, there can be much resistance from the margins.[11] The kind of oppositional consciousness, or "post-oppositional consciousness," as AnaLouise Keating prefers, that can occur when dominant voices are decentered and marginalized perspectives are featured offers us a critical literacy into how power works and strategies for how to respond rather than react.[12] This book intentionally features several voices and analyses that are too often missing from the mainstream yoga "platform" (whether it is the yoga media or the "stars" of yoga) in order to offer greater critical literacy (a point discussed further in part I). We have sought to feature much of the work of social justice being done "on the ground," in communities around the country and the world that are often excluded from that picture. While that is slowly changing at the writing of this book, we hope that the analyses included in this collection will spark ongoing dialogue and help fuel that hopeful trend.

Messages about the body saturate U.S. culture, sending clear messages about whose bodies are valued and devalued. Many of us internalize these messages to such an extent that we start policing our own bodies, creating docile bodies that conform to ideologies about thinness, beauty, and worth.[13] Not only is gender socially constructed, but, as feminist queer scholar Judith Butler noted, gender is constructed through our performance of it; it does not exist prior to our enactment of it.[14] Moreover, both race and class are inscribed on and through our bodies, often in deeply violent ways.[15] Macro and microaggressions impact both marginalized individuals and communities, while also insinuating themselves into the very self-definitions of marginalized groups. E. J. R David's recent work delves deeply into how the historical traumas of oppression inscribe themselves onto the psyches of marginalized groups over generations, something many other feminists of color have long noted.[16] Feminist theorists highlight how power is inscribed on and through our bodies, leaving deep traumas that need to be healed if we are to cultivate healthy, whole, and just worlds. Feminists such as M. Jacqui Alexander, Gloria Anzaldúa, Linda Hogan, Becky Thompson, and Paula Giddings, among others, examine the ways historical traumas have impacted the body and woven themselves into the tapestry of marginalized communities; they also speak to rituals, traditions, and liberatory practices that can help heal and empower communities.[17]

The merger of yoga and feminism, then, invites a turn toward not only the corporeal, but also toward embodied empowerment. Yoga is a critical site for embodiment, as it invites participants sink into their felt sense and reflect upon emotional and physical sensations as well as cognitive ones. It also underscores the realization that feminists, yogis, and body practitioners have known, which is that we hold memory, wisdom, and trauma in our bodies.[18] Since oppression creates deep trauma, it only makes sense that disrupting oppression and healing from it will require more than political and intellectual processes; it will also require embodied ones. At the time of this writing, there seems to be more public awareness of the impact of trauma on our society, informed partly by the important work of Bessel van der Kolk and the Trauma Center at JRI in Boston. It is also important to recognize that many feminists, queer, and critical race scholars and community activists have been addressing trauma and working to heal it in marginalized communities for decades.[19] Like the recent trend in scientific research on the impact of meditation on the brain, we can value and learn from that work but we also need to deeply critique the sudden "credibility" given to ancient traditions or to feminist work once Eurocentric and patriarchal science steps in. While we can learn deeply from the important and valuable scientific work being done, feminists have long been skeptical of the ways that science has historically been used to discredit traditional ways of knowing. As feminist transnational scholar Chandra Talpade Mohanty notes, we need to decenter the white, Eurocentric gaze.[20]

Scholar Michael Yellowbird argues for a "neurodecolonization" and mindfulness, challenging much of the contemporary mindfulness movement in the West to recognize how it perpetuates colonization and instead bringing an indigenous framework to a decolonizing healing process.[21] Moreover, some of the scientific work—though, of course, not all—does not effectively address the roles of oppression in creating this trauma. If we are to truly create embodied social change, we need to understand the role of oppression in creating that trauma for marginalized groups and privilege for dominant groups, and the complexity for those of us whose identity straddle both groups.

Much feminist work in trauma, oppression, and embodied healing points out that bodies are not just sites of oppression, they are also places of knowing, insight, individual empowerment, and social change. People can and do enact resistance through their bodies. These feminists recognize that we cannot create justice by ignoring or trying to transcend our lived experience (in fact, the call to do so is often a privileged one) but by understanding it. As Buddhist writer Zenju Earthlyn Manuel notes, "To acknowledge our pain is to recognize the complexity of our bodies as both the place in which we forge the meaning for our lives, and the location within which we catalyze liberation."[22] Yoga is a prime medium for such embodied resistance because as a tradition, it is a practice for individual and collective liberation.[23] Yoga practices can be key to exploring body knowledge and to a deep, holistic healing.[24] Many yoga practitioners have long recognized the importance of that integration. As feminist Eve Ensler so eloquently says, "You can't dominate a people without separating them from each other and from themselves. The more people get plugged back into their bodies, the more impossible [it] will be for us to be dominated and occupied."[25] The essays in this collection, particularly those in the final section of the book, offer examples of how yoga, when grounded in social justice visions, enable embodied empowerment.

The Parts of This Book

Yoga, the Body, and Embodied Social Change, then, brings together top scholars in the field to explore the connections between yoga, mindfulness, body politics, and embodied social change. The collection is divided into three prominent themes: Inclusion/Exclusion in Yoga Spaces; the Intersection of Yoga, Body Image, and Standards of Beauty; and Yoga as Individual and Collective Liberation. Each section includes interdisciplinary analyses from intersectional feminist perspectives. We have ensured that a diversity of voices are represented by authors and by the subject matter of their articles. *Yoga, the Body, and Embodied Social Change* therefore makes a critical intervention in the field of feminist body politics and social change because it foregrounds yoga as an embodied medium of personal and collective transformation. We hope this book will be one of many to shape these conversations.

The first part of this anthology focuses on issues that make yoga spaces inclusive or exclusionary, including challenging white supremacy and the racialization of bodies and the economic inaccessibility of many yoga classes. This section explores issues of cultural appropriation and ownership that undergird part of the recent controversies around Bikram yoga. The articles address how spaces are often racially exclusionary, outlining what needs to happen in order for yoga spaces to be welcoming and empowering for black women's bodies and queer bodies. This section examines neoliberal constructions of health and the tensions surrounding the integration of yoga in educational systems.

Part II critically examines the stereotypical "yoga body" that saturates the media, looking at advertising that sexualizes women and reproduces the hyperthinness that is so pervasive in the rest of mainstream pop culture. These articles examine rhetoric of weight loss and body vigilance as well as the sexualization of the body through the phenomena of naked yoga. It offers a vision of fat pedagogy that makes yoga classes more welcoming for curvy people who are so often marginalized in the hyperthinness that saturates the Western yoga world. This section also looks at how the blogosphere has opened spaces for marginalized voices to construct and reclaim their own version of wellness.

Finally, the last part looks at how yoga can be a tool for empowering social change. The articles in this section examine whether or how yoga can be feminist and how it can be integrated into various communities to help heal the trauma of oppression. Other articles challenge the cultural appropriation that so often undermines this liberatory potential. Ultimately, this section—and the anthology as a whole—offers possibilities of empowerment through a yoga that is informed by social justice.

NOTES

Special thanks to Becky Thompson for her insightful commentary on this introduction. Your caring insights have greatly strengthened it, and I am honored to be in community doing this work with you.

1. Carolyn Gregoire, "How Yoga Became a $27 Billion Industry—And Reinvented American Spirituality," *Huffington Post*, December 16, 2013, Accessed November 11, 2015. http://www.huffingtonpost.com/2013/12/16/how-the-yoga-industry-los_n_4441767.html.

2. Melanie Klein and Anna Guest-Jelley, eds., *Yoga and Body Image: 25 Personal Stories about Beauty, Bravery, and Loving Your Body* (Woodbury, MN: Llewellyn Publications, 2014); Carol A. Horton and Roseanne Harvey, eds., *21st Century Yoga: Culture, Politics, and Practice* (IL: Kleio Books, 2012).

3. "What Is Kemetic Yoga?" Accessed June 6, 2016. http://kemeticyoga.com/what-is-kemetic-yoga/; Carol A. Horton, *Yoga Ph.D.: Integrating the Life of the Mind and the Wisdom of the Body* (IL: Kleio Books, 2012).

4. Reagan Jackson, "Vitriol Against People of Color Yoga Shows Exactly Why It's Necessary," *The Seattle Globalist*, October 15, 2015. Accessed November 10, 2015. http://www.seattleglobalist.com/2015/10/15/vitriol-against-people-of-color-yoga-shows-exactly-why-its-necessary/42573; Yoga Dork, "Yoga's Diversity Backlash: A Conversation on Including Others (Meaning Everyone) and Creating New Norms," *Yoga Dork*. Accessed November 11, 2015. http://yogadork.com/2015/10/21/yogas-diversity-backlash-a-conversation-on-including-others-meaning-everyone-and-creating-new-norms.

5. Audre Lorde, *Burst of Light* (Ithaca, NY: Firebrand Books, 1988).

6. Susan Bordo, *Unbearable Weight: Feminism, Western Culture, and the Body* (Berkley: University of California Press, 1993); Londa Scheibinger, ed., *Feminism and the Body* (Oxford: Oxford University Press, 2000); Elizabeth Grosz, *Volatile Bodies; Toward a Corporeal Feminism* (Indiana University Press, 1994); Dorothy Roberts, *Killing the Black Body: Race, Reproduction, and the Meaning of Liberty* (New York: Vintage, 1998); Janet Price and Magrit Sildrick, eds., *Feminist Theory and the Body: A Reader* (New York: Routledge, 1999); Katie Conboy, Nadia Medina, and Sarah Stanbury, eds., *Writing on the Body: Female Embodiment and Feminist Theory*, 7th ed. (New York: Columbia University Press, 1997).

7. Barbara Christian, "The Race for Theory," *Feminist Studies*, 14, no. 1 (Spring 1988): 67–79.

8. Kimberlé Crenshaw, "Mapping the Margins: Intersectionality, Identity Politics, and Violence Against Women of Color," *Stanford Law Review* 43 (July 1991): 1241–99. Accessed November 10, 2015. http://socialdifference.columbia.edu/files/socialdiff/projects/Article_Mapping_the_Margins_by_Kimblere_Crenshaw.pdf.

9. Sojourner Truth, "Ain't I a Woman? December 1851," Fordham University Modern History Sourcebook. Accessed June 8, 2016, http://legacy.fordham.edu/halsall/mod/sojtruth-woman.asp; Combahee River Collective, "A Black Feminist Statement," in *Feminist Theory Reader: Local and Global Perspectives*, 3rd ed., eds. Carole R. McCann and Seung-Kyung Kim (New York: Routledge, 2013) 116–22; bell hooks, *Feminist Theory: From Margin to Center* (Boston: South End Press, 1984); Cherríe Moraga and Gloria Anzaldúa, eds., *This Bridge Called My Back: Writings By Radical Women of Color* (New York: Kitchen Table/Women of Color Press, 1983); Paula J. Giddings, *When and Where I Enter: The Impact of Black Women on Race and Sex in America* (New York: W. Morrow, 1984); Daisy Hernandez, "Becoming a Black Man," *Colorlines*, January 7, 2008. Accessed June 7, 2016. http://www.colorlines.com/articles/becoming-black-man.

10. Patricia Hill Collins, *Black Feminist Thought: Knowledge, Consciousness, and the Politics of Empowerment*, 2nd ed. (New York: Routledge, 2000); bell hooks, *Outlaw Culture: Resisting Representations* (New York: Routledge, 2006); hooks, *Feminist Theory*, 1984.

11. hooks, *Feminist Theory*, 1984.

12. Chela Sandoval, "U.S. Third World Feminism: The Theory and Method of Oppositional Consciousness in the Postmodern World," *Genders* 10 (Spring 1991): 1–24; Chandra Talpade Mohanty, *Feminism Without Borders: Decolonizing Theory, Practicing Solidarity*, 5th ed. (NC: Duke University Press, 2003); AnaLouise Keating, *Transformation Now! Toward a Post-Oppositional Politics of Change* (University of Illinois Press, 2013).

13. Sandra Lee Bartky, "Foucault, Femininity, and the Modernization of Patriarchal Power," in *The Politics of Women's Bodies: Sexuality, Appearance, and Behavior*, 3rd ed., ed. Rose Weitz (New York: Oxford University Press, 2010) 76–98.

14. Judith Butler, *Gender Trouble: Feminism and the Subversion of Identity* (New York: Routledge, 1990).

15. Dorothy Roberts, *Killing the Black Body*, 1998; Jael Silliman and Anannya Bhattacharjee, *Policing the National Body: Race, Gender, and Criminalization* (Boston: South End

Press, 2002); Michelle Alexander, *The New Jim Crow: Mass Incarceration in the Age of Colorblindness*, revised edition (New York: The New Press, 2012).
  16. E. J. R. David, ed., *Internalized Oppression: The Psychology of Marginalized Groups* (New York: Springer Publishing Company, 2014); Audre Lorde, *Sister Outsider: Essays and Speeches* (Berkeley, CA: Crossing Press, 2007); Cherríe Moraga, *Loving in the War Years: lo que nunca pasí por sus labios* (Boston: South End Press, 1985).
  17. M. Jacqui Alexander, *Pedagogies of Crossing: Meditations on Feminism, Sexual Politics, Memory, and the Sacred* (NC: Duke Univerity Press, 2006); M. Jacqui Alexander and Chandra Talpade Mohanty, eds., *Feminist Genealogies, Colonial Legacies, Democratic Futures* (New York: Routledge, 1996); Gloria Anzaldúa, *Borderlands/La Frontera: A New Mestiza*, 4th ed. (CA: Aunt Lute Books, 2012); Linda Hogan, *Power* (NY: W. W. Norton & Company, 1999); Becky Thompson, *A Hunger So Wide and Deep: A Multiracial View of Women's Eating Problems*, 2nd ed. (University of Minnesota Press, 1996); Becky Thompson, *Survivors on the Yoga Mat: Stories for Those Healing From Trauma* (CA: North Atlantic Books, 2014); Paula Giddings, *When and Where I Enter*, 1984.
  18. Bessel van der Kolk, *The Body Keeps Score: Brain, Mind, and the Body in the Healing of Trauma* (New York: Viking, 2014).
  19. Becky Thompson, *Survivors on the Yoga Mat*, 2014; Judith L. Herman, *Trauma and Recovery: The Aftermath of Violence: From Domestic Abuse to Political Terror* (New York: Basic Books, 2015); Cathy Caruth, *Unclaimed Experience: Trauma, Narrative, and History* (Baltimore, MD: John Hopkins University Press, 1996); Shoshona Felman and Dori Laub, *Testimony: Crises of Witnessing in Literature, Psychoanalysis, and History* (New York: Routledge, 1991).
  20. Chandra Talpade Mohanty, *Feminism Without Borders*, 2003.
  21. Michael Yellow Bird. "Healing through Neurodecolonization and Mindfulness," Talk at Portland State University. Accessed on Vimeo June 7, 2016. https://vimeo.com/86995336.
  22. Zenju Earthlyn Manuel, *The Way of Tenderness: Awakening Through Race, Sexuality, and Gender*, Foreword by Dr. Charles Johnson (Boston: Wisdom Publications, 2015) 79.
  23. Roopa Singh, "Yoga and Cultural Appropriation," Yoga and Body Image Coalition podcast, 2015. Accessed November 5, 2015. http://ybicoalition.com/roopasingh/.
  24. Thompson, *Survivors on the Yoga Mat*, 2014.
  25. Eve Ensler, "A Second Wind in Life: Inhabiting the Body After Cancer," *On Being* with Krista Tippet, American Public Radio, March 5, 2015. Accessed June 8, 2015, http://www.onbeing.org/program/eve-ensler-the-body-after-cancer/6050

REFERENCES

Alexander, M. Jacqui. *Pedagogies of Crossing: Meditations on Feminism, Sexual Politics, Memory, and the Sacred* (NC: Duke Univerity Press, 2006).
Alexander, M. Jacqui and Chandra Talpade Mohanty, eds., *Feminist Genealogies, Colonial Legacies, Democratic Futures* (New York: Routledge, 1996).
Alexander, Michelle. *The New Jim Crow: Mass Incarceration in the Age of Colorblindness*, revised edition (New York: The New Press, 2012).
Anzaldúa, Gloria. *Borderlands/La Frontera: A New Mestiza*, 4th ed. (CA: Aunt Lute Books, 2012).
Bartky, Sandra Lee. "Foucault, Femininity, and the Modernization of Patriarchal Power," in *The Politics of Women's Bodies: Sexuality, Appearance, and Behavior*, 3rd ed., ed. Rose Weitz (New York: Oxford University Press, 2010) 76–98.
Berila, Beth. *Integrating Mindfulness into Anti-Oppression Pedagogy: Social Justice in Higher Education* (New York: Routledge, 2015).
Bordo, Susan. *Unbearable Weight: Feminism. Western Culture, and the Body* (Berkley: University of California Press, 1993).

Butler, Judith. *Gender Trouble: Feminism and the Subversion of Identity* (New York: Routledge, 1990).

Caruth, Cathy. *Unclaimed Experience: Trauma, Narrative, and History* (Baltimore, MD: John Hopkins University Press, 1996).

Christian, Barbara. "The Race for Theory." *Feminist Studies* 14, no. 1 (Spring 1988): 67–79.

Collins, Patricia Hill. *Black Feminist Thought: Knowledge, Consciousness, and the Politics of Empowerment*, 2nd ed. (New York: Routledge, 2000).

Combahee River Collective. "A Black Feminist Statement," in *Feminist Theory Reader: Local and Global Perspectives*, 3rd ed., ed. Carole R. McCann and Seung-Kyung Kim, (New York: Routledge, 2013) 116–22.

Conboy, Katie, Nadia Medina, and Sarah Stanbury, eds. *Writing on the Body: Female Embodiment and Feminist Theory*, 7th ed. (New York: Columbia University Press, 1997).

Crenshaw, Kimberlé. "Mapping the Margins: Intersectionality, Identity Politics, and Violence Against Women of Color." *Stanford Law Review* 43 (July 1991): 1241–99. Accessed November 10, 2015. http://socialdifference.columbia.edu/files/socialdiff/projects/Article_Mapping_the_Margins_by_Kimblere_Crenshaw.pdf.

David, E. J. R., ed. *Internalized Oppression: The Psychology of Marginalized Groups* (New York: Springer Publishing Company, 2014).

Ensler, Eve. "A Second Wind in Life: Inhabiting the Body After Cancer." *On Being* with Krista Tippet, American Public Radio, March 5, 2015. Accessed June 8, 2015. http://www.onbeing.org/program/eve-ensler-the-body-after-cancer/6050.

Felman, Shoshana and Dori Laub. *Testimony: Crises of Witnessing in Literature, Psychoanalysis, and History*, (New York: Routledge, 1991).

Giddings, Paula J. *When and Where I Enter: The Impact of Black Women on Race and Sex in America* (New York: W. Morrow, 1984).

Gregoire, Carolyn. "How Yoga Became a $27 Billion Industry—And Reinvented American Spirituality." *Huffington Post*, December 16, 2013. Accessed November 11, 2015. http://www.huffingtonpost.com/2013/12/16/how-the-yoga-industry-los_n_4441767.html.

Grosz, Elizabeth. *Volatile Bodies; Toward a Corporeal Feminism* (Indiana University Press, 1994).

Herman, Judith L. *Trauma and Recovery: The Aftermath of Violence: From Domestic Abuse to Political Terror* (New York: Basic Books, 2015).

Hernandez, Daisy. "Becoming a Black Man." *Colorlines*, January 7, 2008. Accessed June 7, 2016. http://www.colorlines.com/articles/becoming-black-man.

Hogan, Linda. *Power* (New York: W. W. Norton & Company, 1999).

hooks, bell. *Feminist Theory: From Margin to Center* (Boston: South End Press, 1984).

———. *Outlaw Culture: Resisting Representations* (New York: Routledge, 2006).

Horton, Carol A. *Yoga Ph.D.: Integrating the Life of the Mind and the Wisdom of the Body* (IL: Kleio Books, 2012).

Horton, Carol A. and Roseanne Harvey, eds. *21st Century Yoga; Culture, Politics, and Practice* (IL: Kleio Books, 2012).

Jackson, Reagan. "Vitriol Against People of Color Yoga Shows Exactly Why It's Necessary," *The Seattle Globalist*, October 15, 2015. Accessed November 10, 2015. http://www.seattleglobalist.com/2015/10/15/vitriol-against-people-of-color-yoga-shows-exactly-why-its-necessary/42573.

Jones, Leslie Salmon. "Afro Flow Yoga." Accessed June 6, 2016, http://www.afroflowyoga.com.

Keating, AnaLouise. *Transformation Now! Toward a Post-Oppositional Politics of Change* (University of Illinois Press, 2013).

Klein, Melanie and Anna Guest-Jelley, eds. *Yoga and Body Image: 25 Personal Stories about Beauty, Bravery, and Loving Your Body* (Woodbury, MN: Llewellyn Publications, 2014).

Lorde, Audre. *Burst of Light* (Ithaca, NY: Firebrand Books, 1988).

————. *Sister Outsider: Essays and Speeches* (Berkeley, CA: Crossing Press, 2007).
Manuel, Zenju Earthlyn. *The Way of Tenderness: Awakening Through Race, Sexuality, and Gender*. Foreword by Dr. Charles Johnson (Boston: Wisdom Publications, 2015), 79.
Mohanty, Chandra Talpade. *Feminism Without Borders: Decolonizing Theory, Practicing Solidarity*, 5th ed. (NC: Duke University Press, 2003).
Moraga, Cherríe and Gloria Anzaldúa, eds. *This Bridge Called My Back: Writings By Radical Women of Color* (New York: Kitchen Table/Women of Color Press, 1983).
————. *Loving in the War Years: lo que nunca pasí por sus labios* (Boston: South End Press, 1985).
Price, Janet and Magrit Sildrick, eds. *Feminist Theory and the Body: A Reader*. (New York: Routledge, 1999).
Roberts, Dorothy. *Killing the Black Body: Race, Reproduction, and the Meaning of Liberty* (New York: Vintage, 1998).
Sandoval, Chela. "U.S. Third World Feminism: The Theory and Method of Oppositional Consciousness in the Postmodern World." *Genders*, 10 (Spring 1991): 1–24.
Scheibinger, Londa, ed. *Feminism and the Body* (Oxford: Oxford University Press, 2000).
Silliman, Jael and Anannya Bhattacharjee. *Policing the National Body: Race, Gender, and Criminalization* (Boston: South End Press, 2002).
Singh, Roopa. "Yoga and Cultural Appropriation." Yoga and Body Image Coalition Podcast, 2015, Accessed November 5, 2015. http://ybicoalition.com/roopasingh/.
Thompson, Becky. *Survivors on the Yoga Mat: Stories for Those Healing From Trauma* (CA: North Atlantic Books, 2014).
————. *A Hunger So Wide and Deep: A Multiracial View of Women's Eating Problems*, 2nd ed. (University of Minnesota Press, 1996).
Truth, Soujourner. "Ain't I a Woman?" December 1851." Fordham University Modern History Sourcebook. Accessed June 8, 2016. http://legacy.fordham.edu/halsall/mod/sojtruth-woman.asp.
van der Kolk, Bessel. *The Body Keeps Score: Brain, Mind, and the Body in the Healing of Trauma* (New York: Viking, 2014).
"What Is Kemetic Yoga?" Accessed June 6, 2016. http://kemeticyoga.com/what-is-kemetic-yoga/.
Yellow Bird, Michael. "Healing through Neurodecolonization and Mindfulness," Talk at Portland State University. Accessed on vimeo June 7, 2016. https://vimeo.com/86995336
Yoga Dork, "Yoga's Diversity Backlash: A Conversation on Including Others (Meaning Everyone) and Creating New Norms," *Yoga Dork*, Accessed November 11, 2015. http://yogadork.com/2015/10/21/yogas-diversity-backlash-a-conversation-on-including-others-meaning-everyone-and-creating-new-norms/.

Part I

Inclusion/Exclusion in Yoga Spaces

Chelsea Jackson Roberts

One of the foundational hallmarks of systems of oppression is the ability to exclude. Whether through explicit laws like Jane and Jim Crow,[1] or twenty-first-century systemic forms of oppression like *The New Jim Crow*,[2] exclusion has been a way to express and expand power and privilege for some, while the oppressed are forced to the under-resourced margins. Within the context of yoga, exclusion creates realities where liberatory thought and practice are policed, culturally relevant images of what a yogi looks like are rare, and the ability for yoga to move Western culture beyond its shortsighted capitalist machinations is stifled. As bell hooks asserts, "Being oppressed means the absence of choices," and in alignment with this belief, this work illuminates the consequences of exclusionary practices within and across yoga communities.

The essays in this section focus on issues surrounding exclusivity across yoga communities and the responsive counter-narratives that offer examples for the ways in which inclusion can be transformative. In an analytically emotional written epoch, Dr. Marcelle Haddix begins the collection with an autoethnographical journey from coming to practice yoga mostly in white privileged spaces to creating liberatory yoga classes for women of color to experience the fullness of yoga.

Encapsulating the justifiable rage many women of color feel when violently and silently marginalized throughout the yoga industry, Haddix's "In a Field of the Color Purple: Inviting Yoga Spaces for Black Women's Bodies" challenges the assumption of Westernized, capitalist yoga that only white female bodies exist and matter.

Dr. Jillian Ford's essay, "I'm Feelin' It": Embodied Spiritual Activism as a Vehicle for Queer Black Liberation," offers personal narrative that illustrates a journey toward liberation. Guided by a theoretical understanding of womanism and yoga, Ford presents a picture for how mainstream yoga looks in relationship with oppression and how yoga can be used potentially as a tool for individual and collective liberation.

Moving through this section's theme of inclusion and exclusion in yoga spaces, Dr. Enoch Page's strong contribution, "The Gender, Race, and Class Barriers: Enclosing Yoga as White Public Space," furthers the scholarly activism within Western yoga communities. Grounding his work in the post-colonial experience, Page posits whether whiteness can be effectively crippled by an understanding of yoga's ancient history of resistance and progressive practice.

Page's writing is urgent, reflecting the impatience of the masses of colonized people of color and white allies who are actively challenging the imperial, capitalist, white privileged yoga spaces through teaching, creating art, and in this particular space, writing.

Drawing from her lived experiences in a desi-American Hindu-Indian family who practiced yoga, in her exploratory essay "Toward Yoga as Property," Roopa Kaushik-Brown, MA, JD, navigates the intricately violent world of ownership and whiteness that seeks to "absorb, own, and feed" off yoga, threatening to erode its healthy potential for wellness and liberation while impaling it on the mechanized machinations of the "free market."

Buttressing her argument in the well-documented legal proceedings involving Bikram copyright and University of Ottawa cases, respectively, Kaushik-Brown "contends that the continued propertization of yoga brings more destruction than creation to the much-needed systems of yoga that embody methods of healing that can help oppressed peoples heal from the lethal effects of racism, colonization, and appropriation based subjugation."

Kerrie Kauer, PhD, poses an important question, "Yoga, Culture, and Neoliberal Embodiment of Health," that speaks to the contradictions and complexities evident as a theme throughout this section. As a tool, a feminist praxis, yoga has enormous potential to allow us to engage in social justice work that does not reproduce "colonial and paternalist notions of service" by embodied and conscious forms of activism. In this way, this model of activism not only becomes more effective by integrating the body-mind as a whole self but becomes a more sustainable way to agitate for social change.

Analyzing the landmark case *Sedlock v. Encinitas*, Dr. Carol Horton's essay, "Yoga is not Dodgeball," extensively summarizes yoga's legal battle for legitimization within the U.S. public educational system. In this stirring commentary, Horton captures the fervor of educators who are eager to witness the potential of yoga to transform students, teachers, administrators, and communities from neoliberal instrumentalist to holistic practitioners of the art of education.

NOTES

1. Pauli Murray, an outspoken woman who protested discrimination on the basis of race and sex. She coined the term "Jane Crow," which demonstrated Murray's belief that Jim Crow laws also negatively impacted African American women. Murray's speech, "Jim Crow and Jane Crow," delivered in Washington, DC, in 1964, sheds light on the long struggle of African American women for racial equality and their later fight for equality among the sexes. Paula Giddings, "Murray, Paula: Fight Jane Crow," *The Nation*, May 23, 1987. Accessed January 30, 2016. http://zinnedproject.org/materials/pauli-murray-fighting-jane-crow/.

2. Michelle Alexander, *The New Jim Crow: Mass Incarceration in the Age of Colorblindness* (New York: The New Press, 2010).

REFERENCES

Alexander, Michelle. *The New Jim Crow: Mass Incarceration in the Age of Colorblindness* (New York: The New Press, 2010).

Giddings, Paula. "Murray, Paula: Fight Jane Crow," *The Nation*, May 23, 1987 Accessed January 30, 2016. http://zinnedproject.org/materials/pauli-murray-fighting-jane-crow/

ONE

In a Field of the Color Purple

Inviting Yoga Spaces for Black Women's Bodies

Marcelle M. Haddix

In early 2014, there was major social media fallout over an essay published on xojane.com, "It Happened to Me: There Are No Black People in My Yoga Classes and I'm Suddenly Feeling Uncomfortable With It." The author of the essay, self-described as a "skinny white girl," wrote about how she became uncomfortable watching a "young, fairly heavy black woman," a new and unfamiliar student in her regular yoga class, "struggle" in a space that was "unable to accommodate her body." In her experience, this white woman described how the heavy, black body threatened her safe, comfortable zone. In response, many black women bloggers, including me, wrote counter-narratives challenging this white woman's privileged attempt at qualifying the black woman's embodied experience with health and wellness. Her essay served to perpetuate the idea that black people do not practice yoga, and if and when they do, they struggle with it because their bodies are not capable of engaging with the *asanas*. Such a flawed perspective negated the full range of yoga and all of its possibilities. It also neglected the intended inclusivity of a tradition that allows for so many white, middle class men and women to participate.

The xojane.com essay made me pause and reflect on my own embodied connection to yoga as a black woman. Why do I continue to practice in spaces that have been co-opted by Western culture as an activity for wealthy, rich white women? How have I come to find myself in a space that is almost always all white with a limited range of body types? Why do so many black women continue to practice yoga despite not seeing representations of her selves and her bodies? How does this reality redefine the yoga tradition that I've learned and studied? What are ways that black female bodies act as a form of resistance to the Westernization of yoga?

In Alice Walker's *The Color Purple,*[1] the character Shug Avery tells Celie, "I think it pisses God off if you walk by the color purple in a field somewhere and don't notice it." Celie then asks, "What it do when it pissed off?" Shug Avery responds, "Oh, it make something else." For me, this passage metaphorically represents what it means for black women, who are "the color purple," to be the only one in dominant white spaces. When black women are under surveillance and constant watch in yoga spaces because they "stand out," instead of being seen for their strength, beauty, and power, black women create counterspaces that both honor and are inclusive of their ways of being and doing in yoga. In this essay, I explore these questions by offering an autoethnographic account of my own experience coming to the practice of yoga and eventually completing my 200-hour yoga teacher training as the only person of color in my program. I draw on black womanist ways of being and knowing[2] to interrogate the ways that my race, gender, class, and embodiment of those identity markers instigated my acceptance within the space, though often times conditionally, and also created moments of marginalization. I then describe my journey beginning to teach yoga classes in community spaces where the majority of the students are black women. There is a freedom and liberation that emanates from my experiences teaching and practicing yoga with black women and other women of color and a desire to honor and love their bodies as I do my own. Despite the countless instances of being "the only one" in yoga spaces, I explore what it means to be a black female body creating an inviting yoga space for other black bodies and how our predominance informs the yoga culture and practice.

BEING THE ONLY ONE

The concept of "being the only one" is quite familiar territory for me. I can easily tap into childhood memories being the only black girl in my entire eighth-grade class that was all white male students and being the only black girl in advanced academic classes during my tracked high school experience. I easily remember being the only black female student in my English teacher preparation classes at a predominantly white university and then going on to be the only black teacher in an all white school. As I now navigate schooling for my own child, a young black adolescent male, I witness him "being the only one" among a predominantly white peer group, and at parent meetings, I am usually the only black mother in the room. I can go on, but there is no need to belabor the point. We live in a society where whiteness is centered and everything that is non-white exists on the margins and even further, outside the borders.

Mine is a narrative that is all too familiar for many. For some, being the "exception" is an acceptable position. One or two black people are allowed into "the club" because they somehow possess "unique" and "superior" qualities than other members of their racial and cultural community. It is seen as desirable to acquire a seat at the table where other members of your group are not invited. This exceptionalism is a strategy to create intracultural division and to maintain white dominance and centrality. In fact, "being the only one" can create the allusion that somehow the lone person of color is unique, special, and deserving of that seat at the table. This location can also result in heightened invisibility—where one walks past the color purple in a field and does not notice it. My own experience has at times meant that I was unseen and that my presence was of no consequence. At other times, my presence has fulfilled a diversity quota and a false sense of inclusivity.

My beginning experiences practicing yoga happened in white dominated spaces. In my early twenties, I began practicing yoga at the local YMCA. I did not know much about yoga when I began practicing—I came to it with the assumptions that this kind of exercise was necessary to balance my cardio and strength training routines and to maintain flexibility and agility. I signed up for a weekly yoga series, and each week, I entered into a crowded YMCA exercise studio, found a space to lay down my mat, and worked my hardest to look like I knew what I was doing. The instructor, a young white woman, would walk around the room as she instructed, assisting people as they attempted each pose. I remember longing for that assistance and reassurance that I was indeed doing it right. Yoga was different from any other exercise I had engaged with—unlike dance, aerobics, cycling, pilates, this was something new and quite different. As an apprentice to this new exercise, I hoped for more guidance from a teacher who might recognize that I was unlike most of the students in the class. One, I was a novice learner. Two, I was the only black woman in the room. Might it occur to the instructor to consider how one might feel being a racially marked body in the space, especially when this is her first time practicing yoga?

Each week, the room was crowded with hundreds of people, yet despite the number of people, I felt alone as the only one in the space. I was hyper visible and invisible at the same time—on one hand, the instructor ignored me while on the other hand, people in the class stared at me and looked away. In these moments, I viscerally understood what it meant to be under the white gaze[3] and to attempt to participate in a yoga practice that centered whiteness. I did not immediately connect with yoga, mainly because I did not feel like it was a space where I belonged. Also, I carried with me cultural and familial messages, having grown up in a black home with deep Christian values, that somehow yoga was "the devil" and that I was engaging in sacrilegious practices. I did not have anyone in my family or community network, at the time, with whom I could share my appreciation for yoga and I was not readily welcomed into the community that was being fostered at my weekly yoga sessions. This initial orientation to yoga left me with the impression that yoga was an individual practice, a journey that I had to travel on my own, that did not necessitate energy with or connection to others. This feeling was substantiated by the stares I received as I walked into the class and by the ways that other students would actively work to make sure they did not have to place their mat next to mine. But, alas, these racial microagressions were only in my head and in my imagination.

Fast forward decades later, I still encounter the same reactions to my presence in predominantly white yoga spaces. In addition to practicing at private yoga studios, I take a regular yoga class at my local YMCA, a space that should foster a more diverse and inclusive community. The class is certainly diverse by gender, class, age, and ability, but I am still the only black woman in the space. When I walk in the large studio, people stare at me as I move toward my preferred spot in the room — in the front, out of view from the mirrors, in the farthest corner. Yoga has become my place of solace and refuge, and now a more experienced yogi, I have learned to go inward to engage in my practice, blocking out expressions of exclusivity, bias and stereotype, and racism. But, again, why should this be the case? Do the other majority white people in the room encounter these same issues? Where are the spaces that honor and value the presence of black and brown bodies? The absence of women of color in these spaces does not confirm that they are not interested in nor capable of practicing yoga. I find irony in knowing that yoga is a deeply spiritual and cultural tradition rooted in India and in the religious principles of Hinduism, Buddhism, Sikhism, and Jainism and practiced by brown and black people all over the world. The Westernization and commodification of yoga has cultivated a popular trend fueled by individualism, competition, and capitalism, and the dominant image in the United States would have most believe that yoga is only practiced by white, middle-class women. To reconcile with the tensions that I experienced practicing yoga in white-dominated spaces, I decided to study more about the historical and spiritual origins of yoga, and to eventually pursue my own yoga teacher certification so that I could better connect with my practice and develop a teaching pedagogy that would welcome and honor the bodies and spiritual offerings of more people like me in my community.

BECOMING A YOGA TEACHER

This was a personal and political act in many ways. When I decided to pursue my yoga teacher training certification, I wanted to do it for me. That year, I turned in my professional dossier for promotion and tenure review at my university, and I celebrated my fortieth birthday. I had returned to my yoga practice and had been practicing consistently for two years at that point. My yoga practice had literally saved me and helped me to navigate through challenging years as a tenure track professor. I decided to pursue my 200-hour teacher training because I wanted to learn more about yoga and to deepen my practice and my commitment to yoga. It was a deeply personal decision and something that I was doing for me.

However, as I began to share with friends and family that I was in yoga teacher training, I realized quickly the power in that declaration. It disrupted misconceptions and long held beliefs expressed through statements I so often heard or reactions I received that "black people don't practice yoga" and "I ain't never heard of a black yoga teacher." Coupling this with the knowledge I had of the ways that white-dominated yoga spaces are exclusive of black and brown bodies, I trained to become a yoga instructor so that I could create spaces to counteract the dominant image of yoga in the United States. Tired of being the only one, this was an important and necessary counterhegemonic act. If the white-dominated spaces presented a narrative that we do not exist or that we do not belong, I needed to create the other space. But, given my geographic limitations, I did not have many options to pursue this training while at the same time working as a full-time university professor. In fact, there were two local options, and both were private yoga studios that catered to a predominantly white demographic. I made a deliberate choice to enroll in a program where I knew that, yet again, I would be the only one and that the information would be filtered through a white-dominated lens. I took an intentional stance to gather the information I needed to teach yoga and to deflect any energy and experiences that would have me believe that I was not welcome.

From January through May, I spent every other weekend with nineteen fellow yoga students completing our 200-hour training and we were the inaugural cohort for this yoga studio, a studio that was gaining increasing popularity in the white middle-class community. We ranged in age, gender, and experience. Some of us were pursuing this training because we wanted to secure teaching jobs at this yoga studio, while others of us wanted to learn more about yoga and strengthen our own practice. In my journal, I wrote twelve individual goals for my training process, and one specifically detailed my desire to create racially and culturally inclusive yoga spaces:

I want to develop a teaching style that is culturally relevant and community based. This intention is what fuels my desire to become a certified yoga instructor. I want to be able to bring more yoga to communities of color, and more specifically, I want to offer classes for Black women and girls in my local community. Deep down, I was hoping that I would walk into YTT this morning and meet at least one other person of color. But, not surprisingly, I am the only person of color in this training program just as I am often the only person of color in yoga classes I take. This has to change, but it changes with creating yoga spaces where people of color feel invited and welcomed. (Journal entry, 1/7/14)

That was my primary reason for enduring yet another experience where I would be the only one, and where I would grapple regularly with what it meant to learn about yoga principles from, with, and through the white gaze.

On the first day of yoga teacher training (YTT), our group of twenty students and one primary instructor settled in to establish a space where each person would be able to be open to this process of evolution and with the necessary process of erosion. We began with the first yama, "ahimsa," to be nonharming and nonviolent, and we discussed how we might practice *ahimsa* in this process of becoming. The instructor invited us to ask ourselves regularly, "what is the loving thing to do?" She went further to ask us to reflect on who we are without the labels; who are the people we love; and who are the people we call our friends. I remain curious about the connections between ahimsa and her questions that proceeded because in my experience as a black woman in this black body, acts of violence and harm that I have endured, from others and from within, are both racialized and gendered. Further, the people and the places where I seek love and safety are with other people of color, and mostly women of color. In that moment, as we were being asked to build a class community, it was painfully clear to me that I was in a space while though familiar was unlike my places of love, and I was being asked to trust that this might become a space where I would not experience harm or violence and instead love among people that I might call friends.

Over the next several weeks, there were several moments when I experienced openings for genuine interactions with the other students. But, this required me to trust in the possibility of establishing nonviolent and nonharming relationships across race and gender. In my yoga journal, I reflected on one instance where I felt this opening:

> Yesterday in my yoga teacher training, we did an activity that was all about building trust and depending on others. In this activity, I stood in the middle of my group with my feet together, arms crossed, and my eyes closed. I was instructed to fall back and allow myself to be passed between my four group members. As I fell back and leaned from side to side, my group members were responsible for catching me and mak-

ing sure that I did not fall. I knew from the beginning that I was going to have difficulty with this activity—you're asking me to close my eyes, fall back, and trust that these folks won't drop me? Oh hell no! is what I was really thinking. Now, I am the person that you want on the outside of the circle—I will not let anybody fall. But, trusting that others will do the same for me has been my challenge. As I began being passed between my group members, I was quite stiff and nervous. I could not relax and let go. At one point, one of my group members paused the passing, held me, and said, "Relax. We got you." And, in that moment, I did just that—I relaxed and trusted that my group had my back, literally. My group members said that my body began to feel much lighter, and I was passed between them with ease and speed. After the activity, I had to work to hold back my tears. I was struck by how someone's simple affirmation of "I got your back" calmed and relaxed me. And, I was also overcome by my willingness to trust that they would. (Journal entry, 1/27/14)

The one group member who told me to "relax. We got you" was a middle-aged white man. Outside of this myth of ahimsa that we were cultivating during our time together in YTT, this was and remains an unimagined possibility. Under the guise of the co-opted principles of yoga, if one is practicing yoga, one should be loving toward others. In the studio during yoga teacher training, this is permissible. However, this is not required in the grocery store, at the local restaurant, or the public library, where being a black woman often renders me invisible and invaluable within the white public sphere.

I was the exception in this space—the one black person who was also paying tuition to complete my 200-hour YTT. Being a certified yoga instructor did not magically change the way that I would be treated when practicing yoga in white-dominated yoga spaces. I still experience other students working feverishly to place their mats as far away from me as possible. I am rarely asked by instructors whether I would like an assist when working through my *asanas*. I am left alone. These experiences only strengthen my resolve to both find and create spaces where bodies of color feel included, welcomed, desired, and affirmed. I long for the moments when I can walk into a yoga class, be seen, and embraced. I remain in search of black yogis like me.

BLACK YOGIS LIKE ME

In early 2014, a video went viral on the internet of Lakeisha Shurn, a black woman in California who took a challenge to videotape her workouts for one hundred days straight. At the time of the video, she weighed in at over three hundred pounds. She shared how, because of her weight and body image, she felt discouraged and depressed throughout her life. At the start of the video, I could sense her feelings of defeat and even despair. But by the end of the two minutes and fifty-nine seconds, I was rejoicing with her. Her attitude and energy just came alive. Over the course of one hundred days, she lost eighteen more pounds and made it out of the "300 club," as she put it. While I would never meet Lakeisha, I wanted to embrace her and let her know that she had my support to keep going. I also wanted to let her know that her story inspired and encouraged me and all of the other millions of people who had watched this video.

Lakeisha's video also represents one example of the ways that black women are presenting counterimages of black women's bodies via social media, digital spaces, and other public platforms. In her blog post "Yoga and the Exclusion of People of Color," Rochelle Robinson observed,

> when I initiated my own Google image search, I found it difficult to spot yoga images (of women) that weren't non-ethnic (I don't consider white an ethnicity). Image after image consisted of white women and men occupying yoga spaces. There were very few images of people of color, and when shown, they were singular images, as with the majority of images displayed, and even fewer images of yogis from India.[4]

I, too, was in search of such images, and more specifically, of examples that pushed back against and resisted dominant narratives that exclude black women's bodies in yoga and in yoga teaching. I sought mirrored representations of myself on blogs and websites and on black yogi Instagram accounts. I subscribed to websites like Decolonizing Yoga, and I joined the Black Yoga Alliance Facebook group. Huffington Post Black Voices associate editor Taryn Finley posted "13 Inspirational Instagram Accounts That Prove Black Yogis Rule" arguing that "though underrepresented, black people practice yoga too."[5]

In response to the essay "It Happened to Me: There Are No Black People in My Yoga Classes and I'm Suddenly Feeling Uncomfortable With It," I wrote on my blog,

> I am always the only Black woman in my yoga classes. *Is this because Black women don't practice yoga?* No. *Is this because Black women struggle with yoga?* No. *Is this because heavy Black women are not comfortable with their bodies in the presence of "skinny white bodies"?* No. Let me offer another perspective, Ms. "Jen Caron." After reading this essay, I reflected on the number of times I have gone into a studio and other students coincidentally avoid placing their yoga mats next to mine. I thought about times when the instructor does not acknowledge my presence, nod or say "hello," or even make eye contact with me. I remembered all the times that I have wanted to stay in child's pose because this is my practice and that is what my body needed in that moment. And, if in that moment we had been in the same yoga class, *would I too have been a threat to you?*
>
> So, why do I continue to go to yoga classes, "shamelessly co-opted by Western culture as a sport for skinny, rich white women" as Ms.

Caron writes, where I am the "only one" (which is not unlike other experiences in my everyday life)? Why do so many women of color continue to practice yoga despite narratives like the one Ms. Caron confesses? Because, as Sweet Brown would say, *ain't nobody got time for that*. Ain't nobody got time to worry about your prejudice, your guilt, or your fear when it comes to taking care of her own body and health. When I practice yoga, I carve out my own space and focus on my flow. Ain't nobody thinking about you. And, health and wellness do not belong to you.

As I complete my yoga teacher training, my friends are like, "girl, when are you going to start teaching your classes? I'm waiting for your class." I have sistafriends who don't feel like being the "only one" in a yoga class taught by the "skinny white girl" who might possess the same attitude as Ms. Caron. And, I don't blame them. For that reason, I am pursuing this training because one, I want to deepen my own practice and two, I want to create yoga spaces where women (and men) of color know that they are welcomed and expected. What is most problematic to me about Ms. Caron's sudden realization is that it is only occurring because of the presence of a Black woman who may have been new to this yoga class. It happens because what is familiar is disrupted by the unfamiliar. Instead, I would want yoga teachers and students to pose these questions and experience this discomfort because these spaces are homogeneous and occupied with people like them. Not when "diversity" appears on the mat behind them. (2/2/14)

I realized that being a black woman yoga instructor meant that I interpreted and understood my training via my own black womanist and feminist lens, and I wanted to connect with other teachers and yogis with similar experiences. In her essay "My Body Is Wildly Undisciplined and I Deny Myself Nearly Everything I Desire," black feminist writer Roxane Gay writes, "I deny myself the right to space when I am public, trying to fold in on myself, to make my body invisible even though it is, in fact, grandly visible. I deny myself the right to a shared armrest because how dare I impose? I deny myself entry into certain spaces I have deemed inappropriate for a body like mine—most spaces inhabited by other people."[6] In her essay "Confessions of a Fat, Black Yoga Teacher," Diane Bondy writes,

> Why is it so shocking that a big person could be a halfway decent yoga teacher? How do we shake up the yoga stereotypes and allow people to see yoga as it really is? We are not all white, able-bodied, super-flexible, thin, heterosexual beings. We are diverse in every way and it's this diversity that makes life interesting.[7]

Black yogis are creating public counterspaces to disrupt the collective witnessing and remembering of being "the only one" in our individual yoga communities. For me, this begins by centering black women's bodies in my yoga practice and teaching.

CENTERING BLACK FEMALENESS IN MY YOGA PRACTICE AND
TEACHING: CREATING A SPACE FOR BLACK WOMEN

I became a yoga teacher because I saw the emotional and physical benefits that I was getting from establishing a regular yoga practice. I felt like
it was a major hypocrisy that the people occupying these spaces were
predominantly white women. With the heightened state of racial violence
toward people of color and the increasing physical and emotional trauma
in communities of color, one could argue our communities would benefit
from yoga the most. My challenge has been to encourage people of color
from my local community to attend my yoga classes despite socially and
historically constructed ideas that this is an activity that they do not
participate in or that these are spaces where they do not belong. To do
this, I was intentional in centering the interests and needs of black wom-
en with a deliberate stance that what is good for black women is good for
all. In essence, this black womanist centering was a form of inclusion.

I began offering yoga classes in community spaces at times for free
and at other times for low fees or on a donation basis. My yoga brand,
"ZenG: Everyday Living Well, Gangsta Style," represents a yoga lifestyle
that is unapologetic and intentional about valuing the soulful and spiritual flavor of communities of color. To invite more women of color to
attend my yoga classes, I relied heavily on my membership in closed
Facebook groups that focused on black women's issues, for example,
affinity groups for black women with natural hair and for black women
who run. I also attended community events and health fairs targeting
communities of color. Largely, I relied on the word of mouth of those
black women who began attending the classes and who invited others to
join our yoga sistercircles. My classes are not solely black women, but
their presence is predominate, and it creates a different kind of experience for those white women and even men who take my classes.

In centering black women's bodies, I am purposeful in thinking about
each aspect of the class—the selection of music, the use of the space, the
flow of *asanas*, the time for breathing, and the passages for meditation.
Each playlist begins with the soulful music of black women like "You Are
Not Alone" by Mavis Staples, "Pack Light" by Erykah Badu, "You Move
Me" by Cassandra Wilson, and Etta James's rendition of "Holding Back
the Years." We center our practice by meditating on the lyrics of songs by
black woman artists that ask us to let go and to release. For sixty minutes,
I ask people in my classes to recognize that while this is their practice,
that we are generating a collective energy to affirm ourselves and one
another. It is my aim to create a space where all bodies feel accepted and
have permission to just be in the moment. This means that my classes are
often filled with laughter, as someone tumbles in and out of a pose, and
with people humming and singing along to the jazz, hip-hop, gospel, and
R&B tunes that make up my yoga playlists. I make sure that I physically

touch and assist each person in the class, in many ways to heal the scars that I still carry from feeling invisible and undesirable in white-dominated yoga spaces. I do not want students in my class to carry that, and I suspect that those are some of the same reasons that many of my students were once deterred from practicing yoga. I end each class by invoking the words of black women writers, poets, and activists to privilege the knowledge production of black women and to establish ancestral connections across generations of women of color. It is essential that we understand that our healing is tied to the healing of our communities.

My goal as a black woman yoga instructor is to bring yoga to more communities of color and to challenge the misrepresentation of people of color and yoga, healthy living, and even healthy eating. While my yoga practice began and remains personal, my identity as a yoga teacher and black woman yogi it also deeply political. It is a health revolution, and my yoga pedagogy and resolve to bring yoga to more communities of color is a counterhegemonic act toward a Westernization of yoga that would have most believe that this is a space for white, middle-class women. As Alice Walker wrote in *The Color Purple:* "If he ever listened to poor colored women the world would be a different place, I can tell you."[8] A black feminist yoga pedagogy benefits all communities.

IN CLOSING: TOWARD A BLACK FEMINIST YOGA PEDAGOGY

I began this chapter with a quote from Alice Walker's novel *The Color Purple*, where the character Shug Avery tells Celie, "I think it pisses God off if you walk by the color purple in a field somewhere and don't notice it." This quote resonates with me because it speaks to the invisibility and hypervisibility of the black female body in predominantly white spaces. For me, it is a statement of resistance against allowing the mainstream population to determine if we exist, if we matter, and if we belong. I continue to practice and teach yoga because the principles of yoga are practiced regularly within communities of color. People of color practice nonviolence, *ahimsa*, within a society where black suffering and racial violence is becoming more normalized. In essence, my role as a black woman yoga instructor is to cultivate the spaces for black people, and black women in particular, to live out full versions of their selves and to honor their bodies in a world that makes that nearly impossible. A black feminist yoga pedagogy assumes that black women's bodies and lives exist, matter, and belong in yoga classes and as yoga teachers. And, when we acknowledge the needs and interests of black women in our yoga spaces, we create spaces inclusive of all.

NOTES

1. Alice Walker, *The Color Purple* (London: Women's Press, 1992) 203.
2. Patricia Hill Collins, *Black Feminist Thought: Knowledge, Consciousness, and the Politics of Empowerment* (Routledge, 2002); bell hooks, *Sisters of the Yam: Black Women and Self-Recovery* (Boston: South End Press, 1993); Audre Lorde, *Sister Outsider: Essays and speeches* (Crossing Press, 2012).
3. Toni Morrison, *Playing in the Dark* (New York: Vintage, 2007).
4. Rochelle Robinson, "Yoga and the Exclusion of People of Color," *Decolonizing Yoga*, http://www.decolonizingyoga.com/yoga-and-the-exclusion-of-people-of-color/.
5. Taryn Finley, "13 Inspirational Instagram Accounts That Prove Black Yogis Rule," http://www.huffingtonpost.com/entry/13-kickass-black-yogis-on-instagram.
6. Roxanne Gay, "My Body Is Wildly Undisciplined And I Deny Myself Nearly Everything I Desire," April 9, 2014. http://www.xojane.com/issues/my-body-is-wildly-undisciplined-and-i-deny-myself-nearly-everything-i-desire.
7. Diane Bondy, "Confessions of a Fat, Black Yoga Teacher," in *Yoga and Body Image: 25 Personal Stories About Beauty, Bravery, & Loving Your Body*, ed. Melanie Klein and Anna Guest-Jelley (Woodbury, MN: Llewellyn Publications, 2014) 73–82.
8. Walker, *The Color Purple*, 199–200.

REFERENCES

Bondy, Diane. "Confessions of a Fat, Black Yoga Teacher," in *Yoga and Body Image: 25 Personal Stories About Beauty, Bravery, & Loving Your Body*, ed. Melanie Klein and Anna Guest-Jelley (Woodbury, MN: Llewellyn Publications, 2014), 73–82.

Collins, Patricia Hill. *Black Feminist Thought: Knowledge, Consciousness, and the Politics of Empowerment* (Routledge, 2002).

hooks, bell. *Sisters of the Yam: Black Women and Self-Recovery* (Boston: South End Press, 1993).

Lorde, Audre. *Sister Outsider: Essays and Speeches* (Crossing Press, 2012).

Morrison, Toni. *Playing in the Dark* (Vintage, 2007).

Walker, Alice. *The Color Purple* (London: Women's Press, 1992).

TWO

"I'm Feelin' It"

Embodied Spiritual Activism as a Vehicle for my Queer Black Liberation

Jillian Carter Ford

Several months ago, a lover of mine and I ventured into a suburban yoga studio to engage in practice and to check out the spot's vibration. She had agreed to accompany me, sensitive to our shared prediction it would be an all-white hetero-normative studio, despite her oft-declared singular devotion to her regular studio in the city. Based on a series of recent eye-opening experiences (in non-yogic spaces), I challenged her assumption that anything this far out of the city would automatically be unwelcoming. The suburban city and county to which I recently moved is notoriously not for people "like us." We entered together: she tall, slim, and chocolate; me short, fluffy, and light-skinned. Upon entry, we noticed three skinny white people, whom we perceived as two cis-women and one cis-man employees. I shot her a glance to indicate something like "let's give it/them a chance." She responded with a look that I interpreted as something like "you better be glad I like you." The white folks did not look our way. To our awkward surprise, they did not even pause their conversation. Caught a bit off-guard by the absence of any human-to-human acknowledgment, we sat down super close to one another on the plush white couch. What unfolded next occurred to me like an SNL parody. For the subsequent ten minutes, the three white people spoke very loudly—in a not-too-big lobby—about their upcoming outreach initiative to a particular community in which yoga was apparently not common. "Well like, what should we start with?" One of the women asked her comrades. The other woman and the man began talking at the same time. He bowed his eyes, and she restarted her sentence. "Well I think the most important thing is that we make them feel welcome," *she declared decisively. "Like, we really have to make them feel like yoga is for* everybody," *she explained, in a tone that buzzed in the back of her neck as she swallowed the last word. The other woman stared, with her lips poked out and a glossy-eyed expression I couldn't decipher. "Yea," the man responded. "This first class is crucial, guys. They'll either dig us or they won't. And after all this we're doing for them, they better dig us!" The women's eyebrows shot up as they chuckled and nodded in agreement. The dialogue continued, and my lover and I turned back to one another. "My bad," I began, and went on to suggest we leave. At this point she persuaded me to stay, figuring we had come this far and already paid online. A few minutes passed before another three white women entered the space. The employees' conversation halted immediately, as the two with their backs to the door spun around enthusiastically to welcome the entering women. The talkative woman rushed the newcomers and hugged two of them excitedly. The quiet woman clapped rapidly with her hands in front of her mouth. This was a cheerful welcome, indeed. Still, no one looked our way. A the previous class let out, the lobby filled with lots of white women in expensive-looking yoga attire, and my lover and I slipped to the back and out of the sea of whiteness and what felt like straightness. I sucked my teeth and she shook her head as we unrolled our mats and laid back into sevasana until class commenced.*

In this chapter, I use the experience described in the opening vignette to outline larger societal trends regarding yoga in relationship to queerness, race, exclusion, resistance, and liberation. As a teacher educator, and as a human committed to a womanist interpretation of social justice, I align with a politic of liberation. Womanist and yogic philosophies offer overlapping conceptions of liberation. One resonate commonality is the principle that energy can be transmuted in the service of liberation.[1] That liberation is possible on a continuum from a microscopic level (e.g., cells)[2] to a cosmic level (e.g., the earth and beyond).[3]

Womanism is a standpoint epistemology that centers black women's logic.[4] Like yoga, womanism posits the most important place to enter for social change creation is the self. Both philosophies, therefore, are embodied. Beginning with self sets yoga and womanism apart from many other social justice endeavors, which commonly identify political, geographical, and institutional places as sites to enter the work. Interconectedness is foundational for using both yoga practice and womanist action as vehicles to create a more just world.[5] Spiritual notions of oneness, such as the oneness of mind/body and the oneness of all people, emerge from both traditions and set in motion a spiritual activism wherein spirituality is engaged to create social and ecological uplift.[6] Entering contested space with a beginners mind and asserting our unfinishedness allows us the space to continue growing.[7] This often requires unlearning a host of harmful messages we have been socialized to believe.

EMBODIED OPPRESSION

One day about a decade ago, in my late twenties, I woke up and found myself unable to take more than a few steps without holding a wall or crumbling to the floor. Arrested by what felt like tremendous weights on my legs and arms, my first thought was that I had the flu; in fact it turned out to be the start of a paralyzing depression. I was fortunate my brother stopped by the following day and found me motionless on my couch. A long time student of Zen Buddhism and meditation, he introduced me to both in the following weeks and months. In so doing, he lit a path of contemplative healing that eventually brought me to yoga. I am no longer baffled, as I was ten years ago, by how suddenly the depression seemed to manifest. In retrospect I realize my inattention to prana had my dulled my chakras tremendously, long before the day I awoke unable to walk.

As an able-bodied, middle-class black queer ciswoman, I was aware mostly of how my privileges had afforded me protection from ableism, classism, and extreme degrees of racism, sexism, and homophobia. What I did not know prior to my first major depression, however, was that my body had actually been cataloguing interpersonal, systemic, and multi-generational traumas since early childhood. Racist, sexist, and homophobic wounds compiled despite my privileges, with no attention to somatic healing. Albeit with different material effects, ableist, classist, transphobic experiences were also being recorded. Embodied responses are common but under-identified consequences of existing within systemic violence. These effects can manifest as body movement constriction (as it did for me), disconnection from the body, heightened startle response, among other manifestations.[8]

One tool of hegemony is to disavow the body as a site of knowledge. By separating one's knowing from one's being, dominant forces can better access oppressed people to internalize standards of morality, success, love, beauty, and so on that serve the interests of those in power. For queer people, these and other standards often become central obstacles based on societal forces that mark queer as deviant. Yoga practice and womanist thought help create portals to other ways of knowing, which are essential tools for contradicting embodied oppression. We develop a consciousness about the value of our inner truths by learning to turn inward. Embodied self-awareness allows us to step outside powerful hegemonic systems that, along with normative prescriptions, include seductive methods to make us believe that the status quo is impermeable. Importantly, our ability to "step outside" systems is most often metaphorical. Real systems do exist that maintain power relations in raced, classed, and gendered ways; consciousness alone does not change this.[9] Thus awareness is a necessary but insufficient element of any liberation struggle. It being an essential starting place for liberation, access to yoga is a question of social justice. Singh offers the following as questions that help clarify links between the personal and political: "Who gets to heal? Who gets to be safe?"[10] Because yoga and womanism direct us inward as a precursor to healing anything outside ourselves, every human being has the ability to participate. Social structures can create pathways and barriers for us to know ourselves and the cosmos in a quest for balance and, ultimately, liberation.

FROM CELLULAR TO COSMIC CONSCIOUSNESS

Contrary to our Western duel foci of money and materialism, ancient yogis believed our bodies were merely a physical manifestation of a much more complex set of internal conditions. Not only was the body understood to be but a shell for the current incarnation of the Self, its importance paled in comparison with that of the life force. The level of one's life-force consciousness largely determines one's capacity for spiritual ascension. Traditionally, the same life force that enlivens our bodies opens flowers, causes rain to fall, and creates ocean currents.[11]

Each of us is made up of trillions of cells, which are affected by chemicals and hormones released from the brain. A major determinant of the chemicals and hormones' qualities is the conscious and subconscious thought cycle. Our nervous system—which served humans well evolutionarily—runs automatically and is vigilant in its duty to protect us from sudden danger. The frenetic pace at which we are socialized to move in contemporary U.S. society creates a context for our nervous systems to remain in protection mode, which is not sustainable for healthy living. Moving from a chemistry of protection to a chemistry of growth allows our cells to align along axes of positivity, which propel us to be well and promote wellness in others.[12]

For decades, yoga in the United States has reflected the deeply entrenched social and economic divisions that capitalism ensures. Below, I discuss growing momentum to resist that exclusion; a force of which this volume is no doubt a part. Despite my academic privileges that created the opportunity for me to contribute to this volume, I am a relative newcomer to regular yoga practice. Thus it was not so long ago that I began surveying the yogic landscape in the United States.

CONTEMPORARY LANDSCAPE

One *might* expect that yoga studios are automatically welcoming places, due to the compassion so central to yoga. In fact, the way yoga has been commodified in the United States makes any assumptions about its contemporary authenticity suspect. Because there is a dearth of empirical research on the extent to which gender, sexuality, and race intersect with yogic spaces in the United States, I began by searching Google, and proceeded to evaluate a catalogued and searchable database of the *Yoga Journal* (YJ) cover images over the last decade.

Google

Googling "gay yoga" yielded over 22 million results. The first several hundred sites generally appeared to be websites for gay men's classes, studios, or trips, with the exception of a sprinkling of sites about yoga as a "cure" for gayness. Googling "lesbian yoga," on the other hand, yielded about 13.5 million results, the first several hundred of which are porn sites! Fascinated and disturbed by the results of those two searches, I proceeded to browse the search yields for "bisexual yoga," "trans yoga," and "queer yoga."

Googling "bisexual yoga" drew the least uniform results. Out of about 1.7 million hits, the first several hundred sites ranged from online discussion forums to erotica, including sites on inclusive classes, pornography, dating, and more. "Trans yoga" and "queer yoga" searches drew noticeably more politicized hits. The most apparent difference between the results of both queries was the number yielded: roughly 4.5 million for the former and just over half a million for the latter. In a quick scan, it seemed the first few hundred on both lists were mostly trans and queer welcoming class advertisements and first person narratives about exclusion experiences. The queer and trans emphasis on resisting exclusion, along with Singh's aforementioned questions about access to healing and safety prompted me to assess what images the YJ—a significant actor in defining mainstream yoga—projects regarding how yoga looks.

Yoga Journal

I analyzed YJ covers spanning the decade between January 2006 and December 2015. This included eighty-five journals. With the exception of 2006 and 2007, when seven and eight issues were published respectively, the *Yoga Journal* published nine issues per year. My findings confirm the frequently cited criticism regarding the target audience for yoga's growing prominence in U.S. society. The vast majority of the images on a decade of YJ issues are of young, white, thin, ultra-flexible, able-bodied, fashionably dressed ciswomen who appear happy and at peace. I searched the cover text for the words "sex," "love," "body," "lesbian," "gay," "bisexual," "queer," "trans" to investigate the YJ's sexuality narrative, and the cover models' appearances to examine the YJ's ideal yogi in regards to race/ethnicity and gender.

The word "sex" appeared one time in the ten-year span I explored. In August 2006 (issue 197), the headline reads "Sex and Yoga: They're Good for the Soul." The article includes four photos of the same white heterosexual couple, which fill up three and a half pages. The first of these pictures is meant to look like the couple is having sex, but a comforter covers the particulars. The other three pictures display the couple practicing joined yogic poses.

"Love" showed up on eight of the eighty-five covers. Of these, only one refers directly to love in the context of an intimate relationship. The headline in February 2006 (issue 193) is "Love Better: How Yoga Can Enhance Your Relationship." The article begins, "When Julie Woodward married her husband, Drew, twenty-three years ago, they were both more or less agnostic" (p. 70). Two headlines refer to loving yoga itself: "Make a Love that Lasts with Yoga" and "Why Surfers Love Yoga." Two cover titles advised us to love the lives we live. Two of the headlines that included "love" were messages to "Love Your Body," and one suggested "Love Your Belly."

Although specific parts of our bodies were mentioned on every cover, I sought to determine what images the YJ chose to convey when they wrote about the "body" in general. The magazine cited "body" eighteen times. Of these, five refer to how bodies look. Titles that alluded to self-acceptance are all connected to articles about "plus size" women, though they did not specifically mention losing weight. There were two covers, however, that did encourage readers to lose weight. It was not until February 2015 (issue 271) that a titular reference to "body" was attached to a body-positive article. The first issue of the final year in my investigation, February 2015, highlighted a recently formed collaborative campaign called the Yoga Body Image Coalition (YBIC) specifically to address these problems. In the first paragraph of the attendant article, gender, sexuality, and race are named as categories that mainstream yoga fails to recognize. The YBIC mission is "to work with all of the ways yoga and body image intersect to create greater access and dignity for all."

One's race, ethnicity, gender, nor any other socially constructed identity category cannot be determined through a photograph. Nor can folks' age, physical ability level, weight, and body type be definitely measured through a photograph. Of course there are other qualities that cannot be conveyed whatsoever, such as disposition, income level, or actual lived experiences. My analysis, therefore, is based solely on categories I assign according to admittedly superficial characteristics. My aim, however, is not to determine the cover models' actual identities but instead how their images might be interpreted by members of larger society.

Every issue depicted a very thin or athletically built person on the cover. Of eighty-five YJ issues spanning the decade, there is one man and eighty-six women. The man appeared in March 2011 (issue 236), and the same year's June issue (238) had three women instead of the typical one. There appear to be about eighteen people of color included over the course of the decade. From 2006 to 2008, three of the four women of color seem to be of East Asian descent, and one woman of South Asian descent.

Then, in 2009, the YJ highlighted four women of color in one year. The women on the February and May covers seem to be of East Asian descent, and the June cover model appears to be of South Asian descent. For the remainder of the decade, no other people of apparent South Asian descent make the cover. Given yoga's origins, this absence is particularly troubling and exemplifies the invisibility some Asian women continue to experience in mainstream U.S. culture (Yamada 2015).

The first woman of African descent appears in September 2009. Another black woman appears on the cover of the 2010 May issue; she is the only person of color included that year. 2011 and 2012 showcase two women of African descent and two women of East Asian descent. The lone person of color in 2013 appears possibly mixed-race, perhaps a person of both African and Asian descent. Two women of East Asian descent and one woman of African descent show up on 2014 covers, and 2015 includes one black woman. The YJ's representation of who can, does, or should have access to yoga is inadequate. It is not surprising, therefore, that a study co-funded by the YJ ignored demographic data about race, income level, and sexuality. The study did illuminate a wider picture of mainstream yoga in the United States, however.

Yoga in America Study 2016.

The study confirmed that yoga is big business. In 2012, yoga practitioners spent $10 billion on clothing, classes, and equipment. That number increased by over 60 percent in the past four years, to a reported $16 billion in 2016. One critique of the capitalist model is the focus on individual benefit. The four years between 2012 and 2016 also indicated rapid growth in yoga awareness in the general population and numbers of practitioners. Specifically, the study indicated increased numbers of male practitioners and practitioners who are older than fifty-five, two of the three tracked demographic categories. Geographical region, the third included category, showed that the South has the highest percentage (32 percent) of any other single region among people who practice yoga. The Northeast, Midwest, and West each constitute approximately 23 percent of the overall U.S. practitioner rate. That gender, age, and region were the only three demographics assessed highlights the critiques regarding contemporary yoga's exclusive environment.

Having a context within which to consider the "queer yoga" and "trans yoga" Google search results helped me understand the multitude of both explicitly welcoming classes and personal narratives of exclusion. Having started my yoga practice in the city of Atlanta (where I lived for fifteen years before my move to an Atlanta suburb about nine months ago), I had access to a much more welcoming yoga community. Also a member of queer and trans/black/people of color/educational justice communities, I was encouraged to begin by people I knew, in spaces I knew. As friends became certified instructors over the past three or four years, they have held classes at a feminist bookstore, a black-owned bike shop, multiple parks, and home studios.

The experience I describe in the opening vignette transpired about a month after I moved. Until that occasion, I had been pleasantly surprised to have my stereotypes of the suburbs debunked as I came into contact with more queer people, people of color, and immigrants than I presumed there would be outside the city. Nevertheless, I was still on guard. Being black and queer in predominantly white and heteronormative spaces can demand energy in ways that are invisible to those with systemic privilege. Deciding whether to go somewhere, calibrating negative energy that may arise from feeling Othered, and working through feelings of disappointment or anger are common examples of energy outflow for people with marginalized identities.

PRE-ARRIVAL NEGOTIATIONS

One benefit of "fitting in"—even if the space is a culturally appropriated version of an ancient spiritual practice constructed and propelled for capitalist gain—is the privilege of ease with which one can decide to show up. The burdens of navigating oppressive social structures is one of the reasons people seek out yoga practice to begin with. It takes vitality, the growth of which is another benefit of yoga for those who can practice in safe and welcoming spaces. A consequence of inequity is energy lost. The measure of energy consumed in preparation for the possibility of being ignored, hyper-seen, unwillingly looped into a conversation, or touched is significant. These and other microaggressions happen so frequently in white heteronormative spaces that cost consideration can become automatic. Whether automatic or conscious, accumulation of constant concern draws on the finite amount of energy that we have as humans.

In the opening vignette, my lover Denisha and I briefly deliberated the possibility of experiencing microaggression-induced discomfort, plus the $15 each, and still we decided to go. Our arrival at the studio was therefore not neutral. The problem of spending energy on concerns about exclusion in a space we were going precisely to increase our vigor and consciousness was not lost on us. Might we achieve access to energy robust enough to thrive instead of only enough to survive?

Marsh distinguishes between humans' biological imperative to survive and our spiritual imperative to thrive.[13] Because our survival is tied to connections with other humans, our thrust for that biological survival when we are very young can include compromising pieces of who we are. This compromise can lead to shame, a feeling that can be contradicted on the yoga mat. Spiritual survival characterized as thriving affords the ability to "know ourselves as [an] expansive possibility of love or grace or wisdom."[14] Individual and collective liberation requires access to these expansive possibilities. No one should have to risk alienation in order to practice connection to breath as informed by learning *asana*.

UPON ARRIVAL: ALIENATION

Queer and trans people trouble binary categories of sexuality and gender. The oft-cited milieu of disapproving judgment often stems from adherence to a sense of "normalcy" as defined by intersecting identities of dominance in heteronormative contexts. Like Denisha and me, many queer people and people of color have experienced disillusionment upon arrival at non-welcoming studios. How might we learn to transmute the anger and pain we carry in our bodies? For some trans people, the principle of detachment from one's body can pose complicated questions.

Overlapping Eastern traditions sometimes bring Zen philosophies to the yoga mat and visa versa. Recognizing non-self is a foundational Zen teaching, along with recognizing the truths of impermanence and suffering. The closer one gets along the path to enlightenment is predicated largely upon one's ability to realize the temporary nature of our bodies and our socially constructed understandings of self. Ehrenhalt described their Zen priest's guidance to seek

> the truth of non-self. No race, no body, no age. No gender. "No eyes no ears no nose no tongue no body no mind," we chant from the Heart Sutra. "Upon awakening," says the priest, "we will return to Buddha-nature, free of conditioned arising states . . ." I wonder silently to myself if gender dysphoria—the experience of dissonance between one's body and mind—in the awakened Buddhist mind, could even exist.[15]

After spending so much time working toward accepting their body, the notion of disregarding it entirely does not come easily for Ehrenhalt.

ORGANIZED MOVEMENTS TOWARD RADICAL ACCEPTANCE

Radical acceptance, or the process of offering radical welcome, moves beyond the simple act of invitation.[16] Radical welcome necessitates the willingness to assess taken for granted practices and to recreate new processes that are safe and affirming for all. Despite the exclusive nature of yoga as depicted by the mainstream YJ, there are growing efforts to critique the problem of exclusivity.

The South Asian American Perspectives on Yoga in America (SAAP-YA) is a network and platform for people in the South Asian Diaspora who are involved in yoga. By providing South Asian-led educational workshops about appropriate forms of cultural production and theology in yogic spaces, SAAPYA's main goal is to promote intrapersonal and interpersonal integration and to dissolve the boundaries that currently create insiders and outsiders in yoga communities.

The members of the aforementioned YBIC promote the transformative power of yoga and consider yoga a tool for movement toward a more socially just world. By articulating that "body positivity is more than a #hashtag, marketing slogan, or commodity," but that instead it is "conscious action and lived practice," the YBIC contradicts the harmful experiences cited by many queer folks. Their podcasts—a mode of communication that itself can be inclusive for folks for whom reading text can be an obstacle—illustrate their broad notions of inclusion. The podcasts address issues of cultural appropriation, disability rights advocacy, aging processes, embodied bodily acceptance, eating disorders, and more. In so doing, they infuse feminist notions of transformative education, time creation, and radical acceptance writ large.

The growing discourse around yoga accessibility has prompted myriad suggestions for how to make previously hostile places safe. By offering free or reduced-price classes to the community, promoting queer- and trans-specific classes, classes for people of color, and body positive classes, more folks are able to experience yoga's benefits. Meditation classes are spaces that offer a respite from the physical element of *asana*, and reintegrate a more holistic and authentic connection to ancient yogic traditions. The yoga accessibility movement is pressing the mainstream yoga establishment to consider who is teaching the classes, and to engage in outreach to diversify instructors. Does your space have instructors who are queer and trans*? Instructors of color? How many fat instructors teach in your space, or people with non-normative physical abilities? What languages do your instructors speak? How old are your instructors?[17]

CONCLUSION

Both yoga and womanism came together to create a roadmap for me to get on a path toward personal liberation. Channeling energy is a practice without which I would not have healed from a series of depressive episodes. Knowing the potential for individual and collective access to freedom, those in mainstream yogic communities should consider the extent to which the spaces they practice are open to those who experience systemic oppressions daily; to do so would align with the most basic yogic principles.

NOTES

1. Delcia Mcneil, "Metaphysical Energy Work & Dynamic Healing: Exploring the Interface of Subtle Energy Healing and Psychotherapy," *Self & Society* 34, no. 4 (2007): 17; Layli Phillips, *The Womanist Reader* (New York: Taylor & Francis), 2006.

2. Charlotte Carnegie, *The Incomplete Guide to Yoga* (Hants, UK: John Hunt Publishing Ltd., 2012) 225.

3. Layli Maparyan, *The Womanist Idea* (New York: Routledge, 2012).

4. Patricia Hill Collins, *Black Feminist Thought* (New York: Routledge, 2000).

5. Tamara Beauboeuf-Lafontant, "A Womanist Experience of Caring: Understanding the Pedagogy of Exemplary Black Women Teachers," *The Urban Review* 34, no. 1 (2002): 71–86.

6. Maparyan, *The Womanist Idea*.

7. Paulo Friere, *Pedagogy of the Oppressed* (New York: Bloomsbury Publishing, 2000) 84; Chelsea Jackson, "Yoga: A Medium for Communication and Learning," interview with Beth Berila. *Every Body is a Yoga Body: Yoga and Body Image Coalition.* Podcast Audio. October 21, 2015. https://itunes.apple.com/us/podcast/ybicoalition/id1036509477?mt=2&i=355052575.

8. Beth Berila, Franz Fanon, and Rae Johnson, "Oppression Embodied: The Intersecting Dimensions of Trauma, Oppression, and Somatic Psychology." *United States Association of Body Psychotherapy Journal* 8, no. 1 (2009): 21.

9. Earthlyn Manuel, "Awakening through Race, Sexuality & Gender," http://www.decolonizingyoga.com/awakening-through-race-sexuality-gender/.

10. Roopa Singh, "Yoga and Cultural Appropriation," interview with Beth Berila. *Every Body is a Yoga Body: Yoga and Body Image Coalition.* Podcast audio. October 21, 2015. https://itunes.apple.com/us/podcast/ybicoalition/id1036509477?mt=2&i=3550525 75.

11. D. Farhi, *Bringing Yoga to Life: The Everyday Practice of Enlightened Living* (New York: HarperCollins, 2004).

12. Bruce Lipton, "The Power of Consciousness," interview with Iain McNay. Consciousness.tv. Accessed February 12, 2011. http://vaccineliberationarmy.com/2011/12/04/bruce-lipton-cellular-biologist-the-power-of-consciousness/.

13. Sarah Joy Marsh, "Reclaiming Your Relationship with Your Body," interview with Beth Berila. *Every Body is a Yoga Body: Yoga and Body Image Coalition.* Podcast Audio. October 21, 2015. https://itunes.apple.com/us/podcast/ybicoalition/id1036509 477?mt=2&i=355052575.

14. Marsh, "Reclaiming Your Relationship with Your Body."

15. Jey Ehrenhalt, "Gender Dysphoria and the Dharma," *Decolonizing Yoga.* Accessed February 6, 2016. http://www.decolonizingyoga.com/gender-dysphoria-dharma/.

16. Tao Drake, "Radical Acceptance and Welcoming Podcast," interview with Beth Berila. *Every Body is a Yoga Body: Yoga and Body Image Coalition.* Podcast Audio. October 21, 2015. https://itunes.apple.com/us/podcast/ybicoalition/id1036509477?mt=2&i=3550 52575.

17. Andi MacDonald, http://www.decolonizingyoga.com/yoga-studios-everyones-welcome/.

REFERENCES

Barkataki, Susana. "Why We Need Safe Spaces in Yoga." *Decolonizing Yoga.* Accessed February 6, 2016. http://www.decolonizingyoga.com/why-we-need-safe-spaces-in-yoga/.

Beauboeuf-Lafontant, Tamara. "A Womanist Experience of Caring: Understanding the Pedagogy of Exemplary Black Women Teachers." *The Urban Review* 34, no. 1 (2002): 71–86.

Berila, Beth. *Integrating Mindfulness into Anti-Oppressions Pedagogy: Social Justice in Higher Education* (New York: Routledge, 2016).

Berila, Beth, Franz Fanon, and Rae Johnson. "Oppresion Embodied: The Intersecting Dimensions of Trauma, Oppression, and Somatic Psychology." *United States Association of Body Psychotherapy Journal* 8, no. 1 (2009): 21.

Collins, Patricia Hill. *Black Feminist Thought* (New York: Routledge, 2000).

Carnegie, Charlotte. *The Incomplete Guide to Yoga* (Hants, UK: John Hunt Publishing Ltd., 2012).

Drake, Tao. "Radical Acceptance and Welcoming Podcast," interview with Beth Berila. *Every Body is a Yoga Body: Yoga and Body Image Coalition*. Podcast Audio. October 21, 2015. https://itunes.apple.com/us/podcast/ybicoalition/id1036509477?mt=2&i=35505 2575.

Ehrenhalt, Jey. "Gender Dysphoria and the Dharma." *Decolonizing Yoga*. Accessed February 6, 2016. http://www.decolonizingyoga.com/gender-dysphoria-dharma/.

Fanon, Franz. *The Wretched of the Earth* [Les damnés de la terre]. trans. Richard Philcox. Paris, France: Présence Africaine, 1963.

Farhi, D. *Bringing Yoga to Life: The Everyday Practice of Enlightened Living* (New York: HarperCollins, 2004).

Freire, Paulo. *Pedagogy of the Oppressed* (New York: Bloomsbury Publishing, 2000).

Jackson, Chelsea. "Yoga: A Medium for Communication and Learning," interview with Beth Berila. *Every Body is a Yoga Body: Yoga and Body Image Coalition*. Podcast Audio. October 21, 2015. https://itunes.apple.com/us/podcast/ybicoalition/id10 36509477?mt=2&i=355052575.

Johnson, R. "Oppression Embodied: Exploring the Intersections of Somatic Psychology, Trauma, and Oppression." *United States Association of Body Psychotherapy Journal* 8, no. 1 (2009): 19-31.

Kumashiro, Kevin K. "Queer Students of Color and Antiracist, Antiheterosexist Education: Paradoxes of Identity and Activism." *Troubling Intersections of Race and Sexuality: Queer Students of Color and Anti-oppressive Education* (2001): 1–25.

Lipton, Bruce. "The Power of Consciousness," interview with Iain McNay. *Conciousness.tv*. Accessed February 12, 2016, http://vaccineliberationarmy.com/2011/12/04/bruce-lipton-cellular-biologist-the-power-of-consciousness/.

Maparyan, Layli. *The Womanist Idea* (New York: Routledge, 2012).

Marsh, Sarah Joy. "Reclaiming Your Relationship with Your Body," interview with Beth Berila. *Every Body is a Yoga Body: Yoga and Body Image Coalition*. Podcast Audio. October 21, 2015. https://itunes.apple.com/us/podcast/ybicoalition/id103650 9477?mt=2&i=355052575.

McNeil, Delcia. "Metaphysical Energy Work & Dynamic Healing: Exploring the Interface of Subtle Energy Healing and Psychotherapy." *Self & Society* 34, no. 4 (2007): 13–22.

Mitchell, S. *Bhagavad Gita: A New Translation* (New York: Three Rivers Press, 2000).

Phillips, Layli. *The Womanist Reader* (Taylor & Francis, 2006).

Singh, Roopa. "Yoga and Cultural Appropriation," interview with Beth Berila. *Every Body is a Yoga Body: Yoga and Body Image Coalition*. Podcast audio. October 21, 2015. https://itunes.apple.com/us/podcast/ybicoalition/id1036509477?mt=2&i=355052575.

Yamada, M. "Invisibility is an Unnatural Disaster," in C. Moraga & G. Anzaldúa, eds., *This Bridge Called My Back: Writings by Radical Women of Color* 4th ed. (Albany: State University of New York Press, 2015).

THREE

The Gender, Race, and Class Barriers

Enclosing Yoga as White Public Space

Enoch H. Page

Yoga and the body converge precisely where subordination, superordination, and markets intersect, but this fact eludes us. Yoga makes us feel better and we feel certain that it will help others, too. We might even believe that yoga will facilitate their spiritual development, as it advances and deepens our own. Appreciating the benefits of yoga, we advocate its adoption, as if offering its wealth to others who we hope will receive it. We presume that yoga can be adopted simply as a private practice that dovetails with a community of practitioners, but this desirable, intimate relationship with yoga reflects the lore of what yoga once was. For today, that lore is merely a myth. Yoga has not been just a private or communal practice for quite some time. The yoga we pass on to others today began evolving in a Western way during the colonial era so it now comes to us with commercial baggage and colonial fears. As a result, we no longer can offer the gift of yoga without the baggage of its promises serving as bait. When others accept our invitation to enjoy the gift of yoga, they do not realize that they have bitten into the bait that we may not have intended to offer them. In any case, we end up participating in how their willingness to receive our gift of yoga hooks their lives on a line that will not let them go. With this taut line, their resources and yoga-refined bodies get reeled onto a capitalist boat—along with other caught fish (consumers)—by a fisherman (marketer) who steers that boat, hunting for profits on the rough waters, not of an open deep blue sea, but of a murky man-made reservoir of commercial yoga markets.

41

Yoga became one of many instrumentalities shaped by colonialization, a larger historic process that produces an order of things, including
yoga. That colonial order does not remain in the past for it continually
reproduces new facets of itself in the present that refract into the future.
Formal colonialism is long gone, but in each racial state[1] that formerly
was embroiled in historic colonial relations, the descendants are living its
postcolonial aftermath. Colonization is a hegemonic process governed by
direct or indirect rule. It entails a capitalist, commercial, and governmen-
tal enclosure of space in which colonized yoga also was enclosed. Colonialism enables a powerful country to seize, by force, the governing apparatus of less powerful countries. Through complicit local elites, it seizes
control over their material, cultural (such as yoga), and labor resources,
in order to project its own authority and to broaden its own power and
wealth. Colonialization is always a capitalist endeavor and the colonizers
are capitalists. They set up what Theo Goldberg calls settler "racial
states" of superordination wherein gender, race, and class dominance
becomes the naturalized order of the day. As Goldberg conceives of the
racial state, it "explicitly, deliberatively and calculatingly takes the lead in
orchestrating the various instrumentalities in the definition and material-
ization of whiteness."[2]

The economies of racial states are driven by the European colonizing
capitalists who capitalize the superordinate property of colonial whiteness[3] by extracting resources in racist ways mainly to be owned by elite
males, colonizing and colonized. This wealth enriches the colonizing nation that parasitically feeds on its resource-rich colonies. Industrial or
entrepreneurial capitalists transform the extracted colonial resources into
commodities for sale. Following Anne McClintock, C. Richard King validates the study of the commodity racism that arises in the nineteenth
century at the nexus of industrial capitalism and colonial imperialism. He
shows how it affirms white supremacy in the public mind through marketing discourses composed of racist language and images that converge
to produce colonizing and colonized consumers who get ranked by gender, race, and class as they participate in the profitable buying of things,
some of which should never have been sold.[4] Yoga is one such commodity. The colonizing capitalists, doing coerced colonial business with the
colonized capitalists, need to produce commodity buyers. To achieve this
goal, they set up markets, in and between the racial states, and rely on an
elite politics of superordinance to create new consumer needs among
elites and to foster the emulation of elite consumption among those who
are subordinated.

Colonized populations made to desire the fulfillment of these new
needs are fashioned into markets—like a yoga market—and complain of
appropriation while the superordinate elites capitalize on the resources
they siphon away from the hands of the colonized who, in such corporate
transactions, no longer are engaged as persons, but only as markets. This

suggests that for populations to be shaped by capitalists into a yoga market is no privilege; rather, the project subjects the colonized masses who are to become the market to the objectifying, alienating, and dehumanizing experiences of a mind-numbing amnesia. Their harsh experiences of being colonized are effaced as the colonizing white marketers seductively represent to the nonwhite colonized the dictated new terms in accordance with which they are now allowed to buy or sell all colonial commodities, including the yoga commodity. The colonizers, as marketers, can represent themselves as the harmless promoters and benign producers of goods and services for sale, no longer to be recognized as the violently usurping colonizers. When the colonial order transforms the bodies, resources, embodied practices, and relationships that once constituted yoga into commodity transactions, we get to see up close, as David Graeber observes, that "the peculiar effect of the market is to erase the memory of previous transactions and create, effectively a veil of ignorance between sellers and buyers, producers and consumers."[5]

We Americans who do yoga stoically stand in mountain pose behind this blinding veil and fail to recognize our position as colonizing yoga instructors or as colonized yoga consumers. As yoga consumers, we comprise a major portion of the commercial yoga market. For 123 years, yoga has been ensnared behind the veil of these exploitative and deceptive colonial processes of yoga commodification and market formation that mainly tend to privilege and enrich European descent elites at the expense of others. That is contrary to what Swami Vivekananda envisioned and promoted. I believe it is high time to reinstitute his vision so that his true mission for yoga can be liberated from capitalist relations and especially from market commodification.

THE IMPERIAL FORMATION OF COLONIZED YOGA IN BRITISH INDIA

Colonies were large-scale nodes of empire, and when looking at the British colony in India, it is hard to observe where the intricately networked establishment of minor exchanges, like personal yoga instruction, take place. Stoler simplifies things when she gazes into empire with a focus on the smaller colonized units that she calls *imperial formations*.

In Stoler's terms, the colonial relations that constitute yoga as an imperial formation can be characterized as "relations of force" as well as "processes of becoming," that are defined by "racialized relations of allocations and appropriations."[6] Expounding further on imperial formations, Stoler claims that "they harbor political forms that endure beyond the formal exclusions that legislate against equal opportunity, commensurate dignities, and equal rights."[7] Most interesting is Stoler's observation that imperial formations organize markets and other policy-making forms of organized power that make promises, but tend not to fulfill them. As Stoler further notes, the imperial formations "are states of deferral that mete out promissory notes that are not exceptions to their operation but constitutive of them." [8] They are forms of organization, including markets, that leave promised things undone and these undone things become inherited *imperial debris*, disappointing seepages that bleed into the present and future. [9]

The prescient mission of Swami Vivekananda, who brought yoga to America, has been compared to liberation theology on twenty-two counts. [10] He set out to launch a decolonizing yoga mission. His goal was to assist the masses to achieve illumination through his conception of yoga; and in order to prepare them to receive and make good use of yoga, he sought, beforehand, to recruit thousands of Western yoga practitioners who would help him to uplift the masses, not one by one, but by eradicating the systems of domination and control that insured their poverty and oppression. If he could accomplish this in India, then it should be do-able anywhere.

It was a workable concept until yoga's colonial trappings undermined Swami Vivekananda's mission by transforming the ascetic yoga he brought to America into a colonizing or market-producing yoga. One views his conveyance of yoga from India to America as a cultural practice moving between two distinct polities. That is what we see if we focus only on the nationality of each country, but we see something deeper when we focus on both countries' shared political economy of colonialism. Significant is how the two polities are linked through the strong informational ties that took form between the British and American colonial agents. [11][12]How does yoga become a colonial resource? Lake and Reynolds[13] establish the idea that in different parts of the world, persons of European descent who sensed they were participating in a common global project of "white racial dominance," faced problems, had questions, and sought information about how to manage their colonized populations, so they "constantly drew on each other's ideas and practices."

Strategies to oppress nonwhites were circulated among whites in different colonies which granted a routine appearance or functionality to colonial systems of domination in different countries. When yoga moves from one nation's colonial system to another one, the conditions are different, but the goals and methods of racial oppression largely remain the same. Consequently, Swami Vivekananda's vision for liberation of the global masses is contained in America. Just as the British were to dismiss and to ruin ascetic yoga in India, Swami Vivekananda's vision for a yoga of liberation in America was to be distorted and deflected into commercialism.

"COLONIZING" AMERICAN YOGA IS ROOTED IN THE RUINATION OF COLONIZED ASCETIC YOGA

British colonial officials had no interest in preserving yoga and refused to acknowledge that Saddhus or the "Accomplished Ones" "were masters of yoga, spiritual heroes, miracle workers and minstrels in ancient times."[14] In British India these ascetic yogis came to be despised and disparaged, much like the Mau Mau of British Kenya came to be regarded by the British and by the entire Western world for much the same reasons.[15] This happened mainly because the ascetic yogis, like the Mau Mau, rightfully refused British colonization and rebelled. These rebels in both colonized countries thereby posed a threat to British colonial authority. The ascetic yogis resisted colonial domination and led the masses to win victories, sign treaties, and demand treasuries. They led discourses, protests, and military actions against alliances between the British colonial elites and their elite Hindu collaborators. They inspired insurrection and resorted to violence where necessary. Additionally, some of their more extreme yoga practices of renunciation were seen as horrifying or self-destructive in western eyes. They generally were radical renunciations that went to the root of self-mastery in ways that shattered the hegemonic limitations of conventional thinking.

Colonial administrators felt compelled to repress and eradicate India's yoga masters from their own communities of practice from which they had been able to threaten British hegemony. Finding them reprehensible and irrepressible, the colonial authorities banned the sadhus (Hindu wandering holy men) and orchestrated an illegalization of the fakirs (ascetic holy men who live solely on alms). Using legal and violent methods, the British colonial administrators sought to invalidate and ruin ascetic yoga in India's spiritual life. A hallmark of the ruination of these ascetic yogis is their loss of "fixed sovereignty"[16] that they formerly enjoyed before the British ripped it away. Even where they were banned from one province, the mighty influence of the ascetic yogis would continue wherever they were relocated or disperse

Stoler affirms that such colonial contests were apt to emerge where the violent colonial order produces imperial formations, like ascetic yoga, and then subjects them to ruin. She regards ruination as "a political project that lays waste to certain peoples and places, relations and things."[17][18] Hence, the ruination of ascetic yoga became a colonial achievement that indelibly registers their historic practice as a spiritual form with political power and strips it of substance in British India *before* it is transported to America. Its ruination in British India displaces the stable, autonomous practices of the ascetic yogis with the slippery slope of the "gradated sovereignty" that yoga practitioners later would enjoy in America. In this way an already ruined imperial formation of ascetic yoga becomes the imperial debris left to the people who live the postcolonial aftermath, and within this imperial debris resides the constitutive promise that colonialism will be good for India. That promise was a theme of British colonial narrative. It was made and gave rise to a new promise of *yoga for all* that would be made by the colonized Swami Vivekananda when he carried a modernized version of ruined ascetic yoga to America, but neither promise would be fulfilled.[19]

Embodiment of ancient yoga knowledge largely was lost to the commons of India when the ascetic yogi's communities got ruined and the value of the wandering yoga master subsequently was thrown into question. Afterward, respectable yogis were more refined and confined. They would become householders who work, and not be yogis who wandered with the support of the commons. This is how Swami Vivekananda modernized the ascetic yogi. In this way ascetic yoga enters America as an exotic but modernized form, with its colonial roots in British India. Its prior ruination serves to degrade and discount the politico-spiritual content of ascetic yoga in America and gives way to commercial yoga, such that its ancient knowledge no longer is taken seriously or regarded as necessary to yoga instruction.

The tendency is to promote yoga for the relaxing and strengthening bodily pleasure it brings, but more than physical strength, bodily ease and happiness is at stake.[20] We lose sight of this when the modernization and commercialization of ascetic yoga fosters this misinterpretation of yoga. It becomes a practice that disciplines the mind through the body while stripping away knowledge of the indispensable role of yoga's austerities in spiritual liberation, but yoga must not be reduced this way. Yoga includes meditation and other means of making discoveries about the illusory self that reveal the union of all things that never were divided, and it does this by helping the aspirant to unveil how the mind projects division. This attainment of the yoga aspirant results in a demolition of the ego, or the 'I-sense' that produces a direct experience of consciousness, a realization, or an uncovering of the eternal isomorphism of the small self with the infinite Self of the irreducible Consciousness. In this regard, yoga is not just for fitness; rather, the mind control required by one's yoga postures is just one narrow aspect of yoga, a larger philosophical system designed to initiate spiritual evolution. Over-focus on the body entails a massive loss of yoga knowledge that becomes a distraction.

Swami Vivekananda intended to deliver a yoga practice not just with ethics, breath, and *asanas*, but also with sexual abstinence and other austerities that westerners would consider rather severe. Patanjali's Yoga Sutra that informed Swami Vivekandana recognizes higher practices besides body postures and so do other yoga practices place mind de-conditioning on a higher plane than body conditioning. A yogi who puts *asana* practice in perspective this way focuses more on the spiritual discipline of the mind which results in their submission and annihilation of ego.

That yogi becomes able to extinguish bodily attachments and all other objects of consciousness that block one's access to identifying with the seer and no longer with myriad sense objects. Removing blocks by choosing not to identify with each pleasurable and unpleasurable mind-wave, disciplines one, eventually, to gain an awareness of consciousness that results in one's illumination. To get there, one assiduously practices all aspects of yoga (for instance, raja yoga, hatha yoga, bhakti yoga, mantra yoga, jnana yoga, etc.) that together will diminish identification with the waves of the mind and gradually will achieve the still mind required. Treating yoga as physical culture or as religion takes one off this path to enlightenment.

Because the ascetic yogis of India resisted colonization and embarrassed the Western-educated Hindus such as Swami Vivekananda, the Swami and other colonized yogis of India would reject some of the more despised elements of Patanjali asceticism and push for the modernization of ascetic yoga. Not knowing, then, that any ascetic yoga tradition steeped in colonialism would fall out of the frying pan and into the fire in America, Swami Vivekananda naively, or optimistically, tries to resuscitate a modulated model of the ruined ascetic yoga in America. Little did he know that his version of ascetic yoga would only become commercial yoga once it became Westernized in America during the enclosure of public space that would characterize nineteenth-century America. Ascetic yoga had been more liberating in India than it would be in America, but when filtered through American colonialism, that yoga from India ends up circulating in both countries, and around the world, as a Westernized exotic commodity, exciting many, de-stressing them, and making them more emotionally sound and physically fit, but illuminating and liberating few, if any. Despite Swami Vivekananda' s mission to bring yoga to everyone, his promise of yoga for all thereby is derailed. It may never be fulfilled yoga subject to market constraints that subject ancient principles to the whims of consumer markets. While ruined ascetic yoga endures its transnational migration, it transforms into a commercial commodity seeking its market immediately upon entering the colonizing space of America, and it is this new space that becomes a key transitional variable

Utilizing my concept of *white public space*,[21] [22] Quentin Lewis hints as to why we normally do not describe yoga or other imperial formations as practice, in terms of a theory of whiteness, rather than identity.[23] In studying historic Deerfield, Massachusetts, Lewis found this town's nineteenth-century residents whitening space by rewriting seventeenth-and eighteenth-century events in order to heroicize the colonizing European Americans who settled there. Their hegemonic narrative practice produces a narrative justifies their holding of that purloined land and whitewashes the settlers' oppressive or genocidal actions in that space toward the Native Americans, African Americans, and poor European immi-

grants. He found the nineteenth century residents of Deerfield committing acts of commemoration that, in effect, "spatialized racial privilege
through a dialectic of exclusion and inclusion," and more to the point of
the whitening of space, they "utilized objects, spaces, and historical
events to assert their white identity in order to reclaim a threatened cultural and economic authority."[24] After delivering his modernized ascetic
yoga to nineteenth-century America, Swami Vivekananda dealt with
comparable racist narratives, racist spatial politics, and whitewashing
practices that provoked him to challenge American racism and rebuke
the conditions to which European America had reduced the formerly
enslaved Africans. In contrast to the Deerfield settler descendants, who
lionized the stolen land holdings of their white ancestors, Swami Vivekananda utilized the objects, spaces, and historical events of his American
sojourn to propagate a spiritual mission, one that sought not only to
possess and enclose space, but also to gift yoga—a practice he saw as
priceless and universal—to humanity. He wanted *yoga for all*, for everyone, but American yoga students had other inclinations. Whitewashing
his efforts to sooth their discomfort with his yoga objectives to suit their
propensities would translate yoga for all only to mean all who can pay.

Swami Vivekananda found space in America only for an evolving
commercial yoga perceived as exotic. This commodity yoga for sale that
emerged in the colonizing American space began to be marketed along
"sliding scales of differential rights" and varied across an emergent global yoga market with sliding scales of ownership or possession. This
yoga would colonize space by expanding yoga markets. That is why
Swami Vivekananda found little or no space for the ascetic yoga that he
desired to inculcate. There was no space even for yoga based on ethical
principles, along with mild renunciation, that jettisons the harsher renun-
ciative practices of radical asceticism. What America adopted was the
asanas and the breathing, along with a bit of meditation, only three of the
eight aspects of yoga. Lost was the student's dedication to embodying all
eight of the ancient yoga teachings (which new yoga seekers reject).[25]
Whites thereby began to enjoy greater access to commercial yoga and
came to possess more of that yoga's material culture, with white women
laying claim to the largest portion of yoga's rights and practices. In other
words, America's colonizing whiteness Westernized the modernized ascetic yoga that Swami Vivekananda brought into racialized space. Space
was being privatized for white middle-class professional enjoyment.
From the space of magazines, to the space of specialized rooms in their
homes, to spaces for entertainment, to space for eating out at restaurants,
and to space for practicing in yoga studios. As Beldstein argues, " Well-
heeled Americans cultivated more and more space for their private uses,"
and he further claims that the space set aside for "professional athletics
and recreational sports" became the "most dramatic quasi-use of defined
space" in the later nineteenth century[26] By commandeering this new

white space, the well-to-do European American yoga instructors (producers) and students (consumers) came to be ranked by what Stoler calls "a gradated sovereignty." They were to be ranked according to the status that accrues to their prowess with *asanas* or to the space where their yoga is practiced or to the cost of their yoga consumption. Rarely would yoga status be determined according to any objective measure of actual spiritual attainment or according to Patanjali's conception of yoga as cessation of fluctuations of the mind.

WESTERNIZING BRITISH YOGA: AN AMERICA IMPERIAL FORMATION

Swami Vivekananda would contend with the whitewashing narratives of colonized America when in 1893 (the same year Ida B. Wells began her campaign for an end to lynching),[27] he arrives in the United States to build a yoga commons, hoping to fuel social development back home in India and around the world.[28] Helping to rebuild India's decimated colonial economy and achieve independence, he hoped to educate the poor by directing the sannyasin (renunciates) under his tutelage to launch mobile education squads that would move from door to door, using the oral tradition to promote the spread of knowledge at the village level. In a letter Swami Vivekananda sent from Chicago to the Maharaja of Mysore, he explains: "This requires an organization, which again means money. There are enough people in India to work out this plan, but alas! they have no money."[29] India's lack of money for social uplift drove him beyond its borders: "After seeking help in my own country and failing to get any sympathy from the rich, I came over to this country through your Highness' aid."[30]

Swami Vivekananda moved about America as a free man while fellow Indian laborers migrating to the United States from India, Africa, the Caribbean, or South America bore the brunt of American apartheid. Many lived in low income neighborhoods and married black women.[31] Indigenous communities annihilated by Andrew Jackson's Indian Wars had their residual populations dispersed and fell under federal control.[32] Millions of the European immigrants who were arriving to seek a better chance in America were greeted with curtailed immigration policies.[33] Once Swami Vivekananda began circulating in America (earning money as a national speaker and collecting donations to support his projects in India), it soon became apparent that things in America were not much better for immigrants from India than they were for poor Indians in British India.

In racially hostile America, Swami Vivekananda himself suffered being diminished and deemed excludable in the eyes of some whites. Well-received by most European American elites who flocked around him, some whites turned away Swami Vivekananda from Southern hotels when they mistook him for an African.[34] The anti-immigrant fervor was as strong as the anti-black sentiment that affronted him. He died in 1902, but white contempt for immigrants was so sharp by 1908 that the San Francisco Call would alert its readers to a "Hindoo Invasion," and by 1917, an act would be passed to close immigration from India.[35]

A few middle-class, high-caste Indians, who later would be granted U.S. citizenship between 1908 and 1922, understood that they could accomplish this goal only by orchestrating events to have themselves legally defined as white.[36] They may have suggested this strategy to Swami Vivekananda. Refusing to proclaim himself white just to gain the advantage, Swami Vivekananda embraced a multiracial heritage, and retorted, ""What! R[sic]ise at the expense of another! I didn't come to earth for that! . . . If I am grateful to my white-skinned Aryan ancestor, I am far more so to my yellow-skinned Mongolian ancestor and, most so of all, to the blackskinned Negritoid!"[37]

Negotiating adverse conditions of the racial state, Americans of color were denied participation in yoga's Westernization during Swami Vivekananda's 1893–1897 and 1899–1902 visits to America. The space left open by their absence enabled the elite whites to flood into the vacuum and seize the wealth of yoga that the nonwhites were not free to grasp seize. It was space that the lower income whites also could not afford to enter and enjoy. Elite whites, in contrast, were free to choose whether or not to join Swami Vivekananda's mission to build yoga in America. Most found his ecumenical outlook charming. He assured the spiritually progressive European American Christians he met that "I do not come to convert you to a new belief," instead, "I want to teach you to live the truth, to reveal the light within your own soul."[38] He did not set Hinduism and Christianity at odds, but sought to highlight the universal content those religions shared. He conveyed not just a yogic message, but also a modernized yogic path to spiritual evolution.

Yoga's Westernization in America would segregate men over women, rich over poor, whites over nonwhites, colonizers over the colonized, and heteronormatives over the sexual or gender minorities. It would not be long before the superordinates in these pairs moved into yoga prosperity. In Photograph 87, archived online by the Swami Vivekananda Vendanta Network, Swami Vivekananda is seated at a South Pasadena picnic surrounded by wealthy white women in 1900. Providing him with material services and resources, these are the kind of women who formed the nucleus of an elite interest in yoga that would evolve into American yoga. Women recommending him to women quickly expanded his national network as they performed as his organizers or public relations managers,[39] and in exchange, he granted audience to their friends and sometimes he wrote them flattering letters. Acknowledging their services, he writes, "Oh, how free they are! It is they who control social and civic duties. Schools and colleges are full of women. . . . I have been welcomed by them to their houses. They are providing me with food, arranging for my lectures, taking me to market, and doing everything for my comfort and convenience. I shall never be able to repay . . . the deep debt of gratitude I owe them."[40] Swami Vivekananda reveled in their collective labor for the collective good.

CAPITALIST REPRODUCTION AND THE IMPERIAL FORMATION OF YOGA'S WHITE WOMANHOOD

Attending the 1900 Paris International Exhibition with anti-capitalist sentiments, Swami Vivekandana conferred with the socialist leader Peter Kropotkin[41] to discuss an incipient socialist movement and declared himself a socialist. Swami Vivekananda identified with that movement, he said, "not because I think it is a perfect system, but because half a loaf is better than no bread."[42] Said another way, he believed that "a redistribution of pleasure and pain is always better than always the same persons having pleasure and pain.[43]

His desire for this redistribution expresses here his hope to see wealth flow from the haves to the have nots. His position on the distribution of wealth stood in sharp contrast that that of some of his European American, elite, and mostly female yoga colleagues. They had their own interest in redistributing wealth from unknown pockets into their own pockets. Some of them were capitalists who saw in Swami Vivekananda's work a chance for women like them to profit.

Sara Bull and Sarah Farmer are the best known examples. They provided Swami Vivekananda with an audience and venue where he made his American reputation speaking at their Green Acre and at the Cambridge Conference.[44] They registered rooms for no payment to those who came to see him. Bull later broke away to set up the Cambridge Conferences on her own and to form a new market comprised of a more academic audience. She initially collaborated with Farmer to create the Green Acre Conference as an unpaid educational program on spiritual and mystical thought in order to pull in paying residents for Farmer's hotel.

The women who Swami Vivekananda met thought yoga to be unwomanly, so they were disinclined to practice any postures, but soon, white woman-led yoga studios grew popular and lucrative. The work of yoga instruction became another enclosure of the commons and a new economic niche for educated white women. Sylvia Federici explains this privatizing enclosure of yoga as a formerly communal relation. She argues that elite white women would be motivated to advance their own economic interests by commodifying yoga.[45] Federici points to the Emancipation Proclamation as a model for how the cost of labor reproduction was relocated away from the slave owner and onto the freed laborers' household. Federici demonstrates that women's domestic labor similarly contributes to capitalist reproduction and also was relocated from the shared female labor of an extended family onto a nuclear family household, often consisting of a single woman living with a spouse. Servants either were nonwhites or lower income whites. Where no servant was held or hired, the woman of the house had to do all of the work.

Capitalist accumulation has been profitable, Federici contends, where employers have relied on "the unpaid domestic work that women have provided," and because this reproductive work of the domestic women had just began to transition during Swami Vivekananda's visit, it took off quickly in the 1920s.[46] Educated white women moved their labor away from the nuclear family household and some relocated it into the profitable, fee-driven yoga studio. Blanche DeVries exemplifies the white women who began making money while also making organizational contributions to the new commercial yoga.[47] Sakai's analysis of racism in the colonized American settler state concurs with and sustains Federici where he notes subsequent cases where female labor relocates itself in the interest of capital: Just as imperialism called Rosie the Riveter and other white women out of the kitchen and into the world of work in World War II, says Sakai, "so in the 1970s were white women again freed by imperialism to enter the labor force in new areas and in unprecedented numbers." White women started to reposition themselves in the 1920s to reproduce capital's labor by instructing yoga-consuming workers in their own self-reproduction by learning how to conduct a relaxing, healthy yoga practice for themselves or as the instructors of others. As Federici interprets such transitions, we can say that formerly unpaid women's domestic" reproductive activities have been reorganized as value-producing services that workers must purchase and pay for."

NEGOTIATING AND TRANSFORMING IMPERIAL DEBRIS

The ruination of ascetic yoga in colonial India would foster in America a commercial yoga seeking to draw untapped populations into the yoga industry to buy an increasingly high-priced yoga commodity. Despite the yoga profits to be earned, the masses did not flock to yoga due to the barriers that impede their access to yoga—religious modernity, racialized gender, and caste/class capitalism. All three factors exemplify what Stoler regards as "structures of dominance." In combination, these three constitute this Westernizing imperial formation of American yoga. Such barriers are not just obstacles to be circumvented. We might view them, as well, as imperial debris to be cleaned up. They challenge the movement for yoga inclusion to become something more, to become instead a movement to liberate yoga in America. In other words, it is incumbent upon

Americans and westerners, generally, to de-commoditize and reinstate ascetic yoga, not just to open up new spaces of diverse inclusion in yoga commodity consumption.

BARRIERS TO THE WEALTH OF YOGA

Western concerns about yoga are often voiced religiously. It may seem to many that a pagan yoga religion is pitted against major religions, like Christianity. What we actually see, however, is the Western dominance of religious modernity. There is less of a religious clash and more of a secular clash of modernizing Western civilization against a yoga tradition from nonwestern civilization the West believes is in need modernization. Secular Westerners see Eastern societies as being steeped in a primitive paganism, or an anti-Christianity, that threatens the primacy of Western ideology in the global arena

Starting with Columbus, the Christian colonizers considered the people they conquered to be backward, sinful pagans needing to be saved. On one hand, they gave the Bible, and the gun in the other hand. Colonials endeavored to take the land in their bid to subjugate the human and material resources of the colonized people. If you were not with them, you were against them, and how lost you were was expressed in the Western religious terminology of having lost salvation—opposing them simply could mean you got no food, you got no job, and you might be jailed or executed.

The yoga barrier of religious modernity is well-guarded by colonized Christian minorities who ally themselves with colonizing Christians. Consider Mack Major, an African American Christian blogger. His stance against yoga suggests that black men may prefer to go to church, where they can lead, than to a yoga studio where white women lead. Major fears that Christians doing yoga are worshipping Hindu gods, not the Christian God, so he warns black Christians against losing their salvation through religious contamination: "Yoga is a Hindu religious practice designed to open one up to visitation and possession by outside spiritual entities, better known as demons."[48] Mack opposes those who defend yoga—intellectuals, white yoga teachers, and seekers who support yoga. Many do not want religion, neither Christianity nor Hinduism, and many seek nonreligious spirituality. As Charles Mudede reports in his coverage of Tiger Lily Yoga, it can be a class indicator where people seeking yoga often avoid local religion because, "Yoga is for a class of people who tend to be spiritual and not religious. As Columbia City gentrifies, it is becoming more spiritual."[49]

A Latina hired by a major advertising agency was assigned to create a yoga market among Catholic Latinos in San Clemente. She discards the white practice of holding *English-only* yoga classes, but found that teach-

ing yoga in Spanish did not draw enough Latinos to report to her corporate office. How to recruit more? As Brittany Levin observes, "She has
stripped away chanting and other aspects of yoga that may be difficult to
connect with for some who are wary of the practice."[50]

A Catholic magazine tells faithful Catholics who desire to do yoga
that they can protect their faith by selecting the yogic exercise and breathing while avoiding the yogic meditation and spirituality that it asserts is
incompatible with Christian spirituality.[51] Playing it safe, some Christians turn to Holy Yoga with its biblically inspired Western meditations
and mantras.[52] Christians of color disdain yoga along with the white
Christians who reject it outright. White Christian parents who think their
children are spiritually misled in school have begun to protest educators
for introducing yoga in the classroom.[53]

A *racialized gender barrier* divorces the secular nonwhite masses from
yoga. Non-Christian African Americans and Latinos often see yoga as
recreational activity devilishly inimical to their subsistence. Some look at
yoga's leisurely white women and see yoga as the luxury activity "they"
do, not as the urgent life-sustaining activity "we" do. Isolation of a sole
nonwhite person exploring yoga in a sea of yoga whites often is an issue.[54] Secular minorities get yoga's whiteness shoved in their faces by
magazines, billboards, and television selling yoga as lean white bodies
assuming exotic poses. Such images place on exhibition the self-indul-
gent narcissism of the white female bodies that populate yoga. The yoga
scene can feel like an egotistical platform for the preening display of
white women.

A *caste/class barrier* distances yoga from Hindu Americans, and them
from others. Urging Hindu American youth to depart from the HinduS-
tudents Council (HSC) that came under conservative control, scholar Vijay Prashad denounces the anti-Muslim tenor of this movement he calls
"Yankee Hindutva" which grew popular by offering a refuge to Hindu
American youth against the racism they encounter on college campuses
and in European American communities.[55] Attempting to outmaneuver
the more abusive encroachments of European American whiteness, HSC
positions its members on par with racially dominate European
Americans by asserting their own *aryaness* and promoting *hindutva* (Hin-
du-ness). On this basis they desire to reclaim yoga for Hindus. They
likely would contest the fact that yoga was created, not by Hindus who
popularized it, but by the Dravidians.[56] It rarely is acknowledged that
yoga knowledge in Sanskrit was best preserved in southeast India where
it was written in Tamil, in documents such as the *Yoga of Tirumilar: Essays
on the Tirumandiram.*[57] Yet, the HSC claims yoga as a Hindu cultural
resource, originating with the more recent Vedic tradition, and those promoting hindutva insist that whites have stolen yoga from Hindus[58]
Hence, the HSC proclaims that yoga is Hindu. Creating this myth that

yoga began with Hinduism, they urge ethnic Hindus to take yoga back from the white Westerners

The racially distancing *caste/class barrier* can generate adverse real-life consequences when minority groups are gazed upon and treated as being low class and loud, just because their cultural background or life experiences assign less value to being quiet.[59] Seen from the viewpoint of whiteness, the capacity of such minorities to benefit from yoga is discounted and they are regarded as people unable to benefit from the meditative state associated with yoga. This is not minority group laziness because it generally reflects the conditioning of capital. That is why most yoga students are less invested in dedicating time for meditation. As workers disciplined by capital, people tend to believe they cannot afford the time for meditation, especially if they already have set aside the time to do the yoga exercise. People under racial oppression are more stressed when they also endure class oppression. While all people are characterized by their yoga habits, capitalists profit more from every person's stressed-out medical visits than they do from peoples' calming meditation.

Genuflecting to how most paying yoga students are so time sensitive, yoga classes or health programs featuring yoga typically offer about ten minutes of meditation after completing a physical yoga session, if any time at all. Yet, medical centers promoting meditation advise their patients, based on recent research, that the most health benefits are gained when yoga students begin their new yoga practice with meditating just five minutes a day and gradually build up to forty minutes a day, with one twenty minute session in the morning and evening.[60] A forty- to forty-five minute meditation is done in some Bikram yoga classes, but in most yoga classes, people prefer the gross sensations of feeling bodily fit to the subtler sensations of also feeling spiritually balanced and inwardly well-meditated. Longer meditation is not likely to be instituted in Western culture under the capitalist production regime of time is money and money is time.

Meditation or yoga sites might provide entry for nonwhite meditators by having nonwhites and other minorities to conduct yoga sessions, instead of the usual white yoga and meditation leaders. Yet, the behavior of whites in the practice space can be so racist that the location or setting is experienced by the nonwhite public as a racially privileged space[61]

It is one thing to report observations of white yoga spaces, but it is another thing to have the racism operative in those spaces to be ratified by whites doing yoga. So, it helps to hear from a couple of white yoga practitioners with whom I informally discussed the issue. Whiteness does occupy privileged yoga spaces, observes Kevin (not his real name). Kevin is a white male in his mid-fifties who recently co-facilitated a workshop at the Kripalu Yoga Center in Massachusetts. He communed there with a black woman, Martha (not her real name). She attended his workshop and shared with him her concerned observation that "the lower you go in this building, the darker the skin color." They agreed it did appear that the people of color hired to work in that building at Kripalu during that workshop largely occupy the menial positions while the hired whites occupy the higher status, more lucrative positions.

A wealthier, white female demographic wields considerable control over commercial yoga and appropriates eastern cultural resources, according to blogger Earth Energy Reade[62] That particular set of white women exercises control even over those included in yoga. An informal phone interview with Dan (not his real name) affirmed this. Dan is a tall, thin, and athletic white male, who at thirty-eight years old emphatically states, "Yoga is quite white and female." Dan is studying to be a yoga teacher. In the seventeen years he has done yoga, Dan reports having practiced in twenty-five different studios across six states, from coast to coast. Some he visited once, but others became his yoga homes where Dan practiced hundreds of times. Dan says he had sixty-two (71 percent) female teachers and eighteen (29 percent) male teachers. He recalls two nonwhite teachers, one Latino and a black woman recently from Africa. They led two of Dan's eighty yoga classes. Every other yoga class Dan took was led by and populated by whites. Asked if his fellow white yoga practitioners ever discussed the absence of people of color in yoga, Dan admitted, "It's never occurred to me, and with those other whites practicing yoga with me, it never comes up in our conversation." Dan reports that he is now meeting people of color who are pursuing his same yoga goal. It is not clear that their recent access mutes dominant white female control. A white male friend shared with Dan his feeling that men in yoga are treated "like second class citizens." Dan says he does not necessarily agree with his friend's assessment.

Blog entries by Maya Rupert[63] and Pia Glenn[64] challenge the whiteness of the yoga space. They engage Jen Caron, a white female blogger, ,[65] who "empathizes" with the heavy black woman doing yoga in front of her at a studio who, in Caron's view, seemed incapable of keeping up with Caron's postural flow. Caron's xoJane blog entry on January 28, 2014, was followed the next day by Glenn, another xoJane blogger. Caron provoked another response three days later when blogger Rupert published an open letter that fueled a heated online debate that jumped from the narrow audience of an online yoga magazine to a national black readership of the HuffPost. In her initial blog entry, Caron upheld her own lithe white body as the yoga standard that she presumed the buxom black woman angrily must envy. Caron exhibited "white fragility" when she presumed that the safety of her yoga studio had been violated by the black female anger that Caron imagined. She regretted that yoga has been "co-opted by white women" and that it was unprepared to accommodate that black woman's needs, but does not question her presumption that the black woman was angry with Caron about her yoga skills. Caron's blog places herself in a dominant racial position and it also might place on exhibition Caron's higher class status. Despite Caron's intentions, the activists' retorts support diversified yoga and defend from Caron's invective a nameless black woman who had been verbally assaulted by Caron's insensitive prose.

Finally, yoga is stereotyped as being healthy for everyone, regardless of the physical condition of the people who show up in yoga class. Some secular minorities fear that yoga alters the mind more than the body. Others wonder if claims about yoga's healthiness could be exaggerated or irrational.[66] [67] A New York yoga master opines that today's urbanized Western bodies sit too much and, thus, are far less flexible than were the bodies where yoga evolved in India. Those people engaged in a wide range of practices that produced far more flexible bodies. With most yoga teachers being unprepared to direct students away from self-harm activity while practicing yoga, demographics reveal a growing number of severe yoga injuries[68]

The Tiger Lily Yoga studio in Seattle[69] reveals a *class/caste* barrier configured as a fee structure that makes yoga unaffordable for the poor local residents who are least able to pay, and this inequitably discriminates against people of color who due, to racism, have less wealth than whites. Higher class/and dominate racial caste yoga elites pay a different rate than do working class and lower income people. Some yoga elites who gentrify the same neighborhood where the studio is locatedmight pay one lump sum of $900 for the special annual fee or pay $1,000 for the regular annual fee. Imagine the savings for the yoga elites when five of them who each pay the regular annual fee of $1,000 altogether would pay the yoga studio just $5,000. According to the studio fee structure, this collective annual fee payment by five elite yoga students would be $400 less than the $5,400 total that would be paid for the same 360 days of yoga by a single lower income and lower class/caste drop-in yoga student. That poor working person's cash flow could be so thin and unreliable that they barely can manage to scrap up the $15 rate per daily class. The yog a studio invites everyone, but the fee structure can shout inequality, as well as exclusivity.

To aid the current movement for yoga inclusion in its drive to foster yoga's liberation, I hereby declare it imperative that exclusionary fee structures be banned and that yoga no longer be for sale, for it must be treated as a commons. To recapture yoga as a commons requires that our yoga behavior must change so we can decolonize our bodies and minds. This way we can build a yoga commons in which there really can be *yoga for all*.

CONCLUSIONS: TOWARDS A LIBERATED YOGA

In yoga, a movement is forming to clear away the imperial debris that makes Western yoga a white public space and prevents it from operating as a commons. The movement stands not just against exclusion, but also against the whiteness cultivated in yoga. It is not a movement against white persons in yoga, per se, but against what Bonilla-Silva defines as "embodied racial power."[70] Embodied racial power refers to the learned behavior of racial dominates and to their enactment of the allocated privileges inherited from the colonial era. It implies a strategic denial that t hose privileges exist while at the same time the space of yoga is being whitened to preserve them. Denial helps to preserve yoga as white public space especially where such claims provoke what Robin DiAngelo calls the "fragility" of whites.[71] This fragility is defensive or protective of whitened yoga. It is displayed by whites in yoga when they are challenged about how they embody dominant racial privilege and are encouraged to make a different choice

The barriers to yoga that make it white public space are mutually constructed on both sides of the power dynamic. The tendency to blame the nonwhite attitude is exemplified when white yoga practitioners like Caron complain of a black woman's attitude while her own white fragility goes unnoti ced in her own line of sight. Postcolonial yoga is blinded by racism where whites who write about Swami Vivekananda understate the racist class dynamic he contended with not just here, in America, but also in India and elsewhere during his travels. Most whites do not recognize that even when trying to be non-racist, their whiteness can trump other concerns and they may commit racist violations that go unaddressed. This blindness to whiteness is structural; it is not the norm only because some people who happen to be white are having personal problems. When the authority and status of yoga's whiteness is challenged by more people of color doing yoga, there is a tendency of whites to join together as a group, however informally, to assert or to defend their hegemonic dominance over that yoga space that they likely intend to control. So, a compassionate heart must coexist with a constant vigilance against racist violations committed in defense of whiteness is required if people of color are to be safe where they go to practice yoga.

The upshot is that we must liberate yoga from whiteness, that is, from the imperial debris embedded in the inherited gender, race and class barriers that preserve yoga as white public space to the benefit of whites, and keep yoga a marketable, profitable monied affair. This is not what most people in yoga want to hear when the current white female yoga managers and instructors stand to gain from the new lucrative yoga markets opening up for men,[72] Latinos,[73] black women,[74]and in various institutions having budgets to pay for yoga instruction. But to neutralize the toxicity of the white public space of yoga, we must help white women to relinquish their damaging control over yoga and wrest yoga out of corporate hands. Recognize that a yoga for all will never be free to produce unwavering ascetic yogis under white control or when brought into institutions that will seek to regulate yoga[75] Under such conditions, the yoga instruction of Patanjali that Vivekananda promoted will continue to be eroded, so we must unleash yoga from its capitalist harness and return it to the commons where it can exist for all of the people, all of the time

NOTES

1. David Theo Goldberg, "States of Whiteness," in *The Racial State* (Malden, MA: Blackwell Publishers, 2002) 160–99.
2. Goldberg, *The Racial State*, 176.
3. Cheryl Harris, "Whiteness as Property," *Harvard Law Review* 106, no. 8 (June 1993): 1707–91.
4. C. Richard King, "Unsettling Commodity Racism," *Studies in Symbolic Interaction* 33, (2009): 255–73.
5. David Graeber, *Possibilities: Essays on Hierarchy, Rebellion and Desire* (Oakland: AK Press, 2007) 102.
6. Ann Laura Stoler, "Imperial Debris: Reflections on Ruins and Ruinaition," *Cultural Anthropology* 23, no. 2 (2008): 193.
7. Stoler, *Imperial Debris*, 193.
8. *Imperial Debris*, 193.
9. *Imperial Debris*, 193, 202.
10. Gopal Stavig, "Swami Vivekananda and Liberation Theology," *Bulletin of the Ramakrishna Mission Institute of Culture* (Novemer–December 2009): 509–15, 556–59. Accessed December 20, 2015. http://americanvedantist.org/2010/articles/swami-Swami Vivekananda-and-liberation-theology.
11. Jonathan Hyslop, review of *Drawing the Global Colour Line: White Men's Countries and the International Challenge of Racial Equality*, by Marilyn Lake and Henry Reynolds, (Cambridge: Cambridge University Press, 2008), *Journal of Global History* 4, no. 1 (March 2009): 75–189.
12. Enoch H. Page, "Information Control: The Past and Present Career of Scientific Thinking in the European and Colonized World." *Reviews in Anthropology* 18 (1991): 259–71.
13. Marilyn Lake and Henry Reynolds. *Drawing the Global Colour Line: White Men's Countries and the International Challenge of Racial Equality*, (Cambridge: Cambridge University Press, 2008).
14. Kamil V. Zevlebil, *The Poets of the Powers* (London, Integral Publishing, 1973), book jacket.
15. John Newsinger, "Revolt and Repression in Kenya: The 'Mau Mau' Rebellion, 1952–1960". *Science & Society* 45, no. 2 (Summer 1981): 159–85.
16. Stoler, *Imperial Debris*, 193.
17. Stoler, *Imperial Debris*,196.
18. Stoler, *Imperial Debris*, 193–94.
19. Banhatti, G. S. *The Life and Philosophy of Swami Vivekananda* (Delhi: Atlantic Publishers & Distributors, 1989) 30.
20. Carol Horton, "The Oprah-fication of Patangali: The Cultural Homogenization of the Yoga Sutr,. *Elephant: Dedicated to the Mindful Life*, November 16, 2010. Accessed March 23, 2015, http://www.elephantjournal.com/2010/11/the-oprah-fication-of-patanjali-culturally-homogenizing-the-yoga-sutra.

21. Enoch H. Page and Brooke Thomas, "White Public Space and the Construction of White Privilege in U.S. Health Care: Fresh Concepts and a New Model of Analysi," *Medical Anthropology Quarterly* 8, no. 1, 109–116.

22. Enoch Page, "No Black Public Sphere in White Public Space," *Transforming Anthropology*, 8, no. 1&2 (2000): 111–28.

23. Quentin Lewis, "Materiality, White Public Space, and Historical Commemoration in 19th Century Deerfield, Massachusetts," in *The Archaeology of Race in the Northeast: Archaeological Studies of Racialization, Resistance, and Memory*, edited by Christopher N. Matthews and Alison Manfra McGovern (Gainesville: University Press of Florida, 2013), 273–90. Accessed November 2, 2015. https://www.academia.edu/17860687/Materiality_White_Public_Space_and_Historical_Commemoration_in_Nineteenth-Century_Deerfild_Massachusetts.

24. Lewis, "Historical Commemoration," 1.

25. Shiva Shahram, "The Yoga Generation Wants Yoga Without Dogma," *GPS for the Soul*, Huff Post, April 9, 2015. http://www.huffingtonpost.com/shahram-shiva/the-yoga-generation-wants_b_7027712.html.

26. Burton J. Bledstein, *The Culture of Professionalism: The Middle Class and the Development of Higher Education in America*, (New York: W. W. Norton & Company, 1978) 64, 60.

27. Ida B. Wells-Barnett, "Lynch Law in America," *The Arena* 23, no. 1 (January 1900), accessed June 17, 2015. https://courses.washington.edu/spcmu/speeches/idabwells.htm.

28. Swami Vivekananda, "Letter to Haripada, December 28 1893," *The Complete Works of Swami Vivekananda*, (Chicago: 1893), https://en.wikisource.org/wiki/The_Complete_Works_of_Swami_Vivekananda/Volume_5/Epistles_-_First_Series/VI_Haripada.

29. Swami Vivekananda, "Our Duty to the Masses, Letter to the Maharaja of Mysore, June 23, 1894," *Complete Works of Swami Swami Vivekananda*, 4: 361–64, http://Swami Vivekananda.org/readings.asp.

30. Vivekananda, "Our Duty to the Masses."

31. Nico Slate, *Colored Cosmopolitanism: The Shared Struggle for Freedom in the United States and India* (Cambridge, MA: Harvard University Press, 2012) 26–27.

32. "Indian Wars Time Table," http://www.u-s-history.com/pages/h1008.html.

33. Beth Rowen, "Immigration Timeline," http://www.infoplease.com/us/immigration/legislation-timeline.html.

34. Sister Nivedita, *The Complete Works of Sister Nivedita* (Calcutta: Advaita Ashrama, 1982), 153.

35. Sister Nivedita, *Complete Works*, 27.

36. Slate, *Colored Cosmopolitanism*, 27–29.

37. Sister Nivedita, *Complete Works*, 153.

38. Makarand Parajape ed., *Swami Vivekananda: A Contemporary Reader*, (New York: Routledge, 2015) 192.

39. Narasingha Prosad Sil, *Swami Vivekananda: A Reassessment* (Cranbury, NJ: Associated University Presses, 1997) 116.

40. Swami Vivekananda, Letter to Haripada, http://www.ramakrishnavivekananda.info/vivekananda/volume_5/epistles_first_series/006_haripada.htm

41. Banhatti. *The Life and Philosophy of Swami Vivekananda*, 111.

42. Banhatti, *Swami Vivekananda*, 200–201.

43. Banhatti, *Swami Vivekananda*, 112.

44. Jacqueline Brady, "Wise Mother? Insane Mother?: Sara Chapman Bull and the Disarticulated Subjectivities of Turn-of-the-Century Motherhood," in *Disjointed Perspectives on Motherhood*, ed. Catalina Florina Florescu (Lanham, MD: Lexington Books, 2013) 201–16.

45. Sylvia Federici, Revolution at Zero Point: Housework, Reproduction and Feminist Struggle, (Oakland: California: PM Press, 2012): 139.

46. Federici, *Zero Point*, 140.

47. "The Film," Yogawoman: Never Underestimate the Power of Inner Peace, http://www.yogawoman.tv/the-film.

48. Mack Major Blog, "Seduced by the Serpent: Yoga and the Devil's Door," *Eden Decoded*. https://www.edendecoded.com/blog-2/item/yoga, accessed August 9, 2015.

49. Charles Udede, "Apparel Store in Columbia," *The Stranger*, May 20, 2015, accessed August 4, 2015. http://www.thestranger.com/blogs/slog/2015/05/20/22250632/the-yoga-studio-thats-replacing-a-black-christian-apparel-store-in-columbia-city.

50. Brittany Levine, "'Got Milk?' Creator Lures Latinos through Yoga," *The Orange County Register*, January 11, 2011, accessed June 3, 2015, http://www.ocregister.com/articles/milk-283097-yoga-spanish.html.

51. Michelle Arnold, "The Trouble with Yoga: A Catholic May Practice the Physical Postures but with Caveats," *Catholic Answers: To Explain and Defend the Faith* 23, no. 3 (May/June, 2012) http://www.catholic.com/magazine/articles/the-trouble-with-yoga.

52. S. Brinkman. "Don't Fall Into the Holy Yoga Trap," *Women of Grace: Authentic Femininity for Such a Time as This*, April 30, 2012, accessed August 4, 2015, http://www.womenofgrace.com/blog/?p=13904.

53. Will Carless, "Yoga Class Draws a Religious Protest," *New York Times*, December 15, 2012, accessed June 12, 2015, http://www.nytimes.com/2012/12/16/us/school-yoga-class-draws-religious-protest-from-christians.html?_r=0.

54. Nadine McNeil, "Is Yoga for People of Color An Oxymoron?" *Elephant: Dedicated to the Mindful Life*, May 22, 2011, accessed June 28, 2015, http://www.elephantjournal.com/2011/05/is-yoga-for-people-of-color-an-oxymoron.

55. Vijay Prashad, "Letter to a Young American Hindu," *Pass the Roti on the Left Hand Side*, May 21, 2007, accessed, July 16, 2015, http://www.passtheroti.com/posts/487.

56. Kumar Buradikatti, "Yoga Was a Contribution of Non-Vedic Dravidian Tradition," *The Hindu*, June 21, 2015, accessed July 16, 2015, http://www.thehindu.com/news/national/karnataka/yoga-was-a-contribution-of-nonvedic-dravidian-tradition/article7339307.ece.

57. Siddhi Tirumular, *The Tirumandiram*. T. N. Ganapathy, ed., St. Etienne de Bolton, Quebec: Babaji`s Kriya Yoga and Publications, copublished with Varthamanan Publications, Theyagaraya Nagar, Chennai, India, 2010) http://www.thirumandiram.net/tirumandiram-about-the-book.html. I thank Sudha Fatima for informing me about the existence and significance of this source.

58. Aseem Shukla, "The Theft of Yoga," *On Faith*, April 18, 2010, accessed August 19, 2015, http://www.faithstreet.com/onfaith/2010/04/18/nearly-twenty-million-people-in/5960.

59. Stephen A. Crockett Jr., "Women Kicked Off Napa Wine Train for Laughing While Black File $11,000 Lawsuit," *The Root*, October 2, 2015, accessed October 2, 2015, http://www.theroot.com/articles/news/2015/10/women_kicked_off_napa_wine_train_for_laughing_while_black_file_11_000_000.html.

60. Sumathi Reddy, "Doctor's Orders: 20 Minutes of Meditation Twice Daily," *Wall Street Journal*, Your Health, April 15, 2013, accessed March 12, 2015, http://www.wsj.com/articles/SB10001424127887324345804578424863782143682.

61. Edwin Ng and Ron Purser, "White Privilege & the Mindfulness Movement," *Buddhist Peace Fellowship: Cultivating Compassionate Action*, October 2, 2015, accessed October 3, 2015, http://www.buddhistpeacefellowship.org/white-privilege-the-mindfulness-movement.

62. Earth Energy Reader, *The Shift Has Hit the Fan*, accessed March 7, 2015, https://earthenergyreader.wordpress.com/2012/05/04/why-i-left-yoga-and-why-i-think-a-helluva-lot-of-people-are-being-duped.

63. Maya Rupert, "An Open Letter to the White Woman Who Felt Bad for Me at Yoga," *HuffPost*, The Blog, January 31, 2014, accessed February 2, 2015, http://www.huffingtonpost.com/maya-rupert/an-open-letter-to-the-whi_b_4692049.html.

64. Pia Glenn, "It Happened to Me: I Read an Essay About A White Woman's Yoga Class/Black Women Crisis and I Cannot," xoJane, January 29, 2014, accessed February

2, 2015, http://www.xojane.com/issues/it-happened-to-me-i-read-an-essay-about-a-white-womans-yoga-class-black-woman-crisis-and-i-cannot.

65. Jan Caron, "It Happened to Me: There Are No Black People in My Yoga Classes and I'm Suddenly Feeling Uncomfortable With It," Xojane, January 28, 2014, accessed February 15, 2015, http://www.xojane.com/it-happened-to-me/it-happened-to-me-th ere-are-no-black-people-in-my-yoga-classes-and-im-uncomfortable-with-it.

66. Swami Jnaneshvara Bharati, "Theism, Atheism, Yoga and Fear," *Traditional Yoga and Meditation of the Himalayan Masters,* n.d., accessed September 2, 2015, http://www.swamij.com/theism-atheism-yoga-fear.htm.

67. Bharati, "Theism, Atheism, Yoga and Fear."

68. William J. Broad, "How Yoga Can Wreck Your Body," *New York Times* Magazine, January 5, 2012, accessed August 12, 2014, http://www.nytimes.com/2012/01/08/magazine/how-yoga-can-wreck-your-body.html?_r=0.

69. Tiger Lily Yoga, "Pricing and Services," n.d., accessed September 1, 2015. http://www.tigerlilyyoga.com/pricing.html.

70. Eduardo Bonilla-Silva, *Racism Without Racists: Color-Blind Racism and the Persistence of Inequality in the United States* (Lanham, MD: Rowman & Littlefield, 2006) 145.

71. Robin DiAngelo, "White Fragility," *International Journal of Critical Pedagogy* 3, no. 3 (2011): 54-70. Accessed February 27, 2012. http://libjournal.uncg.edu/ijcp/article/view/249/116.

72. Joshua Berman "9 Reasons Why You Should Practice Yoga," *Men's Fitness,* accessed October 1, 2015, http://www.mensfitness.com/training/endurance/9-reasons-why-you-should-practice-yoga.

73. Yoga Journal, "The Future of Yoga is in . . . Spanish." *Huff Post: Healthy Living,* July 1, 2014, last updated August 31, 2015, accessed September 1, 2015, http://www.huffingtonpost.com/kwalshyjmagcom/the-future-of-yoga-is-ins_b_55 48826.html.

74. Ashley Weatherford, "Start-up That's Driving Black Women to Yoga," Our Bodies Ourselves, *The Cut,* July 16, 2015, accessed April 3, 2015, http://nymag.com/thecut/2015/07/start-up-thats-driving-black-women-to-yoga.html.

75. Yoga Alliance, "Law," *Yoga Alliance: Many Paths, One Yoga Alliance,* accessed October 2, 2015, https://www.yogaalliance.org/Learn/Article_Archive/Our_Offici al_Stance_on_Government_Regulati.

REFERENCES

Arnold, Michelle. "The Trouble with Yoga: A Catholic May Practice the Physical Postures but with Caveats." *Catholic Answers: To Explain and Defend the Faith.* 23, no. 3 (May/June 2012). http://www.catholic.com/magazine/articles/the-trouble-with-yo ga.

Banhatti, G. S. *The Life and Philosophy of Swami Vivekananda* (Delhi: Atlantic Publishers & Distributors, 1989).

Berman, Joshua. "9 Reasons Why You Should Practice Yoga." *Men's Fitness* n.d. September 1, 2015. http://www.mensfitness.com/training/endurance/9-reasons-why-you-should-practice-yoga?page=4.

Bharati, Swami Jnaneshvara. *Theism, Atheism, Yoga and Fear.* Edited by Swami Jnaneshvara. n.d., September 2, 2015. http://www.swamij.com/theism-atheism-yoga-fe ar.htm.

Bledstein, Burton J. *The Culture of Professionalism: The Middle Class and the Development of Higher Education in America* (New York: W. W. Norton & Company, 1978).

Bonilla-Silva, Eduardo. *Racism Without Racists: Color-Blind Racism and the Persistence of Inequality in the United States* (Lanham, MD: Rowman & Littlefield, 2016).

Brady, Jacqueline. "Wise Mother? Insane Mother?: Sara Chapman Bull and the Disarticulated Subjectivities of Turn-of-the-Century Motherhood," in *Disjointed Perspec-*

tives on Motherhood. Edited by Florescu, Catalina Florina (Lanham, MD: Lexington Books, 2013).

Brinkman, S. *Women of Grace*. April 30, 2012. Accessed August 4, 2015. http://www.womenofgrace.com/blog/?p=13904.

Broad, William J. "How Yoga Can Wreck Your Body." *New York Times Magazine*. January 5, 2012. Accessed August 12, 2014. http://www.nytimes.com/2012/01/08/magazine/how-yoga-can-wreck-your-body.html?_r=0.

Buradikatti, Kumar. "Yoga Was a Contribution of Non-Vedic Dravidian Tradition." *The Hindu*. June 21, 2015. Accessed July 16, 2015. http://www.thehindu.com/news/national/karnataka/yoga-was-a-contribution-of-nonvedic-dravidian-tradition/article7339307.ece.

Carless, Will. "Yoga Class Draws a Religious Protest." *New York Times*. December 15, 2012. http://www.nytimes.com/2012/12/16/us/school-yoga-class-draws-religious-protest-from-christians.html?_r=0.

Caron, Jan. "It Happened to Me: There Are No Black People in My Yoga Classes and I'm Suddenly Feeling Uncomfortable With It," xoJane. January 28, 2014. Accessed February 15, 2015. http://www.xojane.com/it-happened-to-me/it-happened-to-me-there-are-no-black-people-in-my-yoga-classes-and-im-uncomfortable-with-it.

Crockett, Stephen A., Jr. "Women Kicked Off Napa Wine Train for Laughing While Black File $11,000 Lawsuit." *The Root*. October 2, 2015. http://www.theroot.com/articles/news/2015/10/women_kicked_off_napa_wine_train_for_laughing_while_bl ack_file_11_000_000.html.

DiAngelo, Robin. "White Fragility." *International Journal of Critical Pedagogy* 3, no. 3 (2011). Accessed February 27, 2012. http://libjournal.uncg.edu/ijcp/article/view/249/116.

Earth Energy Reader. *The Shift Has Hit the Fan*. Accessed March 7, 2015. https://earthenergyreader.wordpress.com/2012/05/04/why-i-left-yoga-and-why-i-think-a-helluva-lot-of-people-are-being-duped.

Farmer, Jared. "Americanasana." *Reviews in American History* 40 (2012): 145–58. Accessed June 2, 2015. http://www.academia.edu/1475124/Americanasana.

Federici, Sylvia. *Revolution at Point Zero: Housework, Reproduction, and Feminist Struggle* (Oakland, CA: PM Press, 2012).

Glenn, Pia. "It Happened to Me: I Read an Essay About a White Woman's Yoga Class/Black Women Crisis and I Cannot," xoJane. January 29, 2014. Accessed February 2, 2015. http://www.xojane.com/issues/it-happened-to-me-i-read-an-essay-about-a-white-womans-yoga-class-black-woman-crisis-and-i-cannot.

Goldberg, David Theo. *The Racial State* (Malden, MA: Blackwell Publishers, Ltd., 2002).

Graeber, David. *Possibilities: Essays on Hierarchy, Rebellion and Desire* (Oakland, CA: AK Press, 2007).

Harris, Cheryl. "Whiteness as Property." *Harvard Law Review* (June 1993): 1707–1791.

Horton, Carol. "The Oprah-fication of Patangali: The Cultural Homogenization of the Yoga Sutra." *Elephant: Dedicated to the Mindful Life*, November 16, 2015. http://www.elephantjournal.com/2010/11/the-oprah-fication-of-patanjali-culturally-homogenizing-the-yoga-sutra/.

Hyslop, Jonathan. "Review of *Drawing the Global Colour Line: White Men's Countries and the International Challenge of Racial Equality*," by Marilyn Lake and Henry Reynolds (Cambridge: Cambridge University Press, 2009) 175–89.

"Indian Wars Time Table." n.d. October 6, 2015. http://www.u-s-history.com/pages/h1008.html.

King, C. Richard. "Unsettling Commodity Racism." *Studies in Symbolic Interaction* 33 (2009): 255–73.

Lake, Marilyn and Henry Reynolds. *Drawing the Global Colour Line: White Men's Countries and the International Challenge of Racial Equality* (Cambridge: Cambridge University Press, 2008).

Levine, Brittany. "'Got Milk?' Creator Lures Latinos through Yoga." *The Orange County Register*, January 11, 2011. June 3, 2015. http://www.ocregister.com/articles/milk-283097-yoga-spanish.html.

Lewis, Quentin. "Materiality, White Public Space, and Historical Commemoration in 19th Century Deerfield," in *The Archaeology of Race in the Northeast: Archaeological Studies of Racialization*. Edited by Christopher N. Matthews and Allison Manfra McGovern. (Fainesville: University Press of Florida, 2013) 273–90.

Major, Mack. "Seduced by the Serpent: Yoga and the Devil's Door." August 9, 2015.

McNeil, Nadine. "Is Yoga for People of Color An Oxymoron?" *Elephant: Dedicated to the Mindful Life*, May 22, 2011. Accessed June 28, 2015. http://www.elephantjournal.com/2011/05/is-yoga-for-people-of-color-an-oxymoron.

Mudede, Charles. "The Yoga Studio That's Replacing a Black Christian Apparel Store in Columbia City." *The Stranger*, May 20, 2015. Accessed August 4, 2015. http://www.thestranger.com/blogs/slog/2015/05/20/22250632/the-yoga-studio-thats-replacing-a-black-christian-apparel-store-in-columbia-city.

Newsinger, John. "Revolt and Repression in Kenya: The 'Mau Mau' Rebellion, 1952–1960." *Science & Society* 45, no. 2 (1981): 159–85.

Ng, Edwin and Ron Purser. "White Privilege & the Mindfulness Movement," *Buddhist Peace Fellowship: Cultivating Compassionate Action*. October 2, 2015. Accessed October 3, 2015. http://www.buddhistpeacefellowship.org/white-privilege-the-mindfulness-movement.

Nivedita, Sister. *The Complete Works of Sister Nivedita*. Calcutta: Advaita Ashram, 1982.

Page, Enoch. "Information Control: The Past and Career of Scientific Thinking in the European and Colonized World." *Reviews in Anthropology* 18 (1991): 259–71.

———. "No Black Public Sphere in White Public Spaces." *Transforming Anthropology* 8, nos. 1 & 2 (2000): 111–28.

Page, Enoch and Brooke Thomas. "White Public Space and the Construction of White Privilege in U.S. Health Care: Fresh Concepts and a New Model of Analysis," *Medical Anthropology Quarterly* 8, no. 1 (1994): 109–116.

Parajape, Makarand, ed. *Swami Vivekananda: A Contemporary Reader*. New York: Routledge, 2015.

Prashad, Vijay. "Letter To A Young American Hindu." *Pass the Roti on the Left Hand Side*. May 21, 2007. Accessed July 16, 2015. http://www.passtheroti.com/posts/487 .

Reddy, Sumathi. "Doctor's Orders: 20 Minutes of Meditation Twice Daily." *Wall Street Journal*, Your Health. April 15, 2013. Accessed March 12, 2015. http://www.wsj.com/articles/SB10001424127887324345804578424863782143682.

Reynolds, Marilyn Lake and Henry. *Drawing the Global Colour Line: White men's countries and the international challenge of racial equality*. Cambridge: Cambridge University Press, 2008.

Rowen, Beth. "Immigration Legislation." n.d. http://www.infoplease.com/us/immigration/legislation-timeline.html.

Rupert, Maya. "An Open Letter to the White Woman Who Felt Bad for Me at Yoga," *HuffPost*, The Blog. January 31, 2015. Accessed February 2, 2015. http://www.huffingtonpost.com/maya-rupert/an-open-letter-to-the-whi_b_4692049.html.

Sakai, J. *Settlers: The Mythology of the White Proletariat*. 3rd. ed. Chicago: Morningstar Press, 1989.

Shahram, Shiva. "The Yoga Generation Wants Yoga Without Dogma." *GPS for the Soul, Huff Post*, April 9, 2015. http://www.huffingtonpost.com/shahram-shiva/the-yoga-generation-wants_b_7027712.html.

Shukla, Aseem. "The Theft of Yoga." *OnFaith*, April 18, 2010. Accessed August 19, 2015. http://www.faithstreet.com/onfaith/2010/04/18/nearly-twenty-million-people-in/5960.

Sil, Narasingha Prosad. *Swami Vivekananda: A Reassessment* (Cranbury, NJ: Associated University Press, 1997).

Slate, Nico. *Colored Cosmopolitanism: The Shared Struggle for Freedom in the United States and India* (Cambridge, MA: Harvard University Press, 2012).

Stavig, Gopal. "Swami Vivekananda and Liberation Theology." *Bulletin of the Ramak-rishna Institute of Culture* (November/December 2009): 509–15, 556–59). Accessed December 20, 2015. http://americanvedantist.org/2010/articles/swami-Swami Vivek-ananda-and-liberation-theology.

Stoler, Ann Laura. "Imperial Debris: Reflections on Ruins and Ruination." *Cultural Anthropology* 23, no. 2 (2008): 191–219.

Tiger Lily Yoga. "Pricing and Services," n.d. Accessed September 1, 2015. http://www.tigerlilyyoga.com/pricing.html.

Tirumular, Siddhi. *The Tirumandiram.* Edited by T. N. Ganapathy. 10 vols (Theraga-raya Nagar: Babaji's Kriya Yoga and Publications, 2010). Accessed October 2, 2015. http://www.thirumandiram.net/tirumandiram-about-the-book.html.

Udede, Charles. "Apparel Store in Columbia." *The Stranger.* May 20, 2015. http://www.thestranger.com/blogs/slog/2015/05/20/22250632/the-yoga-studio-thats-re-placing-a-black-christian-apparel-store-in-columbia-city.

Vivekananda, Swami. "Letter to Haripada, December 28, 1893." *The Complete Works of Swami Vivekananda* (Chicago: 1893). Accessed March 30, 2015. https://en.wikisource.org/wiki/The_Complete_Works_of_Swami_Vivekananda/Volume_5/Epistles_-_First_Series/VI_Haripada.

———. "Our Duty to the Masses. Letter to the Maharaja of Mysore." *Complete Works of Swami Vivekananda.* Edited by The Vedanta Society of Boston. Vol. 4. (1894). 361–64. Accessed February 15, 2015. http://vivekananda.org/readings.asp.

Weatherford, Ashley. "Start-up That's Driving Black Women to Yoga," Our Bodies Ourselves, *The Cut.* July 16, 2015. Accessed April 3, 2015. http://nymag.com/thecut/2015/07/start-up-thats-driving-black-women-to-yoga.html.

Wells-Barnett, Ida B. "Lynch Law in America." *The Arena,* (January 23, 1900): 15–24. Accessed March 3, 2015. https://courses.washington.edu/spcmu/speeches/idab-wells.htm.

Yoga Alliance. "Law." *Yoga Alliance: Many Paths, One Yoga Alliance.* Accessed October 2, 2015. https://www.yogaalliance.org/Learn/Article_Archive/Our_Official_Stan ce_on_Government_Regulati.

Yoga Journal. "The Future of Yoga is in . . . Spanish." *HuffPost: Healthy Living,* July 1, 2014. September 1, 2015. http://www.huffingtonpost.com/kwalshyjmagcom/the-fu-ture-of-yoga-is-ins_b_5548826.html.

Yoga, Tiger Lily. *Pricing and Services.* Accessed September 1, 2015. http://www.tigerlilyyoga.com/pricing.html.

Yogawoman: Never Underestimate the Power of Inner Peace. Dir. Kate Clere McIntyre and Saraswati Clere. Narrated by Annette Benning. Gravitas. Shadow, 2011. http://www.yogawoman.tv/the-film.

Zevlebil, Kamil V. *The Poets of the Powers.* London: Integral Publishing, 1973.

FOUR

Toward Yoga as Property

Roopa Kaushik-Brown

The forms of yoga practiced by my maternal grandmother (nani ji), Dulari Kaushik, were lived experiences, not studio classes. Nani ji's systems of yogic wellness included strict vegetarianism, Ayurvedic medicinals, and ever present, healing song. The family love of music flows down the generations, and pervades our cultural and spiritual practices of pluralistic Hinduism. One mausi ji (mother's sister) studied classical raga and sitar at a gharana, going on to lead a women's music college in Udaipur. Growing up, I heard my mother sing publicly at weekly bhajan sessions, gatherings where desi-American, immigrant families like our own could come together for welcome social and spiritual refueling. At these bhajans, yoga was not for sale, it was not severable, and it was not white. In almost completely brown spaces, we engaged our yogic practices, which freely pervaded how we sat, how we sang, what we ate, and how we agreed to be breathing, present, and healing together in public space. Now, in the United States, "yoga" is ubiquitous, but the living systems of yoga as practiced by my nani ji can be hard to find.

Popularly, in the West, yoga is synonymous with *asana*, stretching and strengthening postures and motions. Sadly, it is also synonymous with whiteness. Whiteness is absorptive of yoga, which serves to obliterate the pluralizing potential of yoga. What is left is an extremely narrow vision of yoga. The wellness and knowledge systems that comprise yoga are particularly well-situated to funnel important healthful resources to populations at the margins who have little or no access to quality care. Unfortunately, yoga is also fertile ground for appropriation, and not just by whiteness, but also by violent, fundamentalist structures worldwide. But yoga is fundamentally about liberation, through wellness on many levels, with emphasis on a union between the mortal body and immortal energy (which neither dies nor is born). Also, for most of its incredibly long life, yoga has existed as "free," in that it has not been associated with fees that can be prohibitive. Unfortunately, freedom, being free, and yoga are not inseparably braided together, nor have they always been.[1] Herein, the discussion narrowly focuses on U.S.-based, recent yoga-related matters that reveal much about race and the continued experience of colonization in the West. This glimpse reveals how yoga, a potentially liberatory and uniquely accessible wellness structure, is unraveling at breakneck speed.[2]

The current trajectory of American yoga indicates a steep increase in legalized propertization. A comparative look at legalized ownership rights in U.S. yoga over a period of ten years reveals a marked decline in the amount of yoga that remains freely available in the public commons. In 2005, it was reported that in the United States alone, there were: 2,315 registered yoga trademarks, 150 yoga-related copyrights, and 134 patents for yoga inventions.[3] A follow-up search ten years later, conducted by the author, revealed: 3,992 registered yoga trademarks; 2,144 registered copyrights featuring "yoga" as a keyword; and 7,810 domestic patents for yoga-related inventions.[4] This comparative study reveals a 72 percent increase in yoga trademarks, a 1,329 percent increase in yoga copyrights, and a 5,628 percent increase in yoga patents. This indicates an overall 436 percent rise in the legalized propertization of yoga within one decade. Ownership and exclusion are alive and well in American yoga. As Cheryl Harris establishes in "Whiteness as Property," central to propertization is the settled expectation in an ability to own (anything and everything), and to exclude. Whiteness absorbs what can valorize it, in order to shore up defenses to itself, because whiteness is a uniquely valuable resource. Yoga as property is a lens geared to shed light on the ways contemporary yoga exists as an increasingly valued element of de facto and de jur white and Western supremacy.

Thankfully, there are still many ways yoga lives in the world separate from the forces of propertization that pin yoga to an inanimate thing, severable and profitable. But in America, these ways are endangered. Health sciences and healing methods largely emerging out of regions in the global South (i.e., known as former colonies) have great potential for profit making, because wellness is a commodity existing in a fiction of scarcity, and thereby in high demand, ever funneling toward the highest global bidders. Ruth Wilson Gilmore defines racism as the "exploitation of group-differentiated vulnerability to premature death."[5] This chapter takes up the perspective of racialized capital as a health system and argues that if the propertization of yoga continues, it will serve to erode the potential of yoga to increase wellness and thereby liberation, particularly for those "faces at the bottom of the well."[6]

A closer examination of yoga as practiced in the West illuminates what is currently at stake for yoga as an evolving pillar in whiteness as property, and raises new questions around racialized capital and colonization. This chapter looks at two contemporary cases in yoga that saturated Western media, both of which bring transparency to deep tensions around race, colonization, and ownership and use, or appropriation, of yoga. This includes the Bikram copyright case, in which Bikram was denied copyright protection over his signature yoga sequence, and the University of Ottawa case, wherein members of the Centre for Students with Disabilities canceled a free, student-run yoga class due to stated discomfort around proceeding to offer the class without closer consideration of the impacts of cultural appropriation. The cultural narratives constructed by mainstream media around these cases reveals how whiteness spreads tentacles into yoga so as to absorb, own, and feed off of it. Both case studies raise First Amendment concerns around intellectual property and the right to be heard. The chapter offers critical race and decolonizing perspectives on legal protections in yoga expression, and on dominant journalism narratives on yoga that have an arguably law like impact tending to affirm whiteness. These de facto and de jure narratives demand critical analyses of the way ownership and use continue to actualize the historical and ongoing process of colonization. "Toward Yoga as Property," then, interrogates systems of whiteness, colonization, and cultural appropriation as they function in these two pivotal case studies in contemporary Western yoga.

THEORETICAL FOUNDATIONS FOR YOGA AS PROPERTY

Yoga as property is an intersectional project, concerned with the "distribution of political and material resources along racial lines."[7] Intersectionality has never been preoccupied with mere identity or difference, and instead is a generative perspective, aimed at knowing more about "how things work rather than who people are."[8] Healing techniques and abilities are political and material resources, in that healing from personal and political violence enables people to be present and public. The ability to be present and balanced, relatively peaceful and pain free on emotional, physical, and spiritual levels directly affects the ability to participate politically, to know, to have enough, to remember, and to be a self-determined voice in the ongoing struggle for freedoms. As a set of healing, liberatory sciences, yoga can strengthen these basic functions that define all we are as sociopolitical members and shapers.

In "Whiteness As Property," Cheryl Harris states that property as it is understood now was born out of and also helped birth a legal system of subordination, which tried/tries to relegate black people into property.[9] Similarly, the occupation and colonial rule over "Indians" supported white privilege through property rights in land and cultural terrain. A primary function of creating Others and colonies is that these become efficient sites for the lifting of "commodities from point of origin to the imperial center." The extraction never stopped, though it exists in constant metamorphoses. Whiteness is a social construct, an "unstable category" that includes a shifting array of people who benefit from this valuable designation. However real the social value of white supremacy may be, constructions of whiteness, like all races, "are still only human inventions."[10] The discourse of whiteness as property suggests that property is an expectation, one that allows whiteness to develop based on subjugation, which reimagines the world as objects, disposable. In the realm of yoga, that means a vastly pluralistic science is subject to rule of law propertization. In creating an absolute right to use yoga, in constructing within yoga a potentially infinite well of appropriability, the propertization of yoga funnels toward whiteness more cumulative spoils from the continued extraction of intellectual property/expressive wealth and real property/land from within the colonies and the colonized. Use and the ability to profit from use, or appropriation, is a pillar in the bundle of rights that comprise a property interest. This extends to intellectual property, which covers cultural expressions, such as the fields that comprise yoga.

In the *Harvard Journal on Racial and Ethnic Justice* symposium on "Whiteness As Property," Charles Lawrence opens with narrative on his grandmother, as did Harris in the original article, and as is intentionally done herein.[11] Lawrence goes on to describe the evolution of whiteness as property, where old forms are characterized by legalized/de jure segregation and officially sanctioned inequalities. New forms of whiteness as property continue to de facto protect and affirm settled expectations of relative white privilege in practice and effect, though not by stated right. In fact, color blindness is a compelled "abandonment of race-consciousness," which enables the continued lived reality of social inequities being substantively unaddressed. Technically, color blindness is defined as a state of deficiency, a decreased ability in vision. Critical race theorists rebut the color blind, post-racial discourses, asserting these are affirming of whiteness as property through erroneous claims that violent structures do not deny access and bestow no benefit. Lawrence writes of the new color blind narrative that "seeks to seduce and enlist" more people and expressions toward white hegemony. In fact, race does have meaning and does matter in yoga. Where whiteness "functions behind a mask of neutrality in the realm beyond scrutiny," it creates for itself an illusion of unity that hides violence.

Othering and whiteness rely on binary constructions, which by definition are characterized by the extreme. In *Orientalism*, Edward Said shared how these binaries include a West/East construction, a here and there, a solidly illusionary "us" and them.[12] Critical race and decolonizing theory also provide that these binaries encompass black/white, pure/sinful, good/bad, authentic/not authentic, and deserving/undeserving oppositional categories. These binaries serve to enable the stifling creation of an uncivilized, racialized Other who only exists to affirm the delusion of a more civilized West and whiteness. However, binaries simply do not resonate with lived realities of permeable layers in our existence. Porousness and layers, not binary structures, truly define the human experience, in all realms; legal, cultural, social, public, private, and political.

The binary around authenticity and purity in connection with who is deserving of wellness and health is of deep interest to yoga as property analysis because it has been used in particularly violent ways against subordinated peoples. In truth, there is no such thing as microaggressions, in that there is nothing micro about relentless, generational exposure to violence. Any experiences of violence and stressors function in the dominated body to increase proximity to death, creating a "social death" of black and brown peoples. Central to Harris's assertion of whiteness as property is the effectiveness of this analysis in ducking the wearisome discourses on affirmative action that attempt to reduce the discussion to who is pure and deserving of inclusion in things that increase wellness, versus who is a sinner, thereby earning violent exclusion. Linda Tuhiwai Smith writes of the layers around authenticity, and argues that assertions of authenticity can be resonant and even strategic for indigenous peoples.[13] However, she asserts, in general, binary authenticity discourses serve primarily to sever peoples from their indigeneity as one way to justify brutal oppression. In discussing the detrimental impact of unfortunate binaries around mythical purity, Vijay Prashad refers to Gayatri Spivak's "clash of the ignorance" between seemingly opposed sectors who both assert cultural purity, to no strategic effect on increased liberation for all, nor on the undoing of violent systems.[14]

Racial and cultural otherness means that the fact of long-term nurturing or "possession" by South Asia of yoga can be reinterpreted and ultimately erased. Faced with exclusive control over meaning granted to the white and the West, South Asia and India's "possession" of yoga looked different than the dominant definitions of use and enjoyment, and could thereby be determined to exist in states of "waste," and thus the relationship of either to the birth and phenomenon of yoga could simply not exist at all. This process of erasing and retelling the creation stories of yoga in the image of the West/whiteness willfully neglects the way yoga in colonized India was itself othered, made strange and sinful, and thus people were discouraged from any connection to yoga through racist mechanisms of internalized hate and fear. It is as though the entire process of owning people and their ideas that defined/defines colonization and racism have never existed, and sadly, never will come to be real. In *White By Law*, Lopez determines that whites cannot know themselves, and we cannot overcome racism until whiteness is dismantled, but this is highly unlikely.[15] The impact of the continued shoring up of whiteness in yoga is deciphered in important ways by the yoga as property analysis.[16]

STUDY: THE BIKRAM YOGA COPYRIGHT MATTER

The fundamental precept of whiteness, the core of its value, is its exclusivity. This exclusivity is predicated, not on any intrinsic characteristic,
but on the exclusion of the symbolic "other," which functions to "create
an illusion of unity" among whites.[17] Exclusion, appropriation, and propertized ownership are alive and well in yoga. This is because yoga fits
amenably into whiteness claims to superior qualities of goodness, purity,
flexibility, strength, and wellness. Thus, yoga as property is experiencing
exponential growth, as the economic and political forces of accumulated
global capital dictate. A 1,329 percent increase in grants of U.S. copyrights in yoga-related matters over a single decade is simply the tip of the
iceberg in exploring the value of yoga to the West, specifically the racialized American national project.
       Profitable extraction of yoga from the global south continues through
the diaspora of its citizens. Despite status quo media narratives that indicate otherwise, the property-based gold rush on the fields known as yoga
has been and continues to be overwhelmingly initiated outside of India,
and not just by Bikram Choudhury, who remains the only living, brown-
bodied, desi yoga leader-mogul in the West.[18] This study on the Bikram
copyright matter attempts to untwine dominant narratives from the
stark, data-based realities of ownership in and propertization of yoga.
The study presents a summary of the copyright issue at hand, with an
emphasis on yoga as property perspectives that is revealing of a popular,
media judgment of Bikram as a surprisingly sovereign and undeserving
Other.[19]
       Bikram Choudhury and his Bikram's Yoga College of India empire
present a telling and unlikely insight into the propertization of yoga.
Bikram's signature business and wellness method consists of twenty-six
postures and two breathing exercises. This sequence has become one of
yoga's most buzz worthy and profitable commodities in a crowded, overwhelmingly white field. On July 1, 2011, Bikram filed for copyright protection of this style of yoga against Evolation Yoga, which caused a media
outcry and sparked arguably precious critique of his effort to protect a
lucrative business model. Recently, the U.S. Court of Appeals for the
Ninth Circuit ruled that Bikram is not able to secure copyright protections in his popular sequence.[20] This would seem to be a win on the right
side of history, a welcome reprieve in a legal landscape and culture of
over claiming, and owning, intellectual property rights.[21] Media coverage on the matter painted a picture of this "Bad Boy of Yoga," trying to
"own yoga," and that the win meant that no one could "own yoga."[22]
One white, male litigant against Bikram's copyright claim (who settled
out of court prior to this ruling) declared, "I feel complete in the job I set
for myself which was to free yoga from the destructive threat of copyright custody and ownership."[23] Here is just one example of what narra-

tives around the Bikram copyright matter reveal about the propensity of whiteness to insert itself as a perpetual protector of the yoga site (not perpetual profiteer, a more accurate defining characteristic), which indicates how valuable yoga has become as an immensely lucrative developing property in the scope of whiteness.[24]

A closer look at the ruling reveals a few pivotal truths. First, the Ninth Circuit decision was not clear cut, copyright law is a gray area ripe with nuances and contradictions. Second, the Bikram copyright case decision is not indicative of an overall win in "protection" of yoga, or of how the rule of law sanctions ever increasing ownership of yoga.[25] A utilitarian interpretation of copyright protections as provided for in the U.S. Constitution is that the goal is to provide incentive for people to keep inventing and also prevent a depletion of finite goods in the public commons.[26] Thereby, owners of intellectual property can exclude others and appropriate the fruits of their own labor, and it is these two rights that will ensure the utilitarian balance is reached.[27] However, there are convincing arguments that this balance has deeply tipped toward a depletion of the commons and over owning on behalf of so-called inventors.[28] The Evolation case is not the first where Bikram's camp attempted to deploy First Amendment protections against a former mentee who went on to open their own respective studios using the Bikram model. Both times the issue was that they decided to use their former guru's sequence in the exact same order, with the exact same postures, as part of their business models.[29] So, Bikram, who has been diligent about not letting his business model be appropriated without cost, initiated the copyright claim to get these former students to stop using his exact sequence.[30]

In this Ninth Circuit case, Bikram asserted that his lucrative hot yoga industry relied upon a protectable expression of an idea, which was his creation of a set of postures, in a certain order. Similar to choreography, he argued, the Bikram sequence was creatively carved out of a potentially infinite set of *asana* postures. The court disagreed in this case, and said Bikram's poses were not choreography, and were actually a system or method for wellness, which is not protectable under copyright law. However, systems and methods may be patented, which the court noted in the decision, stating that Bikram could better pursue potentially exclusive rights in the sequence via patent application.[31] During the course of this case, the Copyright Office of the Library of Congress issued a statement of policy to explain that they were mistaken when they granted copyright protections in "selection and arrangements of exercises" and "compilations of exercises" in the past.[32] Also, a very similar matter was recently brought before the U.S. Court of Appeals for the Federal Circuit court. The court there used "different reasoning to achieve the opposite result from yesterday's Ninth Circuit opinion.[33] Thus, the Ninth Circuit decision was not an application of an obvious, bright line rule against copyright for *asana* sequences. Instead, it was a ruling that went against past grants of copyright protection, and it was based on reasoning that another court used in the exact opposite way to grant the ownership right. While the Federal Circuit court decision fell under fire for misinterpreting both law and computer science, the fact remains that the Bikram copyright case relies upon nuanced, delicate intellectual property law that perpetually exists in a gray area.[34] Furthermore, Bikram can still potentially own his signature yoga sequence through a patent application.

So, what does the Bikram copyright decision actually mean for stemming the tide of ownership or propertization in yoga? Not as much as it may seem. This ruling was not in line with the trend in intellectual property ownership, which has "vastly expanded" in duration and scope of rights.[35] This indicates an increased propertization of yoga, and more generally a tending toward property in intellectual property itself, evidenced even by calling this realm of creative, idea based expression, "property."[36] A 1,329 percent increase in grants of U.S. copyrights in yoga-related matters over a single decade is simply the tip of the iceberg in exploring the value of yoga to the West, and the racialized American national project. Profitable extraction of yoga from the global south continues through the diaspora of its citizens. These numbers are stark reminders that the Ninth Circuit ruling in the Bikram copyright matter does not in any way indicate that yoga is free or protected from ownership.

WHAT THE BIKRAM COPYRIGHT MATTER MEANS
FOR YOGA AS PROPERTY

A critical race perspective on the realities versus narratives on ownership of yoga that surrounds the Bikram copyright matter implicates a systemic tendency toward popular images and stereotypes that reinforce a sense that the minority "other" is morally wrong and even dangerous, requiring protection from and regulation of them.[37] This, despite the reality that in fact, there are larger forces at hand which are more culpable in preying upon yoga. Indeed, yoga as property informs a strategic, data-based perspective on the subjugation of yoga, as it was brought to the West and consequently begins a marked disappearance from the public commons.

Said's *Orientalism* argues that the East is constructed as a weak, impotent, irrational, feminized Other. So much so that the West is always surprised at the sovereign acts of Eastern peoples. The Other is a binary-based creation, thereby layered existences are not considered. In the Bikram case discussed here, media coverage engages in this form of othering. Mainstream articles from publications such as *The New Yorker, Yoga Journal*, and the *New York Times* consistently convey a sense that Bikram is surprisingly forward in the protection of his business method and yoga system. The creation story of Bikram is shrouded in mystery and intrigue, from childhood immersion in India-based yoga, to a coming to America narrative that is linked to elite, celebrity culture. He is often described as opulent, pimp-like, and garishly masculine. At first glance, this may seem to be a departure from *Orientalism*'s feminization framework. Actually, extremes are engendered by any binary construction, and there is a thin line between extremes, which exist as flip sides of the same coin. Thus, Bikram's hyper and dangerous bad boy masculinity parallels a hyper-feminization of his generally naked, bikini-clad body which populates media imagery.

In truth, Bikram 's successful embrace of capitalism and yoga as property is subject to arguably precious outrage in the media, as though trying to protect and accumulate the profits generated by a powerfully branded sequence is strange. Actually, his financial success in the Western yoga industrial complex reflects a deep understanding of contemporary American commerce. Bikram is not the first to mine yoga *asana* and pranayama for profit potential, though he is the most visible South Asian American man to do so. His actions to copyright and franchise Bikram Yoga are depicted as distinctly uncivilized instead of it being good business sense to, for example, ask any studio calling itself a "Bikram Yoga Studio," to pay him a monthly fee of 1 percent of profits or $1,000, whichever is greater. The franchise deal offered by Bikram's business gives an indication of how profitable his industry actually is. Unfortunately, this propertization of yoga interferes with the spread of any benefits of Bikram yoga to those who cannot afford to pay around $20 a class.

Bikram has long lit a firestorm of media attention. The phenomenon of media narratives and images of Bikram need to be contextualized alongside a long list of minstrelsy characters. As Charles Lawrence describes, he is always in some ways enmeshed in performativity as a black male person embedded in scholarship and academia, and he is never performing alone. Lawrence knows that he is perceived in a context of the Other. Similarly, in analyzing pervasive media narratives on Bikram, it is critical to recall how never is the Other depicted in Western media without catalyzing unfortunate conversation with the expansive repertoire of Orientalizing stereotypes that serve(d) to justify the "artifact" of white and Western supremacy (as it was never the case that whiteness and the West is biologically, geographically superior, or in any way superior to others). In a media narrative which is ever in service to multinational corporate rule and racialized capital, domination over black and brown masculinity through images of the dangerous, hyper-sexual, savage, irrational, swampy, hellacious, ridiculous, alluring, dark male pervade. None of the Bikram media narratives allow representations of him or yoga to be unchained from these depictions.[38]

STUDY: THE UNIVERSITY OF OTTAWA
CULTURAL APPROPRIATION MATTER

Whiteness as a highly valued expectation in property may be virulently enforced and protected, but it is never rational. There is no real, inherent white supremacy, and no justification for the "maldistribution of life chances" that favors whiteness.[39] The maintenance of this twisted social construct requires constant care, affirmation, enabling, and defense. The propertization of yoga represents a relatively new, immensely lucrative weapon in whiteness' ongoing quest for amassing tamperable evidence to alibi its own, purportedly rightful, power. This section examines a recent yoga incident at the University of Ottawa, where young scholars at the Centre for Students with Disabilities (CSD) pressed pause on a free campus yoga class, implicating colonization as an ongoing violence potentially bringing aspects of harm into their *asana* practice space. A deeper look at the backlash CSD received in dominant media narratives, through an analysis of one influential piece of coverage, sheds new light on the fascinating degree to which even a tiny disruption to yoga as (white) property cues deep threat to a quickly settling/settled expectation in commoditized yoga as a trusty tool in the eternal shoring up of whiteness. This segment proceeds with a synopsis of the incident and dominant narratives in media responses. This is followed by an in-depth, intersectional analysis of one influential response piece. The Ottawa study ends with a theoretical discussion as to what is at stake here for yoga as property.

Synopsis

According to student leaders at the University of Ottawa, by November of 2015, the free yoga class offered by CSD had run its course after seven years with just one white, female teacher at the helm. Members of CSD chose to bring closure of that incarnation, with stated hopes for another, more intersectional yoga offering in the future. In the student leaders' words, they needed time to "make it better, more accessible and more inclusive."[40] Three months later, in January 2016, CDS reinstated the yoga class, with a South Asian diasporic female teacher leading the sessions.[41] Clearly, CDS is on a path to making the class as healing as possible for all present, and that path need not be perfect to be powerful, and even positive. The accumulated years of good faith and loyalty by CSD students to long-term yoga facilitator Jennifer Scharf, the white woman they gave a leadership platform to, was not exactly returned by any expression of goodwill in the sensationalized, mainstream press coverage and yoga journalism that followed. Scharf took many opportunities to centralize her outraged voice and image, while marginalizing the CSD perspectives in the ensuing media firestorm.

Yoga in the West is a multi-billion dollar growing industry. Surely the temporary suspension of one free student class is a dwarfed act compared to the giant power of commercialized yoga. Yet, this David and Goliath tiny but mighty scenario is exactly what unfurled as major yoga voices and dominant media outlets moved to silence, shame, and discredit the act. Media pushback overwhelmingly focused on how the CDS leaders dared utter the "unutterable"; namely, race, colonization, appropriation, and the potential for continued political violences in the diaspora vis-à-vis the North American yoga site. A *Wall Street Journal* headline which engages an arguably derisive tone toward "The heightened sensitivities on one campus," is indicative of the way the Centre for Students with Disabilities decision was generally domesticated, feminized, and thereby rendered oddly emotional, ignorant, and even irrational.[42]

Scharf personalized and marginalized the disabled student's political expressions of curiosity about how to contextualize and historicize yoga offerings.[43] Unfortunately, this is a predictable response. Whiteness' settled expectation in the yoga site as needing to be affirming of white personhood and attendant, non-consensual expectations of personal care, are here expressed through Schafer's stated affront at being asked to step up to teach and then step back. What is somewhat surprising is how readily dominant media narratives served up their powerful platforms as echo chambers for imperial and colonial apologist voices angrily denouncing the pausing of the CDS yoga class.

Mainstream media and influential, leading white voices in the yoga business all echoed a single axis version of the story. Innocent yoga teacher gets violated by foolishly strident disabled students who raised irredeemable interest in culture, colonization, and appropriation in relationship to yoga; what's worse, they took away her class. It is important to note that Scharf is in no way stopped from continuing to teach yoga under any other circumstances. Yet, she told the *Ottawa Sun* that she felt the self-identified disabled/disability leaders were people on the wrong side of the "real divide between reasonable people and those people just looking to jump on a bandwagon." Scharf consistently presented herself as one of the "good people getting punished for doing good things." Yet nothing in the coverage pointed to any reason to doubt that the CDS leaders had proceeded with deep intentionality. In fact, at the outset, CDS leaders issued a public statement in which they clarified, "while yoga is a really great idea and accessible and great for students, there are cultural issues of implication involved in the practice," expressing a "need to be mindful of this and how we express ourselves while practising yoga."

THE SLATE PIECE: AN IN-DEPTH LOOK

The imbalanced media pushback is perhaps best epitomized by a popular *Slate* article, "Where the Whole World Meets in a Single Nest: The History Behind a Misguided Campus Debate over Yoga and 'Cultural Appropriation.'"[44] Author Michelle Goldberg recently published a book definitively iconizing a white woman in yoga, *The Goddess Pose: The Audacious Life of Indra Devi, the Woman Who Helped Bring Yoga to the West.* This book positions her as a leading author and popular contributor to media narratives that create a de facto reality of yoga as property. As of this writing, the article has 18.8 thousand likes and 710 comments on the *Slate* site, and it was shared widely over social media, including by leading yoga writers. In the article, Goldberg's byline assures, "No, Westerners Practicing Yoga are Not Guilty of 'Cultural Appropriation.'" This exhibits how whiteness assumes unilateral control over meaning, assured in its own ability to exonerate itself before ever considering whether or not there was a crime.

Due to the construction of whiteness as neutral and the expert, Goldberg can simply say no, continued appropriation or use of the global south, South Asia in particular, for its material and ideational wealth simply does not exist. This negation and self-assured innocence was a popular part of her narrative, echoed frequently in many shares and uses of her article. For example, on Leslie Kaminoff 's Yoga Anatomy public Facebook page, Kaminoff reposted the *Slate* piece with this caption, "Thank you, Michelle Goldberg. Also, it's impossible to 'steal' an idea like yoga from anyone. If I steal something from you, it means that you don't have it any more."[45] This assumption of objectivity, rightness, and authority from leading and white voices in Western, commoditized yoga sadly situates the yoga site as not only a remedy for violence, but also a source of violence.

The violence endemic to colonization reverberates across generations and diasporas. Ongoing effects of colonization include unfairly increased proximity to unwellness. Access to propertized yoga is striated in favor of Western whiteness, so it is the case that some simply do not have yoga anymore, or have less of it than others. One Canadian-South Asian resident of Ottawa told the Canadian Broadcast Corporation that he appreciates the large and primarily all white turnout at local outdoor yoga events, while feeling "a bit ashamed my desi body [isn't] as flexible as theirs."[46] Another stark example of the hierarchical distribution of yoga unequally accumulated by whiteness can be found by an odd trend in the evolving visual culture of yoga. A Google image search for "yoga in slums" reveals a number of photos depicting white women in typically tight, Western yoga clothes striking *asana* poses in narrow alleys of Indian inner cities and slums. These women blithely balance and freely twist in the midst of tight thoroughfares of dehumanizing poverty. Serious, brown faces look on from behind the harsh confines of slum life. Here is a visual reminder that when things like yoga or methods of wellness are used or appropriated by trajectories of colonization, these uses can indeed result in a heightened access for a few, reliant upon a lessened access for a many.

Goldberg uses broad, dehistoricized, and Orientalizing claims to protect commoditized yoga from any connection to inappropriate use, or violences, like racism. Whiteness constantly creates and uses the Other, in any convenient manner, with the goal of defining and valorizing itself. She writes, "The spread of yoga in the West is not just a story about Westerners raiding some pristine subcontinental reservoir of spiritual authenticity." But remaining curious about the layered effects of colonization and imperialism is very different than claiming any "pristine" "authenticity" for the vastly pluralistic layers of the geographies and histories that birthed and nurtured yoga, geographies that factually were mined and subjugated by Western colonization. Goldberg's reductionist and Orientalist assertion that South Asia is not pure suggests that it is undeserving of context, history, or any power analysis that would disturb the peace of a settled expectation in whiteness as just, superior, right, good, inevitable. Her assumed authority gleams with a veneer of objectivity, as though the complicated imbrication of her own white personhood, which relies on being a yoga and South Asia expert, bears no impact on her stance.

This mainstream, bestselling author resoundingly rejects any possibility of violence in the Western yoga site, and seems satisfied with the current yoga whiteout. She dismisses CDS leaders' questioning of the uses of yoga, and casts the disabled youth alongside ignorant, ultra-sensitive "people who know very little of the cultures they purport to protect." There is likely a projection around protection here. Goldberg promotes her book in the midst of the article, she is never not profiting from yoga as she issues these conclusions. Surely her monetized and personhood interest in yoga are valuable to her, and therefore are things she needs to protect. Raising any concern or even curiosity about appropriation as an ongoing, not temporally or spatially static experience is, in her words, "provincialism masquerading as sensitivity." "There's no such thing as cultural purity," she assures her readers, "and searching for it never leads anywhere good." But here, it would seem that she was the one engaged in locating and dislocating notions of purity from the global south. The CDS decision to pause their yoga offering did not hinge on locating India, for example, as "pure," or on some linear temporal and spatial genealogy that can be rewound back to a mythical virginal moment.

Goldberg echoes popular rewrites of yoga creation stories that insert whiteness into all pivotal points in the formation and development of yoga as we know it. She invokes a narrow, depoliticized cosmopolitanism as she relays a creation story of yoga in the West spun as an Indo-

European/American creation. Central to her assertion is this pervasive idea that yoga *asana* is entirely a modern phenomenon, heavily created by white actors from Britain and Scandinavia. She uses Rabindranath Tagore's words to summarize her stance on cosmopolitanism, interpreting, "Where the whole world meets in a single nest," to be an accurate description of this recreated creation story, and on how yoga exists in the the West now. But cosmopolitanism is perhaps better understood as the cosmopolitical, wherein there is no smooth world where goods and people flow freely, ahistorical and depoliticized. A cosmopolitical analysis here would be more present to the accumulation of propertized yoga in the wealthy and the West from the global South as an extension of the dominion-based right of extraction. The colonizing practice is in the realm of mind and body occupation (intellectual property) and physical occupation (real property). In yoga now, it is more about subjugated bodies being physically, visually, and sonically absent.

WHAT OTTAWA MEANS FOR YOGA AS PROPERTY

Invoking depoliticized cosmopolitanisms, Goldberg raises the spectre of a flawed Indian nationalist directive behind India's creation of the United Nations ratified International Yoga Day. It is helpful to recall that perpetual profiteering from whiteness regimes does inform her conclusion that an "impure" "India" cannot possibly be violently subjugated. In *Inhuman Conditions*, cosmopolitanist scholar Pheng Cheah offers helpful, nuanced perspectives on the tendency of former colonies, focusing on South Asia and Africa, to make strident nationalist assertions on the global marketplace of ideas. These layered nationalisms are initially quite extreme, less balanced, which, he relates, is a predictable and even somewhat strategic quality of these first re-emerging steps into cosmopolitical terrains out from under the silencing experiences of colonization. Strategic in that these efforts are directed at regaining power, and expounding narrow nationalisms are one flawed way of directly accessing some kinds of power, like the power to have a sort of sovereign identity. In truth, there is no postcolonial period, Cheng reiterates, de facto colonization continues, as does racial domination, and what we experience from global South nation-states in terms of nationalist assertions is always contextualized by this layered, heartbreaking reality.[47] The dissertation project that Yoga as Property is contextualized within further examines important layers around the impact of right wing Hindu nationalist assertions on the South Asian diaspora, with emphasis on the appropriation of the yoga site, centralizing the growth of anti-Muslim, divide and conquer ideologies masquerading behind hegemonic, anti-terrorist rhetorics.[48]

In propertized social constructions, race and colonization become "unutterable" and "untellable."[49] The CDS student leaders uttered the unutterable and told of the untellable when they spoke of needing and wanting to flesh out their yoga offerings with more context, people's history, and accessible geographies of wellness to promote both personal and political healing. Their graceful pausing of the class, taken to notice and strengthen the offering, became taboo precisely because the students dared to relate an awareness of diasporas charted by the trade of human bodies and ideas, and decided to search and remedy any ongoing avatars of colonization and Western rule showing up in their humble but impactful yoga site.

Key in the propertization of yoga is an occupation of it by whiteness that is almost total, at least in the United States. Even the most potentially allied yoga spaces, such as the Decolonizing Yoga website and prison yoga teacher trainings, are primarily white and white led, leading to affirmations of whiteness as savior and protector. The argument here is not a reductive stance against diversity in yoga, this is not about deriding any and all white involvement in yoga. This analysis seeks to name and understand an obliterative quality that whiteness has had on yoga. The yoga whiteout perpetuates the circumstance of peripheralized populations who need but cannot access this health care system due to mistranslations and predatory exclusivity. This is because when whiteness absorbs yoga for its own mythology of supremacy, the ensuing propertization is overwhelmingly characterized by exclusion and inappropriate use, which in turn cause harm in sites that could have been healing. The recreated, redefined, and whitened yoga creation story is also an extension of the Indo-European myth, whereby structural similarities among languages were assumed to indicate not just similar but the same ancestral roots among humans, which was a move to appropriate or use Sanskrit toward support for European superiority.[50] In regions now known as India, elaborate physical fitness practices such as the wrestling-martial art form Mall-Yuddha or Pehlwani date back to the fifth millennium BC, before Aryan invasions. Importantly, trade in commerce, philosophy, medicine, and the arts was vibrant along river filled regions of the global south including the Indus and Nile valleys.[51] *Asana* teachings from India were present in the building blocks for physical, martial arts practice with the monks of Shaolin. Visual depictions of *asana* practice in yoga exist within North Africa, wherein Egyptian pyramids, hieroglyphs express familiarity and mastery of a range of *asana*. But none of this cosmopolitanism serves to accumulate more whiteness for itself, and thereby it is largely absent from the new yoga creation stories, which are crafted toward ease of use, or appropriation. Cultural appropriation is not a static thing, never a singular event in space or time. Instead, it is ongoing, as evidenced by the continued accumulation of an expectation in ownership and control of yoga for white personhood.

In "Whiteness as Property," Harris writes of how whiteness is "an 'object' over which control was—and is—expected." Harris sheds light on how whiteness is "all bound up in your plans for yourself, then your personhood depends on it, this control of all things." Here, Goldberg exhibits this, as though those curious about healing the violence possible in appropriation need simply to be distracted, like infants, from a politicized truth. This incarnation of a student protest was certainly a layered move, not preoccupied with difference or morally judging the appropriation, but instead a concerted effort to be more inclusive, more just. Yoga as property in this instance is layered by student leaders navigating their own propertization by and at the institution.

The intersectional analyses suggested by the CDS leaders need to be understood in a context that brings transparency to the dynamics of power in operation. This study begins to locate their actions and ensuing responses within race and gender power fields, and notes that while this "context is necessary, it is not sufficient."[52] Intersectional legal theorists write how when racism is defined so narrowly as to exclude it from blame, white entitlement in neutrality has the effect of pushing de facto white supremacy in dominant media narratives under the radar.[53] Reductive interventions like Goldberg's contain and neutralize resistance. The echo chamber of self-serving reassurances as to perfect, persistent non-violence by whiteness and the West in yoga results in intersectional violence. Regardless of the seductive power of these unilateral assurances of no cultural appropriation in yoga sites, "these technologies of gendered racialization cannot be formed into neutral systems."[54]

CONCLUSION: YOGA PESSIMISM AND YOGA FUTURISM IN BALANCE

Yoga as property is an analysis structured to illuminate how yoga is a particularly important site for revealing new developments in the settled property expectation in whiteness. The property lens offered here is less concerned with binary conclusions of good and bad, and primarily aims toward unearthing new, malignant areas where contemporary American racism and its attendant spread of unwellness grows. As stated prior, the arguments presented here are part of a dissertation project much bigger in scope. The larger query asks: How has the South Asian site, with emphasis on yoga, been legally and socially constructed away from a spectrum of blackness toward valorizing whiteness, thereby affirming the U.S. nation-state?

The regions that comprise modern South Asia, and the diasporas that emanate from it, present unique and informative truths about how race and colonization exist in public knowledges and practices. As of early 2016, a search for information on the colonization of India on Wikipedia, the popular public knowledge portal, triggers this message, "The page 'British colonization of India' does not exist."[55] The closest page, "British

Raj," reads like a litany of (tamperable) evidence that the British occupation and pilfering of South Asia was ultimately benevolent and beneficial. After listing so-called civilizing gifts brought by the British to India, this page narrowly relates, "Historians continue to debate whether the long-term impact of British rule was to accelerate the economic development of India, or to distort and retard it." This, despite the undisputed fact that the British instigated partition of South Asia continues to represent one of the bloodiest migrations in human history. Also, India was considered the crown jewel in the British empire. Yet even the Wikipedia page on "India" fails to use the term colonization and instead relates how the British "annexed" India. Situated between and around the black/white binary, South Asian, brown, living histories are high stakes sites in the ongoing battle for equivalent life chances for all.

Vijay Prashad offers an illustrative historical quote from governor general of the Dutch East Indies (1617–1629) Jan Pieterszoon Coen, communicating shortly after the violent occupation of Goa, "[M]ay not a man in Europe do what he likes with his cattle? Even so does the master do with his men, for everywhere, these . . . are as much the property of the master, as are brute beasts[.]"[56] This is an illuminating peek at the propertization of the South Asian site, and the accompanied suffering brought by European occupation of it. As a colonial extension of Britain, America's property theories and practices directly emanate and participate in this legacy of subjugation. The foundational ruling in *Johnson & Graham's Lessee v. McIntosh* (a nation building property case that established the doctrine of discovery, which propelled manifest destiny) affirms the notion that European settler-occupiers were responsible for the perpetual protection of American land and life. But this perpetual protection would be more fittingly described as perpetual profiting. It is instructive to extrapolate these false but dominant doctrinal ideals to the cultural realm of intangible, intellectual property. Michelle Goldberg, in her piece on the supposed inviability of a politicized inquiry into ongoing racisms and yoga, embeds a link directing readers to buy her new yoga book, a bestselling book which is in turn another instrument pulling yoga toward affirming the supposed value of whiteness. She is never not profiting from yoga, even as she, and those powerful voices who echo her, clearly attempt to erase ongoing and nuanced legacies of racial and colonial violence. It should be noted that the power dynamic at play here involves more than domination, and further work on yoga as property will elaborate on the role of agency in the appropriation of and profiteering from cultural objects, commodities, and practices.

In an inquiry into the state of race in America, it is particularly informative to ask, how is yoga being used to support "preservation through transformation?"[57] This is a key phrase from critical legal scholar Angela Harris to describe ways and means that protect white supremacy throughout the transition from formal, legalized racism to de facto racism. It is clear that white supremacy has been preserved in and by the Western yoga site, as discussed in the analyses presented on both the Bikram and Ottowa episodes. Telling, predictable, surprise, and outrage expressed at the sovereign attempts made by Choudhury to maintain commercial control over his name and named yoga products shows a willfully myopic view of intellectual property regimes that are otherwise proliferating at alarming rates. Contemporary America propertizes all things, no realm is off limits, even the Happy Birthday song only recently got "freed after 80 years."[58] Prior to this late-2015 emancipation into the public domain, no restaurant staff could sing Happy Birthday to a celebrating consumer without fear of costly retribution. This is a small hint as to the looming, irrational scope of propertization that underlies all U.S.-based, legal and social, structures and experiences.

The ability to heal has been central to great movements in American popular history. The Black Panthers famously established wellness clinics and free breakfast programs to bring healing to violently marginalized black populations across the country. In the 1970s, youth leaders from across the global south surviving in the South Bronx occupied a hospital to advocate for their family members and elders to get access to care. These youth were characterized in the media as dangerous, criminal gang members. In reality, the heavily marginalized American youth did indeed have intricate social and cultural associations, layered and complex networks or gangs that ideally aided their chances of survival. They had futurism in their hearts, balanced by a poignantly present understanding of their slim chance at sovereign and fully lived lives. These youth and their gangs were the architects of hip-hop as we understand it now, inheritors of Black Panther health initiatives, civil rights struggles, and more.[59] Unfortunately, it appears true that the futurist imagining of justice is primary, and the practice of it secondary. In the hit 1991 song "Everything's Gonna Be Alright (Ghetto Bastard)" the iconic hip-hop group Naughty By Nature rapped about being born into a violent, oppressive society. A memorable verse ends with poignant lyrics, "How will I do it, how will I make it, I won't, that's how." This is evocative of the stark realities of racialized and gendered capitalism, wherein life chances are "maldistributed" toward affirming white supremacy. Imagination, creativity, and culture are key, but perhaps mainly because these are what helps those at the margins in particular to stay present, shining through an everlasting dark.

In this chapter, the central argument contends that the continued propertization of "yoga" brings more destruction than creation to the much needed systems of yoga that embody methods of healing that can help oppressed peoples heal from the lethal effects of racism, colonization, and appropriation-based subjugation. Future work elaborating on yoga as property will establish how yoga, at root, was and is potentially liberatory in intersectional ways. Yoga as property is at once a eulogy to the losses sustained by yoga in the West, and also a celebration of the as yet moderate Western intrusion in the vast timeline of the existence of yogic methods, sciences, and philosophies which continue to spread meaningful healing to so many. Yoga as property is a lens that allows for a better map of yoga, now. This analytical structure will help bring transparency to how much yoga has been extracted from the public commons, where it is already owned exclusively, and how and by whom it is being appropriated.

The cumulative effect of this understanding aims to disrupt the absorptive tendency of whiteness as property, so as to stem yoga' s participation in the maintenance of social death.[60] In narratives surrounding race and yoga matters today, this call for a yoga as property analysis is a fitting instruction for forward movement with increased transparency around political and personal motivations, and rigorous practice in accountability within the emerging fields of contemporary yoga scholarship. In the contemplative practices, we are asked to breathe, notice, and sit with the questions, deeply consider them, and create from them still more questions with "stretch, resonance, and flexibility."[61] We must hold this responsibility dear, and not proceed breathlessly profitable in the modern yoga gold rush; as though there was a color blind, post-racial, post-colonial vacuum in which only yoga exists, forcing yoga into the shape of a perfect alibi for whiteness to persist.

NOTES

1. The liberatory ideal identified here exists as just that, an ideal.
2. This work is an initial step toward a larger and more nuanced dissertation effort. The longer term project will address yoga in a globalized and cosmopolitical context, teasing out layers of appropriation and commercialization both in and outside of whiteness and Western spaces. Also, fuller analysis will be grounded in an exploration and illustration of connections between original yoga systems nurtured in the global south, and critical race theory as well as intersectionality.
3. David Orr, "India Adopts Fighting Position to Hold Onto Ancient Yoga Poses," *The Telegraph*, September 20, 2005. http://www.telegraph.co.uk.
4. *Trademark Electronic Search System*. Accessed December 8, 2015. http://tess2.uspto.gov. *Copyright Catalog*. Accessed December 8, 2015. http://cocatalog.lo c.gov.
5. Dean Spade, "Intersectional Resistance and Law Reform," *Signs* 38, no. 4 (2013): 1031–55. doi:10.1086/669574.
6. Derrick A. Bell, *Faces at the Bottom of the Well: The Permanence of Racism* (Basic Books, 1992).
7. Charles R. Lawrence III, "Passing and Trespassing in the Academy: On Whiteness as Property and Racial Performance as Political Speech." *Harv. J. Racial & Ethnic Just.* 31 (2015): 7, Footnote 15.
8. Sumi Cho, Kimberle Williams Crenshaw, and Leslie McCall, "Toward a Field of Intersectionality Studies: Theory, Applications, and Praxis." *Signs* 38, no. 4 (2013): 785–810, 796.
9. Cheryl I. Harris, "Whiteness as Property," *Harvard Law Review* 106, no. 8 (1993): 1707. doi:10.2307/1341787.

10. Ian Haney Lopez, *White by Law: The Legal Construction of Race* (NYU Press, 2006) xiv.

11. Lawrence, supra.

12. Edward Said, *Orientalism. 1978* (New York: Vintage 1994 [1979]).

13. Linda Tuhiwai Smith, *Decolonizing Methodologies: Research and Indigenous Peoples* (London: Zed Books, 1999) 22.

14. Vijay Prashad, *Everybody Was Kung Fu Fighting: Afro-Asian Connections and the Myth of Cultural Purity* (Boston: Beacon Press, 2001) 16.

15. Lopez, 202.

16. This preliminary literature review offers an initial theoretical survey of the deep legacy of ideas and conversations that a yoga as property analysis enters into. Further expansions will aid in teasing out the layered power dynamics between structure and agency in the globalized phenomenon of propertied yoga. This will include explorations of relevant conceptual realms, such as postcolonial theory, transnational feminism, cultural studies, cosmopolitanism, and global cultural economy.

17. Harris, 1730.

18. This analysis narrowly focuses on Bikram's copyright matters and the attendant coverage and facts of this issue.

19. At the outset it should be understood that this Bikram copyright matter and Bikram himself deserve more attention than can be afforded in this space. This work is one effort in a larger dissertation project, and this portion does not consider the spectre of sexual violence, which is understood as a tool of patriarchal war. This means that consideration of the sexual violence accusations brought against Bikram is not considered here, but certainly deserves trauma informed consideration moving forward.

20. Bikam's Yoga College Of India, L.P. V. Evolation Yoga, LLC) (United States Court of Appeals for the Ninth Circuit October 8, 2015).

21. Michael Barclay, "What Do Yoga and APIs Have in Common? Neither Are Copyrightable," *Electronic Frontier Foundation*, October 9, 2015. https://www.eff.org.

22. Loraine Despres, "Yoga's Bad Boy: Bikram Choudhury," *Yoga Journal*, August 28, 2007. http://www.yogajournal.com. Michael Harthorne, "Court Says Bikram Founder Doesn't Own Yoga Poses," *Newser*, October 10, 2015. http://www.newser.com. Evolation Yoga, "Federal Court Rules That Bikram Doesn't Own Yoga: Copyright Claim Can't Stand the Heat," accessed December 11, 2015. https://www.evolationyoga.com.

23. Gregory Gumucio. Open letter, Bikram Settlement. http://yogatothepeople.com/wp-content/uploads/2012/12/Greg-Letter-Bikram-Settlement.pdf.

24. Other media content reviewed includes Bikram copyright related articles in *The New Yorker, Bloomberg News, New York Times* blogs, *Forbes, The Economist, Mother Jones, Electronic Frontier Foundation, The Atlantic, Huffington Post, Yoga International, Yoga Journal,* and *The Week.*

25. Johnson v. M'Intosh, 21 U.S. 543, 1823.

26. Johnson v. M'Intosh, 16.

27. U.S. Const. Art 1, S ec 8, Cl 8.

28. U.S. Const. Art 1, S ec 8, Cl 8.

29. Jennifer D'Angelo Friedman. "What the Bikram Copyright Rejection Means for Yoga." *Yoga Journal,* October 16, 2015.

30. Ben McGrath. "Steamed." *The New Yorker,* February 6, 2012.

31. Bikram v. Evolation

32. Robert Kasunic. Statement of Policy; Registration of Compilations. *United States Library of Congress. Copyright Office.* 121st ed. Vol. 77. https://www.gpo.gov.

33. Michael Barclay. "What Do Yoga and APIs Have in Common?" *Electronic Frontier Foundation,* October 9, 2015. https://www.eff.org.

34. Barclay. "What Do Yoga and APIs Have in Common?"

35. Michael Carrier. "Cabining Intellectual Property Through a Property Paradigm." *Duke Law Journal* (2004): 1–145; 7.

36. Carrier. "Cabining Intellectual Property Through a Property Paradigm."

37. Again, this analysis narrowly focuses on Bikram's copyright matters and the attendant coverage and facts of this issue. This means that consideration of the sexual violence accusations brought against Bikram is not considered here, but certainly deserves consideration moving forward.

38. Future work on the Bikram matter will specifically illustrate these representations of him in mainstream media, which is an important part of the theoretical critique.

39. Spade, supra.

40. Aedan Helmer. "Free Ottawa Yoga Class Scrapped over 'Cultural Issues.'" *Ottawa Sun*, November 20, 2015. http://www.ottawasun.com.

41. Justin Wm Moyer. "Yoga Class Earlier Put on Hold Over 'Oppression' Resumes—Minus the White Teacher," *Washington Post*, January 26, 2016.

42. Notable and Quotable: "Yoga as 'Cultural Appropriation': The Heightened Sensitivities on One Campus Stretch in a New Direction." *Wall Street Journal*. November 22, 2015.

43. She said the CDS students were "people who don't even have a cursory understanding of the term," intersectionality. Moyer, Justin Wm. "Yoga Class Earlier Put on Hold Over 'Oppression' Resumes—Minus the White Teacher," *Washington Post*, January 26, 2016.

44. Michelle Goldberg. "Where the Whole World Meets in a Single Nest: The history behind a misguided campus debate over yoga and "cultural appropriation." *Slate*, November 23, 2015. http://www.slate.com.

45. Leslie Kaminoff. Facebook page, "Leslie Kaminoff Yoga Anatomy." https://www.facebook.com/LeslieKaminoffYogaAnatomy/posts/891326610963863

46. Andrew Foote, "Yoga Class Cancelled at University of Ottawa over 'cultural appropriation issues.'" *CBCNews* . November 22, 2015. http://www.cbc.ca.

47. Gayatri Chakravorty Spivak and Aleksandur K'osev, *Nationalism and the Imagination*, London: Seagull Books, 2010. 31. Spivak feels differently then Cheah, in terms of his ambivalent take on post/colonial nation states asserting nationalisms. Using the example of elite educational institutions, whereby comparative literatures are absorbed and reduced into the one English medium, she writes, "What a comparativism based on equivalence attempts to undermine is the possessiveness, the exclusiveness, the isolationist expansionism of mere nationalism." Importantly, Spivak also describes the way the study of Indian language literature has become the study of English literature, a nonconsensual creolization, without acknowledgment. "A terrible sociology of knowledge is taking the name 'Indian ' away from them." This very occurrence of whitening continues in all fields of racialized capital, including yoga and wellness. Spivak invokes Edward Said ' s quoting of Hugo of St. Victor, "The man who finds his homeland sweet is still a tender beginner; he to whom every soil is his native one is already strong; but he is perfect to whom the entire world is as a foreign land." This framing is helpful to yoga as property, because in the yoga industrial complex, frequently one encounters the idea that all soils are native, but this finding of a home in India or in yoga by whiteness is not apolitical and is not the same as treating all lands as foreign. Instead, there is a fixation on feeling native, new, reinvented, or uniquely at home in Indian land or practices or property. This fixation in turn affirms and fuels difference.

48. Vijay Prashad, *Uncle Swami: South Asians in America Today* (The New Press, 2012).

49. Cho, supra.

50. Prashad, *Everybody was Kung Fu Fighting: Afro-Asian Connections and the Myth of Cultural Purity*, (Beacon Press, 2002).

51. Prashad, supra.

52. Cho, supra, 789.

53. Spade, supra, 1035.

54. Spade, supra, 1047

55. This discussion point on Wikipedia is situating the site not as a scholarly source, but as an important lens on public knowledge and the production of such knowledges. Out of curiosity, I began a search on the site, and began typing in the search box, "British colonization of," which produced three ensuing options, having to do with the Americas, Africa, and Tasmania. Nothing on India, and then the message that such a page does not even exits. Incredulous, I kept looking for any sign of the British occupation of India being a violent thing that was met with unfathomable human resistance and sacrifice in the name of liberation. I did not find anything of the sort under general terms shared here, not under "British Raj," and not under "India." Only when searching for Indian revolutionaries by name did any of the violence of British rule come through. The Wikipedia page on Bhagat Singh, for example, chronicles the Jallianwala Bagh massacre, which in turn has its own page. But these are specific sites that are likely easily overlooked by those who don't already have exposure to Indian and South Asian resistance movements, exposure of the sort that generally is not built into the world history classes of American public schools.

56. Prashad, supra, 16.

57. Angela P. Harris, "From Stonewall to the Suburbs: Toward a Political Economy of Sexuality." *Wm. & Mary Bill Rts. J.* 14 (2005): 1539.

58. Christine Mai-Duc, "All the 'Happy Birthday' Song Copyright Claims are Invalid, Federal Judge Rules." *Los Angeles Times*, September 22, 2015. http://www.latimes.com.

59. Jeff Chang, *Can't Stop Won't Stop: A History of the Hip-Hop Generation* (Macmillan, 2007).

60. Lisa Marie Cacho, *Social Death: Racialized Rightlessness and the Criminalization of the Unprotected* (New York: New York University Press, 2012).

61. Ruth Wilson Gilmore. "Forgotten Places and the Seeds of Grassroots Planning," in *Engaging Contradictions: Theory, Politics, and Methods of Activist Scholarship* (Berkeley: University of California Press, 2008) 37.

REFERENCES

Barclay, Michael. "What Do Yoga and APIs Have in Common? Neither Are Copyrightable." *Electronic Frontier Foundation*. October 9, 2015. https://www.eff.org.

Bell, Derrick A. *Faces at the Bottom of the Well: The Permanence of Racism* (Basic Books, 1992).

Bikam's Yoga College Of India, L. P. V. Evolation Yoga, LLC (United States Court of Appeals for the Ninth Circuit, October 8, 2015).

Cacho, Lisa Marie. *Social Death: Racialized Rightlessness and the Criminalization of the Unprotected* (New York: New York University Press, 2012).

Carrier, Michael A. "Cabining Intellectual Property Through a Property Paradigm." *Duke Law Journal* (2004): 1–145, 7.

Chang, Jeff. *Can't Stop Won't Stop: A History of the Hip-Hop Generation* (Macmillan, 2007).

Cho, Sumi, Kimberle Williams Crenshaw, and Leslie McCall. "Toward a Field of Intersectionality Studies: Theory, Applications, and Praxis." *Signs* 38, no. 4 (2013): 785–810, 796.

D'Angelo Friedman, Jennifer. "What the Bikram Copyright Rejection Means for Yoga." *Yoga Journal*, October 16, 2015.

Despres, Loraine. "Yoga's Bad Boy: Bikram Choudhury." *Yoga Journal*, August 28, 2007. http://www.yogajournal.com.

Evolation Yoga. "Federal Court Rules That Bikram Doesn't Own Yoga: Copyright Claim Can't Stand the Heat." Accessed December 11, 2015. https://www.evolationyoga.com.

Foote, Andrew. "Yoga Class Cancelled at University of Ottawa over 'cultural appropriation issues.'" *CBCNews*. November 22, 2015. http://www.cbc.ca.

Goldberg, Michelle. "Where the Whole World Meets in a Single Nest: The History Behind a Misguided Campus Debate over Yoga and 'Cultural Appropriation.'" *Slate*, November 23, 2015. http://www.slate.com.

Gumucio, Gregory. Open letter, Bikram Settlement. http://yogatothepeople.com/wp-content/uploads/2012/12/Greg-Letter-Bikram-Settlement.pdf

Harris, Angela P. "From Stonewall to the Suburbs: Toward a Political Economy of Sexuality." *Wm. & Mary Bill Rts. J.* 14 (2005): 1539.

Harris, Cheryl I. "Whiteness as Property." *Harvard Law Review* 106, no. 8 (1993): 1707. doi:10.2307/1341787.

Harthorne, Michael. "Court Says Bikram Founder Doesn't Own Yoga Poses." *Newser*, October 10, 2015. http://www.newser.com.

Helmer, Aedan. "Free Ottawa Yoga Class Scrapped over 'Cultural Issues.'" *Ottawa Sun*, November 20, 2015. http://www.ottawasun.com.

Johnson v. M'Intosh, 21 U.S. 543, 1823.

Kasunic, Robert. Statement of Policy; Registration of Compilations. *United States Library of Congress. Copyright Office.* 121st ed. vol. 77. https://www.gpo.gov.

Kaminoff, Leslie. Facebook page, Leslie Kaminoff Yoga Anatomy. https://www.facebook.com/LeslieKaminoffYogaAnatomy/posts/891326610963863

Lawrence III, Charles R. "Passing and Trespassing in the Academy: On Whiteness as Property and Racial Performance as Political Speech." *Harv. J. Racial & Ethnic Just.* 31 (2015): 7, Footnote 15.

Lopez, Ian Haney. *White by Law: The Legal Construction of Race* (NYU Press, 2006).

Mai-Duc, Christine. "All the 'Happy Birthday' Song Copyright Claims are Invalid, Federal Judge Rules." *Los Angeles Times.* September 22, 2015. http://www.latimes.com.

McGrath, Ben. "Steamed." *The New Yorker*, February 6, 2012.

Moyer, Justin Wm. "Yoga Class Earlier Put on Hold over 'Oppression' Resumes—Minus the White Teacher." *Washington Post*, January 26, 2016.

Notable and Quotable: "Yoga as 'Cultural Appropriation'; The heightened sensitivities on one campus stretch in a new direction." *Wall Street Journal.* November 22, 2015.

Orr, David. "India Adopts Fighting Position to Hold Onto Ancient Yoga Poses." *The Telegraph*, September 20, 2005. http://www.telegraph.co.uk.

Prashad, Vijay. *Everybody was Kung Fu Fighting: Afro-Asian Connections and the Myth of Cultural Purity* (Beacon Press, 2002).

———. *Uncle Swami: South Asians in America Today* (The New Press, 2012).

Said, Edward. *Orientalism. 1978.* (New York: Vintage, 1994 [1979]).

Smith, Linda Tuhiwai. *Decolonizing Methodologies: Research and Indigenous Peoples* (London: Zed Books, 1999) 22.

Spade, Dean. "Intersectional Resistance and Law Reform." *Signs* 38, no. 4 (2013): 1031–55. doi:10.1086/669574.

Spivak, Gayatri Chakravorty and Aleksandŭr K'osev. *Nationalism and the Imagination* (London: Seagull Books, 2010) 31.

Trademark Electronic Search System. Accessed December 8, 2015. http://tess2.uspto.gov.

Copyright Catalog. Accessed December 8, 2015. http://cocatalog.loc.gov.

U.S. Const. Art 1, Sec 8, Cl 8.

Wilson Gilmore, Ruth. "Forgotten Places and the Seeds of Grassroots Planning," in *Engaging Contradictions: Theory, Politics, and Methods of Activist Scholarship.* (Berkeley: University of California Press, 2008) 37.

FIVE

Yoga Culture and Neoliberal Embodiment of Health

Kerrie Kauer

Yoga is a multi-million dollar industry, with approximately twenty million Americans practicing; 85 percent are women. A study conducted by *Yoga Journal* in 2012 found that more than ten billion dollars are spent each year on yoga classes, travel, and equipment.[1] As yoga has increased in popularity in the West, dominant consumer capitalist ideologies have exposed a deep divide between "yoga culture" and yoga as an embodied spiritual practice. In Carol Horton's blog entry "Women in Yoga: Celebration and Critique" to the Yoga Modern website, she states, "In fact, the controversies that divide the yoga community most involve whether the practice has become too entangled with bigger processes of commodifying women's bodies and selling a 'health-and-beauty' agenda."[2] The yoga industry relies on consumer culture and the commodification of the "ideal" body to profit and subsequently reify hegemonic aesthetic ideals.[3] Similar to other forms of movement and fitness, which tend to be quite disembodied, yoga in the West has been guided by neoliberal ideology around one's health and well-being. The lack of one's health, or disease, is often blamed on the individual and their inability to obtain or maintain a healthy body by engaging in carefully prescribed exercise and fitness regimes. Such models of wellness and health reproduce classed, raced, gendered, and sexed bodies that serve the consumer capitalist marketplace (e.g., the weight loss industry, fitness industry, cosmetic surgery, pharmaceuticals, etc.) while simultaneously pathologizing and demonizing transgressive corporeality (e.g., queer, fat bodies). The imagery of health and beauty for women has been equated with a particular kind of body that reproduces hegemonic ideals of femininity. The appearance of a "fit body" rather than the reality of fitness has become a critical determinate of one's social status, and has had a cumulative effect of one's purchases and fitness practices. Yoga in the neoliberal marketplace has, as Sarah Schrank writes, "utterly reshaped an ancient system of Indian spiritual meditation, ripping it from its complex historical roots and replanting it in the shallow earth of corporate profit sharing."[4]

Clearly, yoga has not been unscathed by the neoliberal messaging of health and wellness. For example, *Yoga Journal*, the leading yoga magazine, reaches millions of viewers and subscribers with its magazine alone as well as hosts conferences and events multiple times a year at various locations. Early years of the magazine, particularly in the 1960s, were devoted to women's concerns and women's spirituality, as well as political and feminist issues. Over the past two decades, there has been a sizable shift from feminist issues to neoliberal branding of women's health.[5] Melanie Klein has argued, "As yoga grew in popularity and was absorbed into mainstream culture, it began to reflect many of its toxic values and norms. I found the heart of yoga to be in serious contradiction to the messages perpetuated as the branding and commercialization of yoga exploded."[6] This is an important concept to consider given that the aesthetic of yoga is often viewed by consumers in the Western world through such mediated images. Readers are bombarded with an iconography of sexualized and objectified white women in scantily clad outfits twisting and bending their bodies in incredible postures.[7] This sea of images of white women practicing yoga in a culture that equates yoga with health and wellness sends a clear message about the assumptions of particular bodies. The lack or exclusion of people of color and of fat or queer bodies in the dominant narrative also sends a silent and subtle message about those who are excluded—about the individual responsibility, health, and acceptance of those groups. Images of black and brown bodies, for example, are largely excluded in yoga imagery, simultaneously failing to provide meaningful information about the lack of access to wellness facilities in their community, structural barriers to equitable health care, and systemic obstructions to establishing a regular yoga or mediation practice. The obfuscation of this is problematic given that race, social class, and sexual orientation are critical factors that often impact overall risk, health, access to resources, healing from violence, and the availability and attainment of wellness opportunities.[8] In other words, communities that might benefit the most from yoga are often invisible and excluded. Scores of scientific research have shown that groups who are marginalized and oppressed have higher rates of blood pressure, more stress, are less physically active, and tend to drink and smoke more frequently. In addition to the lack of diverse imagery, the dearth of conversations about systemic and institutionalized forms of racism, classism, heterosexism, and fat phobia is also problematic. It is this silence or omission that reproduces a certain kind of privilege and oppression—a kind that I argue is particularly violent because it is so deeply ingrained and taken for granted as the norm. The goal to better understand the health-related consequences stemming from social inequality is being taken up by various public health initiatives around the United States. As the health care industry moves toward a more integrative model that looks to treat and promote multidimensional wellness, much attention has yet to be given to how oppressive systems within and in conjunction to the health care and fitness industries continue to interlock to create such consequences.

FEMINIST EMBODIED FRAMEWORK

I have been working on a project—collecting data, conducting interviews, gathering documents, and immersing myself in fieldwork—that explores how yoga culture and social justice initiatives can integrate. The following questions guided my project: *How does yoga influence activism? How can the material lived body influence movement toward social justice work? Can embodied social justice movements lead to more conscious and sustainable activism?* I first embarked on this embodied ethnographic project in Big Sur, California at the Esalen Institute in August 2010.[9] The Esalen Institute was founded in 1962 as a center dedicated to alternative modes of education that emphasized the mind, body, spirit connection. The 120 acres of land located between the mountains and the Pacific Ocean was once home to the Esselen Native American tribe and boasts natural sulfur springs as well as an impressive organic garden that is used to feed all of the staff and visitors to the site. I attended my first *Off the Mat, Into the World* (OTM) leadership intensive at the Esalen Institute. The workshop was designed to bring yogis and activists together with an explicit social justice mission. Forty-two participants convened for a five-day workshop lead by four yoga instructors. This chapter is an extension of the ethnographic data collected during the time span that began with that workshop up to present day and includes media analysis, narrative inquiry, participant observation, and interviews.

Feminist scholars, including myself, engaged in gender and Physical Cultural Studies (PCS) work have provided nuanced critiques of the socially constructed body and the myriad ways in which the body has been disciplined and controlled through inequitable social power relations.[10, 11] Our work posits that embodied and sentient experience has been overshadowed by dominant discursive critiques of the body's social relations in society. As Susan Bordo argues in her book *Unbearable Weight*, "While relocation of the body to the culture side of the nature/culture dualism has produced important disruptions to sexist and racist discourse, it has also privileged discourse in ways that sideline the material lived body and suggest that embodiment is solely an effect of language."[12] For this chapter, I attempt to depart from both essentialist readings of the body, as well as the solely discursive deconstructions of the body, invoking the ways in which mind/body, discourse/matter dualisms unite.[13] This approach provides a more thorough and nuanced understanding of *embodiment*, particularly as it relates to oppression and social injustice. Using a feminist embodied approach allows me to anchor into the corporeality of the body, while infusing social and relational experiences; viewing minds, bodies, and societies as thoroughly integrated.[14] As a scholar in the academy, using an embodied approach becomes particularly challenging. As Janet Batacharya further argues, "addressing sentient-social embodiment, especially using Indigenous knowledges such as Yoga, involves challenging Cartesian splits found in both dominant positivist and critical frameworks. It challenges the very idea of academia and the privileging of thought, language and discourse."[15]

EMBODIED SOCIAL JUSTICE

Despite the reticence in embracing "yoga culture," feminists have argued that the practice of yoga can become one that connects us to our own embodiment in spite of dualistic and mechanistic understandings of the body produced by patriarchal capitalism.[16] Luce Irigaray notes that in Western societies, our bodies are educated to forget their sensibilities; that we are indoctrinated to "conquer" our body, reduce it to basic and elementary needs and, in some ways, forget it altogether. She argues that the body becomes cut off from the universe and committed instead to social rules, and yoga can become a tool to reconnect to our carnal experience of love and the divine breaking from detached, disembodied, and patriarchally imposed relationships with the body.[17]

Others have argued that yoga has the ability to counter the heteropatriarchial confines of Western society.[18] [19] Experiencing one's self and the world through embodied movement can potentially make it more difficult to remain passive and rigidly structured around hegemonic social norms.[20] Similarly, Markula argues that if the body is based on a conscious effort to challenge the idealized feminine body, then the body could act as an innovative political statement.[21] Yoga, through breath, movement, and meditation, has the ability to release the psychic pressures of performing learned cultural ethics. When deliberate intention is set in yoga, the limitations within the materialism, power, and state health agendas that guide most sport and fitness practices in the West can be "removed" through the reality of a self-actualized embodied practice.[22] However, as Markula states, "no practice and body shape is oppressive or liberating, but what matters is the intention behind the practice."[23] While not all intention is about liberation, detachment, or social action in every yoga classroom, I argue that the trajectory of modern postural yoga as an embodied form of agency and social justice is occurring simultaneously to the highly commercialized iterations of the practice. For many, yoga "cultivated a sense of empowerment as an inner movement towards a subjective, immanent, sacred, and transcendent dimension from which they have the potential to feel more able to resist oppressive or repressive embodied experiences and enhance their sense of agency."[24]

In addition to yoga's potential for "embodied agency" yoga and other mind/body practices are directly related to involvement in political activities, and moderate levels of spirituality facilitate collective forms of political action.[25] Separate research conduced by Daniel Rothberg as well as Michael Sheridan has demonstrated that personal transformation occurring through spiritual practices such as yoga often fosters broader social action; there is often a connection between individual transformation and structural change.[26] Ancient Hindu texts (e.g., *Bhagavad Gita, Patanjali's Yoga Sutras*) that lay the foundation for yoga define yoga as the interconnectedness or union of all things in nature. *Asana,* or yoga postures, literally translates into "seat" or conscious connection to earth and is a tool for working with the body to renew connection to spirit. Within Patajali's *Yoga Sutras,* the *asanas* are not separated from the rest of the eight limbs of yoga which includes the restraints (*yamas*) and observances (*niyamas*).[27] Mahatma Gandhi, a political activist of India in the 1940s, invoked these principles to ignite independence from British rule specifically drawing from the first Yama of the eight limbs, *ahimsa,* or the tenet to be nonharming. Gandhi's non-violent stance for peaceful revolution was heavily influenced by Patanjali's *Yoga Sutras* that uphold that life requires moral engagement on the field of action. As Stone points out, Gandhi once said, "If you think spirituality and politics are separate, you understand neither spirituality nor politics."[28] Furthermore, in his article on yoga and freedom, Ian Whicher explains,

> Classical yoga acknowledges the intrinsic value of "support" and "sustenance" and interdependence of all living (embodied) entities, thus upholding organic continuity, balance, and integration with the natural and social world. Through yoga one gains proper access to the world and is therefore established in right relationship with the world. Far from being denied or renounced, the world for the yogini, has become transformed, properly engaged.[29]

While some forms of yoga practiced in the West have largely sanitized the embodied spiritual axioms of yoga practice and focus only on the *asana,* there are many teacher trainings, non-profit organizations, and yoga instructors that incorporate the eight limbed path and an embodied spiritual approach that teaches us that yoga not only opens our lives to suffering and pain of ourselves, but to all beings.[30] Additionally, there are many organizations, individuals, and groups that are infusing social justice and feminist activism into their yoga teacher trainings, studios, and workshops. Off the Mat, Into the World became a site for me to explore this connection and engage in an analysis of how social justice initiatives and yoga might unite.

METHODOLOGY

Participants

Workshop participants all shared the practice of yoga, yet participants were diverse in age, gender, race, geographic location, profession, and yoga experience. Of the forty-two participants, four identified as men. The majority of the participants were from the United States, while one participant was currently living and working in Japan, one participant was from Hong Kong, and two participants were from New Zealand. OTM required that participants had been engaged in a regular yoga practice for one year before signing up for the leadership intensive. Participants had practiced varying types of yoga including Vinyasa Flow, Restorative, Yin, Anusara, Ashtanga, Bikram, and Power yoga. Participants came to the OTM intensive with varying experiences in yoga and activism. The diversity of participants included a bestselling author, human rights attorney, graduate student, yoga instructor, secondary school teacher, and massage therapist. Those participants who were formally interviewed ranged in age from twenty-six to fifty-two; seven females and one male participated. All participants were asked if they wished to use a pseudonym, and all participants declined in favor of using their true names. I obtained permission to use my field notes, document collection, and formal interviews from the leaders of OTM in a written document and subsequently gained Internal Review Board approval from my institution. During the intensive a Facebook group was created for the members of the workshop by one of the OTM staff. All participants had permission to read, post, upload images, and comment on the Facebook page.

Interviews and Document Collection

I conducted eight formal semi-structured interviews with participants with whom I attended the OTM workshop at the Esalen Institute. Because I desired to use embodied forms of data collection at the workshop, it required me to also use my own body as a vital resource and immerse myself in the experience.[31] Thus, informal interactions and discussions took place on the site, but I held the formal interviews with participants after the intensive either by phone, teleconference, or in person depending on their location. While phone and teleconference interviews do not reflect an embodied ethnographic approach, I did gain access to my participants through our shared corporeal experience at the OTM workshop and was able to use this level of rapport when conducting formal interviews. Semi-structured interviews lasted approximately thirty to ninety minutes and were recorded with a digital audio recorder, and later transcribed into a word processing program. Transcripts of formal interviews were then entered into Atlas.Ti, a qualitative software program that assists in organizing ethnographic data (e.g., interviews, document collection, photos). Documents were collected over the period of one and a half years, and included websites, blogs, catalogs, and online articles that focused on yoga and activism. Specifically, the OTM and Yoga Activist websites were analyzed as well as blogs from participants from Global Seva Challenges[32] in addition to news articles about yoga and social action.

Using inductive analysis, I found common themes emerging in my field notes, interview transcripts, and documents. Data themes were established by seeking phrases or statements that were repeated throughout the data and I identified consistent themes across my data. As Lee Monaghan noted, the importance of theory lies in interpreting qualitative data[33] and I used a feminist, anti-racist framework to guided my analysis. Without the use of theory to provide a framework, the process of categorizing themes and indexing the data would be virtually impossible. Although this process may be perceived as deductive interpretation, the themes and codes emerged inductively; I sought connections between my own ethnographic observations and important social theory for certain issues and processes within the data.

Analysis

My own body has provided nuanced and existentially based understandings of my data (e.g., the physically exhausting nature of a yoga practice in a five day intensive, viscerally experiencing the mind/body connection through yoga *asana*). Self-reflexivity is integral to an embodied ethnographic approach where one must reflect upon the body and how it is situated within the research process, special arrangements between participants, relationship building, interplay of trust, and friendship and authority.[34] Furthermore, unstructured or informal conversations and participant observation complemented the narrative accounts derived from the formal, structured interviews. These forms of data collection provided a variety of examples and insights on the ways in which yoga and activism are being used together and also examined the ways in which yoga, feminism, and activism are being utilized together. Self-reflexivity is integral to my approach; I reflect upon my own body and how it is situated within the research process, special arrangements between participants, relationship building, interplay of trust, and friendship and authority.

Author Reflexivity

Reflexive accounts of my own bodily knowledge are woven in the findings and analysis, but it is important to acknowledge how I, as a researcher, am situated in this project. I self-identify as a queer feminist, an important piece in how I am perceived throughout the project, as well as how my own identity helps shape my research and analysis. I am white, middle class, and partnered; I have been practicing yoga for approximately seven years and consider myself a retired competitive athlete. My gender as a woman mirrors the broader yoga demographic and most of my participants; this allowed me to fit in easily as a participant observer.

Findings

I will begin my findings with a vignette from my experiences with Off The Mat as it illustrates the embodied work that I, as a feminist researcher, have found to be an important part of the reflexive process of this project. The following is an excerpt from my journal after a morning Vinyasa Flow yoga session led by Seane Corn:

> Today's session was rather intense—the physical piece and the emotional piece. The practice itself did bring up some stuff for me. We learned how to feel in our bodies where we store a lot of tension and old wounds on a cellular, embodied level. At the end we had to journal and share this experience. This process forced me to really be in my body, and not take an "intellectual bypass." A lot came up for me about needing to protect my mom when I was younger by not coming out (as lesbian). I felt where those old tensions were in my body in certain postures that I had thought I resolved and hadn't thought about in years.

As Roxana Ng argues, "Oppression and discrimination are social experiences that have embodied consequences."[35] Power is never enacted as mere intellectual encounters, but for decades I had intellectualized my way around painful heterosexism and homophobia without recognizing the consequences this oppression had on my own body. As a feminist doing queer work, I had spent a decade intellectualizing, theorizing, and thinking my way around topics of heteronormativity, white privilege, racism, queer theory, and sexism all while neglecting the embodied nature of how oppression and power were absorbed by my physical and emotional self.

Initially, participants were asked to formulate their own understanding of conscious activism in small groups of five to six. Each group was responsible for creating words, images, and a definition that reflected their view of activism and each group would then share this with the larger group. Several conversations included ways in which sustainable activism could occur both interpersonally and in the community. We also discussed the ways in which an embodied approach was part of being a spiritual activist, and that drawing from our emotional and social intelligence was equally important to our intellectual and analytical intelligence.

A considerable amount of time was spent on assessing the underlying motives for engaging in activism among participants in the workshop. One of the participants, Nikki, reflected during the workshop, "So, if I'm coming in from a perspective thinking that I'm saving somebody, yeah, I'm gonna get rejected from that community." Another participant, Hala, discussed the approach and conversation that is fundamental to OTM's intensives, "We talk about the distinction between charity and social justice. I feel like that's what yoga is; yoga is helping to inspire that sense of embodiment and empowerment in others." The session facilitator, Seane, discussed the philosophy of the OTM leadership trainings,

> So, the first couple of days [of an intensive] is deep interpersonal work because you cannot do this work of service in the world, it's not sustainable unless you're doing your own interwork. Otherwise, your service very often is based on codependence, meaning let me fix you or change you so I can feel good about me. We teach people the skills so they can go into the service in a much more proactive and healthy way.

This was validated, too, by another participant, TingTing, who had done social activism with a group of yogis in Nepal. Many of the children were orphaned or had been a part of the sex trade industry in the area. Ting-Ting shared her frustration with other individuals who believed giving money to the orphans was enough by saying, "This is yoga off the mat. You know, you're here because you—you want to help the kids in some way, and it's not about you bringing money. It's about you being here, and letting them know that somebody cares, and letting them know that they're no different from us." TingTing went on to discuss many of the issues that arise with *voluntourism*[36] such as the consequential dangers that arise when someone of privilege engages with vulnerable and oppressed groups without having established rapport, awareness, and prior invitation. Consistent with the critiques of many organizations that use SDP models, charity and philanthropy can often dismantle seemingly good intentions of people working with oppressed communities. We engaged in difficult and challenging conversations regarding this throughout the intensive.

SUSTAINING THE COMMUNITY

Throughout my interviews and observations, participants believed that they were aware of the ways in which global activism they were involved in might reproduce neo-colonialist and patronizing ideologies. As Hala stated, "Rather than being presumptuous and coming in and going, 'We think you people need XYZ, and we're going to give it to you and then we're leaving,' it's going into organizations that already have a local presence and asking what they need." Many SDP have taken predominantly functionalist approaches that gloss over institutionalized forms of oppressive power and neoliberal logic of competitive financial and cultural relations.[37, 38] Additionally, many organizations that focus on the "Girl Effect" or empowerment initiatives for girls and women often do so without consulting the communities into which they are entering, and perpetuate imperialist gendered and racial hierarchies.[39] We addressed the problems with entering communities, particularly in the global South, with initiatives that reify the idea that white, Western women "know best" what communities and individuals need. Seane Corn elaborates, "We focus on what the needs of the culture are. Rather than go in there and say we want to build a school and have our name attached to it, we go into the community and say, 'what are your needs?'" These conversations opened critical dialogue for participants and leaders to understand the differences between social responsibility and engaged activism and how the practice of yoga dismantles the "us" vs. "them" rhetoric that ultimately reproduces sympathetic and paternalistic charity work.

This approach to activism has been widely supported in scholarship that is mindful of the harm that some corporate NGOs oftentimes foster when they enter communities in the hopes that sport or physical activity will be a panacea, or worse, an opiate to the important or urgent issues of regions or communities neglecting to address the privilege and ethnocentrism that may be simultaneously presented. In interviews, blogs, and workshops, this theme emerged as an important part of the dialogue within the OTM community. Yet, there was critical dialogue in the workshop about the best way to enter communities, or developing countries without reproducing more harm. Several of the OTM leaders and participants in the workshop described "going into [a community] to empower them," which ends of doing more harm in many of the communities who already feel empowered, but lack tangible resources for survival. It was clear that OTM and many of the people that were more integrated than myself into the organization were still wrestling with "best practices" to engage in social justice work in truly mindful ways.

SUSTAINING THE ACTIVIST

Many of the participants discussed the ways that yoga helped them create more sustainable activism, and served as a reminder for their impetus for social action. As Hala stated, "If we're not willing to go into our own shadow material, our activism can become a way to go around what's going on for us. So for example, say you have a history of sexual abuse but you don't want to look at it, one way to divert it is to deal with other people that have had sexual abuse. That way, you're looking at their issues and staying distracted from your own." Having participants in the OTM intensive practice yoga as a tool for connecting to the reason they are involved with certain social injustices proved useful. We spent time accessing, through our bodies, why certain social justice initiatives were important to us. Social experiences of embodiment are referenced primarily in terms of social relations of power and identity that may be imposed within social hierarchies. In her work on embodiment, Janet Batacharya reminds us that from feminist and anti-racist perspectives, "Sentient social embodiment particularly, healing from violence and oppression is not only about mind, body and spirit wellbeing; nor does it involve solely cognitive understandings of social inequity and its consequences."[40] As many of the OTM participants recalled, power relations that involve oppression and subordination are never purely intellectual, but become stored in the body, as it is experienced and constructed via the body. Nikki stated, "No matter who or where we are, the issues live in our tissues, right? Yoga as embodied practice, which includes underneath it many practices, serve to help release those feelings that live in our tissues." In that light, yoga and its connection to activism becomes a vehicle to present embodiment as an interacting and integrative experience of mind, body, spirit, culture, discourse, and society. Each of these elements cannot be disentangled to fully understand the effects of healing and social justice from oppression as it relates to embodiment. As Ng's work argues, oppression and discrimination are social experiences that have embodied consequences.[41] Challenging and asserting domination is absorbed through one's body and not limited to cognitive experience, but instead is a social, mind related, body inhabited, discursive, and cultural experience. Hala supported this idea by describing how our bodies can serve to educate us on how our activism will be mirrored by understanding embodied emotions,

> Whatever tendencies we have physically, we're going to have in every other aspect of our life. If somebody's physical tendency is to disassociate or be very passive, their activism might be a passivism, a kind of not wanting to acknowledge the shadow and just love and happiness and I don't want to see the bad stuff.

Marianne, a human rights activists and attorney recently working in Afghanistan, expressed how trauma, injustice, and social experiences were deeply felt on an embodied level, and yoga became a tool to counteract the violence, "It was like my ability to do my work to go out every day in Afghanistan and deal with the kind of trauma and suffering that I was dealing with and the kind of secondary trauma that I was experiencing. Every day I had to do my yoga practice." She continued by saying,

> [The] first relationship between yoga and activism for me was that I was already an activist but it became unsustainable because I didn't have ways of properly caring for my—that union between body and mind. I practiced yoga to survive and to be able to keep doing that work and that—and then other time, that's transformed again and yoga became a practice for me of seeing myself more and more clearly.

Several of the participants discussed the ways in which yoga helped them strip down much of sociocultural norms that have been inscribed on their bodies. Marianne discussed the ways in which yoga has helped her work through trauma and see herself clearly despite living in chaos. For individuals or organizations doing activist work around deep social and cultural problems such as war and sexual violence, yoga has been a way to stay grounded and connected to the mission of service. As Nikki stated, "The whole work in activism happens while I'm working with other people, when all my shit comes up, right? So, yeah, so it's being open and willing and honest about looking at my own shit, and that's not easy work." In my interview with Nikki, she suggested that I read her blog about her experience in South Africa from a Global Seva Challenge trip. Being involved in activist work in South Africa that confronted structural forms of racism and sexism unveiled deep layers of oppression that Nikki embodied as a black woman. The following excerpt comes directly from Nikki's blog on the OTM website regarding her experience with race, apartheid, and yoga:

> Later, I realized this moment as the beginning of a breakthrough. After our evening group processing work and especially during the next day's yoga practice, I began to see/feel/experience my inner division and fragmentation as a result of my own misperception (yogis will recognize this as *avidya*). . . . I recognized that apartheid and the system of slavery before it, worked by assigning explicit meaning and standing to each racial classification with Whites superior to all and Coloreds and Blacks respectively more inferior. Even after the outlaw of chattel (physical) slavery, the psychological slavery of inferiority continued. Yoga has helped me understand that everything is energy. Inferior and superior are energies that I embody and can become aware of right down to the level of nervous system sensation.

This particular example illustrates how sociocultural forces are inscribed on the bodies of those who are marginalized or oppressed, and that even through discursive understandings of apartheid and racism that occurred in South Africa, Nikki had to confront, through yoga, how those systemic forms of racism were manifested in her, and how to negotiate trapped energies in her body. It is also important to note that Nikki was one of the only people of color in the entire workshop or who, at the time of this research, had any type of leadership role within the OTM organization. The lack of representation of people of color was a critical observation of the demographic of participants OTM attracted for this particular workshop, and could be an important point of reflection for OTM moving forward as to why this phenomenon might be taking place.

CONCLUSION

As the West has seen a surge in the practice and availability of yoga, competing trends have simultaneously emerged. One trend is that the practice has been subjected to dominant consumer capitalist ideologies. Many yoga studios and teachers rely on the culturally perpetuated "body ideal" to profit—and subsequently reproduce—gendered, classed, raced, and sized messages.[42] Often, these models serve the commercial marketplace (e.g., the weight loss industry, fitness industry, cosmetic surgery, pharmaceuticals), in turn creating a dichotomy wherein the exclusion of disparate bodies (e.g., queer, fat, black) is fueled by their pathologization. Despite this, there is growing evidence of a trend toward embodied, conscious activism. This specific type of conscious activism initiated by yoga offers a new form of progressive body politics that remind us that our bodies are important and inescapable vehicles for social action. And the embodied spiritual foundation from which yoga emerges is "based around the fact that the relation to the self is always constituted in relation to others, as we are radically open to the world."[43]

Many of the participants in the study were deeply involved in collective struggles in their varying spheres of work, family, school, and community. I attempt to understand how yoga can help engender socially responsible activism using embodied sociological and ethnographic approaches. As Batacharya asserts, "Embodiment studies are akin to other disruptions such as critical anti-racist feminism and decolonization that upturn ways of knowing through intricate investigations of lived experience and attunement to sentient-social embodiment."[44] I argue that yoga informed by feminist, anti-racist, and culturally diverse frameworks can offer examples of how social justice work can be affected through progressive body practices. Corporeal knowledge, integrity, and personal transformation that yogic practice engenders *can* serve as a conduit for social justice work. As Burkitt states, "The body is not simply a product of relations to power, but also of relations to communication and transformation. As such, it is equipped with a variety of dispositions, capacities, and potentialities that allow for agency and the constant possibility of social change.[45] Further Zimmerman et al. posit: "Because many social justice movements of the West have relied on secular and intellectual analysis from the Left, largely influenced by Marxist thought that dismissed spiritual or non-secular ideologies, these movements have ignored that fact that indigenous communities have never separated their justice-making from a sense of spirit and Creator."[46] Yoga can provide us with tools to ensure that embodied, sentient, and spiritual experiences fully materialize as equally integral components to doing feminist minded social justice work. Taking an embodied approach where the lived experience is acknowledged in relation to activist projects might also lead to more sustainable and conscious forms of activism without reproducing colonial and paternalist notions of service.

NOTES

1. "Yoga Journal Releases 2012 Yoga in America Market Study," PR Newswire, accessed December 5, 2012, http://www.prnewswire.com/news-releases/yoga-journal-releases-2012-yoga-in-america-market-study-182263901.html.

2. Carol Horton, "Yoga and Feminism: Continuing the Conversation," May 5, 2014, http://Carolhortonphd.Com/Yoga-Journals-Body-Issue-Rebranding/.

3. Pirkko Markula, "Tuning into One's Self: Foucault's Technologies of the Self and Mindful Fitness," *Sociology of Sport Journal* 21 (2004): 302–21.

4. Sarah Schrank, "American Yoga: The Shaping of Modern Body Culture in the United States," *American Studies* 53 (2014): 169–81.

5. Pirkko Markula, "Tuning into One's Self."

6. Melanie Klein, "How Yoga Makes You Pretty: The Beauty Myth, Yoga and Me," in C. Horton & R. Harvey, eds., 21st Century Yoga: Culture, Politics, and Practice, (Chicago: Kleio Books, 2012) 28.

7. Pirkko Markula, "Tuning into One's Self," 57.

8. Liliane Cambraia Windsor, Eloise Dunlap, and Andrew Golub. "Challenging Controlling Images, Oppression, Poverty, and other Structural Constraints: Survival Strategies among African–American Women in Distressed Households." *Journal of African American Studies* 15, no. 3 (2010/2011): 290–306.

9. The Esalen Institute derived its name from the Esselen Native American tribe.

10. Laura F. Chase, "Running Big: Clydesdale Runners and Technologies of the Body," *Sociology of Sport Journal* 25 (2008): 130–47.

11. Pirkko Markula, "Tuning into One's Self"

12. Susan Bordo, *Unbearable Weight: Feminism, Western Culture, and the Body* (Berkeley: University of California Press, 1993) 34.

13. The concept of unity between mind and body as well as discourse/matter dualisms is explored in Janet Batacharya's doctoral work "Life in a Body: Counter Hegemonic Understandings of Violence, Oppression, Healing and Embodiment Among Young South Asian Women."

14. Lee F. Monaghan, "Doorwork and Legal Risk: Observations from an Embodied Ethnography," *Social and Legal Students* 13, no. 4 (2004): 453–80.

15. Janet Batacharya, "Life in a Body: Counter Hegemonic Understandings of Violence, Oppression, Healing and Embodiment Among Young South Asian Women," 18.

16. Michael Atkinson, "Entering Scapeland: Yoga, Fell and Post-sport Physical Cultures," *Sport in Society* 13, no. 7 & 8 (2010): 1249–67.

17. Luce, Irigaray. *Between East and West: From Singularity to Community*, 67

18. Michal Pagis, "Embodied Self-Reflexivity," *Social Psychology Quarterly* 72, no. 3 (2009): 265–83.

19. Lisa R. Rubin, Carol J. Nemeroff, and Nancy F Russo. "Exploring Feminist Women's Body Consciousness," *Psychology of Women Quarterly* 9, no. 1 (2004): 27–37.

20. Michael Atkinson, "Entering Scapeland: Yoga, Fell and Post-sport Physical Cultures," 36.

21. Pirrko Markula, "Tuning into One's Self: Foucault's Technologis of the Self and Mindful Fitness," 319.

22. Aspasia Leledaki and David Brown. "'Physicalisation': A Pedagogy of Body-Mind Cultivation for Liberation in Modern Yoga and Meditation Methods." *Asian Medicine* 4 (2008): 312.

23. Pirrko Markula, "Tuning into One's Self: Foucault's Technologies of the Self and Mindful Fitness," 319.

24. Seil Oh and Natalia Sarkisian. "Spiritual Individualism or Engaged Spirituality? Social Implications of Holistic Spirituality Among Mind-Body-Spirit Practitioners," *Sociology of Religion* 71 (2011): 54–70.

25. Donna Fahri, *Yoga Mind, Body and Spirit: A Return to Wholeness* (New York: Holt, 2005).

26. Daniel Rothberg, *The Engaged Spiritual Life: A Buddhist Approach to Transforming Ourselves and the World.* (Boston: Beacon Press, 2006) 81.

27. 'Asana,' 'Yamas,' and 'Niyamas' are the used terminology originating from Sanskrit

28. Michael Stone and Bellur KS Iyengar, *Yoga for a World out of Balance: Teachings on Ethics and Social Action* (Boston: Shambhala, 2009) 155.

29. Ian Whicher, "Yoga and Freedom: A Reconsideration of Patanjali's Classical Yoga," *Philosophy East and West* 48 (1998): 161.

30. Donna Fahri, *Yoga Mind, Body and Spirit*, 25

31. Alison L. Bain and Catherine J Nash, "Undressing the Researcher: Feminism, Embodiment and Sexuality at a Queer Bathhouse Event," *Area* 38 (2006): 99–106.

32. Global Seva Challenge is a "transformational journey that builds community, provokes awareness and action around global issues, and raises significant funds to support communities in crisis" sponsored by Off The Mat. http://www.off thematintotheworld.org/seva-challenge/

33. Lee F. Monaghan, "Doorwork and Legal Risk: Observations from an Embodied Ethnography," 23.

34. Alison L. Bain and Catherine J Nash, "Undressing the Researcher: Feminism, Embodiment and Sexuality at a Queer Bathhouse Event," *Area* 38 (2006): 99–106.

35. Roxana Ng, "Decolonizing Teaching and Learning Through Embodied Learning: Toward an Integrated Approach," in *Valences of Interdisciplinary: Theory, Practice, Pedagogy* (Edmonton: AU Press, 2012) 45

36. Voluntourism is a growing concept that incorporates community service with international travel.

37. Fred Coalter, "The Politics of Sport-for-development: Limited Focus Programmes and Broad Gauge Problems?" *International Review for the Sociology of Sport* 45 (2010): 295–314.

38. Iain Lindsey and Davies Banda. "Sport and the Fight Against HIV/AIDS in Zambia: A 'Partnership Approach?" *International Review for the Sociology of Sport* 46 (2011): 90–107.

39. Lindsay M. Hayhurst, "Corporatising Sport, Gender and Development: Postcolonial IR Feminisms, Transnational Private Governance and Global Corporate Social Engagement," *Third World Quarterly* 32, (2011): 123.

40. Janet, Batacharya, "Life in a Body: Counter Hegemonic Understandings of Violence, Oppression, Healing, and Embodiment Among Young South Asian Women," 5.

41. Roxana Ng, "Decolonizing Teaching and Learning Through Embodied Learning: Toward an Integrated Approach," in *Valences of Interdisciplinary: Theory, Practice, Pedagogy*, edited by Raphael Foshay (Edmonton: AU Press, 2012) 343–65.

42. Kimberly J. Lau, *New Age Capitalism: Making Money East of Eden*, (Philadelphia: University of Pennsylvania Press, 2000) 345.

43. Jennifer Lea, "Liberation or Limitation? Understanding Iyengar Yoga as a Practice of the Self," *Body & Society* 15 (2009): 86.

44. Janet Batacharya, "Life in a Body: Counter Hegemonic Understandings of Violence, Oppression, Healing, and Embodiment Among Young South Asian Women," 18.

45. Ian Burkitt, *Bodies of Thought: Embodiment, Identity, and Modernity* (London: Sage, 1999) 108.

46. Kristen Zimmerman, Neelam Pathikonda, Brenda Salgado & Taj James, *Out of the Spiritual Closet: Organizers Transforming the Practice of Social Justice*, (Oakland: Movement Strategy Center, 2010) 10.

REFERENCES

Atkinson, Michael. "Entering Scapeland: Yoga, Fell and Post-sport Physical Cultures," *Sport in Society* 13, no. 7 & 8 (2010): 1249–67.

autipacha. "Yoga Justice Playlist Questionnaire." *Black Yogis*. Last modified October 4, 2015. http://blackyogis.tumblr.com/post/130517099262/yoga-justice-playlist-questionnaire

Bain, Alison L. and Catherine J. Nash, "Undressing the Researcher: Feminism, Embodiment and Sexuality at a Queer Bathhouse Event," *Area* 38 (2006): 99–106.

Batacharya, Janet. "Life in a Body: Counter Hegemonic Understandings of Violence, Oppression, Healing and Embodiment Among Young South Asian Women," 18.

Black Yogis. "About." Accessed November 30, 2015. http://blackyogis.tumblr.com/.

Bordo, Susan. *Unbearable Weight: Feminism, Western Culture, and the Body* (Berkeley: University of California Press, 1993) 34.

Burkitt, Ian. *Bodies of Thought: Embodiment, Identity, and Modernity* (London: Sage, 1999) 108.

Butler, Jess. "For White Girls Only? Postfeminism and the Politics of Inclusion." *Feminist Formations* 25, no. 1 (2013): 35–58.

Chase, Laura F. "Running Big: Clydesdale Runners and Technologies of the Body," *Sociology of Sport Journal* 25 (2008): 130–47.

Coalter, Fred. "The Politics of Sport-for-development: Limited Focus Programmes and Broad Gauge Problems?" *International Review for the Sociology of Sport* 45 (2010): 295–314.

Corn, Seane. "Jacoby Ballard: Personal Transformation + Healing Yoga." *Yoga Journal*, March 24, 2015. http://www.yogajournal.com/article/lifestyle/jacoby-ballard-finding-transformation-healing/.

Fahri, Donna. *Yoga Mind, Body and Spirit: A Return to Wholeness* (New York: Holt, 2005).

Hanson, Krista Lee. "When People of Color Say They Want Their Own Yoga, White People Should Listen." *Decolonizing Yoga*. Accessed November 30, 2015. http://www.decolonizingyoga.com/when-people-of-color-say-they-want-their-own-yoga-white-people-should-listen/#sthash.IONQpioc.j3wbj1D8.dpuf.

Hayhurst, Lindsay M. "Corporatising Sport, Gender and Development: Postcolonial IR Feminisms, Transnational Private Governance and Global Corporate Social Engagement," *Third World Quarterly* 32, (2011): 123.

Horton, Carol. "Yoga and Feminism: Continuing the Conversation." *Carol Horton, Ph.D: writer, educator, activist*, blog, May 5, 2014. http://carolhortonphd.com/yoga-and-feminism/.

Iain, Lindsey and Davies Banda. "Sport and the Fight Against HIV/AIDS in Zambia: A 'Partnership Approach?" *International Review for the Sociology of Sport* 46 (2011): 90–107.

Irigaray, Luce. *Between East and West: From Singularity to Community*, 67

Klein, Melanie. "How Yoga Makes You Pretty: The Beauty Myth, Yoga and Me," in C. Horton & R. Harvey, eds., *21st Century Yoga: Culture, Politics, and Practice* (Chicago: Kleio Books, 2012).

———. "Yoga's 21st Century Facelift and the Myth of the Perfect Ass(ana)." *Elephant Journal*. Last modified November 12, 2012. http://www.elephantjournal.com/2012/11/yogas-21st-century-facelift-the-myth-of-the-perfect-assana/.

Krieger, Nick. "Why Queer and Trans Yoga?" *Decolonizing Yoga*. Accessed November 30, 2015. http://www.decolonizingyoga.com/trans-queer-yoga/.

Lau, Kimberly J. *New Age Capitalism: Making Money East of Eden*, (Philadelphia: University of Pennsylvania Press, 2000) 345.

Lea, Jennifer. "Liberation or Limitation? Understanding Iyengar Yoga as a Practice of the Self," *Body & Society* 15 (2009): 86.

Leledaki, Aspasia and David Brown. "'Physicalisation': A Pedagogy of Body-Mind Cultivation for Liberation in Modern Yoga and Meditation Methods." *Asian Medicine* 4 (2008): 312.

Lululemon. "The Lululemon Manifesto." Accessed November 30, 2015. http://www.lululemon.com/about/manifesto

Macdonald, Andi. "Yoga Studios: Everyone's Welcome?" *Decolonizing Yoga*. Accessed November 30, 2015. http://www.decolonizingyoga.com/yoga-studios-everyones-welcome/.

———. "With Your Permission: Yoga, Consent and Authentic Embodiment." *Decolonizing Yoga*. Accessed November 30, 2015. http://www.decolonizingyoga.com/with-your-permission-yoga-consent-and-authentic-embodiment/#sthash.NpTalLWQ.dpuf.

Markula, Pirkko. "Turning into One's Self: Foucault's Technologies of the Self and Mindful Fitness," *Sociology of Sport Journal* 21 (2004): 302–321.

McDonald, Mary G. "The Marketing of Women's National Basketball Association and the Making of Postfeminism." *International Review for the Sociology of Sport* 35, no. 1 (2000): 35–47.

Monaghan, Lee F. "Doorwork and Legal Risk: Observations from an Embodied Ethnography," *Social and Legal Students* 13, no. 4 (2004): 453–80.

Musial, Jennifer. "Engaged Pedagogy in the Feminist Classroom and Yoga Studio." *Feminist Teacher* 21, no. 2 (2011): 2012–228.

Ng, Roxana. "Decolonizing Teaching and Learning Through Embodied Learning: Toward an Integrated Approach," in *Valences of Interdisciplinary: Theory, Practice, Pedagogy* (Edmonton: AU Press, 2012) 45

Oh, Seil and Natalia Sarkisian. "Spiritual Individualism or Engaged Spirituality? Social Implications of Holistic Spirituality Among Mind-Body-Spirit Practitioners," *Sociology of Religion* 71 (2011): 54–70.

Pagis, Michal. "Embodied Self-Reflexivity," *Social Psychology Quarterly* 72, no. 3 (2009): 265–83.

Rothberg, Daniel. *The Engaged Spiritual Life: A Buddhist Approach to Transforming Ourselves and the World*. (Boston: Beacon Press, 2006) 81.

Rubin, Lisa R., Carol J. Nemeroff, and Nancy F Russo. "Exploring Feminist Women's Body Consciousness," *Psychology of Women Quarterly* 9, no. 1 (2004): 27–37.

Schranka, Sara. "American Yoga: The Shaping of Modern Body Culture in the United States," *American Studies* 53 (2014): 169–181.

Siber, Kate. "Your Greatest *Asset*." *Yoga Journal*, May 2015, 78–85.

Stone, Michael and Bellur KS Iyengar, *Yoga for a World out of Balance: Teachings on Ethics and Social Action* (Boston: Shambhala, 2009) 155.

Studio 34: Yoga, Healing, Arts. "Class Descriptions." Accessed November 30, 2015. http://studio34yoga.com/yoga-movement/class-descriptions/.

Valdés, Alisa L. "Ruminations of a Feminist Fitness Instructor," in *Listen Up: Voices from the Next Feminist Generation*. Edited by Barbara Findlen (Seattle, WA: Seal Press, 2001) 25–32.

Windsor, Liliane Cambraia, Eloise Dunlap, and Andrew Golub. "Challenging Controlling Images, Oppression, Poverty, and other Structural Constraints: Survival Strategies among African–American Women in Distressed Households." *Journal of African American Studies* 15, no. 3 (2010/2011): 290–306.

Weber, Brenda R. "Teaching Popular Culture through Gender Studies: Feminist Pedagogy in a Postfeminist and Neoliberal Academy?" *Feminist Teacher* 20, no. 2 (2010): 124–38.

Whicher, Ian. "Yoga and Freedom: A Reconsideration of Patanjali's Classical Yoga," *Philosophy East and West* 48 (1998): 161.

YJ Editor. "Uncovering Yoga's Hidden Eating Disorder Epidemic." *Yoga Journal*, October 8, 2014. http://www.yogajournal.com/food-diet/uncovering-yogas-hidden-eating-disorder-epidemic/

Yoga on High. "Big Asana." Accessed November 30, 2015. http://yogaonhigh.com/classes/specialty-classes/big-asana#sthash.AKuAkmja.dpuf

Zimmerman, Kristen, Neelam Pathikonda, Brenda Salgado & Taj James. *Out of the Spiritual Closet: Organizers Transforming the Practice of Social Justice*, (Oakland: Movement Strategy Center, 2010) 10.

SIX

Yoga is Not Dodgeball

Mind-Body Integration and Progressive Education

Carol Horton

In 2013, Judge John Meyer ruled that it's constitutional to teach yoga in public schools on the grounds that's simply another exercise program, "like dodgeball."[1] In so doing, he rejected the complaint made by a group of conservative Christian parents that their children's school-based yoga program was "inherently and pervasively religious," and violated the California state constitution's separation of church and state. While legally sound, Meyer's "dodgeball" analogy is emblematic of the ways in which the conceptual framing of *Sedlock v. Encinitas* serves to "dodge" critical issues that should be addressed as yoga, as well as closely related mindfulness programs, are increasingly incorporated into U.S. public institutions such as schools, prisons, and V.A. programs.[2]

Sedlock's juxtaposition of "religion" and "exercise" replicates the dominant Western tradition of seeing mind and body as separate parts of our being. Yoga, however, is commonly described as a "mind-body-spirit" practice. In fact, insisting that yoga is "just exercise" presumes precisely the sort of fragmented, mechanistic conception of the body that experienced yoga practitioners reject. Nonetheless, this landmark case perversely pitted yoga advocates likening yoga to "football warm-ups" against anti-yoga plaintiffs contending it's a "spiritual, as well as physical" practice.[3] Rather than challenging their insistence that yoga's spiritual dimensions can only be characterized as religious, the defense simply "dodged" the question of its holistic, multidimensional qualities altogether.

Sedlock's failure to even attempt to square yoga's status as a mind-body-spirit practice with the requirements of secular public institutions isn't unique to this case. On the contrary, it reflects a profound lacuna in American culture. Our educational system has become subsumed by narrowly instrumentalist, neoliberal values, as has our society at large. In keeping with the default mindset this establishes, the defense team in *Sedlock* either championed yoga's ability to improve student "focus, discipline, and behavior" or (rather incongruously) contended that it's simply another exercise program with some extra stretching and breathing thrown in.[4] To have defended yoga in schools on grounds that extend beyond such instrumentalist reasoning would have required taking greater legal as well as cultural risks. Consequently, it wasn't done.

Much is lost in this evasion. Reducing yoga to a mechanistic exercise with some added behavioral benefits eviscerates its true holistic potential, while reinforcing the impoverished understanding of education that dominates our public system. Alternatively, teaching yoga in ways that affirm its status as a mind-body integration practice (adapted as necessary to support secular educational values) offers a means of revitalizing the commitment to educating the "whole child" that once formed the bedrock of our now-marginalized tradition of progressive education. Given that yoga as we know it today has many historical and cultural roots in common with progressive education—both emerged in the early twentieth century with a shared commitment to integrating science, democracy, and the holistic development of "mind, body, and spirit"— integrating them makes sense, and could prove enormously valuable. Doing so with integrity, however, requires dismantling the logic of *Sedlock* and replacing it with an alternative paradigm that affirms the value of holistic practices for individual students, as well as education, culture, and society.

TROJAN HORSE?

Teaching yoga in public schools in ways that maximize its holistic benefits requires a more thoughtful response to parental concerns about its potential entanglement with religion than the "it's just exercise" brushoff provided by *Sedlock*. Indeed, the plaintiff's argument that the Encinitas Unified School District's (EUSD) program was "inherently and pervasively religious" relied in part on the recognition that yoga is a mind-body-spirit practice, not simply "exercise." The conservative Christian parents who brought the case, however, erroneously equated any such practice with the inculcation of religious beliefs. Consequently, rather than seeing the holistic benefits of yoga as potential educational goods, they were regarded as a Trojan Horse for the promotion of religion, specifically a mixture of "Hinduism, Buddhism, Taoism, and Western metaphysics."[5]

The plaintiff's primary expert witness, Dr. Candy Gunther Brown, a Harvard Ph.D. and associate professor of religious studies at Indiana University, framed the issue of the mind-body-spirit relationship exclusively in terms of quasi-religious spirituality. "In the religious origins of yoga, body and spirit are not separable categories (as presupposed by Cartesian mind-body dualism), but aspects of each other, and bodily practices are spiritual as well as physical. From such a perspective," she contended, "it would make little sense to isolate bodily practices from spiritual purposes—as those promoting the EUSD yoga program claim to do." Consequently, Brown argued, stripping any purported religious references out of the EUSD yoga program would not remove its religiosity, which was embodied in the practice itself.

The "Information for Parents" handout distributed by parent activists opposing the EUSD program put the matter more bluntly. "Even according to expert yoga teachers and practitioners, yoga poses are not ever merely exercise, they are different from other forms of systemized practices *because they are inherently religious.*" The leaflet went on to warn parents that students in the EUSD program had received instruction regarding "how to channel energy through a yoga pose to calm anxiety."[6] From their perspective, yoga's purported efficacy in reducing stress wasn't the issue. Even if proved effective, yoga would still be seen as unconstitutional in public school settings on the grounds that teaching children to "channel energy" is a form of religious indoctrination.

This claim was backed up by fact that the EUSD program had been launched and funded by a $533,720 grant from the Jois Foundation, a nonprofit named after the late Indian yoga master Sri Pattabhi Jois.[7] The National Center for Law and Policy, which prosecuted the case *pro bono,* pointed out in a press release that Jois himself had taught that "spirituality means energy, and to meditate on that energy is spirituality." Consequently, the plaintiffs contended, even the seemingly secular dimensions of yoga, such as its ability to reduce stress, were actually part of a religious paradigm.

MUTUAL DISREGARD

Of course, it's possible to provide scientific explanations of yoga's ability to "calm anxiety," rather than "energetic" ones. In fact, scientific research into the neurophysiological processes involved in working with yoga as a mind-body-spirit practice is booming as never before, while becoming substantially more sophisticated and ambitious.[8] Given that *Sedlock* turned on the question of whether yoga is better defined as exercise or religion, however, neither party was motivated to explore such work. On the contrary, Professor Brown preemptively dismissed any scientific claims of yoga's effectiveness as mere "camouflage" designed to disguise its intrinsically religious nature:

> Religious practices such as yoga and mindfulness mediation are often relabeled as scientific techniques, exercise, philosophy, non-sectarian spirituality, commodity, or Christian worship. It is a common promotional strategy to emphasize physical, mental, and emotional benefits. But because the physical and spiritual aspects of practices such as yoga intertwine, failure to acknowledge yoga's religious purposes does not automatically transform yoga into secular exercise. [9]

Brown's contention that scientific claims of yoga's benefits are smokescreens for its essential religiosity was itself easily dismissed by unsympathetic lawyers, judges, journalists, and social media commentators as putting a pseudo-scholarly front on the paranoid fantasies of religious fundamentalists. The defendants' appellate brief, for example, scoffed at plaintiff concerns about the program's source of funding as simply "a concoction of Dr. Brown, who, according to the trial court, believes 'the Jois Foundation is on a sinister mind-control conspiracy . . . to get (students) on a path to become practicing Hindus or Buddhists or Jainists.'" Rather than looking at the situation through "the subjective eyes of an expert who sees religion everywhere," the brief contends, any "reasonable observer" would know that "yoga practices are widely accepted in the Western world, simply for their exercise benefits." [10]

While this is certainly true, it fails to acknowledge that yoga is also commonly embraced "in the Western world" (as well as globally) as a mind-body-spirit practice. Further, experienced yoga practitioners are well aware that the Ashtanga method is exceptionally rigorous, and that those who engage with it seriously would never dream of characterizing yoga as "just exercise." This is no secret. The Jois Yoga website describes Ashtanga as "an ancient system that can lead to liberation and greater awareness of our spiritual potential." Further, the "Philosophy" section of the site provides in-depth discussions of the spiritual and philosophical dimensions of the practice that could be reasonably construed as religious.

Of course, the fact that the Jois Foundation funded the EUSD program is not in itself evidence of unconstitutional "religious entanglement." It does show, however, that parental anxiety about this issue was not simply delusional paranoia. As Douglass (2010) details, preemptively dismissing it as fundamentalist hysteria follows a longer history of liberal scoffing at conservative religious concerns over yoga in schools that dates back to at least 1992. In this sense, *Sedlock* simply continued a preexisting pattern of "vastly oversimplifying" the complex cultural issues involved in teaching yoga (as well as related practices such as mindfulness) in American public schools. [11]

PARADIGM CLASH

Beyond the general tendency to oversimplify complex issues in American culture, the roots of this pattern can be traced back to the emergence of modern forms of yoga and meditation in the early twentieth century. Today, of course, both are popularly understood as "ancient practices" whose meanings and forms haven't changed much in thousands of years. Unsurprisingly, however, recent scholarship demonstrates otherwise. Modern *asana*, or postural yoga practice, emerged in India during the early 1900s, integrating the enthusiasm for meditative yoga and universalist neo-Hinduism sparked by Swami Vivekananda with the holistic health commitments of the transnational "physical culture" movement.[12] In a fascinating historical parallel, modern forms of meditation—which, for the first time, were designed to be simple, accessible, and appropriate for laypeople—were developed by Buddhist monks Ledi Sayadaw and Mingun Sayadaw in early twentieth-century Burma.[13]

Then as now, the dominant cultural frame of Western modernity pitted science and physicality against religion and spirituality. Modern yoga and meditation, in contrast, emerged in conjunction with an alternative paradigm that asserted the harmony of the scientific and spiritual realms. Further, these newly accessible forms of mind-body-spirit practice were understood to be intrinsically "scientific" and "spiritual" themselves. In this formulation, yoga and meditation were understood to be scientific in that their claims to efficacy were based on empirical experience, rather than religious belief. Like scientific experiments, they offered repeatable patterns of movement, attention, and/or breathing that had broadly predictable results.

One such result was a sense of deeper connection to the "spiritual" dimensions of our beings.[14] Because modern yoga grew out of the ancient Indian civilization that also birthed Hinduism, Buddhism, and Jainism, however, the universally accessible spirituality it offered was deeply informed by and entwined with those traditions.[15] This didn't mean that practicing yoga required any particular set of religious commitments; on the contrary, one could practice the "science of yoga" while observing any faith, or none at all.[16] Nonetheless, the historical and cultural connection between the universal spirituality of modern yoga and the particular faith traditions of India demonstrates that the concerns of the conservative Christian parents in *Sedlock* do have some reasonable basis, and deserve to be thoughtfully addressed.

The deeper issue raised here is how best to understand the so-called "spiritual" dimension of modern yoga. This is a complex question. As van der Veer (2014) discusses, scholars have generally avoided the study of spirituality due to its inherent conceptual vagueness (not to mention, its professionally embarrassing associations with New Age "woo"). This is unfortunate, as "spirituality is in fact a crucial term in our understanding of modern society":

> In the later 19th and early 20th centuries the term 'spirituality' received a central significance in understandings of modernity all over the world. One can, obviously, find deep prehistories of spirituality in mysticism, gnosis, and hermeticism, and in a while range of traditions from antiquity, but modern spirituality is something different that cannot be explained terms of these complex prehistories. It is part of modernity and thus of a wide-ranging 19th-century transformation, a historical rupture.

Notably, this same "historical rupture," which incorporated a growing clash between European colonialism and anti-colonial Asian nationalism, not only produced modern forms of yoga and meditation, but also Chinese martial arts and Qigong.[17]

The fact that spirituality is "notoriously hard to define," van der Veer argues, is precisely what "has made it productive as a concept that bridges many discursive traditions across the globe." Rather than having a relatively precise, stable definition, its meaning is part of a "syntagmatic chain" in which the core concepts of "religion, magic, secularity, and spirituality" define themselves against one another. Hence, if the meaning of one shifts, the others must readjust as well. The definitions of religion, secularity, and magic, however, are more circumscribed than that of spirituality, which is particularly fluid and open.

Extrapolating from this insight, it can be said that the cultural framing of modern (and now postmodern) yoga disrupts the West's dominant cultural tendency to assume that science, secularism, and exercise align with each other, but not with religion or spirituality. In this sense, asserting that yoga is simultaneously scientific *and* spiritual clashes with taken-for-granted conceptions of secularity, which is assumed to include the former, but not the latter. It also disrupts the standard conception of exercise, which is presumed to align with secularity and science, but have no spiritual dimension worth noting. In short, the cultural history of modern yoga presents a chain of meaning that links science, spirituality, and mind-body-spirit practice. This set of linked meanings is incompatible with the culturally dominant one, which instead connects science to secularity and "exercise."

SECULAR SPIRITUALITY?

Seen in historical context, the underlying problem of *Sedlock* is that it attempts to adjudicate the question of whether yoga is permissible in public schools exclusively within the terms of the culturally dominant chain of meaning that links science, secularity, and exercise. This paradigm presupposes a natural division between secularity and science, on the one hand, and religion, on the other. And, unlike the alternative chain linking science, spirituality, and yoga (or meditation, Tai Chi, etc.), it has no distinct place for spirituality apart from religion.

Further, the chain of meaning that links science, secularity, and exercise in *Sedlock* is implicitly infused with presumptions of instrumental rationality. This is particularly the case in today's aggressively neoliberal climate, which measures the worth of most individual and social goods, including yoga and education, in the same one-dimensional, economistic terms. Consequently, within the framing of *Sedlock*, it's logical to lump the presumably noninstrumental categories of spirituality and religion together. Such blending of the spiritual and religious is reinforced by their presumed incompatibility with "secularity" and "science" (hence, Professor Brown's claim that scientific evidence of yoga's benefits is simply "camouflage" for its inherently religious nature).

Alternatively, the easiest way to defend the secularity of yoga within the boundaries of this framework is to insist that it's "just exercise," and erase its status as a mind-body-spirit practice altogether—which, of course, is precisely what the defense in *Sedlock* successfully did. Conversely, the logical way to counter this position is to claim that if yoga is a holistic practice that includes a spiritual dimension, then it must be "inherently and pervasively religious." In this sense, the opposing sides in this lawsuit actually shared a common conceptual framework. As such, they inadvertently joined together to "dodge" the deeper question of whether a mind-body-spirit practice such as yoga can be taught in public schools in ways that respect the legal and ethical commitments of secularism.

Reframed in this way, this is not such an easy question to answer. From a historical perspective, the key reason for this is that while there is an established chain of meanings that link science, spirituality, and yoga, there hasn't yet been one that additionally includes secularism. Until recently, this wasn't a problem, as yoga was almost exclusively taught in private settings such as studios, ashrams, and gyms. In such contexts, people are of course free to explore the spiritual side of the practice as they wish (or not), assigning whatever meanings (or lack thereof) to it that they like. Consequently, there's no need to grapple with issues of secularism. Once yoga is shifted into a public school context, however, this is no longer the case.

Expanding on the preceding discussion, it's evident that adding "secularism" to the syntagmatic chain linking yoga, science, and spirituality will necessarily shift the meaning of each of these terms. For example, understandings of "spirituality" that involve metaphysical beliefs would be impermissible in a public school context, as they're not secular. Teaching yoga as a means of revitalizing the "human spirit," however, would be fine. Similarly, the New Age-y conceptions of "science" that are popular in some yoga circles would have to be cut, and replaced with ones possessing solid scholarly credentials. Finally, yoga itself would have to be taught as a practice that's rooted in Indian civilization, but separable from particular religious or spiritual commitments that have historically been central to that culture.[18]

"EDUCATION OF AND THROUGH THE BODY"

In today's neoliberal climate, embracing yoga in public schools as a holistic mind-body-spirit practice, as opposed to emphasizing its instrumental benefits for student fitness, behavior, and achievement, may sound unthinkably radical. As Ennis (2006) notes, however, debates over whether physical education should focus narrowly on the body, or broadly on the mind-body-spirit, aren't new to American public education. Revisiting the evolving status of this issue is important in that it demonstrates that today's taken-for-granted concepts and associated chains of meaning are, in fact, historically provisional and culturally malleable.

Ennis recounts that during the late nineteenth century, intensely vigorous gymnastics systems that "emphasized the 'education of the physical'" and "presaged other forms of fitness-oriented curricula" dominated the public school system. During the early twentieth century, however, "physical educators embraced the innovative perspectives proposed by John Dewey as an opportunity to provide a more enriching atmosphere and a diversified curriculum." The "new physical education" movement that emerged in the early 1900s focused on "educating the complete human being through an emphasis on mind *and* body. Rather than a program of mindless exercise, the new physical education proposed students be educated 'through the physical' such that the mind, emotions, and human body formed a complete action."[19]

In 1923, this growing movement inspired the founding of the American Academy of Physical Education, whose mission was "to advance knowledge in the field of physical education, to uplift its standards, and uphold its honor."[20] Four years later, the progressive approach advocated by the Academy was exhaustively detailed in a 457-page landmark text, *The New Physical Education: A Program of Naturalized Activities for Education Toward Citizenship*, written by movement leaders Thomas Denison Wood and Rosalind Frances Cassidy.[21] This manifesto championed a mind-body-spirit approach to physical education on the grounds of both scientific fact and democratic values.

Wood and Cassidy insisted that "new scientific knowledge . . . proves the soundness of the philosophical treatment of the individual as a whole unit of body, mind, and spirit, by showing that it holds true physiologically." In contrast to today's neoliberal emphasis on the narrowly instrumental benefits of exercise, they insisted that science itself proved the inherent value of holistic movement-based practices. "Even physiology proves that to give the child exercises that have as their only excuse the getting of physiological responses is an unsound practice," they maintained, "based on an unscientific theory."

The New Physical Education additionally insisted that America's democratic commitment to "the worth of the individual allows for no acceptance of dualism, the separate existence of mind and body. On the contrary, the mind, body, and spirit are one; the whole individual—physical and social, intellectual and moral—has infinite worth."[22] In stark contrast to today's neo-liberal assumption of the inevitability of atomistic, competitive individualism, Wood and Cassidy believed that holistic, mind-body-spirit-based physical education could nurture and support democratic values, both within individuals and society at large. "For citizenship in a democracy," they wrote, "individual initiative alone will not suffice. What is needed is the expression of the self in relation to others—to the group; all human beings are interdependent . . . therefore education must aim to develop those bonds which lead to activities for the good of the group."[23]

The holistic philosophy and democratic aspirations of the new physical education never disappeared from the field entirely. They were eclipsed in the post-World War II era, however, in conjunction with new competitive pressures on the public school system following the Soviet Union's launch of the Sputnik satellite. As schools scrambled to increase their core math and science curricula, the cachet of standardized testing increased, while that of holistic physical education diminished. Subsequently, during the 1950s, concerns about the relative "softness" of U.S. students compared with their international counterparts prompted renewed interest in "military drill-oriented gymnastics," with male coaches in particular placing a new premium on becoming "very tough about toughness." Physical educators sought to strengthen their field by developing "hard measures" of fitness, mimicking the standardized tests employed by more prestigious academic subjects. Despite these efforts, however, the social and cultural value accorded to physical education of any sort continued to diminish.[24] By 2013, only 48 percent of American high school students attended physical education classes in an average week.[25]

Holism, Science, and Democracy

Although there was some cross-cultural exchange between those involved in yoga and the new physical education, they were distinct movements rooted in very different societies.[26] Nonetheless, there were important parallels between them. Most notably, this included a commitment to developing a holistic, movement-based practice that spoke to the needs and concerns of modern societies by providing a commonly accessible means of developing the human mind, body, and spirit.

The resonance between the mind-body-spirit language of the new physical education and modern yoga is no accident. Both emerged in conjunction with the transnational physical culture movement of the late nineteenth and early twentieth centuries, which was itself enmeshed in the historic shift toward industrialization and globalization that occurred at that time. As Singleton (2010) demonstrates, modern yoga was a particular manifestation of this broader movement, emerging in early twentieth-century India in conjunction with growing anti-colonial, nationalist ferment. Just as yoga sought to strengthen the Indian nation by supporting its people, honoring its traditions, and sharing a modernized variant of yoga with the world, the new physical education sought to strengthen American democracy by educating the "whole child" and, in the process, cultivating empowered citizens committed to the common good.

Leaders of both movements understood their projects as naturally congruent with science. Given their different cultural roots, however, this connection was interpreted in different ways. Within yoga, there was strong interest in identifying through-lines between pre-modern tradition and modern science.[27] The new physical education movement, in contrast, was located within an entirely different cultural narrative that championed the breakthroughs of modern progress, rather than the continuities of ancient tradition. Nonetheless, both movements were understood as being fundamentally aligned with modern science, in marked contrast to the long-standing division between science and religion in the West. In this sense, each was embedded in a chain of meaning that similarly presumed positive connections between science and the "spiritual" part of the mind-body-spirit equation.

These two early twentieth-century movements also evidenced a common commitment to democratic values that, due to their very different social locations, expressed themselves in very different ways. In India, the development of modern yoga grew out of the "Yoga Renaissance" sparked by Swami Vivekananda in the late nineteenth century, which was strongly linked to anti-colonial nationalism, progressive social reform, and making formerly inaccessible yogic teachings newly available to all. In the United States, the new physical education was directly inspired by the social democratic work of John Dewey, which included but also extended far beyond progressive education per se. While these political projects were different in many ways, both were essentially democratic. Further, both believed that making mind-body-spirit practices maximally accessible to individuals would support collective projects of positive social change.

YOGA, EDUCATION, AND SOCIETY

Almost a century after the advent of the new physical education and modern yoga, the former is a distant historical artifact. The latter, however, is unprecedentedly popular, with over twenty million Americans practicing, and another forty-two million expressing interest in doing so.[28] A recent survey found yoga programs being implemented in over nine hundred schools nationwide, and over 5,400 instructors trained to teach yoga in educational settings.[29] Increasingly, yoga is also being offered in other American public institutions, including prisons and V.A. hospitals. Without doubt, the grassroots movement to increase accessibly to yoga throughout American society is strong, and growing.

In light of these developments, the utter inability of *Sedlock* to recognize, let alone navigate yoga's status as a holistic mind-body-spirit practice is as dismaying as it is instructive. True, it was only one lawsuit, and not necessarily indicative of the entire field. As the only case to consider the constitutionality of yoga in public schools to date, however, it set a critical precedent. Further, while the plaintiff's claim that yoga is "inherently and pervasively religious" wasn't taken seriously outside of particular conservative Christian circles, the defense's argument that it's "just exercise" was greeted with almost universal acclaim.[30] Undoubtedly, much of this was simply pragmatic. Supporters of yoga in schools wanted the EUSD to win the case, and had little motive to contest how that was achieved. Such willingness to uncritically embrace whatever characterization of yoga gets the practice in the schoolhouse door, however, comes at a cost.

To reduce yoga to stretching and strengthening routines, with perhaps a bit of breathing and mindfulness thrown in to facilitate better student behavior, is to eviscerate its true potential. Teaching it as a holistic mind-body-spirit practice in a public school setting, however, requires recalibrating the chain of meaning that has connected it to particular conceptions of spirituality and science for the better part of the past century. Adding "secularity" to this syntagmatic chain necessarily shifts the meanings of each category, as well as the practice itself. Ostensibly, this is not difficult to do. Scientific work on yoga and other mind-body integration practices is booming, and yoga can easily be taught as a means of uplifting the "human spirit" without reference to particular religious tradition or metaphysical beliefs. The current state of American culture, however, makes this difficult. Taking yoga seriously as a holistic mind-body-spirit practice is fundamentally at odds with the entrenched logic of instrumental rationality that dominates our school system, as well as the neoliberal values that suffuse the culture at large.

It's entirely in keeping, however, with our now-marginalized tradition of progressive education, particularly the new physical education movement that flourished in the early twentieth century. This largely forgotten chapter in the history of American education provides a crucial example of how a holistic mind-body-spirit practice can be taught in ways that are not only compatible with secularity, spirituality, and science, but also informed by democratic values. Rethinking today's teaching of yoga in schools from this perspective reveals the narrowness of our current cultural frameworks, and encourages us to imagine more socially informed, ethical, and inspiring alternatives.

Teaching yoga for exercise and behavioral management to students suffering under a regime of excessive standardized testing in a nation whose democratic ethos is in crisis is a colossal waste. The dominant chain of meaning that frames the issue of yoga in schools as a choice between exercise, science, secularism, and instrumental rationality, on the one hand, and religion and quasi-religious spirituality, on the other, is empirically inaccurate and culturally retrograde. Yoga can and should be taught as a mind-body-spirit practice that supports the holistic health and development of students not simply as individuals, but as creative participants in the collective enterprises of education and democracy. Developing a new chain of meaning that links yoga, science, secularism, progressive education, and democratic values has much to offer not only our public schools, but society and culture at large.

NOTES

Many thanks to Mira Binzen, D'Etta Broam, Karma Lynn Carpenter, and Jennifer Cohen Harper for sharing their reflections on teaching yoga in schools with me. Thanks also to Lindsay Bell, Ann Gleig, Kelli Love, Natalia Mehlman Petrzela, Mark Singleton, and participants at the 2015 Society for U.S. Intellectual History (S-USIH) conference for comments on earlier drafts of this paper.

1. Tony Perry, "Judge Rejects Claim that Yoga in Schools is Religious Instruction," *L.A. Times*, July 1, 2013, accessed Sept. 14, 2015, http://articles.latimes.com/2013/jul/01/local/la-me-ln-yoga-ruling-20130701.

2. *Sedlock v. Baird*, No. 37201300035910-CU-MC-CTL, 2013 WL 6063439 (Cal. Super. Ct. C.D. July 1, 2013).

3. Yoga Alliance Amicus, Curiae Brief, *Sedlock v. Baird* (2013), 6; Declaration of Candy Gunther Brown, *ibid.*, 6.

4. YES! Yoga for Encinitas Students Appellate Court Brief, *Sedlock v. Baird*, No. D064BBB (Cal. Ct. of Appeal District 4, Div. 1., C.D. April 3, 2015), 1.

5. Verified Petition for Writ of Mandamus, *Sedlock v. Baird* (2013), 2.

6. Emphasis in original. "Information for Parents: The EUSD/Jois Foundation Yoga Program," accessed Nov. 18, 2015, https://truthaboutyoga.files.wordpress.com/2014/01/eusd-yoga-information-updated-10-03-12.pdf. See, in general, the "Truth About Yoga" website developed by parents opposing the EUSD program, http://truthaboutyoga.com.

7. At the time of the district court trial, the Jois Foundation was part of Jois Yoga (http://joisyoga.com). Subsequently, it was renamed the Sonima Foundation (http://www.sonimafoundation.org). See Carol Horton, "Yoga Train Wreck in Encinitas: Or, What's Up With the Jois Foundation??," *Think Body Electric*, June 1, 2013, accessed Nov. 18, 2015, http://www.thinkbodyelectric.com/2013/06/yoga-train-wreck-in-encinitas-or-whats.html; and Candy Gunther Brown, "Textual Erasures of Religion: The Power of Books to Redefine Yoga and Mindfulness Meditation as Secular Wellness

Practices in North American Public Schools," *Studies in Book Culture* 6, no. 2 (Spring 2015): 34–35, accessed Nov. 18, 2015, https://www.erudit.org/revue/memoires/2015/v6/n2/1032713ar.html.

8. See, for example, the twenty-two-article collection "Research Topic: Interoception, Contemplative Practice, and Health," in Olga Pollatos et al., eds., *Frontiers in Psychology: Consciousness Research* (2015), accessed Nov. 18, 2015, http://journal.frontiersin.org/researchtopic/2251/interoception-contemplative-practice-and-health#overview; and the fifteen-article collection "Research Topic: Neural Mechanisms Underlying 'Movement-based' Embodied Contemplative Practices," in Laura Schmalzl and Catherine Kerr, eds., *Frontiers in Human Neuroscience* (2015), accessed Nov. 18, 2015, http://journal.frontiersin.org/researchtopic/1899/neural-mechanisms-underlying-movement-based-embodied-contemplative-practices.

9. Declaration of Candy Gunther Brown, *Sedlock v. Baird* (2013), 24–25.

10. YES! Brief, 41, 22.

11. Laura Douglass, "Yoga in the Public Schools: Diversity, Democracy and the Use of Critical Thinking in Education Debates," *Religion and Education* 37 (2010): 165–166.

12. Mark Singleton, *Yoga Body: The Origins of Modern Posture Practice* (NY: Oxford University Press, 2010), ch. 4–7.

13. Erik Braun, *The Birth of Insight: Meditation, Modern Buddhism, and the Burmese Monk Ledi Sayadaw* (Chicago: University of Chicago Press, 2013).

14. Such states of awareness can alternatively be described using scientific concepts such as "metacognition." See for example Laura Schmalzl, Chivon Powers, and Eva Henje Blom, "Neurophysiological and Neurocognitive Mechanisms Underlying the Effects of Yoga-Based Practices: Towards a Comprehensive Theoretical Framework," *Frontiers in Human Neuroscience* 9, article 235 (May 2015): 9, accessed Nov. 18, 2015, http://journal.frontiersin.org/article/10.3389/fnhum.2015.00235/full.

15. These religious categories were themselves tremendously impacted as part of this larger historical shift. See Peter van der Veer, *The Modern Spirit of Asia: The Spiritual and the Secular in China and India* (Princeton, NJ: Princeton University Press, 2014) Ch. 3.

16. While the spirituality of modern yoga was distinctive, pre-modern yoga occupied a parallel position as a practice that could be successfully engaged with by practitioners regardless of religious tradition. James Mallinson, "Yoga and Religion," revised text of lecture given at Heythrop College, London (May 8, 2013), accessed Nov. 18, 2015, https://www.academia.edu/3490405/Yoga_and_Religion.

17. van der Veer, *Modern Spirit of Asia*, 35–36, 59, 169, 180.

18. Controversies over yoga in schools and its relationship to Hinduism have been prominent in India as well. See Tarique Anwar, "Yoga in Schools: AIMPLB Goes All Out to Oppose It, But Muslims Aren't Convinced," *FirstPost India* (June 25, 2015), accessed Nov. 18, 2015, http://www.firstpost.com/india/yoga-in-schools-aimplbs-goes-all-out-to-oppose-it-but-muslims-arent-convinced-2312388.html.

19. Catherine D. Ennis, "Curriculum: Forming and Reshaping the Vision of Physical Education in a High Need, Low Demand World of Schools," *Quest* 58 (2006): 41–44.

20. Penn State University Archives, "American Academy of Kinesiology and Physical Education records, 1923–2003," accessed October 4, 2015, http://www.libraries.psu.edu/findingaids/68.htm.

21. Thomas Denison Wood and Rosalind Frances Cassidy, *The New Physical Education: A Program of Naturalized Activities for Education Toward Citizenship* (NY: MacMillan, 1927).

22. Wood and Cassidy, *The New Physical Education*, 49, 29.

23. Wood and Cassidy, *The New Physical Education*, 29, 57.

24. Ennis, "Curriculum: Forming and Reshaping the Vision of Physical Education," 46–47.

25. "Healthy Schools," Centers for Disease Control and Prevention, accessed Nov. 12, 2015, http://www.cdc.gov/healthyschools/physicalactivity/facts.htm.

26. Patricia Vertinsky, "Yoga Comes to American Physical Education: Josephine Rathbone and Corrective Physical Education," *Journal of Sport History* 41, no. 2 (Summer 2014) 287–311.
27. Joseph S. Alter, *Yoga in Modern India: the Body between Science and Philosophy* (Princeton, NJ: Princeton University Press, 2004).
28. Yoga Journal/Sports Marketing Surveys, "Yoga in America, 2012," 7.
29. Traci Childress and Jennifer Cohen Harper, eds., *Best Practices for Yoga in Schools* (Atlanta, GA: YSC-Omega Publications, 2015), xiii.
30. The Appellate Court made little effort to hide the fact they found the plaintiff's complaint ridiculous. Pat Maio, "Lawyers Battle in Yoga Case," San Diego Union Tribune (March 11, 2015), accessed Nov. 16, 2015 http://www.sandiegouniontribune.com/news/2015/mar/11/yoga-dean-broyles-appeal-encinitas/.

REFERENCES

Alter, Joseph S. *Yoga in Modern India: the Body between Science and Philosophy* (Princeton, NJ: Princeton University Press, 2004).
Anwar, Tarique. "Yoga in Schools: AIMPLB Goes All Out to Oppose It, But Muslims Aren't Convinced," *FirstPost India* (June 25, 2015). Accessed Nov. 18, 2015. http://www.firstpost.com/india/yoga-in-schools-aimplbs-goes-all-out-to-oppose-it-but-muslims-arent-convinced-2312388.html.
Braun, Erik. *The Birth of Insight: Meditation, Modern Buddhism, and the Burmese Monk Ledi Sayadaw* (Chicago: University of Chicago Press, 2013).
Brown, Candy Gunther. "Declaration of Candy Gunther Brown," *Sedlock v. Baird* (2013).
———. "Textual Erasures of Religion: The Power of Books to Redefine Yoga and Mindfulness Meditation as Secular Wellness Practices in North American Public Schools," *Studies in Book Culture* 6, no. 2 (Spring 2015): 34–35. Accessed Nov. 18, 2015. https://www.erudit.org/revue/memoires/2015/v6/n2/1032713ar.html.
Centers for Disease Control and Prevention, "Healthy Schools." Accessed Nov. 12, 2015. http://www.cdc.gov/healthyschools/physicalactivity/facts.htm
Childress, Traci and Jennifer Cohen Harper, eds., *Best Practices for Yoga in Schools* (Atlanta, GA: YSC-Omega Publications, 2015).
Douglass, Laura. "Yoga in the Public Schools: Diversity, Democracy and the Use of Critical Thinking in Education Debates." *Religion and Education* 37 (2010).
Ennis, Catherine D. "Curriculum: Forming and Reshaping the Vision of Physical Education in a High Need, Low Demand World of Schools." *Quest* 58 (2006).
Horton, Carol. "Yoga Train Wreck in Encinitas: Or, What's Up With the Jois Foundation??," *Think Body Electric*, June 1, 2013. Accessed Nov. 18, 2015. http://www.thinkbodyelectric.com/2013/06/yoga-train-wreck-in-encinitas-or-whats.html.
Mallinson, James. "Yoga and Religion," revised text of lecture given at Heythrop College, London, May 8, 2013. Accessed November 18, 2015. https://www.academia.edu/3490405/Yoga_and_Religion.
Maio, Pat. "Lawyers Battle in Yoga Case," *San Diego Union Tribune*, March 11, 2015. Accessed November 16, 2015. http://www.sandiegouniontribune.com/news/2015/mar/11/yoga-dean-broyles-appeal-encinitas/.
Penn State University Archives. "American Academy of Kinesiology and Physical Education records, 1923–2003." Accessed October 4, 2015. http://www.libraries.psu.edu/findingaids/68.htm.
Perry, Tony. "Judge Rejects Claim that Yoga in Schools is Religious Instruction," *L.A. Times*, July 1, 2013. Accessed September 14, 2015. http://articles.latimes.com/2013/jul/01/local/la-me-ln-yoga-ruling-20130701.
Pollatos, Olga et al., eds., "Research Topic: Interoception, Contemplative Practice, and Health," in Frontiers in Psychology: Consciousness Research (2015). Accessed No-

vember 18, 2015. http://journal.frontiersin.org/researchtopic/2251/interoception-contemplative-practice-and-health#overview.

Sedlock v. Baird, No. 37201300035910-CU-MC-CTL, 2013 WL 6063439 (Cal. Super. Ct. C.D. July 1, 2013).

Sedlock v. Baird. Verified Petition for Writ of Mandamus, (2013).

Singleton, Mark. *Yoga Body: The Origins of Modern Posture Practice* (New York: Oxford University Press, 2010).

Schmalzl, Laura and Catherine Kerr, eds., "Research Topic: Neural Mechanisms Underlying 'Movement-based' Embodied Contemplative Practices." *Frontiers in Human Neuroscience* (2015). Accessed November 18, 2015. http://journal.frontiersin.org/researchtopic/1899/neural-mechanisms-underlying-movement-based-embodied-contemplative-practices.

Schmalzl, Laura, Chivon Powers, and Eva Henje Blom, "Neurophysiological and Neurocognitive Mechanisms Underlying the Effects of Yoga-Based Practices: Towards a Comprehensive Theoretical Framework." *Frontiers in Human Neuroscience* 9, article 235 (May 2015): 9. Accessed November 18, 2015. http://journal.frontiersin.org/article/10.3389/fnhum.2015.00235/full.

Truth About Yoga website, "Information for Parents: The EUSD/Jois Foundation Yoga Program." Accessed November 18, 2015. https://truthaboutyoga.files.wordpress.com/2014/01/eusd-yoga-information-updated-10-03-12.pdf.

van der Veer, Peter. *The Modern Spirit of Asia: The Spiritual and the Secular in China and India* (Princeton, NJ: Princeton University Press, 2014).

Vertinsky, Patricia. "Yoga Comes to American Physical Education: Josephine Rathbone and Corrective Physical Education." *Journal of Sport History* 41, no. 2 (Summer 2014).

YES! Yoga for Encinitas Students. Appellate Court Brief, *Sedlock v. Baird*, No. D064BBB (Cal. Ct. of Appeal District 4, Div. 1., C.D. April 3, 2015).

Yoga Alliance. Amicus Curiae Brief, *Sedlock v. Baird* (2013).

Yoga Journal/Sports Marketing Surveys, "Yoga in America, 2012." Attachment to YES! Yoga for Encinitas Students. Appellate Court Brief, *Sedlock v. Baird*, No. D064BBB (Cal. Ct. of Appeal District 4, Div. 1., C.D. April 3, 2015).

Wood, Thomas Denison and Rosalind Frances Cassidy. *The New Physical Education: A Program of Naturalized Activities for Education Toward Citizenship* (New York: MacMillan, 1927).

Part II

The Intersection of Yoga, Body Image, and Standards of Beauty

Melanie Klein

The twenty-first century is in large part, if not entirely, characterized by a capitalistic, highly mediated consumer culture. Given the sheer volume and repetitive nature of the carefully constructed messages generated by advertisers to maximize profits by selling desirable lifestyles and identities, it's not a stretch to refer to the media as being at the forefront of the consciousness of culture industry. As Dr. George Gerbner noted in his paradigm on understanding mass communication, the images and messages that we're exposed to have a cumulative impact and actively shape our desires, values, behaviors, and views of the world. And the more we consume, the more deeply we're impacted by what we see and hear.[1]

Internationally recognized author, speaker, and filmmaker Dr. Jean Kilbourne, Ed.D., has spent over four decades examining the narrow and stereotypical ways women and the female body have been presented in media. And what she and other scholars have revealed is that not only is the female body objectified and sexualized, offered as a commodity for public evaluation and consumption, but these images reinforce a standard of beauty few women can exemplify or can obtain without exorbitant costs.[2] For not only is the desired body type one that less than 5 percent of the population has, it's a beauty ideal cloaked in sexism, racism, classism, ageism, ableism, and sizeism as well as heteronormative overtones. It's in the context of this cultural space that yoga practice can offer a respite from the ever increasing barrage of images that sexualize and objectify the female body.

Yet, given yoga's stratospheric rise to popularity in the twenty-first century, the relationship between yoga and the body within our mediated consumer culture becomes more complicated. Once an esoteric activity primarily isolated within spiritual communities and private homes, yoga is no longer simply a spiritual practice or a path to wellness. Yoga is now not only a *practice*, but a *business* and an *industry* embraced by celebrities and advertisers.

The articles in this section seek to critically examine the intersection of yoga practice, media culture, standards of beauty and body image and the complexities, both positive and negative, therein. The authors explore the rise of yoga brands, yoga celebrities, and the role of social media in promoting the myth of the "yoga body" that permeates contemporary yoga imagery.

Dr. Diana York Blaine offers readers an exercise in media literacy by deconstructing yoga advertisements in "Mainstream Representations of Yoga: Capitalism, Consumerism, and Control of the Female Body." She posits that in a culture obsessed with fitness and materialism, it's no surprise that yoga is viewed primarily as exercise and that it is sold using the same tactics. In the process, not only is the female body sexualized and objectified in the mass marketing of yoga, but the very essence of yoga is co-opted and exploited. She offers this analysis as a way to effectively safe guard a potentially sacred and transformative practice from the reach of a consumer culture.

Dr. Jennifer Musial's autoethnographic essay "Work Off That Holiday Meal Ladies!": Body Vigilance and Orthorexia in Yoga Spaces" explores the ways in which the all too common rhetoric of "cleansing" or "detoxing" in yoga spaces is language meant to disguise self-destructive behaviors. She discusses the ways in which this kind of talk potentially triggers those with eating disorders and disordered eating while also allowing new "body projects" to flourish. While yoga practice may be beneficial in healing from distorted body image and/or disordered eating patterns, yoga culture may actually exacerbate orthorexia, an obsession with earing "healthy." Studios and teachers that engage in rhetoric that is reminiscent of diet culture and encourage "clean eating" practices and cleansing not only reflect assumptions about the reasons why individuals and communities come to practice, but they also become race and class markers.

The complexities and frequent contradictions related to yoga practice and the body that exist in contemporary, mainstream yoga continues in "Naked Yoga and the Sexualization of Asana" by Dr. Sarah Schrank. The trend of naked yoga offers a potentially liberatory experience while, simultaneously, oftentimes exacerbating existing issues related to the sexualization and rampant body scrutiny indicative of the dominant culture. The desire to practice naked yoga as a way to experience (and reconnect with) the body as a more "natural physical self" and combat the body festishization that is endemic in consumer culture is further complicated by the rash of sex scandals that have plagued the yoga community over the last few years. Couched in an intersectional framework of sexual politics, readers are offered an in-depth critical history of nudism, yoga and the ways in which yoga and nudity intertwined over the years as well as the author's personal experiences with naked yoga in Los Angeles.

Dr. Maria Velazquez echoes the critiques of yoga culture reproducing oppressive dominant ideologies and marginalizing subordinate groups in "Reblog If You Feel Me: Love, Blackness, and Digital Wellness." Yet, while many critics, scholars, and activists, including authors in this collection, have discussed the ways in which social media reproduces this social hierarchy, we're given an opportunity to examine the ways in which social media platforms have also opened space for marginalized groups to bypass media gatekeepers and define their own experiences.

Finally, in her article "Fat Pedagogy in the Yoga Class," performance artist, writer, and yoga teacher Kimberly Dark, MA, opines on how her body teaches, transforms, and complicates the ubiquitous negative notions of fatness that are pervasive throughout Western culture. Dark moves gracefully and powerfully through her prose to bring forth a vivid picture of what she experiences teaching yoga in spaces where thin bodies are always welcome and other bodies must fight for visibility, which illuminates the restorative power of yoga to help heal trauma from the performance of privilege.

NOTES

1. Michael Morgan, ed., *Against the Stream: The Selected Works of George Gerbner.* (New York: Peter Lang International Academic Publishers. 2002).

2. Jean Kilbourne, *Can't Buy My Love: How Advertising Changes the Way We Think and Feel.* (New York: Simon & Schuster, 1999).

REFERENCES

Kilbourne, Jean. *Can't Buy My Love: How Advertising Changes the Way We Think and Feel.* (New York: Simon & Schuster. 1999).

Morgan, Michael., ed., *Against the Stream: The Selected Works of George Gerbner.* (New York: Peter Lang International Academic Publishers. 2002).

SEVEN

Mainstream Representations of Yoga

Capitalism, Consumerism, and Control of the Female Body

Diana York Blaine

In a nation obsessed with concepts of physical fitness, yoga has ascended in mainstream popularity over the last several decades to one of the most common forms of exercise in the country today. People participate in classes in private studios, large fitness centers, and even college courses taken for credit. This increasing visibility of yoga in the United States has been accompanied by the increasing use of images of yoga in mainstream advertising. But virtually no research analyzes the ways that yoga and the yoga practitioner are represented in this commercial context.[1] Given that the formerly spiritual practice has been transmuted into a commodity consumed by millions and that the representation of yoga engages central issues of gender politics, body image, and capitalist consumption, scholarship must be generated on the narrative framing of yoga when used in marketing.

Therefore, this chapter seeks to contribute to the emerging field of yoga in advertising by closely reading the ideologies embedded in five advertisements by large corporations for products unrelated to the practice of yoga itself.[2] What, I ask, is really being sold? And how does the inclusion of the practice of yoga in the marketing of products affect our understanding both of it and ideas of fitness, spirituality, and success? Analyzing narratives produced in commercials for Carl's Jr., Hyatt Hotels, Aflac Insurance, Victoria's Secret, and Karasil nail fungus treatment, we see three prominent themes emerge: first, that the chaotic female body and its desires must be controlled in order to reproduce heteronormative family dynamics; next, that yoga can be used by consumers to maintain the excesses of patriarchal capitalist consumer culture rather than to resist or reformulate them; and finally, that the Western materialist values of this capitalist consumer culture trump those of Eastern spirituality.

YOGA MARKETING AND THE OBJECTIFIED FEMALE BODY

Despite its origins as a masculine pursuit, yoga has become feminized in the United States both in theory and in practice.[3] Images of yoga in advertising reflect this association between women and yoga, and so promulgate conventional gender dynamics that position woman as the object of the male gaze.[4] By doing so, these advertisements market yoga not as a means of resisting sexism but as a mechanism for achieving the bodily perfection necessary to meet with male approval and access to men's resources. While many women actually report a reduction in body dysmorphia after regular yoga practice,[5] the representations of this activity in advertising promote a pathological relationship between females and their appearance.

The first example comes from Carl's Jr., a company that has openly embraced sexist themes in its advertising. Many of its television commercials conflate the female body with the product being consumed, thereby reifying a relationship between women and products.[6] Its Great Buns ad is no exception to this practice, as the hamburger buns are explicitly associated with the slang term for the associated body part, the buns, or buttocks. The ad begins during a class in a yoga studio filled with fit young white women. The setting reflects material privilege, with the clean bright space nicely appointed, and the background music offering a vaguely exotic sitar riff to help set the tone of Eastern spirituality. But the camera quickly zooms in on the anxious face of one of the young white women prone on her mat. She turns to her friend and whispers, "So suddenly Todd wants me to get great buns." This line is spoken during the Up Dog posture. "He's a buns guy?," her friend responds with surprise. The camera cuts to a frontal shot of a row of thin, young, white women in tiny shorts and bra tops. The two females who have spoken then move into Down Dog, and the camera cuts to a tight shot of their buttocks stuck up in the air.

There can be no mistaking the thrust of the scene: that this female is the heterosexual partner of a male who, while off camera, holds the power over her. She is not focused on her own practice; she is not represented as bonding with her female friend; and her body becomes nothing more than a vehicle for male pleasure, both in appearance and in the punning connection between her buns and the buns that will carry the hamburger patty into the male consumer's mouth. Yoga has been reduced to a means of reshaping the natural female body into something more palatable for male consumption. The next scene makes this male entitlement even more explicit as the camera pans from a tight shot on two women's bottoms clad in tight formal wear bumping together slowly and provocatively to two white men seated together, one middle-aged, one young. The older man, clad in a tuxedo, speaks with a possessive, confident air. "It's nice having another guy who likes great buns in the family," he says to the younger man. His posture exudes comfort and privilege as he takes up space with his arms thrown across the chairs. It becomes apparent that he is the father of the bride, one of the two women bumping on the dance floor, and he is speaking to his new son-in-law. The other woman is apparently his wife. "Thanks, Mike," replies the younger man. "Call me *dad*," he says, with expansive emphasis on the final word.

As these two men's patriarchal kinship ties are solidified, the camera cuts back to the dance floor where the younger of the two women eats a burger seductively as she thrusts erotically in her slinky wedding gown. As with the women in the yoga studio, she is thin, young, white, and displayed for the male gaze. No men are shown practicing yoga in the ad, nor are they shown dancing. White masculinity in this advertisement is associated with possessive ownership and femininity with performance for male approval. No ties between women are represented without the male as mediator, whether the absent disapproving boyfriend insisting the female alter her appearance, reducing yoga to a practice that sculpts women's bodies for men's sexual pleasure, or the present smug patriarch welcoming the young man into the ownership of his women who both silently gyrate on the dance floor.

The final vignette reveals the inevitable results of women being shown as dependent on male approval. A white couple is depicted riding up an escalator. The camera cuts in for a tight shot of the man's face as he does a double-take at the sight of the jeans-clad buttocks of the woman riding up in front of them. His date (wife?) holds onto his arm. We hear him say, "Whoa, great buns," as the camera cuts to a tight shot of her rear. His female partner turns to him with a bemused look on her face as he continues, "so smooth and round, you know. . . ." The camera cuts to the strange female eating a bite of burger as we hear the male make a guttural sound, "ooooh," and we see the three triangulated, the sexualized woman licking her fingers, the couple staring from below. The dynamics of this scene encourage us to enjoy the female partner's humiliation as she is powerless over the male's sexual satisfaction, expressed both in his hearty spoken approval as well as the orgasmic noise he emits while watching the other woman. The final shot brings the narrative full circle as we see rising buns on a baking sheet in an oven, zooming in on one exactly as the camera has zoomed in on women's posteriors in the three vignettes. "Eat like you mean it," reads the superimposed tagline.

This ad positions the "you" who eats as male. Women do not possess power absent the ability to attract male attention, depicted as an ability both provisional (Todd does not find her body satisfactory and she must work on it in yoga or presumably he will move on) and transitory (the bottom on the escalator now has the male's attention despite his own woman being present while he oozes desire for some other set of buns). In between these two humiliating scenes of female desperation lies the marriage narrative, offering to women one possible hope of obtaining scarce male resources by becoming man's nominal possession. Women can desire to be whatever they want, as long as they desire only to be an object of male pleasure. Associating this hegemonic heteronormative masculine dominance with the practice of yoga subverts its potential for female empowerment. It is represented instead only as a vehicle for achieving male approval. And while the ad shows several women consuming hamburgers, and the tag line is "eat like you mean it," the actual context can only produce a pathological relationship between females and food. It is males who are permitted satisfaction, both sexual and dietary. Woman is the consumed, not the consumer. The spiritual aspects of yoga practice are eliminated entirely from this narrative.

Mainstream advertising has a long history of co-opting potentially liberating practices and, as this commercial demonstrates, the case of yoga is no different.[7] Despite its anti-Western emphasis on yoking the mind, body, and spirit, yoga is now used by multi-national corporations to fetishize consumption and the perfected white (female) body rather than offering an alternative to patriarchal consumer capitalism. The spiritual aspects of it are either dropped entirely in mainstream advertising or, as we shall see in this next case, transformed into a means of transcendence that offers physical, not metaphysical, perfection.

FINDING TRANSCENDENCE THROUGH OBJECTIFICATION

The Victoria's Secret fashion show has become a cultural phenomenon compared with the Super Bowl, heralded by much pre-show publicity and viewed by many in large celebratory parties. Given the tsunami of attention it receives, one might easily lose sight of the fact that it is at its center merely a feature-length commercial for products. Young scantily clad females parade down the runway, marketing lingerie to the masses. But something more than underwear is being sold. The Victoria's Secret model promotes a particular ideal to the female consumer, one of bodily perfection and an emphasis on the female as the object of the male gaze. As with the Carl's Jr. advertisement, it is hard to imagine how yoga fits in to this conventionally sexist context. But in 2013, as part of the publicity to advertise the program, Victoria's Secret runway model Lindsay Ellingson taped a promotional piece that featured her at Equinox gym in New

York (advertising that high-end fitness brand as well). Clips of this package were picked up by *Inside Edition*, which ran a feature story on the upcoming fashion show. "How do those gorgeous models stay in such fantastic shape?," asks the *Inside Edition* anchor as clips of the models swaying provocatively in their elaborate garb play behind her. The answer, it turns out, is yoga.

In this marketing campaign, the practice seamlessly aligns with production of the female body as (erotic consumable marketed) object. Ellingson is shown doing Tree pose behind a headline reading "Angel workout." "Before Supermodel Lindsay Ellingson slips on her angel wings," says the voice-over, "she hits the Equinox Health Club to get runway ready." We are then shown the young thin white woman performing a series of yoga postures at the gym, interspersed with images from the fashion show itself. While her simple presentation of "some of her favorite yoga poses" in a relatively unglamorous setting might be viewed as an opportunity to promote the practice as empowering for a woman both physically and spiritually, the context instead emphasizes yoga as a means to become the impossible, to attain the unobtainable. "If you want a toned tummy and legs like a Victoria's Secret model, try the Downward Dog," says the announcer while a nearly naked woman wearing a smiley face on her back struts toward the viewer. In spite of the conditional mood, "*if* you want," there actually can be no room for resistance. Of course the female viewer is to want what this advertisement markets, which is self-transformation through physical, not spiritual, change.

At the same time that this marketing campaign explicitly offers results to the viewer, it paradoxically advertises fictional ideals as concrete goals. At least four levels of metaphor operate in this narrative: angel, model, commodity, and celebrity. Angels come from Judeo-Christian theology, mythical figures who bring messages from gods. Models are definitively aspirational but not actually beings. The young woman who models, in other words, is not actually a model. The model is itself the inanimate ideal. Commodities, which is what the Victoria Secret fashion shows market, and which is what the Victoria's Secret models also become, are again not actual beings. They are cultural productions. And finally the notion of celebrity itself operates on a fictive register, as the synonym "star" suggests. These are ideas, not people, unreal products of a culture in love with the fantasy of a person who is more than human. But the insistence that the female viewer become these fictions obscures the very fictional aspects of the narrative. Yoga then can only be a means to failure, not because the female consumer lacks self-will, but because attaining the unreal is not possible.

In the Victoria's Secret campaign, yoga becomes a method to transform into a sacred object, an angel, albeit one whose ultimate function operates on a decidedly earthly plane. These young women are promoted

as masturbatory fantasies for males. Just as in the Carl's Jr. advertisement, the control of the female body and the production of it is fodder for
the male gaze that profoundly undermines the possibility of female agency. While the audience for the Carl's Jr. ad is clearly men, and the audience for the Victoria's Secret yoga ad is clearly women, the construction
of femininity remains identical in each. According to these commercials,
women need yoga to be visually appealing to males, and being visually
appealing to males is shown as women's main purpose.

CORPORATE USES OF YOGA TO REPRODUCE CAPITALISM

This next advertisement differs from these first two insofar as it represents woman as professional, operating in the public sphere, and facing
traditionally masculine challenges. In this ad, yoga becomes not a way to
produce the desirable female body but as a means for women to cope
with the pressures of patriarchal capitalism and the double demands of
being responsible both in the home and workplace. Many corporations
have adopted such yoga-friendly marketing practices in order to attract
women to their businesses both for leisure and corporate travel.[8] This
particular piece ran as part of a series in the *New Yorker* promoting Hyatt
Hotels to businesswomen as friendly to their individualized needs.[9] In
these cartoons, "Alexa," a thin, young, white woman, must juggle her
personal fitness goals with her family obligations and her work respon-
sibilities. She is depicted as on the road in each segment, with Hyatt
offering what she needs to successfully meet the myriad challenges of her
privileged, professional existence.

Part two, "Emotional Rescue," shows Alexa in the first frame literally
wearing her baggage on her head, with a suitcase filled not with the work
attire she will need for this business trip, but with various family and
friends all demanding pieces of her as she tries to prepare to leave. We
see five people seated in her luggage, pressing down on her skull, all of
whom she is responsible for in some way: "the husband-daughter, baby,
mother, best friend before you leave town pile-on." A young girl sobs,
rubbing her eyes in tantrum mode, a young husband with a clueless
expression holds a wailing infant at arm's length, and two adult women
finish out the group, one scolding Alexa with her hand in "I-told-you-so"
posture, the other on the phone, arm flung out as she presumably holds
forth to Alexa about something she needs or wants.

In the next scene, Alexa has checked into her hotel room only to discover that amid the chaos she has forgotten her curling iron, described as
an "essential business tool," and notes also that she had no room to pack
her yoga mat. Help soon arrives in the form of a nameless young female
hotel employee in uniform bearing both items. The final frame shows
Alexa literally floating in the air on her mat in lotus position, curling iron

aloft beside her in space. "And now the only thing I've left behind is stress," the caption reads. Given that the business trip was described in the first scene as "make-or-break," we are meant to experience great relief that she is going to be able to manage the experience and perform successfully on the job.

Certainly in comparison to the toxic messages of the Carl's Jr. ad and the Victoria's Secret campaign, the narrative here seems far more benign. Yoga is not yoked to production of the female body as sexualized object and the woman experiences such transcendence via her practice that she actually leaves the earth. While her body is drawn as thin, and her stylish fitted matching yoga togs emphasize her cleavage, we are not primarily focused on her as the object of the male gaze but as a working woman who is also a wife and mother and friend and daughter. Yoga might be viewed in this ad as part of her balanced existence, one that has spiritual, as well as physical and material, components. And she is not depicted as needing a man to support her financially. Clearly someone on a business trip such as this has a professional career, implying female agency that equals that of man's.

But this ostensible solution to her problems obscures the gendered nature of Alex's stress, and in fact serves to naturalize it rather than delineating the impossibility of finding work-life balance for employed females who are expected to do both shifts, professional and domestic. She has not only "left behind" stress, as she claims, she has left behind a private life that feeds off of her, revolves around her, and will most certainly be there when she returns from her trip. Instead of representing the male as an equal, and equally adept, partner in parenting, for example, the ad shows the man helplessly holding the baby, eyebrows raised in confusion and shock. One can only imagine the urgency with which he will hand over that infant when Alexa walks through the door. Yet yoga is shown as a solution to this impossible situation, one in which even her friend and mother "pile on" her with needs rather than being represented as sources of nurture and support.

The gender binary also manifests in her need to worry about her appearance on the business trip. That the curling iron is referred to as an "essential business tool," while clearly meant to be tongue-in-cheek, actually underscores the conventionally masculine context of the public sphere and woman's uncomfortable fit in that environment. Again yoga might offer a respite from the realities of sexism in the workplace, and she is not reduced to underwear model in this narrative, but the curling iron that floats in the air alongside her as she practices in her hotel room offers a fantasized transcendence of these very real issues that women who want to, or have to, function in the public sphere must grapple with on a daily basis.

More pressingly, perhaps, the questions of what corporation she works for and what business practices she promotes go entirely unexplored, as do the class and race disparities suggested by the presence of the worker who obligingly delivers her the accoutrement she requires to be in balance. Who is this nameless worker? Does she get to do yoga? Does the business Alexa works for contribute to increasing global inequities? Perhaps she works for the military-industrial complex. These issues might seem to be beyond the scope of a discussion of representations of yoga, but actually highlight ways in which this practice can be mutated into one that actually serves to reproduce hierarchal materialist and antispiritual Western lifestyles rather than revealing them and resisting their toxicity.

In ads like this, and through other means like mindfulness campaigns, corporate America increasingly co-opts yoga to keep its army of workers working, dumping their stress in boardrooms temporarily converted to yoga studios instead of demanding change. As Sandra Ignani describes it:

> The recent explosion of yoga, in light of state and market discourses that stress *individual* responsibility for coping with what could be considered social problems, serves only to offer a market-based response to work-life conflict, one that cannot redress the raced, classed and gendered dimensions that underpin the changing and increasingly insecure nature of work. . . .[10]

If only a yoga mat could solve the problems caused by modern consumer corporate capitalism, as this ad asserts, but in actuality the "stress" that we are asked to accept instead might signal the need for real and fundamental changes in our homes and workplaces and nations. Yoga might make it possible for privileged Westerners to stand our lives. But should it? And why are Alexa's problems personal and not political?

The quasi-spiritual transcendence this cartoon character experiences thanks to her relationship with corporate America is made even more explicit in an Aflac advertisement which uses yoga to sell insurance. Part of a series in which the Aflac duck appears incongruously in fitness situations, this ad shows people practicing in a yoga studio increasingly distracted by the animal's presence. As in the other representations of yoga studios, this one is bright, clean, well-appointed, and features sitar music in the background to add an "exotic" element. Those practicing yoga in this commercial are more varied than other ads we have looked at insofar as there is one male featured (as well as a duck), although the preponderance of class members are young, thin, white women, as is the yogi. While she gives instructions, the duck makes loud noises suggestive of both a quack and the word "Aflac." This gets the attention of two women, one white one African American, who give each other sidelong glances, bemused by the interloper's presence.

The duck continues to do the postures albeit in comical form.[11] As the male gets assistance with his Down Dog, he glances up in surprise due to the distraction caused by the animal, who looks between his legs and quacks "Aflac" at the man. Eventually his antics cause the African American woman to speak. "Not that great at yoga," she says, referring to the duck. "Yeah," agrees her friend, "but when I slipped a disk he paid my claim in just four days." The woman is incredulous. "*Four days?*" "Yep," she says, staring at him with shining eyes. The last shot of the class shows savasana, resting pose, with the duck snoring contentedly on his mat. A final frame depicts the duck's picture superimposed directly on a rolled yoga mat sitting next to two lighted candles.

This last image suggests a shrine not to a deity but to the duck and the corporation which he represents. Transcendence and power in this context do not lie in the practice of yoga, which for all we know is what caused the woman to slip a disk. The miracle here is Aflac insurance, shown as taking the place of the sacred and superseding it in strength. The yogi and her class are no match for the magical powers of a multinational corporation. The marketing campaign further attributed the insurance company with metaphysical power by appending this statement to the commercial on YouTube:

> One path to inner peace is getting your claim paid fast. And while the Aflac Duck might not be great at Yoga (it's hard to touch your toes when you don't have any,) he'll bend over backwards to pay your claim in just four days. Now everyone exhale together: "Aaaflaaaaaac."[12]

"Inner peace" might well be a goal of yoga practice, yet in this ad it comes not from inner work but outside corporate systems. Instead of emphasizing the impersonal nature of these multinational businesses, the quotation offers corporate unity, as the reader imagines a community exhaling "together," not in Sanskrit, but in company-speak, promoting the name of this business.

YOGI AS CORPORATE SHILL

In each of these preceding instances, yoga has been co-opted by patriarchal capitalist interests in order to promote profit rather than personal wellness. These messages emphasize aspects of existence that modern consumers are encouraged to feel anxious about and then offer a product — whether hamburgers, lingerie, hotel rooms, or insurance policies — that purports to alleviate them. Yoga as a cultural symbol operates as context in these advertisements but not as agentic. The final ad under consideration also markets a solution to a problem using yoga as the context but not the answer, in this case going even farther by having the yogi herself promote consumption. Thus this narrative thoroughly elides the possibility of yoga as a method of alleviating anxiety about appearance and permitting the infiltration of market forces into the very practice space itself. In this commercial for a toe fungus ointment a young, thin, white woman in a yoga studio, surrounded by other similar females, is in the middle of a seated posture while the yogi comes around to assist. The young woman has her right leg bent over her left knee. She holds her right foot in her hands and grimaces not with pain but with shame. "My nail fungus in so embarrassing," she says anxiously to the yogi, who immediately squats down next to her and replies, "You need Kerasal Nail Fungal Nail Renewal Treatment." The shot cuts to an image of the product in a box and then to a yellow toenail. A male voice speaks about "clinically proven" results as we see a tube applying ointment to the toe. Promises of improved appearance in two weeks are made. Fine print below suggests up to six months of use is typical. The last shot shows the product and a smaller embedded screen where we see the yogi looking at us. She is holding up a package of the product and saying "Kerasal Nail. Have them looking at your pose, not your toes." She beams a glorious smile.

In many ways this ad embodies the various themes we have found in the other yoga advertising. The female body is represented as chaotic and in need of control, here literally diseased. The solution comes via yoga, but not the practice itself. Rather than suggesting she resist her culture's insistence upon superficial appearances, the yogi validates the young woman's shame over her body. Instead of suggesting transformation of her anxiety, the yogi's wisdom encourages it and offers a solution.[13] This solution is a corporate product, promoting a culture of consumption that reduces females to objects. The "them" who looks at her holds the power. Her yoga session, indeed her very embodiment, is always already mediated by the external gaze, inescapable even when doing a personal spiritual discipline.

Yoga has been and continues to be a life affirming practice for millions of Americans. Yet as this initial examination of its use in advertising reveals, it can also be exploited for purposes diametrically opposed to those that the adherents of yoga avow. In one sense, its increasing prevalence in marketing narratives suggests a growing awareness of the importance of yoga in people's daily lives, but it also reveals a need to continue to resist dangerous messages about women's bodies and the reach of corporate consumer culture into our most private and sacred spaces.

NOTES

1. The few projects that use yoga advertisements as their primary text focus on images in *Yoga Journal*, a publication aimed at those with a previous interest in the topic. One is an unpublished thesis, "Female and Male Yogis in Media: An Analysis of Gender Stereotypes in Yoga Advertising," by Daria Kamalipour, Southern Illinois University, Edwardsville, December 2013. The thesis analyzes advertisements in the

magazine. The other analyzes images on the cover. See Pirkko Markula, "Reading Yoga: Changing Discourses of Postural Yoga on the *Yoga Journal* Covers," *Communication and Sport* 2, no. 2 (2014): 143–71

2. Also useful but beyond the scope of this current essay would be quantitative studies of the frequency of yoga in advertising and comprehensive coverage of the various products yoga is shown in conjunction with. The ads analyzed here were observed and collected by the author in the course of daily life, selected for analysis as they are widely viewed by mainstream audiences and therefore have the possibility of influencing large numbers of people.

3. For the history of yoga, see Beatrix Hauser, *Yoga Traveling: Bodily Practice in Transcultural Perspective* (New York: Springer, 2015); for the demographics, see Crystal Park et al., "Who Practices Yoga?: A Systematic Review of Demographic, Health-related, and Psychosocial Factors Associated with Yoga Practice." *Journal of Behavioral Medicine* 38 (2015): 460–71.

4. I use the term here following Laura Mulvey.

5. For example see Susanne Hafner-Holter et al., "Effects of Fitness Training and Yoga on Well-being, Stress, Social Competence, and Body Image," *Neuropsychiatrie: Klinik, Diagnostik, Therapie und Rehabilitation: Organ der Gesellschaft Österreichischer Nervenärzte und Psychiater* 23, no. 4 (2009).

6. For a discussion of the feminizing of meat in U.S. culture see Carol Adams, *The Sexual Politics of Meat: A Feminist-Vegetarian Critical Theory* (Continuum, 2000).

7. For example, see Jean Kilbourne, *Deadly Persuasion: Why Women and Girls Must Fight the Addictive Power of Advertising* (The Free Press, 1999).

8. See Renuka Methil, "Women Only: For the Jet-setting Female Executive it's the Details that Matter," *Business Insights: Essentials*, October 15, 2015.

9. A box at the bottom of part 3 notes that these cartoons were "created in collaboration with the artist Marisa Acocella Marchetto. To see her in action and view the complete series, go to NewYorkerOntheTown.com/Hyatt."

10. Ignani, Sandra. "How Far Can the Market Stretch?: Yoga as a Limited Response to Work-Life Conflict in Canada," *Studies in Political Economy*(2006): 11.

11. Tellingly there's a remix of this ad on YouTube that includes hearty fart sounds emitting from the duck and the male's body as they bend.

12. This comment was published August 5, 2014. The ad has since been removed from YouTube.

13. Anyone who has ever done a yoga class knows how preposterous it would be for someone to announce her embarrassment over her feet in the middle of a session and even more preposterous for a yogi to endorse some product in response.

REFERENCES

Adams, Carol, *The Sexual Politics of Meat: A Feminist-Vegetarian Critical Theory* (New York: Continuum, 2000).

Hafner-Holter, Susanne and Martin Kopp and Verena Gunther. "Effects of Fitness Training and Yoga on Well-Being, Stress, Social Competence and Body Image." *Neuropsychiatrie: Klinik, Diagnostik, Therapie und Rehabilitation: Organ der Gesellschaft Österreihischer Nervenärzte und Psychiater* 23 (2009).

Hauser, Beatrix, ed., *Yoga Traveling: Bodily Practice in Transcultural Perspective* (Cham and New York: Springer, 2013).

Ignani, Sandra. "How Far Can the Market Stretch?: Yoga as a Limited Response to Work-Life Conflict in Canada." *Studies in Political Economy* (2006): 11.

Kamalipour, Daria. "Female and Male Yogis in Media: An Analysis of Gender Stereotypes in Yoga Advertising" (MA thesis, Southern Illinois University, 2013).

Kilbourne, Jean, *Deadly Persuasion: Why Women and Girls Must Fight the Addictive Power of Advertising* (New York: The Free Press, 1999).

Markula, Pirkko. "Reading Yoga: Changing Discourses of Postural Yoga on the *Yoga Journal* Covers." *Communication and Sport* 2 (2014): 143–71

Methil, Renuka. "Women Only: for the Jet-setting Female Executive it's the Details that Matter—Even a Safety Pin, Skirt Hanger or Yoga Mat in the Hotel Room Can Make a World of Difference." *Business Insights: Essentials*, October 15, 2015. Accessed November 14, 2015. http://bi.galegroup.com.libproxy1.usc.edu/essentials/article/GALE/A190747371?u=usocal_main

Mulvey, Laura. *Visual and Other Pleasures* (Houndmills, Basingstoke: Palgrave Macmillan, 2009).

Park, Crystal and Tosca Braun and Tamar Siegel. "Who Practices Yoga? A Systematic Review of Demographic, Health-Related, and Psychosocial Factors Associated with Yoga Practice." *Journal of Behavioral Medicine* 38 (2015), 460–71

EIGHT

"Work Off That Holiday Meal Ladies!"

Body Vigilance and Orthorexia in Yoga Spaces

Jennifer Musial

Vignette One: It was the 1980s. Growing up, my Mom insisted we couldn't eat until my Dad joined the dinner table. As a workaholic perfectionist, my Dad was always engaged in a task that prevented him from sitting down when the meal was served. I developed a feminist sense of inequality and normalized food denial at the same time. I learned that I can't eat when I'm hungry and that one doesn't eat until all the work is done.

Vignette Two: It was 2011. I was visiting my partner's family over the winter holidays. My partner's father offered me a bag of pretzels, a staple of Pennsylvania snack food. I politely declined because I'd given up eating gluten earlier that year. I was so upset that I later cried in the basement. I was so hungry.

Vignette Three: It was 2015. As I'm preparing to teach a yoga class, one of my students brings me two pumpkin muffins. She carefully tells me all of the ingredients and makes a point of saying she opted for tahini instead of peanut butter. She remarks,"now they are 'clean' food." After class, students invite me to lunch at the new organic cafe. Later in the day, the studio co-owner posts a photograph on Facebook with the hashtag #cleanliving.[1] I wonder if my orthorexic thinking will be triggered teaching here.

In the edited collection *Yoga and Body Image: 25 Personal Stories about Beauty, Bravery, and Loving Your Body,* authors Melody Moore, Melanie Klein, Seane Corn, Chelsea Jackson Roberts, Alanis Morrissette, Claire Mysko, Dawn M. Dalili, and Kerrie Kauer admit to using yoga to help heal from disordered eating. These anecdotes are supported by research that finds disordered eaters who deny consumption affect (i.e., hunger pains, tummy "growling," becoming "hangry," or feeling "full") can benefit from body mindfulness that sensitizes them to somatic messages prompting nourishment.[2] Through personal narrative and empirical studies, yoga is described as a positive adjunct therapy for disordered eating.

Upon encountering this literature, I was wary of the triumphal tone. Surely yoga advertised as a way to lose weight or manage hunger can trigger negative body/self image. Robin Boudette, a yoga teacher and treatment provider, concurs, "Some yoga classes could reinforce the very self-destructive beliefs and cultural values that we are trying to extinguish. A competitive, perfectionistic [sic] patient does not need a class where she would be vulnerable to pushing too hard, ignoring personal limits and becoming overly focused on physical results. . . ."[3] Yoga teachers who emphasize control (of the breath, body, mind, energy, or diet) can be detrimental to those trying to relinquish control of their bodies. In this case, the unruly body becomes a project "to be managed and maintained"[4] through yogic discipline. Unlike projects that order the body according to white, thin, ableist, cisgendered ideals of gendered sexuality, these body projects cloak themselves in spiritual liberation[5] wherein ascetic pursuit maps onto contemporary capitalism and healthism that invites yoga students to buy into a "pure" body, literally and epistemologically speaking.

While I was initially interested in how yoga spaces may be triggering for those recovering from eating disorders, it was my personal experience with disordered eating and teaching yoga that led me to question how fasting, restrictive eating, and other "self-destructive behaviors under the guise of detoxing [or] cleansing"[6] become new body projects in yoga spaces. In this autoethnographic essay, I pair my experiences as a yoga teacher and practitioner who struggles with disordered eating habits, most recently manifesting as orthorexia (a disordered eating practice marked by preoccupation with the quality of food one consumes), with a discussion of neoliberal body vigilance that triggers self-shaming affect. While yoga can be healing for those with disordered eating patterns, I argue detox practices, cleanses, and the rigor of "disciplined" power/hot yoga practice contribute to orthorexic thinking that encourages a fixation on healthful eating and "correct alimentation,"[7] which can be triggering for those (like myself) oriented to control their bodies. Beyond the individualized, and often pathologized, practice of orthorexia, I query: to what degree is yoga-related orthorexia connected to class- and race-based gentrification when the yoga studio and the natural foods/Whole Foods/ Trader Joe's/organic restaurant become markers of neighborhood transformation? This question identifies privilege attached to being able to practice in a yoga studio and purchase detox products, cleanse programs, and organic foods promoted by studios and individual yoga teachers. Therefore, one must ask: what, or who, are we cleansing ourselves from? I use Foucauldian Discourse Theory and autoethnographic storytelling to unpack orthorexia in yoga. By drawing on my journal entries, canonical yoga texts, and popular yoga materials (i.e., corporate messaging, blogs, magazines) as primary source material, I capture the yoga world I live in, which is not relegated to one space or forum. Discourse, like experience, oscillates between personal interaction, self-inquiry, and material artifacts gaining meaning through a circulatory process. Hence, I avoid a positivist rendering of orthorexia in favor of a "messy text" that more authentically captures "narrative truth" not "historical truth";[8] in so doing, I avoid analytical closure and "le[ave] dangling and messy" the "ambiguity of the phenomenon represented."[9]

Autoethnography compliments an essay devoted to orthorexia in yoga spaces because it "adds blood and tissue to the abstract bones of theoretical discourse."[10] It is somatic and affective; and, like yoga, autoethnography pays attention to the quotidian nature of everyday life while demanding self-reflexivity. As tools of exploration, autoethnography and yoga require vulnerability that is unsettling because "confronting things about yourself that are less than flattering generates a lot of fears and self-doubts—and emotional pain. . . . Then there's the vulnerability of revealing yourself, not being able to take back what you've written or having any control over how readers interpret it."[11] As a discourse analyst trained to listen for what is *not* being said as well as being a yoga teacher increasingly uncomfortable with negative food talk in yoga spaces, particularly because I recognize myself in recent blog posts about orthorexia,[12] I felt compelled to take up this subject.

DEFINING ORTHOREXIA

From its conceptual introduction, orthorexia has been tied to yoga because it first appeared in *Yoga Journal* in 1997. Coined by medical doctor and alternative health practitioner Steven Bratman, orthorexia refers to "a fixation on eating healthy food"[13] that manifests in an inflexible diet, diligent food label reading, scrutiny of food sourcing, ritualizing food preparation, or stringent vitamin consumption that ensures "pure" or "clean" eating. Orthorexia often begins as a mechanism to lose weight, manage illness, or alter (perceived) negative eating habits, but adherence to strict dietary ideals leads to a preoccupation with "what to eat, how much, and the consequences to dietary indiscretion come to occupy a greater and greater proportion of our mental life."[14] Over time, orthorexic individuals become entangled in a cycle of "lapses, self-praise for success, strict self-control to resist temptation, and conceited superiority over anyone who indulges in impure dietary habits."[15] The aforementioned self-flagellation and shame results in self-corrective action. Diversion from the routine leads to:

> intense frustration when their food-related practices are disrupted or thwarted, disgust when food purity is seemingly compromised, and guilt and self-loathing when they commit food transgressions . . . dietary violations may prompt a desire for self-punishment, manifested by an even stricter diet, or purification via supposedly cleansing fasts. [16]

Orthorexic practice is demonstrated by my journal entry, which illustrates eating preparedness and nutritional consequences:

> I love airports, but I dislike traveling through small regional ones. I ensure I have many snacks on hand because there are too few vegetarian gluten-free options. Sometimes I will go hungry rather than eat French fries, which may be the only food option available.

Orthorexia may result in social isolation, malnutrition, nutritional imbalances, or self-starvation. Though some individuals may become very ill, orthorexia is rarely fatal. [17]

There is a lack of professional consensus on orthorexia. [18] Psychiatric health professionals, medical doctors, alternative health practitioners, and researchers alike question whether it is a psychiatric illness, a manifestation of obsessive compulsive disorder, an addiction, representative of the new "healthism," or simply a lifestyle choice. In "The Clinical Basis of Orthorexia Nervosa: Emerging Perspectives," Nancy S. Koven and Alexandra W. Abry compare orthorexia, anorexia, and obsessive compulsive disorder by saying these conditions share an orientation toward perfectionism, cognitive rigidity, impaired functioning, poor external monitoring, trait anxiety, and impaired working memory. [19] In addition to perfectionism and a predisposition to high anxiety levels, Biswajit Chaki et al. find that orthorexic and anorexic individuals need to control their environment. [20] I use myself as an example here:

> While I have had disordered eating patterns since I was a child, orthorexia manifested for me when I started volunteering at a local yoga studio. I was in the later stages of my PhD, and I couldn't afford a yoga membership. I lucked out when I was able to volunteer in exchange for a studio membership. After one year, I decided to complete yoga teacher training coinciding with the last year of my PhD. The final dissertation push was stressful, my romantic relationship was strained, my dissertation supervisor was mostly absent, and I was teaching as an adjunct professor at multiple universities. Further, I was living in a community with few friends. The yoga studio became my "happy place." Being around kind and supportive people was a gift. I started to internalize that a dedicated yogi/ni makes certain lifestyle choices. Many fellow teachers and practitioners were vegetarian, and went through cycles of "detoxing" from caffeine, sugar, dairy, and wheat. During my time at the studio, I gave up eating "processed" foods, [21]

and eventually I went gluten-free by choice. I exhibited control over my diet and my *asana* (physical postures) practice because my life was out of control otherwise. To this day, I am gluten-free by choice. It is the last major remnant of orthorexia that I hold onto. I often wonder if my "irrational" fear of reintroducing gluten is connected to my precarious labour status. With more stability in my life, would I relax my eating habits?

In *Health Food Junkies*, Bratman differentiates orthorexia from bulimia and anorexia by saying, "whereas the bulimic and the anorexic focus on the quantity of food, the orthorexic fixates on its quality."[22] Recent literature suggests this distinction is inaccurate. For instance, A. Kummer et al. contend that anorexia may begin with red meat avoidance, vegetarianism, veganism, or loyalty to an organic food diet[23] while Cristina Segura-Garcia et al. maintain that after eating disorder treatment, some women develop orthorexia, which "can hide the real attempt to control the amount of food intake with the excuse to eat high-quality foods."[24] This research suggests a more fluid continuum between various eating disorders than previously theorized.

Another way researchers separate orthorexia from recognized eating disorders is through positing that orthorexics do not espouse weight-associated anxieties whereas many anorexics and bulimics fear gaining weight.[25] However, Bratman argues that healthy eating can be a form of "covert conformity" wherein individuals, typically women, "'accidentally' live up to the Barbie image" without intentionally setting out to do so.[26] Orthorexia that results in weight loss may be socially affirmed. As Kaila Prins reveals, "People were mostly commenting on how healthy I was, how great I looked, and how they wished they could be like me as I lost weight . . . everyone praised me for how clean I was eating and how much they wanted my willpower."[27] Claudia McNeilly received a similar response when she adopted an orthorexic Paleo diet. She writes, "Since I was eating only vegetables, coconut oil, and lean meat, the ten pounds came off quickly. Soon, people who hadn't spoken to me in years started praising me for how great I looked. The compliments were addicting— they would become my justification for enduring what evolved into a fear of half the food groups."[28] Prins and McNeilly's narratives point to the difficulty of identifying an orthorexic practice: since eating "clean" is prescribed as the healthful way to lose weight, orthorexics are swimming with the cultural current. Indeed, sometimes individuals with orthorexia must declare an "against health"[29] stance to heal from this disordered eating practice, which is to say orthorexics unapologetically consume processed foods, sugary foods, or "fatty" foods without fear, regret, or self-punishment.

However, focusing on the psychological nature of orthorexia tends to pathologize this eating practice, and may reinforce neoliberal healthism, which places "the blame for health problems and the burden of their solutions" on the individual.[30] Fewer academic studies examine the soci-ocultural nature of orthorexia. In "'Orthorexic Society' and Media Narrations: Advertising and Food Labelling," Guido Nicolosi suggests that we live in an "orthorexic society" that is "obsessed [with] correct alimentation" because there is an increasing disconnection between traditional foodways and contemporary living in the Euro-Western world.[31] When met with a neoliberal expectation to live an orderly life according to healthism, a discourse of "personal responsibility [that] demands that individuals achieve health, avoid risk factors, and prevent ill health" with "regular exercise" and "healthy eating habits,"[32] it is unsurprising there is growing food anxiety manifesting as orthorexia.

CLEAN BODY, CLEAR MIND

A focus on eating healthfully finds a home in yoga, particularly because certain yoga traditions dictate consumption practices. For instance, in *Light on Yoga*, B.K.S. Iyengar outlines an ideal eating schedule by recommending that students should conduct their *asana* practice on an empty stomach. If this is not possible, a light meal one hour before practice will sufficiently nourish the body; if one has heavy meal, he/she/ze/they should wait "at least four hours" before starting *asana* practice. Food is best consumed half an hour after *asana* practice concludes.[33] My journal entry demonstrates how meals are scheduled around *asana* practice:

> I find that a banana is a perfect snack before heading to a hot power-vinyasa class. After practice, I do not have much of an appetite but I notice that I crave "clean" foods: it is not uncommon for me to eat a hearty salad or edamame. I realize this means I have skipped an entire meal; *asana* seems to have nourished me. I do not want to put junk food back into this clean body after a sweaty practice.

In yoga, cleanliness is not "next to Godliness"; cleanliness is the *route* to spiritual liberation. Atman (God, highest self) will not inhabit an impure temple, Swami Svatmarama writes in the *Hatha Yoga Pradipika*.[34] Discourses of cleanliness, purification, and clarity emerge through discussions of Niyamas (i.e., Shaucha), Yamas (i.e., Ahimsa), Kriyas, and fasting, among other topics, in classical yoga texts. Yoga traditions that posit the mind can be stilled by disciplining the body reinforce a body/mind epistemology that may inculcate the body is "dirty or imperfect [thus] reinforcing the negative self-belief that underlies eating disorders."[35]

It is through an interpretation of yoga scripture that teachers and studios often urge body vigilance. For instance, Iyengar draws upon Shaucha (purification) when he writes, "Besides purity of the body, thought and word, pure food is also necessary. Apart from cleanliness in the preparation of food it is also necessary to observe purity in the means by which one procures it."[36] The Jivamukti yoga tradition speaks definitively to this point. For Jivamukti practitioners, vegetarianism (and preferably veganism) is the ideal way to preserve the purity of life.[37]

Food fixation in the name of Shaucha or Ahimsa is reinforced by Kriyas (cleansing actions) designed to help the yogi/ni find clarity. In May 2015, *Yoga Magazine* came under fire for publishing an article on Vyaghra Kriya (aka "The Tiger"). Responding to a reader inquiry, columnist Dr. Malik outlines how to complete Vyaghra Kriya, which involves "self-induced vomiting as a means of self-purification" that coincidentally "tones the muscles of the abdomen" and "burns off excess fat and trims the waist." Blogger YogaDork and others swiftly critiqued the advice, calling it "reckless" and "irresponsible."[38] While Malik's discussion of "The Tiger" was recognized as harmful, contemporary yoga teachers like Baron Baptiste advocate fasting as a Kriya to cleanse the body with minimal critical attention.

For Baron Baptiste, who has popularized the Baptiste Power Vinyasa method, fasting is a physical way to "reset" the body. Baron Baptiste created the 40 Days to Personal Revolution Program "to lead [participants] home to mental clarity, lightness of body and illumination of spirit that comes with whole-life health."[39] In addition to routine power yoga *asana* practice, meditation, and journaling, students are asked to be mindful of their eating patterns leading to a three-day fruit fast occurring in week four. Baptiste prefaces the fruit fast by saying, "the sweat in the room smells very thick—it's almost as though a cloud of toxicity is hanging in the air as the impurities are coming up and out through the students' pores. The physical rocks of poison are slowly rising to the surface of their gardens to be removed."[40] This body-shaming language sets up the fruit fast, which promises to "leave you lighter, cleaner, and infused with more energy."[41] To further motivate participants, Baptiste says, "active cleansing or fasting is a way to allow your body to fully empty out and get clean, giving your metabolic organs a chance to rest and renew themselves." After the fruit fast, people "literally start to glow" and they are "able to receive the radiance."[42]

Having taught at two studios that offer hot Baptiste Power classes and the 40 Day Revolution program, I observed the fruit fast become a major topic of conversation:

> During the fast, students excitedly disclosed their experiences and frustrations as well as their food preparation tips and tricks; "remember, avocados and tomatoes count as fruit!," said one participant to another who lamented she was running out of creative eating options. Many of us checked in with students by asking how it was going. I secretly wanted their resolve, but I knew that if I committed to a fast, I would become self-competitive and try to hold out for longer than three days.

The following exchange demonstrates how the fruit fast dominates yoga spaces that offer the 40 Day Revolution program:

I was teaching an afternoon Hatha class when I walked into the practice room. While on their mats awaiting the start of class, students were
talking about what they "can and can't eat." Rather than eliminating
foods due to allergies or sensitivities, there was an unstated list of
forbidden foods. Knowing the 40 Day Revolution program had commenced, but wanting to probe deeper than consumption practices, I
asked "Aside from our eating, how are you doing?" to which one student gleefully replied, "I'm not doing this" (referring to the 40 Day
Revolution program). I responded "me neither!" Given the predominance of food restriction discussion that framed this yoga space, we felt
like outsiders who found each other in that moment. During one section of class, I asked students to curl into a ball, and I must have
likened it to an egg because one participant sarcastically responded,
"we can't eat eggs Jen!" I offered a sympathetic, "awwww" then followed with "well, I don't eat eggs anyway." Reflecting back, it was a
strange way of offering solidarity. I reflect in my journal later, "not a
day goes by where there isn't talk of food here."

The hyperfascination with being "clean" extends beyond the Baptiste 40
Day Revolution program. Recently, Gaiam began a "Conscious Cleanse"
program that promises participants will "have more energy," "shed excess weight," "sleep" soundly, and "be your vibrant shiniest self."[43] I
take the online quiz "How Clean Are You?," which indicates I am a
"clutter bug," a nonsensical phrase that generates an email saying, "Alright, so maybe there was a bit of carb-loading lately, who can really say
no to sugary sweet doughnuts or nachos stacked high with melting
cheese? We've all heard that we are what we eat—why not make ourselves a treasure trove of brilliance and sparkle?"[44] I recall the effects of
nutritional de-cluttering in the past·

Roughly six weeks into giving up processed foods, someone told me I
looked like I was glowing. I felt validated.

MAKE OVER, TAKE OVER

Refashioning the self into a vibrant, shiny, glowing, and pure (neoliberal)
subject requires more than food negation. One must be able to afford the
40 Day Revolution Program, the Conscious Cleanse, and whole foods
that are typically recommended. Living in a food desert with limited
finances or without the cultural capital to read nutritional labels/recipes
hampers one's ability to #eatclean.

Though we had a vegetable garden when I was a kid, meals were more
likely to include frozen or canned veggies than fresh ones from the
farmer's market. I taught academic classes at a prestigious university
and yoga classes at a studio that catered to an economically and racially
privileged student demographic when I became orthorexic. I'm starting
to wonder if my orthorexia was tied to internalizing a bourgeois atti-

tude towards "the right" kind of food. Maybe orthorexia was the key to class-passing in the neoliberal academy. Could I eat my way to academic success?[45]

Orthorexic society does not exist in a vacuum. In order to practice orthorexia, one must have access to "pure" foods. The natural food store, farmer's market, vitamin shop, free-trade café, and organic restaurant become the geographical beneficiary of orthorexic thinking supported by yoga spaces. While we are cleansing our bodies, we are also cleansing the neighborhood and rebuilding it in the image of a healthy community: we are gentrifying.

I have taught in six yoga studios[46] spanning three different cities ranging in size. All were locally-owned businesses; three were located downtown while the remaining three were in strip malls not far from the city center. The clientele of each space ranged in age and practice level, but was homogenously white. A few studios offered reduced-price classes to appeal to practitioners who could not afford a drop-in fee; however, most practitioners had disposable income, health insurance subsidies, or parental support to afford studio memberships. Some students had additional monies to participate in programming like the 40 Day Revolution, which cost extra. The first studio I taught at literally sat at the corner of a major intersection that divided the bourgeois/affluent south from the working class/gentrifying northern neighbourhood; the studio represented the tip of downtown revitalization, which was robust to the east and developing to the west. The studio was surrounded by a Pizza Pizza (fast food), Dairy Queen, french fry shop, three bars, Vietnamese restaurant, El Savadoran take-out, bubble tea joint, sushi restaurant, and expensive grocery store catering to those who need just a few items. We always had to leave the outdoor light on post-classes to deter intoxicated people from hanging around the stoop. Sometimes I'd arrive to teach an early morning class and find vomit on the front step. Or left-over pizza crust.

Leslie Kern writes, "notions of detoxifying, cleansing, balancing, aligning, beautifying, and purifying are applied to bodies that seek to be transformed, inside and out. Simultaneously, these bodies are actively consuming environmental gentrification in the new neighbourhood spaces."[47] Through cleaning the front entrance to a studio, purifying the body through orthorexic eating, or attending detox hot yoga classes, students engage in a neoliberal body project that maps the city as well as corporeality.

When I ask two different yoga studio owners what they dream for their studios, they each say they wish they had a bigger space to accommodate a fresh juice/smoothie bar. One studio co-owner fantasized about making healthy juices with no added sugars unlike Panera located one block away. Little did she know that I'd recently begun purchasing Panera's Green Passion Power Smoothie before teaching at the studio. I saw it as a positive step to ensure I was healthfully hydrated before class. Now I felt guilty about my sugar consumption. I haven't purchased a Panera smoothie since.

Commercial yoga studios typically imagine their community as open-minded individuals who are committed to health and wellness rather than marginalized people seeking relief from systemic trauma, poverty, colonialism, or white supremacy; it is the latter who are often ostracized from revitalization efforts that facilitate the arrival of yoga studios in the first place. Urban change occurs "through the removal of symbolically 'dirty' bodies and practices and their replacement with symbolically 'clean' bodies and practices"[48] like yoga. Right now, few commercial yoga spaces operate in the messiness that defines community;[49] instead, they are more likely to desire a "sanitized" practitioner who purchases a healthful smoothie as opposed to one who volunteers to run a community kitchen out of the studio.

CONCLUSION

The last yoga studio that employed me was fixated on healthy eating. In preparation for this essay, I documented orthorexic normativity at the studio. As a result, I had daily notes and a full archive. During orientation with a new student, one of the co-owners remarked, "we talk a lot about food here but not in a bad way," by which she meant they do not talk about junk food. She looked to me for affirmation. I remained silent.

During the two-part telephone series "How Yoga Brings Healing to Those who Struggle with Negative Body Image and Disordered Eating," Melody Moore advises participants to avoid food shaming exemplified by saying "because I'm going to be doing x later, I can't eat y now." Narrating food choices in this way contributes to disordered eating.[50] Preparing this essay was illuminating because it heightened my criticality toward food shame and normalized orthorexia. The process of writing was "self-consciously therapeutic [because] it opens up a conversation, and when it works well, the conversation continues to be therapeutic for the writer."[51] Beyond Svadhyaya (Self-Study), I hope this essay provokes radical honesty about the harmfulness of purity in our bodies, our relationships, and in our communities.

NOTES

1. As of November 2015, there are 25.5 million images on Instagram under #EatClean and 17.1 million images appear when one searches #CleanEating. See Kellie Galentine, "Orthorexia and Social Media: What You Need to Know about the 'Clean' Eating Disorder," http://bust.com/orthorexia-social-media-what-you-need-to-know-clean-eat

ing-disorder.html.

2. See Robin Boudette, "Question and Answer: Yoga in the Treatment of Disordered Eating and Body Image Disturbance," *Eating Disorders* 14 (2006): 167–70; Laura Douglass, "Thinking Through the Body: Conceptualization of Yoga as Therapy for Individuals with Eating Disorders," *Eating Disorders* 19 (2011): 83–96.

3. Boudette, "Question and Answer," 169.

4. Joan Jacobs Brumberg, *The Body Project: An Intimate History of American Girls* (New York: Vintage Books, 1997) xxi.

5. By which I do not mean to suggest that body vigilance is de-gendered. White women of economic privilege dominate U.S. yoga spaces. See Crystal L. Park, Tosca Braun, and Tamar Siegel, "Who Practices Yoga? A Systemic Review of Demographic, Health-Related, and Psychosocial Factors Associated with Yoga Practice," *Journal of Behavioral Medicine* 38, no. 3 (2015): 460–71.

6. Chelsea Roff, "Starved for Connection: Healing Anorexia Through Yoga," in *21st Century Yoga: Culture, Politics, and Practice*, edited by Carol Horton and Roseanne Harvey (Chicago: Kleio Books, 2012) 92.

7. Guido Nicolosi, "'Orthorexic Society' and Media Narrations: Advertising and Food Labelling," *EurSafeNews* 9, no. 1 (2007): 10.

8. Carolyn Ellis, "Evocative Autoethnography: Writing Emotionally About Our Lives," in *Representation and the Text: Re-framing the Narrative Voice*, edited by William G. Tierney and Yvonna S. Lincoln (Albany: State University of New York Press, 1997) 129.

9. George E. Marcus and Dick Cushman, "Ethnographies as Texts," *Annual Review of Anthropology* 11 (1982): 117.

10. Ellis, "Evocative Autoethnography," 117.

11. Carolyn Ellis, "Heartful Autoethnography," *Qualitative Health Research* 9.5 (1999): 672.

12. See Claudia McNeilly, "When Does 'Eating Clean' Become an Eating Disorder?," last modified November 3, 2015, *Vice*, https://broadly.vice.com/en_us/article/orthorexia-eating-clean-eating-disorder and Chelsea Roff, "Yoga's Shadow Side," *Yoga Journal*, October 2014, 96–99, 113–118.

13. Steven Bratman, *Health Food Junkies: Orthorexia Nervosa: Overcoming the Obsession with Healthful Eating* (New York: Broadway Books, 2000) 9.

14. Bratman, *Health Food Junkies*.

15. Bratman, *Health Food Junkies*, 10.

16. Nancy S. Koven and Alexandra W. Abry, "The Clinical Basis of Orthorexia Nervosa: Emerging Perspectives," *Neuropsychiatric Disease and Treatment* 11 (2015): 385.

17. Bratman, *Health Food Junkies*.

18. Orthorexia is not listed in *The Diagnostic and Statistical Manual of Mental Disorders* (DSM-5). Despite its absence from the DSM-5, the National Eating Disorders Association features orthorexia on its website.

19. Koven and Abry, "The Clinical Basis of Orthorexia Nervosa," 387.

20. Biswajit Chaki, Sangita Pal, and Amit Bandyopadhyay, "Exploring Scientific Legitimacy of Orthorexia Nervosa: A Newly Emerging Eating Disorder," *Journal of Human Sport and Exercise* 8, no. 4 (2013): 1045–1051.

21. This meant eliminating food with notable chemical additives. I became a strident food label reader. I gravitated to the "organic," "natural" food section of the grocery store, and I began shopping at the health food store and farmer's market.

22. Bratman, *Health Food Junkies*, 10.

23. A. Kummer, F. MV Dias, and A.L. Teixeira, "Letter to the Editor: On the Concept of Orthorexia Nervosa," *Scandinavian Journal of Medicine and Science in Sports* 18 (2008): 395.

24. Cristina Segura-Garcia, Carla Ramacciotti, Marianna Rania, Caroleo Aloi, Mariarita Matteo, Antonella Bruni, Denise Gazzarrini, Flora Sinopoli, and Pasquale De Fazio, "The Prevalence of Orthorexia Nervosa Among Eating Disorder Patients After Treatment," *Eating and Weight Disorders* 20 (2015): 162.

25. See Anna Brytek-Matera, Lorenzo Maria Donini, Magdalena Krupa, Eleonora Poggiogalle, and Phillipa Hay, "Orthorexia Nervosa and Self-Attitudinal Aspects of Body Image in Female and Male University Students," *Journal of Eating Disorders* 3, no. 2 (2015): 1–8; Chaki et al. "Exploring Scientific Legitimacy of Orthorexia Nervosa"; Koven and Abry, "The Clinical Basis of Orthorexia Nervosa."

26. Bratman, *Health Food Junkies*, 65.

27. Michelle Ng, "Drawing the Line Between Eating Healthily and Being Obsessed with Healthy Eating: A Chat with Kaila Prins (Part One)," *I am #FedUpWithFood*, last modified October 15, 2015, https://iamfedupwithfood.wordpress.com/2015/10/15/a-chat-with-kaila-prins-ex-orthorexia-sufferer-turned-wellness-coach/.

28. McNeilly, ."When Does 'Eating Clean Become an Eating Disorder?'"

29. See Jonathan M. Metzel, "Introduction: Why Against Health?," in *Against Health: How Health Became the New Morality*, edited by Jonathan M. Metzel and Anna Kirkland (New York: New York University Press, 2010).

30. Linn Håman, Natalie Barker-Ruchti, Göran Patriksson, and Eva-Carin Lindgren, "Orthorexia Nervosa: An Integrative Literature Review of a Lifestyle Syndrome," *International Journal of Qualitative Studies on Health and Well-Being* 10 (2015): 10, 12.

31. Nicolosi, "'Orthorexic Society' and Media Narrations," 10.

32. Håman et al., "Orthorexia Nervosa," 2.

33. B.K.S. Iyengar, *Light on Yoga* (New York: Schocken Books, 1972) 57.

34. Pancham Sinh, trans. *Hatha Yoga Pradipika*. 1914: iii. http://sacred-texts.com/hin/hyp/index.htm.

35. Roff, "Yoga's Shadow Side," 112.

36. Iyengar, *Light in Yoga*, 38.

37. Sharon Gannon and David Life, *Jivamukti Yoga: Practices for Liberating Body and Soul* (New York: Ballentine Books, 2002) 50.

38. YogaDork, "Yoga Magazine Slammed for Encouraging Eating Disorders in How-To Article," *YogaDork*. Last Modified May 12, 2015. http://yogadork.com/2015/05/12/yoga-magazine-slammed-for-encouraging-eating-disorders-in-how-to-article/

39. Baptiste Institute, "40 Days to Personal Revolution," http://www.baptisteyoga.com/pages/40-days-program.

40. Baron Baptiste, *40 Days to Personal Revolution: A Breakthrough Program to Radically Change Your Body and Awaken the Sacred Within Your Soul* (New York: Simon and Schuster, 2004) 119.

41. Baptiste, 156.

42. Baptiste, 171.

43. Gaiam, "The Conscious Cleanse," *Gaiam* 2015 http://www.gaia.com/lp-joincc.

44. Gaiam (yoga company) through email with the author, November 23, 2015.

45. See Gary Bridge and Robyn Dowling, "Microgeographies of Retailing and Gentrification," *Australian Geographer* 32, no. 1 (2001): 93–107; Julie Guthman, "Fast Food/Organic Food: Reflexive Tastes and the Making of 'Yuppie Chow,'" *Social and Cultural Geography* 4, no. 1 (2003): 45–58; Sarah Squire, "The Personal and the Political: Writing the Theorist's Body," *Australian Feminist Studies* 17, no. 37 (2002): 55–64.

46. Two studios were owned by the same person but served different areas of the city.

47. Leslie Kern, "From Toxic Wreck to Crunchy Chic: Environmental Gentrification Through the Body," *Environment and Planning D: Society and Space* 33 (2015): 74.

48. Kern, 68.

49. This does not account for yoga classes that run out of religious spaces, recreation centers, or YMCAs/YWCAs, which are more rooted in community wellness.

50. Melody Moore and Seane Corn, "How Yoga Brings Healing to Those who Struggle with Negative Body Image and Disordered Eating," Telephone Workshop, July 28, 2015.

51. Douglas Flemons and Shelley Green, "Stories that Conform/Stories that Transform: A Conversation in Four Parts," in *Ethnographically Speaking: Autoethnography, Literature, and Aesthetics*, edited by Arthur P. Bochner and Carolyn Ellis (New York: Altamira Press, 2001) 190.

REFERENCES

Baptiste, Baron. *40 Days to Personal Revolution: A Breakthrough Program to Radically Change Your Body and Awaken the Sacred Within Your Soul* (New York: Simon & Schuster, 2004).

Baptiste Institute. "40 Days to Personal Revolution." Accessed November 28, 2015. http://www.baptisteyoga.com/pages/40-days-program.

Boudette, Robin. "Question and Answer: Yoga in the Treatment of Disordered Eating and Body Image Disturbance." *Eating Disorders* 14 (2006): 167–70.

Bratman, Steven. "Health Food Junkie." *Yoga Journal* (September/October 1997): 42–50.

———. *Health Food Junkies: Orthorexia Nervosa: Overcoming the Obsession with Healthful Eating* (New York: Broadway Books, 2000).

Bridge, Gary and Robyn Dowling. "Microgeographies of Retailing and Gentrification." *Australian Geographer* 32, no. 1 (2001): 93–107.

Brumberg, Joan Jacobs. *The Body Project: An Intimate History of American Girls* (New York: Vintage Books, 1997).

Brytek-Matera, Anna, Lorenzo Maria Donini, Magdalena Krupa, Eleonora Poggiogalle, and Phillipa Hay. "Orthorexia Nervosa and Self-Attitudianal Aspects of Body Image in Female and Male University Students." *Journal of Eating Disorders* 3, no. 2 (2015): 1–8.

Chaki, Biswajit, Pal, Sangita, and Amit Bandyopadhyay. "Exploring Scientific Legitimacy of Orthorexia Nervosa: A Newly Emerging Eating Disorder." *Journal of Human Sport and Exercise* 8, no. 4 (2013): 1045–1053.

Douglass, Laura. "Thinking Through the Body: Conceptualization of Yoga as Therapy for Individuals with Eating Disorders." *Eating Disorders* 19 (2011): 83–96.

Ellis, Carolyn. "Heartful Autoethnography." *Qualitative Health Research* 9, no. 5 (1999): 669–83.

———. "Evocative Autoethnography: Writing Emotionally About Our Lives." In *Representation and the Text: Re-framing the Narrative Voice*. Edited by William G. Tierney and Yvonna S. Lincoln (Albany: State University of New York Press, 1997) 115–39. .

Flemons, Douglas and Shelley Green. "Stories that Conform/Stories that Transform: A Conversation in Four Parts," in *Ethnographically Speaking: Autoethnography, Literature, and Aesthetics*. Edited by Arthur P. Bochner and Carolyn Ellis (New York: Altamira Press, 2001) 187–90.

Foucault, Michel. "Technologies of the Self," in *Lectures at Vermont University in October 1982*. Edited by Martin H. Luther, Huck Gutman, and Patrick H. Hutton. (University of Massachusetts Press, .1988) 16–49. http://foucault.info/documents/foucault.technologiesofself.en.html.

Gaiam. "The Conscious Cleanse." *Gaiam*. Accessed November 23, 2015. http://www.gaia.com/lp-joincc.

Gaiam, email message to author, November 23, 2015.

Galentine, Kellie. "Orthorexia and Social Media: What You Need to Know about the 'Clean' Eating Disorder." Accessed November 7, 2015. http://bust.com/orthorexia-social-media-what-you-need-to-know-clean-eating-disorder.html.

Gannon, Sharon, and David Life. *Jivamukti Yoga: Practices for Liberating Body and Soul* (New York: Ballentine Books, 2002).

Guthman, Julie. "Fast Food/Organic Food: Reflexive Tastes and the Making of 'Yuppie Chow'." *Social and Cultural Geography* 4, no. 1 (2003): 45–58.

Håman, Linn, Natalie Barker-Ruchti, Göran Patriksson, and Eva-Carin Lindgren. "Orthorexia Nervosa: An Integrative Literature Review of a Lifestyle Syndrome." *International Journal of Qualitative Studies on Health and Well-Being* 10 (2015): 1–15.

Iyengar, B.K.S. *Light on Yoga* (New York: Schocken Books, 1972).

Kern, Leslie. "From Toxic Wreck to Crunchy Chic: Environmental Gentrification Through the Body." *Environment and Planning D: Society and Space* 33 (2015): 67–83.

Koven, Nancy S. and Alexandra W. Abry. "The Clinical Basis of Orthorexia Nervosa: Emerging Perspectives." *Neuropsychiatric Disease and Treatment* 11 (2015): 385–94.

Kummer, A., F. MV. Dias, and A. L. Teixeira. "Letter to the Editor: On the Concept of Orthorexia Nervosa." *Scandinavian Journal of Medicine and Science in Sports* 18 (2008): 395–96.

Marcus, George E. and Dick Cushman. "Ethnographies as Texts." *Annual Review of Anthropology* 11 (1982): 25–69.

McNeilly, Claudia. "When Does 'Eating Clean' Become an Eating Disorder?" *Vice*. Accessed November 4, 2015. https://broadly.vice.com/en_us/article/orthorexia-eating-clean-eating-disorder.

Metzel, Jonathan, M. "Introduction: Why Against Health?" In *Against Health: How Health Became the New Morality*. Edited by Jonathan M. Metzel and Anna Kirkland (New York: New York University Press, 2010) 1–25.

Moore, Melody and Seane Corn. "How Yoga Brings Healing to Those who Struggle with Negative Body Image and Disordered Eating." Telephone Workshop. July 28, 2015.

Ng, Michelle. "Drawing the Line Between Eating Healthily and Being Obsessed with Healthy Eating: A Chat with Kaila Prins (Part One)." *I am #FedUpWithFood*. Accessed October 19, 2015. https://iamfedupwithfood.wordpress.com/2015/10/15/a-chat-with-kaila-prins-ex-orthorexia-sufferer-turned-wellness-coach/.

Nicolosi, Guido. "'Orthorexic Society' and Media Narrations: Advertising and Food Labelling." *EurSafeNews* 9, no. 1 (2007): 8–11.

Park, Crystal L, Tosca Braun, and Tamar Siegel. "Who Practices Yoga? A Systemic Review of Demographic, Health-Related, and Psychosocial Factors Associated with Yoga Practice." *Journal of Behavioral Medicine* 38, no. 3 (2015): 460–71.

Rangel, Cristian, Steven Dukeshire, and Letitia MacDonald. "Diet and Anxiety: An Exploration into the Orthorexic Society." *Appetite* 58 (2012): 124–32.

Roff, Chelsea. "Starved For Connection: Healing Anorexia Through Yoga," in *21st Century Yoga: Culture, Politics, and Practice*. Edited by Carol Horton and Roseanne Harvey (Chicago: Kleio Books, 2012) 73–94.

Roff, Chelsea. "Yoga's Shadow Side." *Yoga Journal*, October 2014, 96-99, 113–18.

Segura-Garcia, Cristina, Carla Ramacciotti, Marianna Rania, Matteo Aloi, Mariarita Caroleo, Antonella Bruni, Denise Gazzarrini, Flora Sinopoli, and Pasquale De Fazio. "The Prevalence of Orthorexia Nervosa Among Eating Disorder Patients After Treatment." *Eating and Weight Disorders* 20 (2015): 161–66.

Sinh, Pancham, trans. *Hatha Yoga Pradipika*. Accessed November 28, 2015. http://sacred-texts.com/hin/hyp/index.htm.

Squire, Sarah. "The Personal and the Political: Writing the Theorist's Body." *Australian Feminist Studies* 17, no. 37 (2002): 55–64.

YogaDork. "Yoga Magazine Slammed for Encouraging Eating Disorders in How-To Article." *YogaDork*. Accessed November 7, 2015. http://yogadork.com/2015/05/12/yoga-magazine-slammed-for-encouraging-eating-disorders-in-how-to-article/

NINE

Naked Yoga and the Sexualization of *Asana*

Sarah Schrank

This essay considers the current popularity of naked yoga classes in the United States as an expressive desire to liberate the body and experience a more natural physical self but also as a troubling symptom of the sexualization of the body within contemporary yoga culture. Naked yoga is generally practiced in mixed-gender groups, although sometimes in single-sex classes, and is often organized through social networking sites such as Facebook and Meetup. Naked yoga classes can be exhilarating bonding experiences but can also leave practitioners, and especially women, open to competitive body scrutiny and unwelcome sexual overtures. Moreover, naked yoga's online imagery is disconcertingly close to pornography, with its artificially enhanced bodies and keen eye for exposed genitalia.

As beauty standards rigidify, and the pathologizing of the body becomes commonplace in our national discourse about health care access, ageing, fitness, and "fatness," many Americans across class and ethnic lines have been seeking sanctuary from the relentless judgment of how they look, eat, and move. This anxiety is exacerbated by our current culture of "wellness," which makes caring for body and mind a personal issue rather than a publicly supported concern.[1] The desire to escape our intensified body fetishism, an unpleasant byproduct of advanced capitalism and contemporary globalization, partly explains the rapid expansion of the American yoga market in the past twenty years.[2] The nature of consumer economics has increasingly made yoga a commercial enterprise with the same strategic niche appeal as any other commodity. As enterprising yogis trademark competing products like AcroYoga®, Core-PowerYoga®, YogaFit®, BROga®, and YogaLean®, the commodification and sexual objectification of the body within yoga culture intensifies.

Our bodies have become so laden with signifiers of status, sexuality, and consumer possibility that it is quite easy to feel simultaneously dissociated from our physical selves and obsessed with how our physical selves look and perform. Since neither bodies nor fashion trends are stable, shaping and reshaping ourselves can feel like a relentless obligation to meet an ever-elusive goal. The weight of this pressure is especially pronounced for women, who have been taught since the nineteenth-century beginnings of urban-industrial capitalism that access to the public sphere came with patriarchal and misogynistic expectations that their bodies' physical appearance and presumed sexual availability were key gauges of character and social standing.

In the United States, of course, capitalism's commodification and objectification of the body also has deep roots in the institution of slavery. Its racist legacies overtly sexualized women of color and have made the black female body a particular object of social scrutiny and fetishized desire. As bell hooks wrote in the early 1990s, "representations of black female bodies in contemporary popular culture rarely subvert or critique images of black female sexuality which were part of the cultural apparatus of nineteenth-century racism and which still shape perceptions today."[3] In their work on the experience of black women in 1920s urban America, Hazel Carby and Cheryl Hicks document that the mere presence of African American women in the public sphere could mark their bodies as sexually available or socially degenerate, thus subjecting them to harassment, assault, and even incarceration.[4] White women were never subject to the same type of racialized surveillance but the combination of late-Victorian gender ideologies about separate spheres and sexual purity (especially for wealthy women), and a lack of any political power, also made their public presence at the turn of the twentieth century fraught with sexual overtones. The sexual objectification of working-class women was further complicated by new patterns of courtship (dating) that mingled sexual possibility with the treats of the consumer economy.

With the historically entrenched categories of race, class, and gender playing such key roles in the sexual objectification of the female body in the United States, it is not surprising that yoga, with its emphases on the present, the mind-body connection, and paths to enlightened being, would have held such appeal for American women, from Swami Vivekenanda's first crowded lectures in the 1890s to the present-day yoga studio. But yoga, like most things, is imperfect and its very embodiment, which offers such joy and release to so many, can also tether us to expectations of physical prowess, beauty, and sexual attractiveness that counteract yoga's most blissful effects.

The uncomfortable relationship between sex and yoga has surfaced recently in disturbing media scandals about abusive student-guru relationships, sexual harassment, and rape within international yoga schools, as well as in feminist scholarship critiquing contemporary yoga's objectification of young, white women and exclusion of women of color. The commodification and concomitant sexualization of *asana* (physical postures) is interpreted as a problematic deviation from yoga's meditative origins, its healing potential as a therapeutic tool for body and spirit, and the presumed goals of community, enlightenment, and embodied self-acceptance. The website Yoganonymous' ongoing discussion about the prevalence of online "selfies" that privilege the extraordinarily fit, young, and nimble is one example, as is the criticism of former model-turned-yoga-teacher Tara Stiles for her emphasis on the body beautiful in her bestselling book *Slim Calm Sexy Yoga*.[5] Judith Hanson Lasater, founding co-editor of *Yoga Journal*, made waves in 2010 when she publicly criticized the current incarnation of the magazine for using sex to sell yoga: "I am confused because I do not understand how photos of naked or half-naked women are connected with the sale of practice products for *asana*, an important part of yoga. These pictures do not teach the viewer about yoga practice or themselves. They aren't even about the celebration of the beauty of the human body or the beauty of the poses, which I support. These ads are just about selling a product."[6]

While yoga is held up as a spiritual and meditative practice that transcends material and physical desires, it has had a long and conflicted relationship with human sexuality. Anthropologist of religion Joseph S. Alter explains, "until the beginning of the twentieth century—and in sharp contrast to what it has become over the course of the past hundred years—hatha yoga was magical, mystical, structured with reference to the physiology of sex, and concerned with embodied immortality. It was inherently physiological rather than metaphysical, even in its most philosophical articulation."[7] Yoga's physicality was inherent to its practice, as well as the cosmology that supported it, so much so that Alter argues "yoga fetishizes the body as a whole and parts of the body in relation to one another."[8]

This argument is echoed in the now classic essay "Sex and Yoga: Psychoanalysis and the Indian Religious Experience," in which J. L. Masson argues that the very physicality intrinsic to yoga harbors the contradictions of desire and transcendence: "Hence yoga is unhappy with the body, and at the same time, all Yogins are obsessed with the body and its products. So we find that the . . . Tantrics have various ceremonies that involve sexual intercourse, but that the sexual content [of] such activities can be consciously denied because of the fact that they take place in a ritual context."[9] In short, sexuality and its denial, whether explicit or subliminal, *and* the fetishization of the body are deeply interwoven into the corporeality of *asana* practice. In our contemporary moment, this historical repudiation plays itself out as a dialectical tension between a yearning to link yoga seamlessly to a past, however checkered, in order to uphold its spiritual authenticity and the hope that tethering yoga to modern body culture will somehow transcend Western society's profound and paradoxical anxieties about sex. Naked yoga has the potential to address this tension by shedding the worst elements of our competitive body culture and encourage healthy intimacy; however, its overt corporeality sexualizes the space in which participants practice and clouds yogic interpretations of physicality and community. In jettisoning the markers of commodity fetishism by forgoing the clothing, jewelry, and decorative props ubiquitous in contemporary yoga culture, naked yoga also leaves the body bare and vulnerable.

In this essay, I argue that the expectation that yoga, unlike swimming or aerobics classes, for example, is a natural fit for a naked body practice has ancient origins in India and more recent historical roots in American social nudism dating back to the 1930s. Modern yoga and nudism emerged in the United States as closely coupled body practices harnessed to pursuits of health and natural living. I also argue that there is confusion within the current practice of naked yoga as to where the liberated body ends and the sexualized body begins, reflecting broader societal hang-ups about nudity and sex that yoga alone cannot remedy. The problem is less that yoga is an inappropriate site to work these issues out; rather, we are asking a lot of a body practice, albeit a sophisticated one, to resolve the social fallout of misogyny, the competitive scrutiny of capitalism, and body commodification.

A HISTORY OF YOGA AND NUDITY

An Internet search for naked yoga will get hundreds of hits, most of which fall into three categories: 1) pornography that uses naked yoga as the ruse to have sex on film (in the old days, it was pizza delivery or plumbing mishaps, but in today's marketplace, why not yoga?). Even when not showing explicit sex, these sites feature pornographic bodies, complete with airbrushed skin, surgically enhanced breasts, and hairless *mons pubis* in yoga positions highlighting these eroticized physical features. Cable networks and streaming services also feature naked yoga films, which are generally amateurish and focused on how many crotch shots can be crammed into a scene. *Natural and Nude Techniques*, available on Amazon Prime, is a case in point;[10] 2) sleekly marketed yoga studios that either offer regularly scheduled naked yoga classes or specialize in the genre, with celebrity teachers like New York's Aaron Star, who also runs a swift business in naked, and erotic, yoga videos. These studios are, for the most part, directed toward gay men and often restricted to male participants; and 3) women-friendly nude yoga classes that are usually mixed-gender and oriented toward yogis and yoginis interested in achieving an enhanced body-awareness and experiencing the physical freedom of nudity in a safe environment. These classes often claim deep roots in nude yoga's ancient tantric and sadhu traditions evoking nudity as the key to yogic authenticity and the sacred feminine.

Just like clothed yoga, which draws from myriad cultural traditions, Indian, European, and American, naked yoga has no one continuous route from the ancients to the present but neither is it a twenty-first century invention nor a consumer novelty. Digambara Jain monks, members of one of India's, indeed the world's, oldest religions, do not wear clothes and follow a series of vows and duties that resemble Patanjali's yamas and niyamas, the ethical commitments of yoga.[11] Dasnami ascetics, the naga sadhus, are holy men who live naked and are easily recognizable by their long dreadlocks and ash and paint-coated bodies.[12] To many British colonials in the nineteenth century, it was these naga (naked) ascetics who represented yoga, indeed, India, and appeared to be practitioners of a kind of black magic with their bodily contortions and seeming ability to live without food, water, or even air.[13] And it was Indian nationals in the early twentieth century who placed distance between the ascetics and modern *asana* practice in what would be a successful effort to "clean up" yoga for an international market, which, in the exchange of Eastern spirituality for Western capital, could challenge British colonialism.[14] Nudity was thus purposefully severed from the modern yoga practices that would leave India to find a welcome audience in the West, and particularly in the United States. But unlike the contemporary practice of naked yoga in the west, which aspires to liberate and encourage self-realization, Philip Carr-Gomm points out "the nakedness of the Jain saints [was] designed to demonstrate their renunciation of physical attachments and pleasures rather than their celebration."[15] Moreover, the Digambara Jains do not believe women can participate: "A woman cannot gain enlightenment because she cannot totally fulfill the vows of Aparigraha and Ahimsa since she is obliged to wear clothes. To achieve moksha she must reincarnate into a man's body that can then remain naked."[16] The goals and demography of contemporary naked yoga bear little resemblance to its Jain origins in deeply religious, celibate asceticism; nevertheless, it is useful to remember that nudity and yoga are intricately linked historically and that the very nakedness which draws sensational attention to the material body now originally signified a *renunciation* of material and sexual desires.

One of the earliest references to naked yoga in the United States is in a 1938 essay entitled "The Mental Element in Our Physical Well-Being" by Marguerite Agniel, a yoga enthusiast and author of the successful yoga guide *The Art of the Body: Rhythmic Exercises for Health and Beauty* (1931). Her essay, published in *The Nudist*, the flagship magazine for organized nudism in the United States, featured nude women in a variety of yoga postures along with Agniel's suggestions for focusing attention on breathing to improve concentration and foster a healthier relationship between one's thinking and spiritual selves.[17] The marriage of nudism and yoga made perfect sense: both were exercises in healthful living; both were countercultural and bohemian; both highlighted the body; and both were sensual without being explicitly erotic. Moreover, in both practices, the health and beauty of the body were paths to better living but not necessarily ends in themselves.

As Elizabeth De Michelis, Mark Singleton, and Stefanie Syman have documented, it was in the 1950s that modern yoga took shape as a popular physical practice in the United States and when it became especially attractive to female practitioners.[18] Fascination with the *Bhagavad Gita*, Hinduism, and the meditative benefits of *raja* yoga, of course, has a much earlier American history, going back to Ralph Waldo Emerson, Henry David Thoreau and the nineteenth-century intellectual and cosmological pursuits of the Transcendentalists.[19] The creative and elite vanguard of the 1920s and 1930s also experimented with yoga, following the teachings of such celebrities as the flamboyant guru Pierre Bernard, his handsome and serious nephew Theos, and the mystic leader Jiddu Krishnamurti, but it was in the wake of World War II that yoga *asanas* became a regularly practiced form of exercise.[20] Paramhansa Yogananda's wildly successful *Autobiography of a Yogi*, and his ingenious mail-order yoga courses, embedded yoga in American popular culture along with myriad other postwar consumer fads like paint-by-numbers and coonskin caps. And it was Indra Devi's Hollywood studio, famous clients, and bestselling publications like *Yoga For You* and *Forever Young, Forever Healthy* that solidified the physical practice of yoga in the postwar United States as a key to keeping fit, staying slender, and achieving an overarching sense of well-being, particularly for women.[21]

The 1950s were, in fact, ripe for anything Americans could interpret as a new kind of exercise; the decade was laden with messages generated by the federal government, U.S. military, and medical doctors that Americans were growing soft as a result of postwar prosperity. As Shelly McKenzie argues, freeways, car culture, and suburban homes full of conveniences and convenience foods were making Americans lethargic and overweight while a male business culture of cocktails, smoking, and stress was causing a lethal "cardiac crisis" with men in its sights. Together, doctors and Eishenhower's President's Council on Youth Fitness promoted physical exercise as a way not just to prevent soft bodies but also any political ideologies that might be "soft on communism."[22]

Women, of course, were also in the crosshairs of the new postwar fitness market. If they were to be good American suburban housewives and keep their husbands satisfied enough to return to the family home, they had better keep their girlish figures. Between Jack LaLanne's televised calisthenics and nutritional tips and Indra Devi's popular books and LPs for cultivating a home yoga practice, white, heterosexual, middle-class women were expected to be thin and in shape. While there were plenty of spurious gadgets on the fitness market in the 1950s (the electric slimming belt being one of the most famous), LaLanne's scissor kicks in leotards and Devi's clear directions for stretching, twisting, and balancing were inexpensive and easy to replicate. By the time white suburban housewives were practicing *suptabadacanasana* in their rumpus rooms, American yoga had been pretty much shorn of its spiritual and meditative qualities. It had also been feminized, but only to the extent that yoga was a conduit to shaping a sexually appealing female figure.

One of the most interesting cultural responses to the emphasis on health and fitness in the 1950s, not to mention the decade's fascination with sex, was social nudism. With its American origins going back to Kurt Barthel's 1929 nudist retreat in upstate New York, by the postwar period the American Sunbathing Association had thousands of members and hundreds of nudist clubs and colonies located all over the country. An effort to promote natural living and escape from a prurient sexual fascination with the body, American nudism had its golden age in the fifties as cars and leisure time allowed for travel while lengthy court battles over the legality of private nudist camps were finally won. And as prefab suburban homes and tract housing swept over the landscape, nudists also began reshaping their houses and living areas to allow for year-round naked living that drew in sunlight but protected residents from their neighbors' suspicious gaze.[23] These cheap DIY nudist homes were invisible to the public eye but celebrated in nudist magazines where photographs and design plans were shared and traded.[24] It was also in these very magazines that American nudists learned about yoga, expanding their quest for health and well-being; in suburbia, nudism and yoga came together as a syncretic modernist exercise in natural living through the body.

By the early 1960s, yoga was a regular feature in *Sunshine and Health*, a later incarnation of *The Nudist*. Ads for a mail-order "Yogism Course" promised "power is the secret of success. In Yogism, now adapted to needs of Western Man, is the power you've always wanted! Banish anxiety, worry, fear, and frustration! Take vitality from the air . . . cleanse mind and body of defeatist poison. . . . Strengthen your spine and nervous system, control your emotions." For twenty-five cents, an interested reader could order Lesson 1 from the Insight School.[25] A 1961 *Sunshine and Health* pictorial displayed women practicing yoga poses at a nudist camp while a 1962 issue of *Nude Living*, which featured an interview with architect Richard Neutra, made a point of explaining that the interviewer, Audre Hardy, was a nudist and a practitioner of "Hindu yoga."[26] In each of these examples, what was foregrounded was *not* that yoga needed to be practiced naked to be beneficial but rather that yoga's meditative and physical tools had a sympathetic overlap with nudism's goals of health, mental and emotional well-being, and progressive social change through a corporeal practice.

Yoga and nudity became more intrinsically entwined with sex in the 1970s when yoga became an integral part of the Human Potential Movement, a new age outgrowth of both the counterculture and popular psychology that taught that ultimate happiness and fulfillment could be reached through the self-actualization of one's true talents and desires. In 1972, Malcolm Leigh published a short, heavily illustrated guide to postural yoga featuring nude women and, in 1974, the short film, *Naked Yoga*, written and directed by Paul Corsden, fully captured the aesthetics of new age yoga nudity, with gelled lenses creating a psychedelic aura, flowing water, and ethereal female yogis evoking the early twentieth-century nymphs of Fidus fame.[27] A German symbolist painter and practicing Theosophist, Fidus (Hugo Reinhold Karl Johann Höppener, 1868–1948) depicted a phantasmagoric *art nouveau* world of nudity, sex, and nature popular with early nudists and yogis in Europe and, later, the American counterculture.

The most famous institution grounded in the credo of human potential was Esalen in northern California's Big Sur, where naked yoga classes have been led since the 1960s, but Elysium, a nudist colony in Los Angeles' Topanga Canyon, was another key site for what the founder Ed Lange called a "Human Awareness Growth Center."[28] Opened in 1968 and surviving for over thirty years, Elysium featured, along with its clothing-optional grounds, amenities, and accommodations, a rich catalog of self-help seminars and workshops that delved into yoga, group massage, touch therapy, meditation, and sexual health.[29] Yoga, like every other activity, could be practiced nude or clothed but, unlike the yoga described in *Sunshine and Health*, at Elysium, many of yoga's benefits were tied to its nakedness. To reach one's full potential, one had to be comfortable in one's skin and the key was to allow oneself to feel vulnerable and absorb the vulnerability of others. While some of Elysium's yoga offerings suggested that participants would be more comfortable wearing clothing, others, like "Energy, Breath, and Movement" and "The Body Learning Workshop," were purposefully naked and promised "through a process of sensory awareness, therapeutic touch and gentle movement exercises, the learner will have the opportunity to answer questions regarding sexuality, healing, stress, pain, and the connection between mind and body."[30] No one who attended these classes expected to have sex, or if they did, they were sorely disappointed. What the Elysium workshops did do, however, was integrate nudity and yoga in ways that expressly promoted healthier sexuality through mind-body awareness. Nakedness, and the sensuality it generated, was thus integral to the yoga practice of this new age context.

NAKED YOGA IN THE CONTEMPORARY UNITED STATES

However popular yoga may have been with suburban housewives in the 1950s and hippies in the 1960s, there has been no precedent for the main-streaming and mass marketing of yoga in the twenty-first century. Yoga is now a multibillion dollar industry that has been assimilated into medi-cal, therapeutic, fitness, and fashion cultures in ways unimaginable a generation ago. Why yoga has become such an economic juggernaut and hugely popular cultural trend is widely debated but the major reasons can be tied to innovations in yoga marketing specifically and broad de-velopments in globalized lifestyle and wellness consumerism more gen-erally. As the body increasingly carries the status signifiers of wealth, health, and well-being, yoga has proven an exceptionally malleable com-modity: a marker of urban hipness, a badge of alternative lifestyle pur-suits, a sign of socially progressive political leanings, evidence of a spiri-tual quest, and a ticket to fitness. A Marxist cultural analysis of the body under global capitalism would suggest that our social relations have be-come so tied to commodity consumption, and their concomitant signifi-ers, that we have completely naturalized the labeling of the body. We derive "common sense" from how people look no matter how hard we work and how much we spend to produce a desirable body.[31] Yoga, both as corporeal practice and a commodity, also naturalizes these relation-ships, which can be hierarchical and unjust. Indeed, yoga's prevailing link to physical fitness makes it difficult to separate from the surveillance and categorization, indeed, fetishization, of bodies in American culture.

Yet, despite their concerns about contemporary yoga's privileging, and marketing, of young, fit, white, and thin female bodies, feminist scholars, yogis, and activists alike also see yoga as liberating and empow-ering, and the disproportionate number of women in yoga classes cer-tainly upholds that view. While we cannot escape the essential embodi-ment of the yoga experience, we can use it to challenge restrictive societal norms and take our bodies back.[32] As the medical socialist Gayle Sulik argues, "corporeality is entangled in culture and biology, meaning and substance, identity and lived experience, mind and matter. Yoga can be a window into these varied dimensions of feminist conceptualization."[33]

As tightly tied to a global consumer marketplace as they may be, yogis, and their pursuits, are sincere. In *Selling Yoga: Counterculture to Pop Culture*, Andrea Jain argues that the economics of yoga has not necessari-ly altered the importance of *asana* for modern yogis: "[P]ostural yoga systems, in all of their various manifestations, cannot be judged as au-thentic or inauthentic relative to one another or to ancient or so-called classical yoga traditions. They must be understood in terms of the collec-tive and divergent meanings and functions their practitioners attribute to them. According to the history of postural yoga, these include the sacral-ization of the body, the mystic-erotic union with divinity, pleasure, the path to self-actualization or self-realization, as well as modern notions of health, beauty, sex appeal, and fitness."[34] These are certainly contradictions few serious yogis can fail to notice since narcissism, immodesty, competition, and profit fly in the face of yoga's most cherished ethics. Yet challenges to the commercialism bloom in communities all over the United States including free yoga classes in local parks and beaches, donation-only studios, and organizations like the Yoga and Body Image Coalition and Off the Mat, Into the World, which encourage the application of yoga principles to social and economic ills. I would argue that the contemporary practice of naked yoga also serves to challenge the commercialism and sexism of modern *asana* practice but, as I've established above, naked yoga's sensuality and hyper-corporeality makes it more complicated than a simple stripping of yoga's flashy trappings.

The naked yoga studio that has received the most press is New York City's Bold and Naked, founded by Joschi Schwartz and Monika Werner. Offering coed, male-only, and tantric massage classes, Bold and Naked's website states that "naked yoga changes and reshapes your muscles and gives them more endurance and flexibility, but you will agree, one of the coolest things about it is that it changes your perception and understanding of your own body. Join us and have fun! Pierce the illusion of whatever holds you back to reveal that you can accept, appreciate and celebrate yourself."[35] Perusing the studio's website and accompanying blog, it is clear that Bold and Naked is positioning itself as a serious yoga center for studying meditation and yoga philosophy, while simultaneously exploring varied elements of human sexuality. Bold and Naked's owners are also actively focused on attracting gay men to the studio. While the nudity of their classes is not supposed to be about sex—rather, "it's about being comfortable in your own skin and the amazing confidence that comes with it"—the studio explicitly promotes naked yoga as beneficial for sexual health.[36] Within the visual online context of Bold and Naked, a high-end urban yoga studio, being naked is sexy and the inherent promise of a Bold and Naked physical practice is a body that others will find sexually appealing. And the offerings of naked (male) tantric massage certainly drive home the point that feeling good in one's body is a sensual and erotic enterprise. Yet the Bold and Naked blog also puts forth a pretty straightforward feminist self-loving credo: "Part of yoga is to honor and connect with your body. Practicing yoga naked frees you from negative feelings about your body and allows you to be more accepting of your physical imperfections. You will find a deeper connection with yourself and the world around you."[37]

There is nothing wrong with Bold and Naked's yoga offerings; in fact, the studio's website and the press's positive coverage promise a safe, exciting, and athletic yoga experience that likely can go a long way to making yogis—male or female, queer or straight—feel good in their skin. My concern is that Bold and Naked's framing of yoga as both liberating and sexy is symptomatic of contradictory messages within contemporary popular culture that confuse liberated bodies (those that are free of signifiers, categories, judgments, and scrutiny; Bold and Naked even states it bluntly: "You can't do anything without being labeled")[38] with bodies that are sexually desirable. A key part of marketing *any* element of our body culture, whether fashion, fitness, or health, is tying the commodity to sex appeal, making the enterprise of body improvement fundamentally a narcissistic one. This process fetishizes the body, sublimating anxieties about sex, aging, and death, and instead foregrounds the body's desirability as the main signifier of successful socioeconomic relations. By making the body itself a commodity fetish, and not simply a vessel for selling other commodities, our cultural economy collapses the distinction between liberation and sex.[39] Of course, for many people, the two can be mutually inclusive, but they are not the same. For many women, for example, feeling liberated in one's flesh is to *not* feel sexualized. Feminist critics of beauty culture in the United States have debated for decades over whether or not participating in the consumer economy of beauty and the body allows the agency of choice or is simply an exercise in sublimation and gender oppression intrinsically tied to the body's sexual objectification.[40]

The conundrum for contemporary yoga is that it is presumed to be outside the sexual corporeal realm yet, as has been noted by many observers critical of how yoga is currently marketed, its popularity and growth as both a cultural movement and a consumer market is inherently tied to the body, both its perception and its performance. In the United States and, indeed, in most of our globalized world, it is increasingly difficult to untether the corporeal from the sexual. Yoga offers an opportunity to at least try, although yoga is itself subject to sexual fetishism, as is made evident in recent online posts about the sexiness of yoga pants, an uptick in labiaplasty to rid one of "camel toe," or the staging of Australian *Yoke* magazine's provocative cover of a young, topless female yogini posing in *uttanasana*, with her polka-dot underpants-clad posterior in the air.[41]

While Bold and Naked is an example of how contemporary yoga can combine sexuality and *asana*, other naked yoga classes and studios are more women-centered, less commercial, and less focused on athleticism and fitness. Their relationship to sex and the eroticized body, however, can vary. Katrina Rainsong is a performance artist, nudist, and model who teaches naked yoga classes in Scottsdale and Tempe, Arizona. Her branded practice R.A.W. Nude Yoga (the acronym standing for revealed, authentic, and wise) encourages us to think of our bodies as "living temples." She argues "to feel our own nudity in a non-sexual, non-medical construct can be new and very healing. To perceive other people's nudity in a non-sexual setting can be healing not only for the individual, but also for the collective."[42] In her artfully produced book *R.A.W. Nude Yoga:*

Celebrating the Human Body Temple, Rainsong features a combination of black and white photographs of male and female yogis, a brief, but thoughtful history of nude yoga, poetry, descriptions of the postures, and treatises on the significance of practicing nude. For example, she writes, "nude yoga allows your whole body to breathe; to feel the air on every inch of your skin. It allows you to indulge in your physical perceptions. And while it is sensual, it need not be erotic. In practice we consciously engage all of our senses, all of our chakras, our entire being."[43] In fact, the images are not erotic. The yogis are young, attractive, fit, and have extraordinarily glowing skin but Rainsong states in her introduction that the photographs have not been digitally altered or airbrushed; the people are real. The yoga postures are impressive and tastefully shot and the sense of empowerment emitted by the photographs is that of remarkable grace and physical control.

Megan Leigh Kobzeff, a protégé of Katrina Rainsong, also teaches naked yoga classes in Tempe. Twice a week, she leads a series called "Love the Skin You're In," a *yin* (gentle) yoga practice that is clothing optional for participants. With a more modest promotional style than that of Rainsong, Megan Leigh presents images of herself lying peacefully on the floor under a string of Tibetan prayer flags. With long dreadlocks, tattoos, and a beautiful Earth Mama physique, this naked yogini imparts a feeling of authentic pleasure in her own body and a yoga practice that approaches something natural and uninhibited. Rather than even evoking the issues of sex or sensuality, in an online interview, Megan Leigh states, "both practicing and teaching naked yoga have transformed me into a more body-positive and self-loving person. It is beautiful to see a group of people of varying body types, age groups, and cultures all feeling comfortable enough in their own skin to strip away their ego and their clothing."[44] Here, naked yoga really does seem healing. Fitness, the body beautiful, and sexual health are not part of the conversation in the way they are for Bold and Naked or even Katrina Rainsong's more women-focused practice.

MY NAKED YOGA EXPERIENCE IN LOS ANGELES, CALIFORNIA

Long before I ever knew I would be writing about naked yoga, I decided to attend a naked yoga class. For several years, I had been studying American nudist culture for a book on natural living and the body and had managed, over the previous decade, to rack up thousands of hours of regular *asana* practice; the articles and blogs I had seen on my feed about naked yoga ultimately piqued my curiosity about this peculiar nexus of my two main interests. I conducted online searches for naked yoga classes in the Los Angeles area but the ones I could find initially were too far away or male-only. Using Facebook, I contacted Katrina Rainsong, who I knew led coed naked classes in Arizona, and asked her where I could find similar classes near me. She made a couple of suggestions, including using Meetup, the social networking site, to find a group of like-minded yogis. Rainsong herself moderates who attends her own classes through email or personal references from students she already knows.[45] I followed her advice, joined Meetup, and quickly found a newly formed group of yogis who had just started holding naked classes at an art gallery and dance studio on Los Angeles' west side. Classes cost $25 for men, were free for "females," and promised a "sexy" female yoga teacher. The address would be provided once my Meetup profile was accepted and I could join the group.

Given how much I dislike the sexualization of my regular studio (to this day, I steer clear of gossip about which students are having sex with which teacher, or each other, and "Om" my way through any flirtations I prefer to avoid), it speaks to how badly I wanted to give naked yoga a try that I overlooked the glaring red flag of a yoga practice marketed as "ladies night." After a couple of emails via Meetup, which protects your anonymity, with the male organizer, I had the information I needed to attend. And so a couple of weeks later, I drove twenty-five miles to a busy part of Los Angeles for a 7:30 p.m. class. I got there early to secure a spot but found myself, and a few other yogis, loitering outside, mat rolled under arm, as the previous drawing class hadn't let out yet. As I was the only woman, other than the teacher, I felt awkward, looked-at, and unsure this was turning out to be the great idea I had envisioned. Further doubt crept in when I was asked if I would be able to bring any female friends with me to the next session. I said, "probably not," and quickly entered the studio as soon as the last art student left.

Once inside, I felt better. This was the type of space I'd been in a million times. Mirrors on one wall, flexible dance floor below my feet, track lighting, and a Bose stereo in the corner. The teacher set up her mat, I set up mine to face her, and the others set theirs up accordingly. By the time everyone showed up, there were probably ten of us altogether: three women, seven men. No one took their clothes off until the teacher instructed us to and at that point everyone grew very focused on her instructions. I didn't find being naked to be uncomfortable but I certainly felt compelled to stare at my mat. That strategy got a little messed up when we were all in downward-facing dog (*adho mukha svanasana*) with our heads looking back toward the mirror. At that point, it was impossible to look away and everything was on display. But the atmosphere was friendly, a bit silly, and I was delighted that my practice was so strong. When the class ended, and we were all pulling our jeans and t-shirts back on, I received many compliments about my dancer pose and kick-ass *chattaranga* push-ups and nary a comment about my body. I decided that this might actually be fun and promised to show up the following week.

For about two months, I regularly attended this class, which grew by a couple of yogis each time. By far, the majority were men but increasingly more women joined the group. Ages ranged from about twenty-five to fifty-five and the ethnic makeup reflected Los Angeles' own extraordinary diversity. White men and women made up about 40 percent of the class, there were several African American men and women who attended regularly, an equal number of Asian American men and women took part, as well as a few Latinas and mixed-race participants whose ethnicity was difficult to guess. To the best of my knowledge, there were no Latinos in attendance when I was there. Overall, the class consisted of a representative multiethnic cross-section of the city. There was a group of us regulars, who practiced together, while new attendees laid out their mats around our cluster. It was friendly; I made a point of introducing myself to everyone, especially new women, in an effort to keep up the good vibe we had been cultivating. For several weeks, this strategy worked. I found the physical practice to be easy compared to my usual hot vinyasa routine but the focused concentration was much more intense and the post-class endorphin rush was stronger than in a clothed class. I felt protected by my group of regular male attendees, who were respectful, polite, and overly worried about the safety of the walk to my car and my solo drive home. In true Los Angeles fashion, traffic was a frequent topic of conversation as everyone commuted a fair distance to get there. I told almost no one that I had taken up naked yoga and I enjoyed having a secret practice that brought me a lot of pleasure. What could go wrong?

By the time I attended what would be my last class, I had been feeling great about naked yoga. It made me feel good in my body, I liked the community I was helping to create, it felt a little risqué, and it was a way to feel sexy and attractive in a safe space without any sexual pressure. I felt adored by my little crew and I enjoyed programming the music and helping to set up the room. I fielded online inquiries about the class during the week and encouraged those who approached me through Meetup to give it a try. The whole thing, even the lengthy drive to get there and home, felt good. It was a new routine, something private and my own, and a nice distraction from a variety of unpleasant complications in my life at that time. Unfortunately, good things sometimes come to an end.

The last class I attended started badly. It was crowded, with easily twice as many people as usual, and with a number of new, young, female participants in their early twenties who were jockeying to get their mats as close to the young men as they could. I guessed this was what was happening when I was told a couple of times, rudely, to move my mat. In modern American yoga culture, there is a complex etiquette dedicated to personal space and mat placement. Shoving an experienced yogini out of the way so you can rub your stuff on the boy you think is hot is not part of it. To their credit, my older male friends in the class explained that this was "Sarah's spot," and offered to move their own mats to allow the women space. But, of course, that was not the issue. The young women wanted to be near the other young men, not my rotund middle-aged naked yoga buddies. Finally, I just asked the Alpha One cute guy who was causing the hubbub if he would shuffle his mat in such a way that would allow him an entourage of admirers while I could keep my spot. He agreed, mats were rearranged, and the class, mercifully, began.

Once underway, the class was fine, even if the room felt overcrowded, but I was bothered by what had happened at the beginning. It marked a significant change in the room's atmosphere and I realized that until that particular class, I had not experienced naked yoga as sexualized. Sexy, sure. But not sexualized in the sense that a sexual encounter was a natural outcome of practicing naked yoga next to someone or that a hypercorporeal experience, as naked yoga certainly is, had to be about sexual attractiveness. In fact, I had been enjoying naked yoga so much precisely because I felt brave, liberated, and appreciated, but not sexualized. I was annoyed by what I felt was a glitch in my routine but an important part of yoga is keeping the mind focused even while thoughts race and I decided to ignore the class's irritating start and work on my half-moon pose. Midway through a set of flowing postures, I felt a familiar tug and painful pinch near my right shoulder blade, the flaring of an old injury, and dialed it down until class ended.

As I got dressed as quickly as I could so I might make it home in time to put an icepack on my shoulder before it became a painful mess, a member of the class ran across the room to talk to me. It was a man, about my age, who had attended a couple of times, but who gave off bad vibes. I didn't like him and I definitely did not feel like talking to him. "I see you're rubbing your shoulder. I'm a massage therapist and might be able to help," he said, and reached over to press on my back with his right hand while his left hand grabbed my breast. I froze and just said, "Uh . . . no thanks. I've got a massage therapist." As I grabbed my mat and prepared to flee, he stuck his card in my hand and suggested I call him. I was so startled by the whole encounter, I put the card in my pocket and left the studio as fast as I could. Later that evening, I looked him up to see who had done the old "reach-around" and realized he was a pornographer. But lest I still not get the message that my naked yoga experience had nosedived, on the drive home, I received a Meetup text from another man in the class who, while not one of my buddies, was a regular. I knew his name, had chatted with him a couple of times, and had declined his invitation from a few weeks earlier to check out another yoga studio with him. This text, however, was sexually explicit, graphic, and, let's just say, a different kind of invitation. It was awful and I felt more violated by the text than by the groper. That night I yanked my Meetup profile, which prevented anyone from the naked yoga group from contacting me, and never returned to the class.

I have subsequently talked to friends about what happened, asking for thoughts on what changed, and why. This is not a scientific sampling by any means, but most women I tell express profound disappointment that an activity I had enjoyed and found empowering was now gone because it was unsafe, uncomfortable, and, frankly, sexist. The takeaway point was that I was not going to be allowed to show my body in a way I could control. If I wanted to practice yoga naked, with men, the message was clear that I was physically vulnerable, sexually available, and subject to assault. Male friends express surprise that I didn't have trouble earlier and have suggested that it was the sexualization of the space by the young women—the creation of an overtly sexually competitive environment—that sent up signals that the game was on.

The bad experience did not take away the pleasure I had taken in naked yoga before things went haywire and I would absolutely practice naked yoga again, but in a different environment, one more akin to what Katrina Rainsong and Megan Leigh offer in Arizona. I would prefer a more experienced teacher, a studio with dedicated nude classes, and a more women-oriented focus, although I would still be comfortable with men in the room. I would also want a class that addressed the relationship of yoga to nudism—one of the problems with the Meetup group is that I doubt anyone there knew much about either—and the rules of engagement, which are that there is a difference between nudity and sex and that certain behavior would not be tolerated. This is true at nudist camps, nude beaches, clothed yoga studios, and spas—it should be true in naked yoga.

The body exposed can be very empowering for women and men. As the social theorist, Donald M. Lowe has simply put it, "sexual energy is power."[46] This specific form of empowerment, in our globalized, late-capitalist world, is closely tied to patterns of consumption, the visual, sexualized power of advertising, and the objectification of the body. Because claiming the body as a site of personal empowerment is so difficult to then disentangle from the heightened expectations and scrutiny of our commodified body culture, naked yoga makes sense as a practice that promises to do just that: empower the self by severing ties to the social and sexual signifiers of clothing. The body, at its most vulnerable, can also be its most potent, self-actualized state. Yet, naked yoga, while challenging the sexual *materiality* of the body, cannot alone address the sexual *politics* of the body without a clear, consensual agenda incorporating the intersectionality of race, class, and gender. It is not sensible to rely on any body practice to do this for us, especially one that demands an individualistic and economically entitled position from its practitioners. Nevertheless, naked yoga does have tremendous experiential value for women and if practicing it can be the springboard for a positive body image, self-empowerment, or a new way to express a feminist consciousness, then it may be time to lose the yoga pants.

NOTES

1. Carl Cederström and André Spicer, *The Wellness Syndrome* (Cambridge, UK: Polity Press, 2015) and Charlotte Biltekoff, *Eating Right in America: The Cultural Politics of Food and Health* (Durham, NC: Duke University Press, 2013).

2. Jon Stratton, *The Desirable Body: Cultural Fetishism and the Erotics of Consumption* (Chicago: University of Illinois Press, 1996); Donald M. Lowe, *The Body in Late-Capitalist USA* (Durham and London: Duke University Press, 1995); and Mike Featherstone, "Body, Image, and Affect in Consumer Culture," *Body and Society* (March 2010), 193–221.

3. bell hooks, "Selling Hot Pussy: Representations of Black Female Sexuality in the Cultural Marketplace," in *Black Looks: Race and Representation* (Boston: South End Press, 1992) 114.

4. See Hazel Carby, "Policing the Black Woman's Body in an Urban Context," *Critical Inquiry* 18, no. 4 (Summer 1992): 738–55 and Cheryl Hicks, "'Bright and Good Looking Colored Girl': Black Women's Sexuality and 'Harmful Intimacy' in Early-Twentieth-Century New York," *Journal of the History of Sexuality* 18, no. 3 (September 2009): 418–56.

5. Tara Stiles, *Slim Calm Sexy Yoga: 210 Proven Yoga Moves for Mind/Body Bliss* (New York: Rodale Books, 2010); Lizette Alvarez, "Rebel Yoga," *New York Times*, January 21, 2011. YogaDork, "Tara Stiles Launches 'Slim, Calm, Sexy' Yoga to Acclaim, Insult, Revolt," August 31, 2011. Accessed August 17, 2015.

6. Judith Hanson Lasater, Letter to the Editor, *Yoga Journal*, September 2010.

7. Joseph S. Alter, "Yoga and Fetishism: Reflections on Marxist Social Theory," *The Journal of the Royal Anthropological Institute* 12, no. 4 (December 2006): 764.

8. Alter, "Yoga and Fetishism."

9. J. L. Masson, "Sex and Yoga: Psychoanalysis and the Indian Religious Experience," *Journal of Indian Philosophy* 2, no. 3 (March–June 1974): 312.

10. *Natural and Nude Yoga Techniques*. Dir. Optik Dave, 64 mins. 2005.

11. Philip Carr-Gomm, *A Brief History of Nakedness* (London: Reaktion Books, 2010); David Gordon White, *Sinister Yogis* (Chicago: University of Chicago Press, 2009).

12. James Mallinson, "Yogis in Mughal India," in *Yoga: The Art of Transformation* (Freer-Sackler: Smithsonian Institution, 2013), 76.

13. White, *Sinister Yogis*.

14. See White, *Sinister Yogis* and Sarah Strauss, *Positioning Yoga: Balancing Acts Across Cultures* (New York: Berg, 2005).

15. Carr-Gomm, *A Brief Histor of Nakedness*, 58.

16. Carr-Gomm, *A Brief History of Nakedness*, 59.

17. Marguerite Agniel, "The Mental Element in Our Physical Well-Being," *The Nudist: Sunshine and Health* 7, no. 6 (June 1938): 18–21.

18. Elizabeth De Michelis, *A History of Modern Yoga: Patañjali and Western Esotericism* (London and New York: Continuum, 2004); Mark Singleton, *Yoga Body: The Origins of Modern Posture Practice* (Oxford and New York: Oxford University Press, 2010); and Stefanie Syman, *The Subtle Body: The Story of Yoga in America* (New York: Farrar, Straus, and Giroux, 2010).

19. See Philip Goldberg, *American Veda: From Emerson and the Beatles to Yoga and Meditation—How Indian Spirituality Changed the West* (New York: Harmony Books, 2010).

20. See Goldberg and Robert Love, *The Great Oom: The Improbable Birth of Yoga in America* (New York: Viking, 2010).

21. Michelle Goldberg, *The Goddess Pose: The Audacious Life of Indra Devi, the Woman Who Helped Bring Yoga to the West* (New York: Alfred A. Knopf, 2015).

22. Shelly McKenzie, *Getting Physical: The Rise of Fitness Culture in America* (Lawrence: University Press of Kansas, 2013).

23. Sarah Schrank, "Naked Houses: The Architecture of Nudism and the Rethinking of the American Suburbs," *Journal of Urban History* 38, no. 4 (July 2012): 635–61.

24. Schrank, "Naked Houses."

25. Advertisement for the Insight School, Evanston, IL. *Sunshine and Health*, 29, no. 1 (January 1960): 3.

26. *Sunshine and Health* 30, no. 4 (April 1961): 23; *Nude Living* 1, no. 6 (April 1962), Richard and Dion Neutra Papers, Box 1476, Folder 14. Department of Special Collections, Charles Young Research Library, University of California, Los Angeles.

27. Malcolm Leigh, *Naked Yoga* (New York: New American Library, 1972) and *Naked Yoga*, dir. Paul Corsden. 24 mins. 1974.

28. Gary Mussell, "Remembering Elysium," 2011, 1. Southern California Naturist Association Archives, Moorpark, California.

29. Elysium Institute, "Ongoing Seminars," *Journal of the Senses*, no. 67 (Spring 1984): 26–42. Southern California Naturist Association Archives. Moorpark, California.

30. Elysium Institute, "Ongoing Seminars," 36.

31. Chris Shilling, *The Body in Culture, Technology, and Society* (London: Sage Publications, 2005) 35–37.

32. There is a growing feminist literature that addresses the potential of yoga for female empowerment and emotional, as well as physical healing. See Carol Horton and Roseanne Harvey, editors, *21st Century Yoga: Culture, Politics, and Practice* (Chicago: Kleio Books 2012); Melanie Klein and Anna Guest-Jelley, editors, *Yoga and Body Image: 25 Personal Stories about Beauty, Bravery, and Loving Your Body* (Woodbury, MN: Llewellyn Publications, 2014); and Carol A. Horton, *Yoga PhD: Integrating the Life of the Mind and the Wisdom of the Body* (Chicago: Kleio Books, 2012).

33. Gayle Sulik, "Yoga: A Window into Feminist Theories of the Body," *The Society Pages*, April 16, 2015. Accessed October 3, 2015.

34. Andrea R. Jain, *Selling Yoga: From Counterculture to Pop Culture* (Oxford and New York: Oxford University Press, 2015) 173.

35. Bold and Naked Studio. http://boldnaked.com/. Accessed July 5, 2015.

36. Bold and Naked Studio.

37. Bold and Naked Blog. http://boldnaked.com/mag/why-naked/. Accessed July 28, 2015.

38. Bold and Naked Blog.

39. For more on the commodification of the body and the commodity fetish, see *The Desirable Body*, 25–57.

40. Sheila Jeffreys, *Beauty and Misogyny: Harmful Cultural Practices in the West* (London and New York: Routledge, 2005) 5–10.

41. *Yoke Magazine*, Issue 02: Balance, 2014. Cover image.

42. Katrina "Rainsong" Messenger, *R.A.W. Nude Yoga: Celebrating the Human Body Temple* (Phoenix: Bridgewood Press, 2013) 8.

43. Messenger, *R.A.W. Nude Yoga*, 9.

44. Naked Yoga Alliance, *Interview with Megan Leigh*, June 5, 2015. Accessed July 1, 2015.

45. Leslie K. Hughes, "Nude Yoga Classes Catch On In Valley," *AZ Big Media*, June 11, 2014. Accessed July 28, 2015.

46. Lowe, *The Body in Late-Capitalist USA*, 133.

REFERENCES

Agniel, Marguerite. "The Mental Element in Our Physical Well-Being," *The Nudist: Sunshine and Health 7*, no. 6 (June 1938): 18–21.

Alter, Joseph S. "Yoga and Fetishism: Reflections on Marxist Social Theory," *The Journal of the Royal Anthropological Institute* 12, no. 4 (December 2006): 763–83.

Biltekoff, Charlotte. *Eating Right in America: The Cultural Politics of Food and Health* (Durham, NC: Duke University Press, 2013).

Carby, Hazel. "Policing the Black Woman's Body in an Urban Context," *Critical Inquiry* 18, no. 4 (Summer 1992): 738–55.

Carr-Gomm, Philip. *A Brief History of Nakedness* (London: Reaktion Books, 2010).

Cederström, Carl and André Spicer. *The Wellness Syndrome* (Cambridge, UK: Polity Press, 2015).

De Michelis, Elizabeth. *A History of Modern Yoga: Patañjali and Western Esotericism* (London and New York: Continuum, 2004).

Featherstone, Mike. "Body, Image, and Affect in Consumer Culture," *Body and Society* (March 2010): 193–221.

Goldberg, Michelle. *The Goddess Pose: The Audacious Life of Indra Devi, the Woman Who Helped Bring Yoga to the West* (New York: Alfred A. Knopf, 2015).

Goldberg, Philip. *American Veda: From Emerson and the Beatles to Yoga and Meditation— How Indian Spirituality Changed the West* (New York: Harmony Books, 2010).

Hicks, Cheryl. "'Bright and Good Looking Colored Girl': Black Women's Sexuality and 'Harmful Intimacy' in Early-Twentieth-Century New York," *Journal of the History of Sexuality* 18, no. 3 (September 2009): 418–56.

hooks, bell. "Selling Hot Pussy: Representations of Black Female Sexuality in the Cultural Marketplace," *Black Looks: Race and Representation* (oston: South End Press, 1992) 113–28.

Horton, Carol A. *Yoga PhD: Integrating the Life of the Mind and the Wisdom of the Body* (Chicago: Kleio Books, 2012).

Horton, Carol and Roseanne Harvey, eds. *21st Century Yoga: Culture, Politics, and Practice* (Chicago: Kleio Books 2012).

Jain, Andrea R. *Selling Yoga: From Counterculture to Pop Culture* (Oxford and New York: Oxford University Press, 2015).

Jeffreys, Sheila. *Beauty and Misogyny: Harmful Cultural Practices in the West* (London and New York: Routledge, 2005).

Klein, Melanie and Anna Guest-Jelley, eds, *Yoga and Body Image: 25 Personal Stories about Beauty, Bravery, and Loving Your Body* (Woodbury, MN: Llewellyn Publications, 2014).

Leigh, Malcolm. *Naked Yoga* (New York: New American Library, 1972).

Love, Robert. *The Great Oom: The Improbable Birth of Yoga in America* (New York: Viking, 2010).

Lowe, Donald M. *The Body in Late-Capitalist USA* (Durham and London: Duke University Press, 1995).

Mallinson, James. "Yogis in Mughal India," in *Yoga: The Art of Transformation* (Freer-Sackler: Smithsonian Institution, 2013) 69–83.

Masson, J. L. "Sex and Yoga: Psychoanalysis and the Indian Religious Experience," *Journal of Indian Philosophy* 2, no. 3 (March–June 1974): 307–20.

McKenzie, Shelly. *Getting Physical: The Rise of Fitness Culture in America* (Lawrence: University Press of Kansas, 2013).

Messenger, Katrina "Rainsong." *R.A.W. Nude Yoga: Celebrating the Human Body Temple* (Phoenix: Bridgewood Press, 2013).

Schrank, Sarah. "Naked Houses: The Architecture of Nudism and the Rethinking of the American Suburbs," *Journal of Urban History* 38, no. 4 (July 2012): 635–61.

Shilling, Chris. *The Body in Culture, Technology, and Society* (London: Sage Publications, 2005).

Singleton, Mark. *Yoga Body: The Origins of Modern Posture Practice* (Oxford and New York: Oxford University Press, 2010).

Stiles, Tara. *Slim Calm Sexy Yoga: 210 Proven Yoga Moves for Mind/Body Bliss* (New York: Rodale Books, 2010).

Stratton, Jon. *The Desirable Body: Cultural Fetishism and the Erotics of Consumption* (Chicago: University of Illinois Press, 1996).

Strauss, Sarah. *Positioning Yoga: Balancing Acts Across Cultures* (New York: Berg, 2005).

Syman, Stefanie. *The Subtle Body: The Story of Yoga in America* (New York: Farrar, Straus, and Giroux, 2010).

White, David Gordon. *Sinister Yogis* (Chicago: University of Chicago Press, 2009).

TEN

Reblog If You Feel Me

Love, Blackness, and Digital Wellness

Maria Velazquez

In 2014, an article in *The Nation* on "Feminism's Toxic Twitter Wars"[1] instigated a larger conversation among black feminists working in and outside of the academy on the role academics should take in online feminist conversations. Some black feminist bloggers, such as Dr. Brittney Cooper of *Crunk Feminist Collective*, described the role many white feminists have taken in both erasing the theoretical contributions of feminist women of color working online,[2] and reducing the importance of the collaborative works produced by multi-ethnic feminist collectives, such as the #femfuture report, to a mere anomaly.[3] At the same time that this public, online conversation among prominent black feminists came to a head, *XOJane* published "There Are No Black People In My Yoga Class and I'm Suddenly Feeling Uncomfortable With It."[4] Written by a white woman, this "It Happened to Me" article struck a peculiar, racist, and voyeuristic note as the author speculated about the emotional well-being of an overweight black woman she observed in her yoga class. Shocked, she realized that part of her discomfort was the introduction of a visceral and unruly blackness in her sacred yogic space.

The online response[5] to this post by yoga students, practitioners, and teachers of color was vocal and immediate. These responses incorporated circulating images of black and brown women practicing yoga through micro-blogging platforms such as Tumblr, referencing online memes, and reflecting extensively on yoga as a culturally appropriative example of mind/body work that is itself imagined as racially exclusive.[6] Using humor and honesty, these responses lambasted a progressive mind/body practice whose practitioners ignored the realities of racism, classism, and imperialism framing the American experience of yoga.

Yoga may seem like an odd way to explore digital activism and wellness. However, stories like this showcase the "missing steps"[7] in the utopian fantasy of the digital commons, demonstrating how these discursive absences create an unbridgeable gap in the stepping-stone process of addressing racism, misogynoir,[8] and colonialism in ostensibly safe spaces. It's important to recognize that the erasure the *XOJane* piece demonstrated is two-fold. First, the publication of this article dismisses the possibility of black women as an online audience, able to read, respond, and object to a think-piece that centered whiteness as a normative gaze. Second, it reiterates the misogynistic and racist stereotype that black women are unconcerned with wellness. This two-pronged attack on black women's technological fluency and embodiment is not only untrue, it dismisses that "fitness is another area where black women have created something new in the absence of others caring about what they need."[9] This something new developed online.

CROWDSOURCING SELF-LOVE: BLACK WOMEN
AND WELLNESS ONLINE

During the 1990s and early 2000s, sites like MotownGirl.com, Carol's Daughter, the Long Hair Care Forum, and BlackGirlLongHair began circulating images of black women loving their bodies and their blackness — hrough yoga, natural hair care products, meditation, and crafts. This mingling of spirituality, handicrafts, and political resistance reflected the long history of black wellness practices in the United States, where "acts of healing became arts of resistance, inscribing the vital link between personal health and collective freedom."[10] The creators of these black holistic health websites suggested that this leisure-based resistance was especially critical to *black women's* survival — loving ourselves, healing our souls, and relishing our bodies — had become a matter of life and death. The very breath we breathed was in danger because of our literal weight[11] and our shared metaphysical[12] burden of racist histories and cultural erasure.

In *Body Language*, Kimberly Lau argues that organizations like Sisters in Shape and other black women's wellness groups make a specific kind of claim to identity politics.[13] This claim complicates both race and gender, using a "health and exercise project for black women [to act as] a community, a culture, and a movement."[14] In particular, when connecting black women's emotional and physical wellness to a sense of black community, shared cultural mythos, such as the stereotype of the strong black woman, are reshaped into an engagement with "the black woman's

strong body."[15] This reimagining of black women's strength as an investment in self-care, wellness, and health "represent[s] a mode of cultural
activism and open[s] up new ways of imagining the strong black woman."[16] Here, I build on Tara Brabazon's article "Fitness is a Feminist Issue," in which she highlights the fact that "[t]o move fitness beyond the
self-help discourse, *self making* must transform into *sense making*."[17] This
is in part the mission of blogs like *The Black Girl's Guide to Weight Loss*,
where Erika Kendall writes,

> Why do I write this for you? Because I, along with every other Black
> woman who has even a passing interest in fitness, can relate. It's what
> we go through every day, and I think it's only fair that I address you
> and your concerns in a way we wish ours were addressed. . . . The
> reason my blog carries the title it does is not because it is a guide to
> weight loss for Black girls; it is a guide to weight loss by a Black girl.[18]

Kendall's explicit engagement with race and racism is reflected in her
posts on eating disorders, black women's experiences of sexual harassment, her reflections on the controversy regarding Michelle Obama's
booty, and her analysis of the editing of Shirley Sherrod's NAACP speech
on black farmers. Kendall's blog has been largely embraced in the black
blogosphere, garnering praise from *Afrobella* and *Black Enterprise*.[19] She
has also contributed to *Madame Noire,* another beauty and lifestyle blog
focused on black women. Tracing the movement of *A Black Girl's Guide to
Weight Loss* provides an opportunity to reflect critically on the web of
connections in which anti-racist, anti-sexist discourse "moves" online.
Kendall, and the "web of connections"[20] with which she participates,
creates a forum for a conversation that explicitly links wellness to political wellbeing and human rights.

In order to analyze these, I offer the concept of a digital praxis of love.
This concept incorporates the idea of *praxis* as a mingling reflection and
action directed toward infrastructural or social change, as well as *digital*
to reflect the branching of the technological, material, and imaginative
worlds of the online activist. *Love* emphasizes the role of affect in propel-
ling these projects forward. What I found attractive about this idea is that
it provides an analytical framework for the labor fans and bloggers do for
free, an analysis that moves beyond the curator/creator framework offered by the PEW Research Center's work on Internet use. I look at gifsets
and image manipulations in order to trouble the easy divide between
curator/creator, to highlight an evolving conversation on race and wellness. These virtual and material labors of love—blogging projects, metasites collecting historical research, and Tumblrs blurring the line between
the personal and the political—often participate in larger social justice
movements centered around body positivity, wellness, and well-being.
Blogging, image-making, and participating in online discussions are

ways to stretch those few hours in the studio into something longer, something both more tangible and more ephemeral.

The rise and development of websites, blogs, and forums created to share information about natural hair and holistic pampering created a space where black women began exchanging wellness tips that incorporated yoga and meditation as part of a critical aesthetics that centered *feeling good* as a criteria for evaluating wellness. Picking up the lost strands of "black is beautiful," these online communities combined an acute awareness of race, racism, and the impact infrastructural oppression has on black women's health with a conscious commitment to critical aesthetics as self-care. In the following section, I present a brief history of black wellness as an embodied form of resistance in order to situate the political significance of this online work.

DEFINING WELLNESS DURING A #BLACKOUT

I link the histories of bodily transcendence, cultural survival, and technology in order to connect the rise of public, accessible scholarship centering the experiences of marginalized subjects with the exhortation to *feel good*. In particular, I engage the movement of images associated with wellness, self-care, and cultural survival, focusing on their connections to anti-racist and anti-sexist conversations online. In doing so, I illustrate the continued salience of the body in the age of the digital as a signifier of identity and labor. The 2014 *XOJane* article "It Happened To Me: There Are No Black People In My Yoga Classes And I'm Suddenly Feeling Uncomfortable With It," incited a series of online conversations about black women, white privilege, and yoga, many of which incorporated images of black women engaged in yoga or other movement-based wellness practices. The author of this *XOJane* article literally could not imagine a fat black woman loving her body or doing yoga. While the author's ignorance is hilarious, her shock over the presence of a black woman in her yoga class as well as her apparently sincere surprise that black women read stuff online illustrates that blogging about wellness blurs into blogging about embodiment and politics. In this section, I offer a definition of wellness and situate that definition in a larger history of black wellness in the United States.

I define "wellness" as multifaceted, incorporating individual agency, physical health, mental health, a sense of physical well-being, and a sense of social well-being. This definition draws on *Body & Soul: The Black Women's Guide to Physical Health and Emotional Well-Being* by Linda Villarosa and the National Black Women's Health Project; the universal definition suggested by the President's Council on Physical Fitness and Sports; and Angela Hissong's "Feminist Philosophy: A Beginning Point for Adult Educators Promoting Women's Wellness Education." Even though it is a contested term because of its association with alternative medicine, I use the term "wellness" instead of "fitness" because of its conceptual emphasis on individual agency, self-care, and ownership of one's bodily autonomy. Fitness is typically defined as "strength, flexibility, and stamina,"[21] incorporating metabolic, cardiovascular, and body composition.[22] In contrast, wellness is a state of being, and the sum total of many aspects of the individual's life. Fitness focuses solely on the body, giving little attention to psychological, emotional, and social well-being, but each of these elements is incorporated into the concept of wellness.

This definition of wellness is particularly useful because its emphasis on agency and bodily autonomy is a direct contrast to the antebellum concept of "soundness."[23] "The marriage of professional medicine and slavery put a price on black health" and explicitly tied the fitness of black bodies to their ability to labor and not to the quality of their lives.[24] A slave who was declared "sound" by a doctor was more marketable; some slaves would do what they could to make themselves "unsound" in order to avoid being sold away from their families. In contrast to this focus on labor and value, black wellness practitioners, often women, treated physical ailments as part and parcel of a broader network of possible psychic, spiritual, and social ills, any of which could influence the unwell person's material being. This conscious willingness to love and care for black bodies, selves, and relationships directly contrasted with the cruelty of slave owners and the indifference of white medical practitioners.

After Emancipation, the political and social struggles over black bodies, definitions of black health, and the political significance of *feeling well* continued. Black middle-class women's participation in the growth of the YWCA continued this trend; creating a safe space for black women to play tennis and swim also entailed providing moral guidance from community leaders.[25] Unfortunately, much of the history surrounding black women's contributions to early physical fitness, nutrition, and wellness movements have been lost or muddled because of the academic dismissal of such work as mere respectability politics or class-passing.[26] By 1983, however, the black feminist movement began to push against the focus on beauty, poise, and class as the major requirements for "polishing black diamonds."[27]

In 1983, Bylle Y. Avery founded the Black Women's Health Imperative at the First National Conference on Black Women's Health.[28] In her foreword to *Health First!: The Black Women's Wellness Guide*, Avery describes how the National Black Women's Health Project combined the concerns of the civil rights movement with the women's rights movement. Over the next decade, this black feminist movement impacted public health strategy as well as the wellness opportunities available to black women across the United States. In fact, "in 1988, there was some kind of Black women's health activity going on somewhere in the United States almost every weekend."[29] By 1990, the Black Women's Health Project

launched Walking for Wellness.[30] The 1990s would also see the publication of *Body and Soul*, as well as *The Black Women's Health Book*. By 2002,
Essence Magazine launched its "War on Girls" series, which made a direct
and explicit connection between black girls' health outcomes, their own
perception of their quality of life, and the implication these two factors
held for the black community. Sadly, despite this activism, "Black wom-
en's lives play out within a 'perfect storm' of distress, oppression, and
misguided optimism. . . . So when our well-being wanes, it rocks the
foundations of the whole Black community."[31]

Black blogs on wellness are part of this ongoing struggle. These histories, and their connection to a larger wellness movement active online,
offer an opportunity to consider trauma as a "structure of feeling" endemic to living in a racist and classist police state.[32] Through the body,
trauma is both imagined and made visceral and viscera. Engaging with
these structures of feeling is as much about grappling with the somatic
experience of oppression as it is the sensory and material.[33] However,
there is little work that connects the evolving black women's wellness
movement to this critical geopolitical moment. This lack of research is
particularly troubling because of the ways in which the militarization of
national and public policy disproportionately impacts black women's
quality of life and access to health care.[34]

The archival practices associated with creating, curating, and recircu-
lating online images of black women engaged in wellness practices is a
powerful example of the amorphous boundaries of these bloggers' virtual lives, where understandings of the body vacillate between the material
and the virtual. In an interview with *The Atlantic*, Robin Rollan, the blogger behind BlackYogis, emphasizes that African Americans "don't have a
great track record when it comes to preventative health. Wellness is not
really valued."[35] In an email interview with *Chelsea Loves Yoga*, a blog
centered on making wellness practices accessible to black Americans,
Rollan explicitly links her commitment to circulating images of black
yogis as part of a larger social justice mission. She writes,

> I quickly noticed that there were barely any images online or in maga-
> zines of yogis of color and in particular *Black* yogis. This is by no means
> a unique situation but just a symptom of a larger issue of how images
> of people of color are handled in the main stream. Aside from Russell
> Simmons and the amazing Faith Hunter, there was virtually a "black-
> out." For the most part, "blackouts" are the norm in the media except
> when it comes to the ills of society, in which case images of black
> people are ridiculously over represented.[36]

Is Rollan a creator or a curator of online content? Is her emphasis on the
recirculation of gifs and still images a critical making project? The easy
answer is *no*—after all, she neither created nor contributed to Tumblr's
design. I don't like that answer. It's too narrow, and dismisses the affec-

tive and intellectual significance of the work black bloggers contribute to online conversations about race, ethnicity, and wellness. In particular, it dismisses the significance of Rollan's tagging practices, which mark black bodies as practitioners of yoga in a political and social moment where black women are neither imaged as technologically fluent nor as having an investment in wellness. For example, figure 10.1 shows BlackYogis' tagging practices, their emphasis on black yoga practitioners as yoginis and instructors, and their engagement with the naming of yoga postures as a taxonomic practice that reinforces both a practitioner's authority and their membership to a larger group of yoga practitioners. Rollan's continuous focus on yoga as a community activity adds a complexity to the ostensibly simple mission of image recirculation. In this case, image, text, and indexing become part of a larger conversation on black bodies, wellness, and black community online and off.

Rollan's archive of black yogis captures images of bodies whose mortality has become national myth, whose unwellness has become the dark face of obesity in America, and whose creator is supposed to be technologically ignorant. Because of this, I argue that a digital praxis of love mingles the creative and the political, the technological and the embodied, and the affective and the analytical. It is about keeping conversations moving, and insisting on the right to speak honestly and vulnerably about pain and survival. I came to this definition because for me it holds a kind of explanatory power; it provides a larger context for the work of bloggers such as BlackGirlinMaine and the Tumblr user BlackYogis. These bloggers use their online work to discuss the commingled effects of racism and sexism on black women's bodies, as well as black women's activist work to address these physical and psychic ills. For example, a May 1, 2015, post on BlackYogis features a black woman (identified by *USA Today* as Dream Reiki Project founder Shameeka Dream) dressed all in white like a *santera* doing a sage smudge in front of a row of police in riot gear. This image, originally from a *USA Today* article on peaceful protests in Baltimore, visually gathers layer upon layer of meaning: the clothing calls up a larger history of syncretic, African-influenced religions in the United States; the police officers in their riot gear with their looming shadows are a concrete manifestation of state power and violence; and the sage smudging itself is a specifically American indigenous practice. Textually, Rollan links this image of benediction and purification in the wake of the Baltimore protests following the murder of Freddie Gray to a longer history of black activism and spirituality through her use of the tag #SoulPower.[37]

BlackGirlinMaine,[38] known offline as Shay Stewart-Bouley, uses her blog to reflect on parenthood and experience of being black in Maine. In her blog, she talks about aging, parenthood, and living in an overtly racist and sexist society. She is deliberately and consciously honest about

Photo   April 13, 2013   32 notes

Bound Triangle Pose *Baddha Trikonasana*

Here I go getting that triangle in...with a bind.

Tags: Bound Triangle Pose Baddha Trikonasana, black yogis, black women yoga, black yoginis

Figure 10.1.   Triangle Pose. Credit: Robin Rollan
Robin Rollan, Black Yogis Tumblr, 2013, Digital Image. Available from: http://
blackyogis.tumblr.com/post/47864696000/bound-triangle-pose-baddha-trikona-
sana-here-i (accessed January 16, 2016).

feeling alone, isolated, and angry as a result of being a black woman. She writes,

> I am a woman living in a body that some deem to be inferior and in a world where I must always be on guard. It's tiring. . . . Why I didn't

have a large panic attack before is a testament to the strength of yoga in my life.[39]

In this blogpost, Stewart-Bouley describes liveblogging her ER visit as a result of a panic attack, her feelings of isolation, and her anger at well-meaning acquaintances who comment on her supposed stress. She highlights that she's not stressed; she's angry. She writes, "What I feel most days when I am sitting with myself is rage, rage at a world that seeks to invalidate my very existence . . . rage that I must wear a mask for my own safety and protection. My struggle is the struggle of many Black women in a country that doesn't honor or respect Black bodies."[40]

TOWARD A DIGITAL PRAXIS OF LOVE: WHEN DOES BLOGGING ABOUT WELLNESS BECOME WRITING ABOUT POLITICS?

As I write this, it is the spring of 2015, and #blackout is trending on Twitter, Tumblr, and Facebook. It's a day to celebrate blackness, to post selfies tagged #blackout, to celebrate black digital communities, and black love. There has been a flurry of beautiful brown and black faces on my Facebook timeline, in the secret POC and Fashion group I subscribe to, on my Tumblr dashboard. These images range from the tongue in cheek (for example, one of my favorites is a clip from *School Daze* with *a toast to my family/BLACK TUMBLR/#blackout* flickering in neon green)[41] and the poignant.[42] As her #blackout contribution, Tumblr user SeduceMyIntellect included a photo series of herself doing yoga, writing "Embracing the power of yoga through the beauty of my black skin."[43] This celebratory series of images, seen in figure 10.2, is tagged with #blackout, #blackyogis, #blackgirlsrock, and #melanin. These last two are particularly interesting; like #blackout they are associated with a radically black politic. Unlike #blackout, they are specifically associated with a call to arms to prioritize the emotional, spiritual, and intellectual well-being of black women and girls. Coupled with the tags #ebonyfitness and #blackfitness, these tags tell a story of revolution, self-care, and self-love as political and social priorities.

Both #blackout and #blacklivesmatter became opportunities for users to contribute visually to conversations on both yoga and race. For example, an Instagram post by rollinmyyogawheel demonstrates the crossing of the indexical streams so prevalent in black images of wellness. Scratched and gritty, the user's picture features a black woman in a one-legged standing pose with her fingers touching behind her twisted back. In a sharp contrast to other images featuring this particular contributor, she is neither smiling nor dressed in the bright jewel tones she prefers, and is seen wearing in her other posts. As a caption, she has written,

Figure 10.2. Embracing the Power of Yoga through the Beauty of My Black Skin.
Credit: Vanessa Chambers
Vanessa Chambers, SeduceMyIntellect Tumblr, 2015, Digital Image. Available from: http://seducemyintellect.tumblr.com/post/115433747362/embracing-the-power-of-yoga-through-the-beauty-of (accessed January 6, 2016).

I decided to do something a little different today. Because when we say that Black Lives Matter. That includes other things besides just police brutality. . . . Being a young black rape victim myself I was very much able to identify with the struggles the little girl in the movie [*A Time to Kill*] was dealing with . . . the scene that stuck out to me the most was when Matthew McConaughey (the lawyer) described in detail to the jury the horrific things that little girl had endured. . . . [A]fter he described everything, he said "now imagine she's white. . . ." It had never occurred to me that no one would care about a hurt child just because she was black. But in that moment I realized that maybe this, this racism played a part in no one ever helping me . . . I was failed by a system built to fail me . . . .

Before getting reblogged by BlackYogaSuperstars,[44] this image's tags on Instagram included #blacklivesmatter, #ferguson, and #michaelbrown. Other yoga images tagged as #blacklivesmatter include KatSoulKoi's digital illustration of a black yogi crying as she sits in an interrupted half lotus.[45] Her hands are raised above her head with the slogan "Hands Up Don't Shoot" framing her pose. Included as figure 10.3, this particular image emphasizes both the woman's tears and the spiraling swirls of her afro. The tags include #mckinneytexas, suggesting that this image was drawn at least partly in response to police brutality directed specifically toward black girls and women.

Figure 10.3. Black Lives Matter. Credit: Kat Sol
Kat Sol, KatSoulKoi Tumblr, 2014, Digital Image. Available from: http://katsoulkoi.tumblr.com/post/103744586226/black-lives-matter-katsoulkoi-art (accessed: January 6 2016).

In these digital projects, love is defined as a politic of *self*-care that heralds a call to *communal* care. The same elements are present in each of these Tumblr posts: an insistence that black bodies deserve love, deserve care, and that this care must emerge from an engagement with both infrastructural oppression and the chronicling of individual experiences with trauma. My use of love as a kind of political and social activist work draws on Chela Sandoval's arguments in *Methodology of the Oppressed*, where she describes love as a "set of practices and procedures that can transit all citizen-subjects toward a differential mode of consciousness."[46] "Love," for Sandoval, "is enacted by revolutionary, mobile, and global coalitions of citizen activists who are allied through the apparatus of emancipation."[47] My goal is not to suggest that love is a cure-all or that there's something utopic when people write about wellness online. Instead, I argue that these virtual and material labors of love—blogging projects, metasites collecting historical research, and Tumblrs blurring the line between the personal and the political—participate in larger social justice movements centered on body positivity, wellness, and wellbeing.

NOTES

1. Michelle Goldberg, "Feminism's Toxic Twitter Wars," *The Nation*, January 29, 2014, accessed February 17, 2014, http://www.thenation.com/article/178140/feminisms-toxic-twitter-wars#.

2. See, for example, Amanda Marcotte's uncredited use of blogger Brownfemipower's work on immigration. Tara L. Conley of *The Feminist Wire* offers a sustained analysis of this controversy in an open letter to Marcotte (http://thefeministwire.com/2013/03/an-open-letter-to amanda marcotte/)

3. The discursive erasure of this shared project produced by a multi-ethnic feminist collective echoes the historical amnesia associated with interthnic feminist mobilizing in the 1960s and 1970s as described in Katie King's *Theory in Its Feminist Travels: Conversations in U.S. Women's Movements* (Bloomington: Indiana University Press, 1994).

4. Jen Caron, "It Happened To Me: There Are No Black People In My Yoga Class and I'm Suddenly Feeling Uncomfortable With It," *XOJane*, January 28, 2014, accessed August 15 2014, http://www.xojane.com/it-happened-to-me/it-happened-to-me-there-are-no-black-people-in-my-yoga-classes-and-im-uncomfortable-with-it.

5. The online response to this blogpost, as well as its movement within and without feminist online spaces, may have been impacted by its circulation by other online publications, such as Slate.com and Salon, as well as its reblogging through Facebook, Tumblr, and Twitter.

6. For example, Demetria L. Lucas released a post in response immediately afterward. Entitled "Dear Yoga Girl, You Know that Most of Us Don't Envy Your Shape, Right?" Lucas uses her blogpost to zero in on the concept of body envy as framing black women's engagement with wellness practices. She writes, "Black women really don't spend that much time thinking about white women," arguing that black women approach wellness practices with their own goals in mind, goals that exist independently of white women. In "It Happened To Me: I'm a Big Black Girl Around Small White People & I'm Suddenly Feeling Uncomfortable With It," CeCe Olisa writes a profound reflection on how Caron's response to the black woman's body reveals

Caron's own anxieties about race and weight, astutely observing that it "would be racist and weird to say 'OMG! You're so big and black!' so instead she says 'OMG! I'm so white and small.'"

7. Cliff Pervocracy, "The Missing Stair," *The Pervocracy: Sex, Feminism, BDSM, And Some Very, Very Naughty Words*, published electronically June 22, 2012, accessed August 15, 2014, http://pervocracy.blogspot.com/2012/06/missing-stair.html.

8. This term was coined by Moya Bailey to describe the specific hatred directed toward black women, in "They Aren't Talking About Me," *Crunk Feminist Collective*, 2010. Published electronically March 18, 2010, accessed August 18, 2014. http://www.crunkfeministcollective.com/2010/03/14/they-arent-talking-about-me/.

9. Tamara Winfrey Harris, *The Sisters Are Alright: Changing the Broken Narrative of Black Women in America* (Oakland, CA: Berrett-Koehler Publishers, 2015) 110.

10. Sharla M. Fett, *Working Cures: Healing, Health, and Power on Southern Slave Plantations* (Chapel Hill, NC: The University of North Carolina Press, 2002).

11. Restrictive lung disease is one of the physical effects of obesity, and is a condition where your weight constricts the expansion of your lungs.

12. The social significance of breathing, its legislation, and its connection to living within institutions of power has been demonstrated most poignantly in the activism following the murder of Eric Garner by a police officer in December 2014, who gasped, "I can't breathe," as he was choked to death. This powerful phrase helped to inspire the hashtags #icantbreathe, #blacklivesmatter, and #wecantbreathe on Twitter, as well as protest chants, posters, and t-shirts. In response, the New York Police Department and their supporters wore "I CAN Breathe" hoodies at a pro-police rally (Alfred Ng, Barry Paddock, and Thomas Tracy, "NYPD Supporters Wear 'I Can Breathe' Hoodies at City Hall, Sparking War with Opposing Demonstrators," *New York Daily News*, December 19, 2014). This response may itself reflect the institutional role breathing, fitness, and bodily worth take in military cultures, as described by Brian Lande in "Breathing Like a Soldier: Culture Incarnate" (*The Sociological Review* 55 (2007): 95–108). Further, because of the disproportionate impact food deserts have on the black community (leading to increased rates of obesity) and the disproportionate impact environmental racism has on the black community (leading to increased rates of asthma), Garner's *ongoing* struggles to breathe were only made *visible* during his fatal encounter with the police. For more on the intersectional consequences of these forms of institutionalized racism, please see Shaya Mohajer, Tayefe, Liz Dwyer, and Willy Blackmore's "What Baltimore Has in Common with Ferguson and Other Protest Flash Points" (*Take Part*, April 30, 2015) and Max Ehrenfreund's think-piece for *The Washington Post*'s Wonkblog, entitled "The Racial Divide in America Is This Elemental: Blacks and Whites Actually Breathe Different Air" (*The Washington Post*, December 4, 2014).

13. Kimberly J. Lau, *Body Language: Sisters In Shape, Black Women's Fitness, and Feminist Identity Politics* (Philadelphia, PA: Temple University Press, 2011).

14. Kimberly J. Lau, *Body Language*, 6.

15. Kimberly J. Lau, *Body Language*, 10.

16. Kimberly J. Lau, *Body Language*, 10.

17. Brabazon, "Fitness is a Feminist Issue," 77 (emphasis in original).

18. Erika Nicole Kendall, "Blogging While Black: On Having An Accidentally Controversial Blog Title," *Black Girl's Guide to Weight Loss: The Op-Eds* (2012), http://blackgirlsguidetoweightloss.com/the-op-eds/blogging-while-black-on-having-an-accidentally-controversial-blog-title/.

19. In a 2013 blogpost, Patrice Yursik of *Afrobella* describes Kendall as one of her "biggest fitness inspirations"; *Black Enterprise* described *A Black Girl's Guide to Weight Loss* as one of 2013's top twenty digital entrepreneurs (Suncear Scretchen, "Black Blogger Month: *Black Girls' Guide to Weight Loss*, from Fat to Fit," *Black Enterprise* (2012). Published electronically May 17 2012. http://www.blackenterprise.com/lifestyle/black-blogger-month-black-girls'-guide-to-weight-loss/).

20. Dianne Rocheleau and Robin Roth, "Rooted Networks, Relational Webs, and Powers of Connection: Rethinking Human and Political Ecologies," *Geoforum* 38, no. 3 (2007).

21. Linda Villarosa and National Black Women's Health Project, *Body & Soul: The Black Women's Guide to Physical Health and Emotional Well-Being* (New York: HarperPerennial, 1994), 36.

22. Charles B. Corbin, Robert P. Pangrazi, and Don B. Frank, "Definitions: Health, Fitness, and Physical Activity" (Washington, DC: President's Council on Physical Fitness and Sport, 2008).

23. Fett, *Working Cures: Healing, Health, and Power on Southern Slave Plantations* (Chapel Hill: University of North Carolina Press, 2002).

24. Fett, *Working Cures*, 20.

25. Jennifer H. Lansbury's *A Spectacular Leap: Black Women Athletes in Twentieth Century America* (University of Arkansas Press, 2014) provides an in-depth description of the impact the 1918 opening of the Germantown YWCA had on the black community in Philadelphia and the founding of the American Tennis Association. Lansbury's work also situates the black women's athleticism in the social and political contexts of their time. Her discussion of the black community's shifting attitudes toward black women's athleticism is particularly useful because she highlights the role of classism in the evolving stereotypes surrounding strong black women.

26. Ava Purkiss's dissertation "'Mind, Soul, Body, and Race': Black Women's Purposeful Exercise, 1900-1939" (University of Texas at Austin, 2015) is one of the few historiographies that interrogates the erasure of black women's wellness-based activism from America's history of physical culture movements.

27. Laila Haidarali's "Polishing Brown Diamonds: African American Women, Popular Magazines, and the Advent of Modeling in Early Postwar America" (*Journal of Women's History* 17, no. 1 [2005]: 10–37) describes the role black women's appearance, skin color, weight, and poise took in both respectability politics and class mobility.

28. Eleanor Hinton Hoytt, Hilary Beard, and the Black Women's Health Imperative, *Health First!: The Black Women's Wellness Guide* (New York: Smiley Books, 2012).

29. Byllye Avery, "Who Does the Work of Public Health?" *American Journal of Public Health* 92 (2002): 574.

30. Avery, "Who Does the Work," 574.

31. Hoytt et al., *Health First!*

32. Ann Cvetkovich, *An Archive of Feelings: Trauma, Sexuality, and Lesbian Public Cultures* (Durham, NC: Duke University Press, 2003), 17.

33. Ann Cvetkovich, *Depression: A Public Feeling* (Durham, NC: Duke University Press, 2011) 11, emphasis in original.

34. Angela Davis, "Sick and Tired of Being Sick and Tired: The Politics of Black Women's Health," in *Women, Culture & Politics* (New York: Knopf Doubleday Publishing Group, 2011) 53–65.

35. Rosalie Murphy, "Why Your Yoga Class Is So White," *The Atlantic* (2014), published electronically July 8, 2014. Available at http://www.theatlantic.com/national/archive/2014/07/why-your-yoga-class-is-so-white/374002/.

36. Robin Rollan, "Yogi in the Community: Robin Rollan (Black Yogis Tumblr)," *ChelseaLovesYoga: Activism & Yoga* (2013), http://www.chelsealovesyoga.com/yogi-in-the-community/.

37. Robin Rollan, "Peace Be Still," *Black Yogis*. May 1, 2015. Tumblr. Accessed: June 29, 2015. Available at http://blackyogis.tumblr.com/post/117861447857/peace-be-still-soulpower-healer-baltimore.

38. Shay Stewart-Bouley, "About Me," *Black Girl in Maine* (2008), http://blackgirlinmaine.com/about/.

39. Shay Stewart-Bouley, "Laying My Burden Down or the Struggle of a Black Woman," *Black Girl in Maine* (2014), published electronically April 15, 2014, accessed August 25, 2014. http://blackgirlinmaine.com/racial-and-cultural/laying-my-burden-down-or-the-struggle-of-a-black-woman/.

40. Shay Stewart-Bouley, "Laying My Burden Down or the Struggle of a Black Woman."
41. Olivia--Nope. "#blackout." *Olivia Nope*. March 6, 2015. Tumblr. Accessed March 6, 2015. Available at http://olivia--nope.tumblr.com/post/112949258202/phuckindope-squaddddd.
42. For example, inaudible-reign wrote, "Whether you get 5 notes or 7 million tomorrow, you are all beautiful black people. . . . The black community loves you and want to see you shine" ("Reminder:" Maristoviante. March 6, 2015. Tumblr. Accessed March 6, 2015. Available at http://mariareadsalot.tumblr.com/post/112849130199/reminder). The original post by inaudible-reign has been deleted; however, it was reblogged over sixteen thousand times, including to my own Tumblr. I have created an archived webpage of this post and the other Tumblr posts described in this article using the Wayback Machine. These archived links will be included in the bibliography.
43. SeduceMyIntellect, "Embracing the Power of Yoga through the Beauty of My Black Skin," Tumblr, Accessed January 6 2016. Available at http://seducemyintellect.tumblr.com/post/115433747362/embracing-the-power-of-yoga-through-the-beauty-of.
44. BlackYogaSuperstars and Jermil Sadler, "Photo by Rollinmyyogawheel," *BlackYogaSuperStars- Where Black Yogis Shine!*. December 16, 2014. Tumblr. Accessed: January 6 2016. Available: http://blackyogasuperstars.tumblr.com/post/105332042845/photo-by-rollinmyyogawheel.
45. KatSoulKoi, "Black Lives Matter," *Soul Koi*. November 27, 2014. Tumblr. Accessed January 6 2016. Available at http://katsoulkoi.tumblr.com/post/103744586226/black-lives-matter-katsoulkoi-art.
46. Chela Sandoval, *Methodology of the Oppressed* (Minneapolis: Univeristy of Minnesota, 2000), 139.
47. Sandoval, *Methodology of the Oppressed*, 183.

REFERENCES

Avery, Byllye. "Who Does the Work of Public Health?". *American Journal of Public Health* 92, no. 4 (2002): 570–75.
Bailey, Moya. "They Aren't Talking About Me." *Crunk Feminist Collective* (2010). Published electronically March 18, 2010. http://www.crunkfeministcollective.com/2010/03/14/they-arent-talking-about-me/.
Brabazon, Tara. "Fitness Is a Feminist Issue." *Australian Feminist Studies* 21, no. 49 (2006): 65–83.
Caron, Jen. "It Happened to Me: There Are No Black People in My Yoga Class and I'm Suddenly Feeling Uncomfortable with It." *XOJane* (2014). Published electronically January 28, 2014. Accessed January 6, 2016. http://www.xojane.com/it-happened-to-me/it-happened-to-me-there-are-no-black-people-in-my-yoga-classes-and-im-uncomfortable-with-it.
Conley, Tara L. "An Open Letter to Amanda Marcotte." *The Feminist Wire* (2013). Published electronically March 4, 2013. Accessed January 6 2016. http://thefeministwire.com/2013/03/an-open-letter-to-amanda-marcotte/.
Corbin, Charles B., Robert P. Pangrazi, and Don B. Frank. "Definitions: Health, Fitness, and Physical Activity." Edited by the Department of Health and Human Services. Washington, DC: President's Council on Physical Fitness and Sport, 2008.
Cvetkovich, Ann. *An Archive of Feelings: Trauma, Sexuality, and Lesbian Public Cultures* (Durham, NC: Duke University Press, 2003).
———. *Depression: A Public Feeling* (Durham, NC: Duke University Press, 2012).
Dastagir, Alia E. "The Part of the Baltimore Protests You Haven't Seen." *USA Today* (2015). Published electronically April 29 2015. Accessed January 6, 2016. http://

www.usatoday.com/story/news/nation/2015/04/28/baltimore-protests-peaceful/ 26510645/.

Davis, Angela. "Sick and Tired of Being Sick and Tired: The Politics of Black Women's Health," in *Women, Culture & Politics* (New York: Knopf Doubleday Publishing Group, 2011) 53–65.

Ehrenfreund, Max. "The Racial Divide in America Is This Elemental: Blacks and Whites Actually Breathe Different Air." *The Washington Post: Wonkblog* (2014). Published electronically December 4 2014. Accessed January 6 2016. https:// www.washingtonpost.com/news/wonk/wp/2014/12/04/asthma-like-so-many-other-factors-in-eric-garners-death-is-correlated-with-race/.

Fett, Sharla M. *Working Cures: Healing, Health, and Power on Southern Slave Plantations* (Chapel Hill: The University of North Carolina Press, 2002).

Goldberg, Michelle. "Feminism's Toxic Twitter Wars." *The Nation* (2014). Published electronically January 29, 2014. Accessed January 6 2016. http:// www.thenation.com/article/178140/feminisms-toxic-twitter-wars#.

Haidarali, Laila. "Polishing Brown Diamonds: African American Women, Popular Magazines, and the Advent of Modeling in Early Postwar America." *Journal of Women's History* 17, no. 1 (2005): 10–37.

Hoytt, Eleanor Hinton, Hilary Beard, and the Black Women's Health Imperative. *Health First!: The Black Woman's Wellness Guide* (New York: Smiley Books, 2012).

inaudible-reign. "Reminder." *Maristoviante*. Tumblr. Electronically published March 6, 2015. Accessed: March 6, 2015. Available: http://mariareadsalot.tumblr.com/post/ 112849130199/reminder. Archived: https://web.archive.org/web/20160105230045/ http://mariareadsalot.tumblr.com/post/112849130199/reminder

KatSoulKoi. "Black Lives Matter." *Soul Koi* (2015). Tumblr. Published electronically November 27 2014. Accessed January 6 2016. http://katsoulkoi.tumblr.com/post/ 103744586226/black-lives-matter-katsoulkoi-art. Archived: http://web.archive.org/ web/20160106001109/http://katsoulkoi.tumblr.com/post/103744586226/black-lives-matter-katsoulkoi-art

Kendall, Erika Nicole. "Blogging While Black: On Having an Accidentally Controversial Blog Title." *Black Girl's Guide to Weight Loss: The Op-Eds* (2012). Published electronically January 11, 2012. Accessed January 6 2016. http://blackgirlsguidetoweightloss.com/the-op-eds/blogging-while-black-on-having-an-accidentally-controversial-blog-title/.

King, Katie. *Theory in Its Feminist Travels: Conversations in U.S. Women's Movements* (Bloomington: Indiana University Press, 1994).

Lande, Brian. "Breathing Like a Soldier: Culture Incarnate." *The Sociological Review* 55, no. s1 (2007).

Lansbury, Jennifer H. *A Spectacular Leap: Black Women Athletes in Twentieth-Century America.* (University of Arkansas Press, 2014).

Lau, Kimberly J. *Body Language: Sisters in Shape, Black Women's Fitness, and Feminist Identity Politics* (Philadelphia, PA: Temple University Press, 2011).

Lucas, Demetria L. "Dear Yoga Girl, You Know That Most Black Girls Don't Envy Your Shape, Right?" *A Belle in Brooklyn* (2014). Published electronically January 30, 2014. Accessed January 6 2016. http://www.abelleinbrooklyn.com/dear-yoga-girl-know-black-girls-dont-envy-shape-right/.

Mitchell, Stacey Ann and Teri D. Mitchell. *Livin' Large: African American Sisters Confront Obesity* (Roscoe, IL: Hilton Publishing Company, 2004).

Mohajer, Shaya Tayefe, Liz Dwyer, and Willy Blackmore. "What Baltimore Has in Common with Ferguson and Other Protest Flash Points." *Take Part*. Published electronically April 30 2015. Accessed January 6 2016. http://www.takepart.com/article/ 2015/04/30/baltimore-and-other-flashpoints.

Murphy, Rosalie. "Why Your Yoga Class Is So White." *The Atlantic* (2014). Published electronically July 8, 2014. Accessed January 6 2016. http://www.theatlantic.com/ national/archive/2014/07/why-your-yoga-class-is-so-white/374002/.

Ng, Alfred, Barry Paddock, and Thomas Tracy. "NYPD Supporters Wear 'I Can Breathe' Hoodies at City Hall, Sparking War with Opposing Demonstrators." *New York Daily News*, December 19 2014. http://www.nydailynews.com/new-york/nyc-crime/suspect-arrested-assault-cops-brooklyn-bridge-article-1.2051361.

Olisa, CeCe. "It Happened to Me: I'm a Big Black Girl around Small White People & I'm Suddenly Feeling Uncomfortable with It." *Plus Size Princess* (2014). Published electronically January 29, 2014. Accessed January 6 2016. http://www.plussizeprincess.com/2014/01/happened-black-girl-around-small-white-people-suddenly-feeling-uncomfortable-with-response-carons/.

Olivia--Nope. "#blackout." *Olivia Nope*. Tumblr. Electronically published March 6, 2015. Accessed March 6, 2015. http://olivia--nope.tumblr.com/post/112949258202/phuckindope-squaddddd. Archived: https://web.archive.org/web/20160105225943/http://olivia--nope.tumblr.com/post/112949258202/phuckindope-squaddddd

Pervocracy, Cliff. "The Missing Stair." *The Pervocracy: Sex, Feminism, BDSM, and Some Very, Very Naughty Words* (2012). Published electronically June 22, 2012. Accessed January 6, 2016. http://pervocracy.blogspot.com/2012/06/missing-stair.html.

Purkiss, Ava. "'Mind, Soul, Body, and Race': Black Women's Purposeful Exercise, 1900–1939." Dissertation, University of Texas at Austin, 2015.

Rocheleau, Dianne and Robin Roth. "Rooted Networks, Relational Webs, and Power of Connection: Rethinking Human and Political Ecologies." *Geoforum* 38, no. 3 (2007).

Rollan, Robin. "Peace Be Still." *Black Yogis*. Tumblr. Electronically published May 1, 2015. Accessed June 29, 2015. http://blackyogis.tumblr.com/post/117861447857/peace-be-still-soulpower-healer-baltimore. Archived: http://web.archive.org/web/20160107035657/http://blackyogis.tumblr.com/post/117861447857/peace-be-still-soulpower-healer-baltimore.

———. "Yogi in the Community: Robin Rollan (Black Yogis Tumblr)." *ChelseaLovesYoga: Activism & Yoga* (2013). Published electronically June 16, 2013. Accessed January 6, 2016. http://www.chelsealovesyoga.com/yogi-in-the-community/.

Sadler, Jermil and Black Yoga Superstars. "Photo by Rollinmyyogawheel." *BlackYogaSuperStars-Where Black Yogis Shine!* (2014). Published electronically December 16 2014. Accessed January 6, 2016. http://blackyogasuperstars.tumblr.com/post/105332042845/photo-by-rollinmyyogawheel. Archived: http://web.archive.org/web/20160105235150/http://blackyogasuperstars.tumblr.com/post/105332042845/photo-by-rollinmyyogawheel

Sandoval, Chela. *Methodology of the Oppressed* (Minneapolis: Univeristy of Minnesota, 2000).

Scretchen, Suncear. "Black Blogger Month: Black Girls' Guide to Weight Loss, from Fat to Fit." *Black Enterprise* (2012). Published electronically May 17 2012. Accessed January 6, 2016. http://www.blackenterprise.com/lifestyle/black-blogger-month-black-girls'-guide-to-weight-loss/.

SeduceMyIntellect. "Embracing the Power of Yoga through the Beauty of My Black Skin." *SeduceMyIntellect*. Tumblr. Accessed January 6, 2016. http://seducemyintellect.tumblr.com/post/115433747362/embracing-the-power-of-yoga-through-the-beauty-of. Archived: http://web.archive.org/web/20160105231340/http://seducemyintellect.tumblr.com/post/115433747362/embracing-the-power-of-yoga-through-the-beauty-of.

Stewart-Bouley, Shay. "About Me." *Black Girl in Maine* (2008). Accessed January 6, 2016. http://blackgirlinmaine.com/about/.

———. "Laying My Burden Down or the Struggle of a Black Woman." *Black Girl in Maine* (2014). Published electronically April 15, 2014. Accessed January 6, 2016. http://blackgirlinmaine.com/racial-and-cultural/laying-my-burden-down-or-the-struggle-of-a-black-woman/.

Villarosa, Linda, and the National Black Women's Health Project. *Body & Soul : The Black Women's Guide to Physical Health and Emotional Well-Being* (New York: Harper-Perennial, 1994).

Winfrey Harris, Tamara. *The Sisters Are Alright: Changing the Broken Narrative of Black Women in America* (Oakland, CA: Berrett-Koehler Publishers, 2015).

Yursik, Patrice Grell. "My Biggest Fitness Inspirations | Afrobella." *Afrobella.* Published electronically March 3, 2013. Accessed January 6, 2016. http://www.afrobella.com/2013/03/28/my-biggest-fitness-inspirations/.

ELEVEN

Fat Pedagogy in the Yoga Class

Kimberly Dark

This is a story about what it means to allow the body to be seen. To be seen in movement, to be seen in pleasure, to be seen as the model for the *asana*, for alignment, for peace. It's about beauty and acceptance as tools for teaching others, consciously wielded and constantly part of unconscious exploration. It's about vulnerability, persistence, and strength. In addition to *talking* to help bring students into the experience of the body, teachers are *examples* of being in our own bodies. During teaching, we are each internal subjects, in addition to being seen by students. We can never fully understand what we're offering, except through contemplation of our experience, and of the comments and non-verbal responses we receive from others. We model presence and confidence and vulnerability. Indeed, we offer a holistic experience of being as a model. I am a fat woman—among many other identities—and therefore, I offer a fat pedagogy, whether or not I ever articulate it in the yoga studio.

The body is the significant artifact. Consider the definition at dictionary.com.

> Artifact, *noun*
> 1. any object made by human beings, especially with a view to subsequent use.
> 2. a handmade object, as a tool, or the remains of one, as a shard of pottery, characteristic of an earlier time or cultural stage, especially such an object found at an archaeological excavation.
> 3. any mass-produced, usually inexpensive object reflecting contemporary society or popular culture:

The body itself may be a different kind of noun, an organic form. But what we make of bodies socially—the ways in which we socially construct the meaning of bodies—becomes the artifact. We are performative creatures; our bodies are both product and process, and our ways of being influence others. As Judith Butler described, performativity is ". . . that reiterative power of discourse to produce the phenomena that it regulates and constrains."[1] When my fat body teaches yoga, the expectation of what media culture has taught us that fat bodies can and should do (things like sitting, eating, crying, rolling over, being sick, sad, and dying) is disturbed by the fact of my body moving and speaking in the yoga teacher role. The resulting dissonance becomes part of the teaching space I hold for students. Even if we never speak of it (though sometimes we do), my body is enacting fat pedagogy.

Every yoga teacher comes to terms with what it means to be seen. And that's no small matter, for women in particular. Already positioned as "the weaker sex," women often reach an unassailable pinnacle of whatever form of fitness they practice before they allow the body to be seen. As sociologist Erving Goffman explained, back in the 1950s, we manage identity using a variety of artful means.[2] We manage our identities to find basic comfort, to maximize privilege, and to minimize oppression. The body is always teaching, and even more so in classes, like yoga, where the body is demonstrating form. Even when teaching topics, like sociology, which ostensibly involve only the minds of students and teachers, my body is teaching. People think they can overlook my body, but it's never true. I am still providing an example of how varying vehicles can carry the mind. As a yoga teacher, I am providing an example of how varying vehicles can show *asana*. My "performances" of self always involve the body as significant artifact. And students manage the dissonance using linguistic constructions like this: She's fat, but she's brilliant. She's fat, but she's graceful. She's fat, but she's beautiful. The fat body remains the significant artifact because it's so powerfully salient to every aspect of social life for women. We are socialized to live in constant relationship to fat—either being fat, avoiding being fat, or being glad we're not fat. No matter what I do, so long as it doesn't conform to the pre-set cultural standards for fat bodies—sloth, gluttony, dull-mindedness, disease, and death—there will always be a "but."

Through my work as a writer, storyteller, and performance-poet, I've learned about the significance of embodied storytelling. My embodiments are varied of course—I speak from a fat body, a queer body, a female body, a mixed-race-white-privileged body, etc. I started touring my first solo theater show in 1998, titled *The Butch-Femme Chronicles: Discussions With Women Who Are Not Like Me (and Some Who Are)*. I thought the success of that show derived from how audiences engaged with the stories and poems I'd written. Over time, I realized that my on-stage presence was also an important element of the show's success. It's not just that I was telling stories about lesbian lives; I was an actual lesbian, on stage for ninety minutes, available for viewing. This may sound strange nowadays, but remember that the visibility of gay and lesbian people who actually talk about being gay and lesbian has exploded in the last decade. I started performing before Ellen DeGeneres "came out" on television. I was a breathing, moving artifact, animating stories that offered emotion, detail, and analysis.

Maya Maor's article "Becoming the Subject of Your Own Story: Creating Fat Positive Representations"[3] discusses the "politics of the ordinary and familiar"[4] in an analysis of my performance work. I bring to life, on stage, the ambiguity and complexity of a stigmatized appearance. Maor explores the ways in which my fat embodiment is "ambiguous," along with how the intersections of my various identities complicate the external gaze. The ways in which students are both disturbed and comforted by complexity are similar when I teach yoga.

Really think this through: my body type is normally seen as a cautionary tale, not as a site of peace and practice and beauty, action and joy. My fat body is more readily pictured on a sofa, or if working, behind a desk. If I ask you to picture an American woman, nearly fifty years old, weighing more than three hundred pounds, you are not likely to picture her in a range of pursuits. You are not likely to say, "Well, I need more information than that to be able to picture her. What does she like to do?" She is not assumed to like to do anything (except maybe eat). She is static and it pains you to move her, just as you imagine it pains her to move.

The predetermined ontology of the body is already in play when one considers the fat body. And I disrupt it directly by being physical in many specific settings, manners, and pursuits. I also reinforce it at times. I allow myself to be seen in my limitations and in the modifications I take doing yoga, that less bulky bodies do not need to take (at least not for the sake of navigating fat).

There comes to be a pedagogy that derives from the ontology of bodies—whether they are super-fit or soft and motherly, or fat or old or disabled or beautiful, or any combination of these. Whether consciously or not, we each enact a pedagogy of embodiment in addition to whatever other approaches we take to teaching. It's just that slender bodies are rendered "neutral" in the yoga studio, much as all privileged identities become invisible as social defaults of normalcy. No one's body is neutral; we are each enacting a pedagogy of form. My fat pedagogy is as conscious as I can make it. I explore it in the hopes that a) others' embodied paradigms and pedagogies become more visible and so that b) it becomes easier to respect the wisdom and necessity of diverse bodily paradigms and pedagogies.

ALLOWING THE BODY TO BE SEEN

People often talk about yoga practice as having liberated them from
something they couldn't name. Yoga is more than fitness and yet hatha
yoga is rooted in movement of the breath and body. People often speak of
yoga as having freed them and allowed them to see more beauty in
themselves and in others. That's why the poet John O'Donohue's[5]
thoughts on beauty come to mind as I consider the process of allowing
the body to be seen.

> Beauty isn't all about just nice, loveliness-like. Beauty is about more
> rounded, substantial becoming. And I think when we cross a new
> threshold, that if we cross it worthily, what we do is we heal the pat-
> terns of repetition that were in us that had us caught somewhere. And
> in our crossing, then we cross into new ground where we don't just
> repeat what we've been through in the last place we were. So I think
> beauty in that sense is about an emerging fullness, a greater sense of
> grace and elegance, a deeper sense of depth and also a kind of home-
> coming for the enriched memory of your unfolding life.

It is indeed a process. I am always the artifact, and the unfolding, as I
occupy the teacher's mat. Our socially constructed views on body shame
and worthiness are indeed a threshold that must be crossed if we are to
move toward peace and acceptance.

I choose how I allow my body to be seen. So do you. We are always
living two lives: one as the subject of our own stories, in which we make
meaning of who we are, what we do and say. This life-as-subject is still a
socially mitigated life, and it also contains an internal flair and flavor. It
contains choice. We dress or undress, adorn or simplify, follow or reject
cultural standards for appearance, show up in a range of settings, or
remain in private space only. These are our choices. The second life is as
the object of external interpretations. Those interpretations can bring
privilege or pain, include or exclude us in specific settings, and sometimes limit how we are able to receive help or remain part of a community. When external interpretations sanction us, the results can be trivial
or deadly. This is no game. I choose how I allow my body to be seen and,
when I can stay conscious about it, I choose when and how I allow others'
interpretations to affect me.

I am continually crossing a threshold within myself regarding social
interpretations, expectations, privileges, and the possibility for oppression. Sure, in the studio where I teach, I have a reasonable amount of
comfort. I have the credibility of simply occupying the teacher role. Athletic credibility also assists the fat body in finding comfort. I had that
through my thirties and into my early forties—the credibility of what
people called "an impressive practice." That's waning for me, though a
trained eye can often see a long-term yoga practice in my body. I notice

that when I'm a student in other studios, my emotional stability can waver depending on how welcome I feel, how out of place I feel. This is true even though I also teach. Indeed, after decades of nearly always being the fattest participant in the yoga studio, in the gym, or on the hiking trail, my own visibility can still exhaust me. This visibility in the student role is complex. Jeannine Gailey explores this complexity in her book *The Hyper(in)visible Fat Woman*, in which she investigates individual perceptions and social expectations. Specifically, she names the phenomenon of "hyper(in)visibility," which is the seemingly paradoxical social position of being paid exceptional attention—often negative, sanctioning attention—while simultaneously being erased.[6] As a student, I'm often expected to fend for myself when it comes to posture modifications, and still I can feel scrutinized by the teacher and other students. I recall once, during my first class with a particular teacher, being told I wasn't capable of downward dog and should simply take a resting pose. Even as I explained that I had practiced downward dog daily for decades, the teacher's simultaneous scrutiny and erasure of my practice prevailed through class.

I am aware that I choose to cross the threshold of exhaustion into comfort and peace not only for myself, but for others as well. It's helpful when I remember that I disturb stereotypes for the common good, as well as for my own sake. Being slender or fit or young or hegemonically beautiful does not exempt one from the physical and emotional trauma of body tyranny and expectations of conformity. I practice peace and pleasure in a fat, aging, queer, female body for the good of all. And I do so publicly. In the teacher role, my "hyper(in)visibility" and I become fully visible. Students are supposed to look at my body and consider its positions.

My body is vulnerable to social interpretations, and in being vulnerable, I draw subtle attention to everyone's vulnerability. All bodies experience social critique—and some are more vulnerable to sanction or actual injury than others. Female bodies more than men's, people of color more than white bodies, genderqueer bodies more than cisgender bodies. Fat bodies more than thin ones, to name a few. Can the vulnerable body be powerful?

As a yoga teacher, I allow my body to be seen in movement, to be seen in pleasure, to be seen as the model—not of a laudable body type, but of specific movements, joint rotations, muscular effort, states of being. Allowing my body's limitations to be seen by saying things like "This doesn't work on my body, but you may be able to . . . " can be powerful for students who can't take every "further" modification suggested. I specifically tell students not to take every option. Accept when "it's not your pose." Accept the modification. You are not invited to every party. Neither am I. We're going to be fine sometimes staying home or going to another party. And too, sometimes it's great to accept an invitation you wouldn't normally consider. The pose is like a party—a choice, something to enjoy, perhaps a challenge, but not an expectation, a way to judge human worth.

I also allow my body to be in community. I participate in the creation of the community I occupy. I teach in a retreat center where large, mixed-level classes are the norm. We also offer private and small group classes. My students include athletes and fitness beginners, yoga teachers, and those who've never practiced before. The people who come through are mostly young to middle-aged and fairly active (the retreat is not a resort; there is walking involved on the campus) and they are also, fat, thin, young, old, able, and disabled (to the extent that they can still navigate the uneven terrain of the property). I help people focus on the specifics of doing *asana* safely, to notice pleasure in the body, the information in the body. I am teaching specific people, not just teaching yoga *asanas*. We use props and modifications in every class.

When I reveal my vulnerability, along with the steadiness of my practice, I'm offering the possibility of finding strength and solid ground within a vulnerable position. My social position (related to body stigma) is not likely to change much in my lifetime. Indeed, it's likely to intensify with age. The fact is, if we're lucky enough to live long lives, we'll all be stigmatized by age and declining ability. I often remind students that there are good reasons why we practice corpse pose at the end of every class. That's where we're all heading, and so learning acceptance and peace in the body now is relevant for all. I can't control how others see me, and I can influence community. I can develop a solid yet malleable understanding of myself. Often, students report that this modeling allows them to rest their own pursuit of perfection—not just in the postures, but in various aspects of life. All of that is part of my fat pedagogy.

YOGA IS FOR THE BODY YOU HAVE TODAY: A PEDAGOGY OF OMISSION

I often say some version of this in hatha classes: "Yoga is for the body you have today, not the body you had yesterday or last year or fifteen years ago. Not the one you will have tomorrow or next week or next year after you've practiced every day, or after you've learned to love yourself, or after you've given up ice cream." There are endless humorous and poignant comments I can squeeze from examples that convey this truth: now is all we have. No matter how the mind negotiates and avoids this fact, now is all we have. If you want to be present, then accepting exactly this body is part of that. If you place value on ahimsa, on stilling the waves of the mind so that you can rest in true consciousness, the body is part of that. We are not separable from our bodies during hatha yoga (and arguably, not at any other time before death). And yet, how often do people conditionally accept their bodies, all while claiming to be present? The body from which I speak matters when I say, "This is the only body you have. Yoga is for this body. Accept this body." I know that some students are wondering, how I can mean that, while other students are thinking, wow, I think she really means she accepts her body. In either case, they are truly considering bodies—mine, and their own in relationship to mine, others, and social standards. Similarly, when a slender teacher, or a visibly muscular teacher says such things, the student may think, wow, look how clear thinking, liberated, and advanced she is. Or conversely, sheesh, of course she can love and accept herself; look at those abs. We are never speaking—or thinking—from the mind alone. The body is involved.

In my classes, I talk more about the body than about philosophy. I include some of the yoga sutras and chants and stories about Hindu mythology, but minimally. According to my eclectic training (including Iyengar-style teaching), I talk more about alignment than affirmations. I draw attention to bodies that show clear examples of good posture, including my own, and I look for a range of body types to use as examples when I do this. Any body can potentially be a clear example of positioning, effort, variations on the pose. A huge part of pedagogy lies in what we choose to exclude in each sixty-, seventy-five-, or ninety-minute class. So much of popular culture can be replicated in spaces like yoga studios, or we can consciously choose to omit the aspects that are incongruent with the yoga sutras, the yamas, and the niyamas. We each bring our sum of self, our opinions (even subtly conveyed in the way we hold our bodies, glance, dress, etc.). No one is teaching "pure" yoga. Indeed, I don't believe such a thing exists. We combine lineage, training, and innovation. Thus has yoga progressed from its beginning into the present day.

I often attend classes that include contemplations, affirmations, and I'm not against them. Indeed, "Yoga is for the body you have today" is an affirmation of sorts. I specifically don't use affirmations that reference the appearance of the body, outside of positioning in the *asana*. The kundalini teacher in a class I recently attended said "If you want to get ripped abs, keep practicing breath of fire!" He seemed to truly believe that the appearance of his abs originated in breath of fire. Consider how absurd it would be for me to point to my fat arms and say, "this is the result of twenty-five years practicing plank pose!" I'm very careful about language and causation, though many teachers link appearance and practice without care.

In another example, my yoga teacher friend used to routinely say, "Come into your body and feel gratitude. You have two arms, two legs, your sight and hearing!" I asked him once, privately, if he really meant that's why we should be grateful. Conversely, did he mean that blind students or amputees could not experience gratitude in a yoga practice?

He saw my point. And this type of verbal encouragement—in part because yoga is routinely practiced by a relatively privileged group in the United States—is endemic to studio banter.

We have to work at awareness, phrasing, and word choice. For instance, I exclude comments about bodies that are often seen as laudable, unless it's about the pose. "Let's see what's going well in this trikonasana!" I might say. Though it's sometimes tempting, especially when someone is well-dressed, or particularly graceful in that lithe, willowy way we're taught to admire, I don't comment on beauty, fitness, style, etc. We may indeed share an ideal image of these things, but I don't choose to reinforce that association. I prefer to point out how everyone can enjoy the experience of the body. The appearance of the body is simply not of concern, unless it's about posture and modification.

The first teacher with whom I learned to teach, Sherri Jones, was an Iyengar-style instructor. She mentored me, apprentice-style, during a span of two years in which time I assisted in classes she taught, and subbed for classes when she was away. My learning with her included fewer sessions in which she taught me to teach, and more opportunities to observe and adjust and teach in actual classes with a range of bodies. After I taught, she would prompt my reflections on my teaching, and also on the specific bodies with which I had contact during that class. Observation and presence were key elements in her teaching, and she showed me their importance by example. I recall the first time I ever witnessed her kneel down next to someone's body, in a pose, and contemplate it, as though looking for the internal logic of that body in that *asana*. I was impressed with the strategy and also felt as though I was witnessing something rare—not just in a yoga class, but in regular life: the ability to be present to the truth of another person's body.

What I didn't see, and what I try to eschew in my own classes, is fear. If I don't know how to teach a certain body how to do yoga, I look to that body itself for cues. I do my informed and intuitive best. If a student becomes a regular in my class, I take the invitation to learn more about the specifics of that body. How does that person's cerebral palsy affect the yoga practice? How does that person's fat distribution affect the yoga practice? How does that person's inflexibility affect the yoga practice? We are not just teaching poses, after all. We're teaching people.

I also learned from how Sherri managed the entire class climate with regard to student judgments of one another. Establishing the culture of the room is primarily about the teacher. It also includes the physical setup, how students are allowed or encouraged to interact with each other, and how they refer to or discuss themselves within that setting. For instance, I recall a regular student in our studio who was transitioning her gender, male to female. Over a period of months and years, other students witnessed the changes in her appearance. It's reasonable enough to think that gender should simply not be an issue in yoga and yet, the responses from students were a profound reminder that our instruction is always situated in a specific location, in specific bodies, and in cultural interpretations of bodies. As social creatures, we don't escape the burden of making meaning of one another, and this can be troubling when also juggling the aims of yoga. We're coming more deeply into our own bodies, after all, putting aside many of our other social identities for a while in favor of participation in the yoga community. That can feel vulnerable to anyone in the room. One day, in class, as we held a seated twist and Sherri came around to provide adjustments to our upright postures, a student who appeared to be male, white, and in his early sixties looked at the transitioning woman with a sneer and in a whisper (intentionally audible to all) said to the teacher, "So, is that a man or a woman?" Sherri answered, calmly but firmly, as she applied her adjustment to the man's spine, "Yes. Now breathe."

This is how class culture is established, little by little. Certain things are encouraged, others are accepted, and some things are not tolerated at all. Based on this culture, the studio attracts its clientele. Of course, the appropriateness of these interactions depends, in part, on the lineage in which one teaches. In some classes, the student's inner wisdom is thought to be the best guide for modifications. Teaching can be very proscribed. And still, what the teacher chooses to add—or omit—helps to establish the class pedagogy.

EXPLORATIONS OF BEAUTY AND WORTHINESS

I asked Sherri recently for her reflections on how my body and practice were accepted in the teaching role when I first began offering classes in her studio. Fat yoga and fitness instructors are still not at all the norm at this printing, but we were a downright unusual sight in the 1990s. She replied via email.[7] "As I think back on that era, I'm not remembering any negative reactions or comments. What I do recall is that some people commented on your flexibility—that they were impressed! And I remember other comments having to do with your poise and your skill in teaching a comprehensive practice session. So—a positive experience is what people reported back to me."

Predictably, part of my acceptance in the teacher role had to do with my physical abilities. The super-capable fat body, especially one that can do unexpectedly laudable things involving strength and focus, is often temporarily exempted from the usual ridicule fat bodies receive. I've sometimes additionally felt students use me as "inspiration porn" which is quite different than simply finding my practice holistically empowering. The term "inspiration porn" is often used to describe feelings of gratitude, relief, or empowerment when viewing disabled people accomplish heroic or even common tasks with courage, grace, and aplomb. I didn't specifically feel that students viewed me that way in Sherri's studio, though I have felt it on occasion since then. At the retreat center where I currently teach, I've had students who—thinking they're saying something complimentary—tell me that if I can love my body, then surely they can too. Or that if I can do a headstand, then there's still hope for them too. There's a certain starry-eyed, "wow, I guess I have nothing to complain about" element in these comments.

Actual appreciation and admiration for me as a mentor is also sometimes present and has a different feel entirely. For instance, Sherri commented on her own process of deciding that I was ready to teach in her studio. She said, "I could tell you had a steady practice yourself and that you had, additionally, the awareness and insight, the sensitivity and knowledge to begin teaching. I definitely loved that you had the courage to step into the teacher role for me—the courage and the confidence to face head on whatever thoughts the students might have going on inside of them."

These elements are not about the body, and yet, the body is always in play. It's possible for multiple and even conflicting perceptions to play out at once. Recently, a student who was new to my class scrutinized my posture in a way I found familiar and then gaped with disbelief when she couldn't do what I was doing. This type of response to my body in the teacher role comes up infrequently, and fairly predictably nonetheless. She seemed to think that she was failing because I (a fat woman) could do something she couldn't. It's easy to see how this mindset can arise. Our culture has taught us that bodies line up along a hierarchy of worth, and fat bodies are among the most devalued. If the fat yogi or the old yogi or the disabled yogi can do something considered "advanced," chances are it's impressive to most.

Sometimes it's simply not possible for clear instructions or a steady practice or even the authority of the role to override the culturally sanctioned dismissal and derision of the fat body. Again, the culture of the yoga studio can either confirm or reconstruct the cultural norms and values we've been given regarding bodies. As Sherri shared, "The fact that you were a very regular part of the group classes I taught and that many of the students at my studio knew you, I feel, helped a lot in them accepting you into the role of the one leading the class. And for sure they saw me treat you with respect as I did them. . . . So all of those factors helped the transition to be smooth."

She further commented on how students bring their own bodies and ideas about bodies and cultural values into the yoga studio, and the value in my body's ability to disrupt negative norms. "I loved that you with your big, beautiful, graceful, and limber body just broke all to pieces the *Yoga Journal* image of what a yoga teacher was supposed to look like. . . . One of the biggest comforts for me when you were holding the space in my absence was that I knew you would be competent in handling whatever came up among the students—whatever the particular dynamics would be for a given group I was sure you'd be able to direct in a good way. That's such a key strength for any teacher to have, you know? The ability to stay calm, to stay engaged, to move the group forward through weird comments or off-colored jokes or who knows what, and to bring the class to a successful completion."

What does it mean for a yoga class to come to a successful completion? I often comment about how much of what we do on the mat is a metaphor for other areas of our lives. Balance, steadiness, strength, flexibility—we take them all with us into our other endeavors. Awareness and practice help make this so.

When it comes to "fat pedagogy," somehow I want to ask students: Are you able to see beauty in me, in my body? And what does that do for your ability to see beauty in yourself? How do we approach one another with the same appreciation (or even reverence) with which we approach nature, the forms of beauty that we can most readily recognize?

When it comes to everyday things like yoga, sex, movement, athleticism, eating, dancing, etc., what matters is the *experience* of the body, not the *appearance* of the body. Yes, we have to reject the whole media machine (and sometimes friends and family) to truly grasp this. And it's vital to a good life and a better world. Of course appearance seems to matter, because there are well-documented rewards and privileges attached to all types of culturally normative appearance. There's no wisdom in staying out of the body's experience though, no deep pleasure or understanding. It only makes us easier for others to control when we seek privilege and revel in the kind of hierarchies that prop up our sense of self-worth. I realize that people don't like to think of themselves as controllable, but we are. We need community. And it's the wisdom of the body, the wisdom of experiencing the body, that can lead us out of all manner of trouble when we fall in. It can lead us to stronger community, wiser culture. Again and again, in our continuing social evolution.

NOTES

1. Judith Butler, *Bodies that Matter: On the Discursive Limits of Sex* (London and New York: Routledge, 1993) xii.

2. Erving Goffman, *The Presentation of Self in Everyday Life* (Edinburgh: University of Edinburgh, 1956).

3. Maya Maor, "Becoming the Subject of Your Own Story: Creating Fat-positive Representations," *Interdisciplinary Humanities* 30, no. 3 (2014): 7–23.

4. Zoe C. Meleo-Erwin, "Disrupting Normal: Toward the 'Ordinary and Familiar' in Fat Politics," *Feminism & Psychology* (2012) doi: 10.1177/0959353512445358.

5. John O'Donohue and Krista Tippett, "The Inner Landscape of Beauty," "Speaking of Faith."

6. Jeannine Gailey, *The Hyper(in)Visible Fat Woman* (Palgrave MacMillan, 2014).

7. Sherry Jones, email to author, August 30, 2015.

REFERENCES

"artifact," in Dictionary.com, 2015. http://dictionary.reference.com/browse/artifact. September 29, 2015.

Butler, Judith. *Bodies that Matter: On the Discursive Limits of Sex* (London and New York: Routledge. 1993) xii.

Gailey, Jeannine. *The Hyper(in)Visible Fat Woman* (Palgrave MacMillan, 2014).

Goffman, Erving. *The Presentation of Self in Everyday Life* (Edinburgh: University of Edinburgh, 1956).

Jones, Sherry. Email to author, August 30, 2015.

Maor, Maya. "Becoming the Subject of Your Own Story: Creating Fat-positive Representations." *Interdisciplinary Humanities* 30, no. 3 (2014): 7–23.

Meleo-Erwin, Zoe.C. "Disrupting Normal: Toward the 'Ordinary and Familiar' in Fat Politics." *Feminism & Psychology* (2012) doi: 10.1177/0959353512445358.

O'Donohue, John and Krista Tippett. "The Inner Landscape of Beauty." "Speaking of Faith." National Public Radio. February 28, 2008. Accessed September 3, 2015. http://www.onbeing.org/program/john-o-donohue-the-inner-landscape-beauty/2031.

Part III

Yoga as Individual and Collective Liberation

Beth Berila

The earlier sections of this anthology discuss how yoga in the West is rooted in histories of colonization and at the center of many contemporary debates over education, body image, sexuality, consumerism, health, and wellness. Mainstream Western yoga is clearly both reflective of and embedded in contemporary racial, gender, sexual, economic, and cultural power dynamics. But it is also a vibrant site of social change. Indeed, the science and philosophy of yoga offer unique tools for liberation, both on individual levels and on collective ones.

Yoga offers ways to heal from the trauma of oppression. When taught in informed ways, it can provide safer spaces for marginalized communities to sink into their embodiment, heal from oppression, and build empowered selves and communities. Indeed, the rise of classes for people of color and LGBTQAI+ communities, along with adaptive yoga programs, indicate the need for not only creating spaces for marginalized communities but also integrating yoga philosophy and training with social justice awareness. This integration is not new, of course, as yoga in India has historically been connected to social change. But its manifestation in the West, with the emphasis on capitalism and *asana*, makes this social justice connection controversial for some and deeply transformative for others.

The essays in this section examine yoga's potential for revolutionary change. Thalia González, JD, and Lauren Ecktrom's (E-RYT-500) essay, "From Practice to Praxis: Mindful Lawyering for Social Change," starts the section with a discussion of how the eight limbs of yoga can inform a more liberatory approach to law. They discuss how social justice, mindfulness, and yoga can offer a more compassionate, relational, and transformational praxis of law that can empower marginalized communities by helping us embody and connect the ideals of "working for justice" and "living justly."

Punam Mehta, MSc, in her chapter "Embodiment through Purusa and Prakrti: Feminist Yoga as a Revolution from Within," describes the model of feminist yoga that she has developed while working with indigenous pregnant women and new mothers abusing substances during pregnancy in Winnipeg, Manitoba, Canada. Situating her work within histories of colonization that affects both yoga and the communities with whom she works, Mehta describes how feminist yoga can be taught in ways that help indigenous women empower both themselves and their communities.

Dr. Steffany Moonaz writes of her work with people living with chronic illnesses. In her chapter, "Yoga and Dis/Ability," Moonaz traces some of the historic references about the body in classic yoga texts to build a foundation for yoga therapy. She then analyzes her research and teaching with communities living with dis/ability to argue for yoga as a deeply healing tool for healthy embodiment. In particular, she focuses on yoga as a way for people living with arthritis and other chronic illnesses to reframe their relationship with their bodies and learn techniques to help them enhance their quality of life.

"Yoga as Embodied Feminist Praxis: Trauma, Healing, and Community-Based Responses to Violence" furthers this discussion by exploring how yoga can be combined with feminist awareness to help heal from trauma and build stronger communities. Drawing on their work with two community-based organizations, Urban Yogis in New York City and Project Air in Kigali, Rwanda, Dr. Beth S. Catlett and Mary Bunn, MA, note how yoga can shape transformative service projects while also noting some of the potential pitfalls of working with communities different from one's own.

Dr. Ariane Balizat and Dr. Whitney Myers discuss the potential for integrating feminism and yoga. Their chapter, "Yoga, Postfeminism, and the Future" analyzes the tendency in much Western yoga to reflect the postfeminist tenet that gender equality is already achieved, even while it reproduces problematic classist, body image, and racialized ideals. They conclude their chapter with a discussion of how intersectional feminism and yoga can inform one another as we work to heal from oppression and create more socially just worlds.

Finally, in their chapter, "Queering Yoga: An Ethic of Social Justice," Jacoby Ballard (E-RYT-500) and Karishma Kripalani, MA, trace the colonialist, heteronormative, white supremacist capitalist patriarchal roots of much mainstream yoga that excludes all people who do not fit the "norm." Placing in dialogue their rich and distinct identity locations, they describe their experiences of marginalization of yoga worlds but also offer yoga philosophy and counter-cultural yoga spaces as powerful modes healing. They offer a vision of queering yoga for social justice transformation. Taken together, the articles in this section create an invaluable dialogue for the potential and the limitations of yoga for individual, collective, and societal transformation.

TWELVE

From Practice to Praxis

Mindful Lawyering for Social Change

Thalia González and Lauren Eckstrom

This chapter considers a new way to explore, contextualize, and expand yoga as an embodied lived practice. We seek to reveal how yogic practices can intentionally expand the domains in which law students and lawyers see themselves acting. Our work is intended to contribute to the diverse body of scholarship that broadly considers the intersection between mindfulness and law, and more importantly, to add a new dimension to the discourse. Thus, our chapter has twin goals. First, we aim to position legal practice as relational. By this we mean a formal practice not solely concerned with responding to legal wrongs, but rather seeking to respond to the harms and effects that legal practice can have on relationships at multiple levels: the lawyer with self, the lawyer with client, the lawyer with community, and the lawyer with systems of justice. We believe an evolution in the conversation regarding legal identity as inherently relational is integral to understanding how collective struggles and commitments are at the foundation of lasting social change. As bell hooks explains, the importance of feminist, anti-racist, and intersectional activism is to fight against the interlocking systems of oppression (imperialism, white supremacy, capitalism, and patriarchy), not treating them in isolation from each other but as different manifestations of the same dominator culture.[1] Second, we aim to show how yoga, as an embodied lived practice, offers principles that can define, guide, and ground legal practice as a relational conception of people and the world we inhabit. To do this, we draw on the *The Yoga Sutras of Patanjali*, paying particular attention to how the Eight Limbs of Yoga can ground lawyers seeking to reimagine conceptions of identity, solidarity, justice, equality, dignity, and respect. For example, how might one look at a practice of *Ahimsa* to thoughtfully consider the language used when navigating the complexities of difference. When viewed in this intersectional context, yoga connects, not separates, ideas of "working for justice" and "living justly." As such, the practice of lawyering mindfully is to see social justice work with steadfast attention to interconnectedness.

THE CONTEMPLATIVE LAW MOVEMENT

The integration of mindfulness into legal practice and pedagogy has become increasingly prevalent over the last twenty-five years.[2] The first wave of the contemplative law movement began in 1989 when Jon Kabat-Zinn offered a program in mindfulness-based stress reduction for judges, which was followed by similar trainings for mediators.[3] Ten years later the American Bar Association published Steve Keeva's book, *Transforming Practices: Bringing Joy and Satisfaction to the Legal Life*, which identified the efforts of lawyers to integrate contemplative practices into the profession.[4] In 2002, the movement garnered mainstream attention when the *Harvard Negotiation Law Review* hosted a symposium on mindfulness meditation and alternative dispute resolution and published Leonard Riskin's seminal piece "The Contemplative Lawyer: On the Potential Contributions of Mindfulness Meditation to Law Students, Lawyers, and Their Clients."[5] This article presented Riskin's conception of the "Lawyer's Standard Philosophical Map," which connected mindfulness meditation and legal education and practice, arguing that meditation is essential to the development of alternative skills (personal and professional) needed for a sustained and effective practice.[6]

Contemplative practices have emerged in higher education as an important pedagogical approach to connect students with new ways of thinking, listening, writing, and engaging in society. As Arthur Zajonc has observed, this "quiet revolution" has gained significant recognition over time, by affirmatively declaring that "change, growth and transformation of the human being" are hallmarks of a genuine education.[7] Similar to other disciplines, the contemplative law movement has grown in scope and content. Over the last decade, the Center for the Contemplative Mind in Society's Law Program has led the field in developing a "common understanding of what is meant by contemplative practices and how it might apply to the practice of law."[8]

While much of the early pedagogical work was done "under the radar," in courses associated with individualized well-being, upon the release of the Carnegie Report in 2007 the need for a curriculum that integrates contemplative practices became apparent.[9] In a discipline where students are taught to distance themselves from their emotions, values, clients, and even authentic selves, scholars and commentators have made clear connections in how contemplative practices serve to reshape personal, ethical, and professional foundations.[10] For example, Douglas Codiga argues that mindfulness meditation offers lawyers a method for cultivating deeper insights that "touch upon the whole lawyer's life."[11] In this way, contemplative practices can promote "more ethical conduct, more compassionate and empathic judgment, social justice, and transforming the world in support of the more altruistic tendencies with human nature."[12] Today, a variety of contemplative practices are introduced to law students at more than twenty law schools, in presentations, workshops, classes, externships, or student groups.[13]

As a movement, contemplative or mindful lawyering[14] continues to center on the individual, with scant attention focused on how such practices can be embedded in, shape, and be shaped by community-based and social justice legal practice. This is not surprising as it follows the similar patterns identified by Kimberlé Crenshaw with respect to identity politics and conceptions of social justice in which liberatory objectives are to be devoid of categories of social significance.[15] While a handful of scholars that have rejected this construction, their voices have not been reflected in the mainstream dialogue. For example, Rhonda Magee has argued that contemplative practices can "provide a bridge to deep reconsideration of how to more meaningfully, ethically, and effectively law in service to clients and community"[16] and begin to address the critiques of legal education by critical race scholars. We agree. Mindful lawyering, when advanced as a critical pedagogy, challenges students to develop not only the legal knowledge to deconstruct issues of power, privilege, inequality, and subordination, but an intersectional view of how existing social categories and constructions replicate and perpetuate subordination. Instead of simply looking at one layer of experiences or relationships, mindful law students (and lawyers) seek to create new structures and relationships that promote equality and inclusion, resist subordination, fostering self-expression and self-determination, respect the intelligence and agency of individuals and communities, and at the most foundational level, ground their work in approaching others with dignity and respect. This translates into a radically different form of learning that stresses critical self-reflection, deconstructs dominant patterns of knowledge production, and connects to historical and contemporary realities of power and privilege. As Roxana Ng argues, such embodied learning is essential as an anti-oppressive pedagogy in higher education.[17] For Ng such pedagogy dissolves the "boundaries between the self and collectivity, between the individual and the system."[18] When viewed as embodied learning, mindful lawyering forces students to face their own biases, prejudices, stereotypes, egocentric, or sociocentric tendencies.

In 2007, Angela Harris, Margaretta Lin, and Jeff Selbin offered a new approach to the practice of mindful lawyering that reflects a more embodied approach to practice. Their work positions mindfulness to address a "central tension in our work: how best to advocate on behalf of subordinated and disenfranchised communities within the existing political economy while holding fast to a clear vision of a more diverse, democratic, egalitarian, transparent, and participatory civic life."[19] From this space, they posit a theory of practice in which lawyers engage in "collective work of peacemaking" in disenfranchised communities without reinforcing patterns of subordination and oppression.[20] By aligning community lawyering and principles of engaged Buddhism they offer the first glimpse into the potential for mindfulness to decenter lawyers as the central focus of a contemplative movement in law, and instead position *relationships* with clients and the community as the heart of mindfulness. For example, they thoughtfully note, "Mindfulness does not dictate a particular relationship between lawyer and client; indeed, it does the opposite. It requires the lawyer to be aware of and intentional about the layers of relationship with the client and situation involved."[21]

Given that our work seeks to expand the theory and practice of mindful community lawyering, and likewise mindful legal education, we do so with keen attention to the groundbreaking nature of Harris, Lin, and Selbin's vision, and in alignment with the idea that "mindfulness can transform lawyers and communities alike as we work together toward a more just and equitable future."[22] In this way, we look to holistic yogic practice as a place from which lawyers can more fully develop their capacity to critically self-reflect, engage in knowledge production, connect to historical and contemporary realities of power and privilege, and foster individual and collective empowerment. Such transformation aligns with what hooks provocatively calls "releas[ing] the attachment to dominator thinking and practice."[23] We believe developing such capacity is essential for lawyers to build bidirectional and accountable relationships not only with their clients, but as importantly, with themselves. By approaching law as a mindful embodied practice, lawyers seeking social change can more effectively draw upon the strengths of others to develop a shared vision, exercise the power required to necessitate change, and work in collective solidarity. Moreover, instead of exercising power in ways that replicate marginalization, they do so with deliberate attention to intersecting axes of identity and power. We do not suggest such critical transformation will happen after one single yoga posture or even after a thousand hours of yogic practices, but rather when one is able to step on and off the mat with a presence of mind to navigate the complex and contradicting forces of social justice lawyering. For example, what might it look like to consider the often repeated phrase in a yoga class "root to rise," not only as a signal for transition from one pose to the next, but a commitment to being rooted in a transformational practice that moves toward a vision of liberation for all. As Angela Davis has powerfully noted, the cultivation of mindfulness can become a revolutionary force if embedded in social movements that target oppressive systems.[24]

FROM PRACTICE TO PRAXIS

Before it is possible to discuss the intersection between yoga and lawyering, it seems first necessary to introduce not only the practice of yoga itself, but also how we understand yoga. Contemporary Western yoga practice is widely perceived as the performance of physical yoga postures. This is a limited understanding of yoga as a somatic practice. As the *Yoga Sutras* set forth, yoga postures or *asanas* are only one component of a larger philosophy that extends to thoughts, actions, behaviors, and the senses.

We define yoga more expansively: as a practice that is not simply marked by the execution of *asana*, but a holistic approach that embodies all of the eight limbs to develop, and sustain, a multiplicity of relationships with self and others. Thus, the practice of yoga includes *asanas*, but are not limited to *them*. As Kay Gendron has noted, "[We are] citizens of two worlds: the external world of relationships, work, family, and community, and the internal work of our deepest inner reality."[25] By approaching yoga as an embodied living practice, we seek to emphasize its inherent relationality. For example, in living all eight limbs, one can begin to move past simply looking at the external, such as status, race, gender, or ability, and embrace a more intersectional approach that captures the full diversity of human experiences, expressions, and relationships. In releasing illusion or *Maya* from reality, one can also begin to view power as more than an external concept and instead as a reflection of an ethos present within each living person.

It is in operating from this broader definition of yoga, we believe that yoga, like social justice lawyering, reflects the praxis of mindfully exercising power.[26] We draw on the simplest definition of power, from its Latin root, as meaning "to be able." Similar to experiencing a difficult moment as a social justice lawyer, to sustain a challenging yoga posture exemplifies powerfully sitting with a challenging case, while remaining free of harmful reaction and fully embodied with truthfulness and contentment. Thus, the multiplicity of experiences that define yoga practice and social justice lawyering reflects a dynamic interplay of processes by which power is created from living in relationship with self and others.

Certain principles define, guide, and ground yoga, such as conscious self-care, healthy boundaries, honesty in word and action, collaborative living, compassion for self and others, and self-reflection. The foundation of such principles lay in *The Yoga Sutras of Patanjali*, more specifically the Eight Limbs of Yoga.[27] Formally defined, the Eight Limbs of Yoga include: *Yama* (Awakened Qualities), *Niyama* (Codes for Noble Living), *Asana* (Postures), *Pranayama* (Breath Control), *Pratyahara* (Sense Control), *Dharana* (Focus or Concentration), *Dhyana* (Meditation), and *Samadhi* (Absolute Oneness). Similar to Harris, Lin, and Selbin, who grounded their theory of mindful community lawyering in the fourteen principles of engaged Buddhism, we turn to the eight limbs as a foundation for how one might choose to inhabit the world of social lawyering from a subtly, or perhaps radically, reoriented space of personal and professional identity. In doing so, one would approach their legal practice with a greater intentionality and attentionality to the complex layers of relationships that shape the experience of working for justice. Furthermore, while the eight limbs do not dictate the set of ideas or theories about issues of power, privilege, bias, or oppression, they provide a framework for thinking critically and self-reflectively about the relationship and boundaries between the self and the collective, the individual, and the system. The development of such critical reflexivity supports a deeper connection between one's own mind and body, as well as the realization that no body can be divorced from its lived experiences, including the constructions of race, sex, gender, class, and ability. Thus, to work and live justly is to think and act in ways to challenge dominant structures of subordination.

Yama (Awakened Qualities)

Yama, the first limb, is composed of five qualities of Awakened Living: *Ahimsa* (Non-Violence), *Satya* (Truthfulness), *Asteya* (Non-Stealing), *Brahmacharya* (Celibacy), and *Aparigraha* (Non-Grasping).[28] The *Yamas* are practiced both inwardly and outwardly, manifesting as relationships to oneself and in relationships in one's community and the world. Therefore, the *Yamas* are inseparable from professional identity, and as such, are instructive when considering a more relational approach to lawyering by provoking lawyers to sit with difficult questions not only about the nature of individual work, but the ever changing meaning of working for justice in an unjust society. This is particularly true when striving to serve the needs of individuals and communities that have experienced systemic oppression, without reinforcing patterns of behavior that perpetuate subordination.

While all of the five qualities are equally important, we turn our attention to *Ahimsa*, *Satya*, and *Aparigraha*. *Ahimsa* or Non-Violence means "not causing pain."[29] Nonviolence is widely translated as not killing, and while this is an obvious and integral component of nonviolence, *Ahimsa* extends far beyond to include the subtle realms of personal experience such as not causing pain to others or oneself in thoughts, words, and actions. For example, if thoughts, revealed aloud, inflict pain on self or others then even the thought itself moves against the principle of *Ahimsa*.

From a practical standpoint, committing to *Ahimsa* means to learn to listen without judgment or reaction and to refrain from speaking in ways that create disharmony. A practice of *Ahimsa* also requires nonreactivity in the face of adversarial actions of others in order to elevate human connection and experience; it asks practitioners to engage in clear and compassionate communication.

Broadly speaking, the ideas of *Ahimsa* are represented in the legal literature. In the late 1980s and early 1990s a thoughtful body of scholarship[30] emerged challenging traditional notions of public interest lawyering and emphasizing egalitarian collaboration between community lawyers and clients. It is in this discourse that we position *Ahimsa* as central. While a connection has never been explicitly drawn to *Ahimsa*, clear and compassionate communication aligns with models of lawyering that seek to disrupt dominant frames of communication between lawyers, clients, and communities. For example, when considering lawyer-client collaboration Gerald López, in his influential book *Rebellious Lawyering: One Chicano's Vision of Progressive Practice*, argues: "[A] client and a lawyer do not want simply to add to each other's knowledge. . . . [I]nstead, they desire to challenge what each knows-how each gained it, what each believes about it, and how each shares and uses it."[31] For López, this requires rebellious lawyers to develop a capacity to listen deeply, share more openly, reflect more critically, and cultivate deeper social awareness. Similarly, for Harris, Lin, and Selbin, the mindful lawyers asks, "Do we speak and treat one another in ways that are compassionate and reflect the humanity in all of us? Do we take the time to muster the courage to resolve the inevitable conflicts that arise when people work together closely? Do we mindfully create campaign strategies that understand the inter-relationships between people and actions?"[32]

Furthermore, as Chip Hartranft translates, "being firmly grounded in nonviolence creates an atmosphere in which others can let go of their hostility."[33] Thus, by practicing *Ahimsa* lawyers can learn to let go of their defensiveness and generate powerful connections and communication free of self-interest. As angel Kyodo Williams writes, "There is a place that we find when we look deeply into ourselves" and "that allows us to be completely free of our histories, our stories, our hang-ups. . . . We actually have a freedom spot in our brains."[34] Such connectivity reflects what Anthony Alferi has identified as the legal-political enterprise of democracy promotion, whereby cooperative lawyer-client roles and relationships forge alternative divisions of labor in advocacy and restore abandoned narratives of citizenship.[35]

The second Yama, *Satya* or Truthfulness, is the basic principle of not lying. Again, it is important to move beyond a narrow construction of *Satya* and recognize that nonviolence and truthfulness are inherently connected. As Hartranft explains, "one's truthfulness toward self and others (*satya*) not only enables one's personal actions, but also removes the pressure to deceive."[36] In considering *Satya* in relationship to social change work, a legal practice grounded in truthfulness is not simply about being honest with oneself or with clients, allies, or collaborators, but the willingness to be collaborative rather than divisive when imagining solutions. As the embodiment of collaboration, *Satya* reinforces a central idea we set forth at the beginning of this section: the exercise of power. Working for justice requires a commitment to the sharing of power in order to work in solidarity with others. Drawing on social movement literature, solidarity is built through "a sustained series of actions between power holders and persons successfully claiming to speak on behalf of a constituency lacking formal representation"[37] as well as through connective structures and shared identities that sustain collective action. Thus, *Satya* challenges governing norms of power and privilege traditionally associated with litigation-centered practice where power circulates and finds its only expression in the doctrinal structure of law and legal analysis. Consider the example of working in coalition. When embodying *Satya* one may pause for before simply rendering a legal assessment and instead elevate the voices of community members most affected by the harm to ensure bidirectional power sharing and truly engaged dialogue, as opposed to one-sided solutions. In this example, *Satya* helps to narrate new social meanings of knowledge and power as lawyers let go of conventional understandings of their roles and privileges. Acting as a mindful lawyer, one no longer views legal practice as an individualistic enterprise divorced from the exercise and maintenance of power in multiple and complicated forms, but as a shared lived experience that has been marked by conditions of oppression.

Non-Grasping, *Aparigraha*, is the fifth Yama that considers the significant personal, internal suffering caused by thoughts of grasping—for money, status, objects, relationships, and careers that are perceived as missing or lacking. *Aparigraha*'s ultimate aim is "freedom from the compulsion to have [which] allows us instead to seek the true source of happiness, which is wisdom."[38] The simplest lesson of *Aparigraha* can be expressed in two interconnected ideas: first, lawyers are not the only agents of social change, and second, lawyers are at their best when seeking to learn from and connect with others. By fighting against the powerful and subtle forces of "cultural encapsulation"[39] (all the unconscious ways that race, gender, and class background, as well as professional socialization and the privileged status of being a lawyer, shape thoughts and actions) through a deliberate practice of *Aparigraha*, lawyers can restructure the relationships in which they act, the tactics and strategies they employ, and transform their visions of social change. In this way neither the lawyer, client, nor system alone sets the terms or goals of the relationship.

Niyama (Codes for Noble Living)

Niyama is the second limb of yoga and includes five Codes for Noble Living: *Saucha* (Purity), *Santosha* (Contentment), *Tapas* (Purification), *Svadhyaya* (Self-Study), and *Isvarapranidhana* (Celebration of the Divine).[40] While the Yamas are guidelines for behavior toward others, the Niyamas are guidelines for how to treat oneself. Again, we acknowledge all of the Niyamas, but choose to focus on two specifically for purposes of our discussion: *Santosha* and *Svadhyaya*.

Santosha or Contentment is the second Niyama. In the plain terms, *Santosha* means to cultivate a steady state of presence. As is the case with all of the Eight of Limbs, *Santosha* requires constant diligence to develop an internal state of contentment, despite external challenges, stresses, tensions, and distractions. As a practice, *Santosha* also challenges a focus on the multiple ways in which one can create internal accountability for a healthy relationship to self. In this manner, a relationship or connection between *Santosha* and *Aparigraha* (Non-Grasping) become clear. For example, similar to non-grasping, *Santosha* "brings joy . . . because letting go of our attachment to externals as the source of happiness allows us to abide in the here and now."[41] For lawyers working for social change, *Santosha* supports a more deliberative practice of self reflection aimed at understanding what it means to work for justice. It also promotes an internal assessment of the dynamic and multidimensional impacts that social justice lawyering can have on individuals over the course of a day, month, or lifetime. For example, *Santosha* asks lawyers to consider how to bring balanced attention to the suffering one sees in daily work, as manifested in the experiences of individuals and communities facing injustice, without developing into a state of despair or indifference. Similarly, when one's work is met with opposition, a practice of *Santosha* can invite a moment of introspection to look at the long view of social change to recognize that the intense conflict or contestation may create new opportunities, rather than barriers. Furthermore, *Santosha* provides a critical reminder for lawyers engaged in social justice work that internal anger, while a powerful catalyst to incite and motivate, is also a barrier to transformation at the individual, interpersonal, and community levels. Yet, all of this being said, one should not manifest *Santosha* as complacency or entrenchment. Nor should moving through adversity embrace an idea of helplessness or fuel a sense of hopelessness. This final idea is of particular significance when considering the countless narratives of the difficulties that those working for social justice face in a system that remains fundamentally unequal and unjust.

Svadhyaya, Self-Study, is the fourth Niyama. *Svadhyaya* sets forth that practitioners should acquire knowledge for continued personal growth throughout their lifetime. But *Svadhyaya* does not merely mean self-study or knowledge acquisition for the sake of learning; rather, at the heart of

Svadhyaya lies a critical question of how knowledge is applied to one's life. From this perspective the provocation of *Svadhyaya* is to obtain deeper wisdom and integrate this wisdom into daily living. When understood from this broader context, *Svadhyaya* speaks directly to understanding the struggles of the past to better grasp where we stand, how we got here, the roads others have walked, and the paths we might pursue. Knowledge enables change. We wish to be clear that the gathering of knowledge is not limited to academic study, though there is an extensive literature from the past thirty years addressing lawyering and social change. Rather, it encompasses the act of listening to and honoring the narratives of others. As López reminds us, lawyers "[m]ust open themselves up to being educated by all those with whom they come into contact, particularly about the traditions and experiences of life on the bottom and at the margins."[42]

Asana (Pose)

Asana is the most widely recognized limb of yoga, and the yogic postures are often considered the most direct means to convey yoga as an embodied lived philosophical practice. Like other mindfulness practices that have become popular as part of the contemplative law movement, the physical practice of yoga encourages practitioners to assess embodied somatic feedback loops through a process of introspection toward their own bodies. Yet the execution of yoga postures comprises only one small aspect of the practice of all eight limbs. In their original understanding, yoga postures were to help ascetics sit in meditation for long periods of time with the goal of freeing practitioners from the distractions of bodily sensation and pain. But *asana* also translates as a "posture that brings comfort and steadiness."[43] Thus, to apply *asana* as an embodied lived philosophy is to cultivate comfort and seek steadiness in all situations. This captures the true essence of yoga, which extends *asana* beyond one's mat and into all aspects of living. Regardless of the specific posture, *asana* translates into an ability to see and feel the world in a nonreactive, engaged, and deliberative manner. Simply put, in *asana* one must do less to be more.[44]

When aligning *asana* with all forms of legal practice, the connection becomes quickly apparent. For example, developing the inner and outer strength to approach (and hold) a difficult physical pose is analogous to the ability of a lawyer to see and identify strong emotional reactions in a specific moment, and then to think through those reactions in a mindful way to promote a positive relationship. Furthermore, given that much of legal practice is underpinned by physical experiences, such as interviewing a client, engaging in a negotiation, writing with another lawyer, or presenting arguments before a court, the development of increased awareness of the various external forces impacting the body allows lawyers to grow their abilities to view these forces with the nonjudgmental eye that emerges from holding postures. Given that lawyers are embodied actors that enter and engage with their client's diverse worlds, the relationship of an *asana* practice to legal practice is inescapable.

Separate from physical and emotional stamina, *asana* demonstrates the importance for social justice lawyers to become in tune with their own internal state. There is tremendous benefit to simultaneously and consciously monitoring one's response to the experiences of others, becoming open and less reactive, and yet remaining cognizant of one's own well-being. The development of greater physical awareness is a hallmark of the contemplative law movement, as lawyers (and law students) are often asked to consider how various forms of stress impacts their bodies, and likewise their mental capacities.[45] But what the movement has not asked is how greater awareness of linked physical and mental experiences can transform lawyers to work more collaboratively *with*, not simply *for* clients, thus widening their vision of the possibilities for meaningful social change. We raise this fundamental question in hopes that the movement will seek to expand its view of the critical mind-body connection created in diverse mindfulness practices from a single focus (the lawyer as an individual) to a relational focus (the lawyer in connection with others). Furthermore, this question also seeks to provoke a thoughtful discussion considering how relationships of power are never enacted merely in the form of intellectual encounters. As Ng reminds us, "Most intellectual encounters entail a confrontation of bodies, which are differently inscribed. Power plays are both enacted and absorbed by people physically, as they assert or challenge authority, and the marks of such confrontations are stored in the body."[46]

In addition to negotiating the physical world of legal practice, we wish to draw attention to how lawyers must also engage in narrative methodology (or story-telling), thus navigating their clients' physical experience as well. Not only does narrative methodology require lawyers to control their physical awareness, e.g., listening without being distracted by external stimulations, but more importantly, it requires that once the narrative has been collected, lawyers must embody the role of translator. This embodied role of translator, telling and retelling a client's narrative, requires a careful balance between exercising the power to translate lived experiences into law, and ensuring that such power does not rewrite narratives in a false way. As Harris, Lin, and Selbin note, when "lawyers fail to be mindful of the power imbalance between them and community residents and activists, [they] can drive rather than partner in community struggles."[47] When considering the connection between such physical acts and necessary reflective capacities, the relationship between *asana* and the other eight limbs, such as the Yama *Ahimsa*, delivers a powerful message to social justice lawyers. Through a broad expression of *asana* one can engage in a transformative process that changes how to both physically and mentally move in the world with a deeper recognition of what it means to work *with*, rather than *for* individuals and communities seeking social change.

Lastly, *asanas* can also be understood as a means to relieve limiting internal definitions. This idea resonates deeply with social justice lawyers and is reflected across the work of such scholar-activists as Gerald López, Bill Hing, Luke Cole, Lucie White, Anthony Alferi, Ascanio Piomelli, and Bill Quigley. Their scholarship is marked by a critical view of the traditional prescriptive notions of relationships between lawyers and clients, and contemplates alternative power-sharing processes that build sites of democratic accountability internally and externally. Further, these scholars' models of lawyering for social change embrace the vastness of the work as a means to understand not only the current struggle, but to look at its historical roots with an intention of considering a world of new possibilities. They all acknowledge that though lawyering for social change is difficult, there is much to learn from understanding the legal outcomes in a given moment as well as the collaborative process that yielded those outcomes.

Pranayama (Breath Control) and Pratyahara (Sense Control)

Emotional experiences and mental states are reflected in the breath and the wider senses. For example, as anger, fear or stress arise, the breath pattern becomes unpredictable, rigid, and short, and the eyes dart around. Similarly, as happiness, well-being, and joy arise, the breath pattern becomes long, deep, and steady and vision calmly settles. *Pranayama,* Breath Control, is the fourth limb of yoga and requires practitioners to more deliberately notice their breath cycles, to regulate their mind and energetic states, and control *prana* or life force. *Pratyahara,* Sense Control, is the fifth limb and involves controlling the five senses. The application of *Pranayama* and *Pratyahara* supports all of the guiding principles of Yama and Niyama. By developing a keen awareness of the different states of one's breath and senses, practitioners can move more freely and think more clearly when adversity, challenges, or stress arise. Moreover, the intentional witnessing of changes in the breath or senses allows one to decenter from the external experience, and instead look inwardly to establish balance or regain steadiness in an effort to be nonreactive in the face of difficult situations.

The idea and practice of *Pranayama* and *Pratyahara* has been a foundational aspect of the contemplative law movement, whether or not explicitly expressed in such terms. Beginning in 2002 with Riskin's seminal work on mindfulness and law, scholars have consistently articulated a clear connection between the calming of the mind and the ability to engage more effectively in legal practice. For example, Scott Rogers, the founder and director of the University of Miami School of Law's Mindfulness in Law Program, notes that when one develops more attentional awareness to the senses, "Thoughts and feelings arise, but do not dictate an impulsive reaction. An open and receptive capacity emerges that attends to moment-to-moment experience without assuming what it means or how to respond."[48] In the context of community lawyering Harris, Lin, and Selbin draw connections between mindful awareness and thoughtful communication. They write,

> It is a truism that effective lawyers must learn how to listen to and communicate with their clients, and that this is not as easy as it seems. It is difficult partly because communication flows through a number of channels, not all of them verbal and not all of them conscious. In addition, especially in a community practice, lawyer-client communication often crosses lines of power and privilege. The work of listening across difference and across boundaries of power and privilege is difficult. The mindful lawyer can learn to be aware of these matrices of power without being defeated by them, and even can learn to employ them in transformative ways.[49]

Mindful breath and sense control allows social justice lawyers to bring greater attentional focus on their reactions and connections to the experience of the outer world. In this manner, a focus on breath and senses not only calls attention to the internal state of being, but develops greater awareness of the layered relationships and reactions to self, others, and systems of justice. As López reminds us, "When we act together, we appreciate the advantages of standing shoulder to shoulder."[50]

Dharana (Concentration), Dhyana (Meditation), and Samadhi (Absolute Oneness)

While independently distinct, we have opted to combine the final three limbs together, given their interconnected nature. When considered as interconnected ideas, they demonstrate that when a practitioner is fully focused and mindfully aware, a timeless state evolves where tasks are completed with ease, conflicts effortlessly fall away, and one sees through the illusionary veil of separateness to understand that we are all one. Oneness represents the ultimate state of collaboration with all of life where we are joined together in union. As Hartranft reflects, "the forms and distinctions that had individuated these entities fall away, leaving just their essential natures, recognized as the same stuff."[51] For us, one simple idea captures *Dharana, Dhyana,* and *Samadhi*: by thinking and acting with intention, social justice lawyers no longer see themselves as simply working for change, but rather as mindful collaborators building the power of others to fight against structures that perpetuate legal, political, economic, and social subordination.

CONCLUSION

This chapter is a beginning. First, it seeks to expose the practice of law as complex series of relationships. Second, it introduces a new way of thinking about the intersections between practicing yoga and practicing law. In placing our work simultaneously *within* and *outside* the contemplative law movement, it presents an entry point for a vibrant discourse that repositions relationality (with self, others, and systems of justice) at the center, rather than at the margins. While we concentrate on social justice lawyering, our ideas and arguments are meant to resonate with both lawyers and non-lawyers, in hopes of catalyzing new conversations about the inter- and intra-personal conditions necessary for lasting social change. We believe these ideas also sit squarely within the evolving pedagogy and practices of contemplative or mindful legal education. We are grateful for the early work of Harris, Lin, and Selbin in framing a theory of mindful community lawyering that moves past notions of mindfulness or contemplative practice seen as beneficial for the individual, but not connected to relationships with communities or system of justice. For us, their work was instructive when considering an alternative vision of mindful lawyering grounded in the Eight Limbs of Yoga. We see the eight limbs as guiding not only the actions of an individual relationship to self, but more importantly, in relationship to others by fostering more inclusive ways of interacting and connecting. By grounding social justice lawyering as an embodied yogic practice that engages multiple voices, connects diverse talents and perspectives, and unleashes new energies, a transformation occurs which links individualistic enterprises and collective actions. In this way, lawyers become agents of change committed to embodying an alternate view of the practice in which change occurs both internally, within relationships, and externally, in the conditions experienced by those most often marginalized.

NOTES

1. bell hooks. *Teaching Community: A Pedagogy of Hope*. New York: Routledge, 2003.
2. Rhonda Magee. "Educating Lawyers to Meditate." *University of Missouri–Kansas City Law Review* 79 (2011): 535–94.
3. Magee. "Educating Lawyers to Meditate," 535–94.
4. Steven Keeva. *Transforming Practices: Finding Joy and Satisfaction in the Legal Life*. Illinois: American Bar Association, 1999.
5. Leonard Riskin. "The Contemplative Lawyer: On the Potential Contributions of Mindfulness Meditation to Law Students, Lawyers, and Their Clients." *Harvard Negotiation Law Review* 7 (2002): 33–65.
6. Riskin. "The Contemplative Lawyer," 33–65.
7. Arthur Zajonc. "Contemplative Pedagogy: A Quiet Revolution in Higher Education." *New Directions in Teaching and Learning* 134 (2013): 83–94.
8. The Working Group for Lawyers has primarily adapted meditation practices from the mindfulness and insight traditions within Buddhism.

9. Scott Rogers. "The Role of Mindfulness in the Ongoing Evolution of Legal Education." *University of Arkansas at Little Rock Law Review* 36 (2014): 387–412.

10. Magee. "Educating Lawyers to Meditate." 535–94.

11. Doug Codiga. "Reflections on the Potential Growth of Mindfulness Meditation in Law." *Harvard Negotiation Law Review* 7 (2002): 110–124.

12. Rhonda Magee. "Contemplative Practices and Renewal of Legal Education." *New Directions for Teaching and Learning* 134 (2013): 31–40.

13. Magee. "Contemplative Practices and Renewal of Legal Education," 31–40; Rogers. "The Role of Mindfulness in the Ongoing Evolution of Legal Education," 387–412.

14. We acknowledge that contemplative or mindful lawyering is not homogenous in its practices, forms, and foundations. As such, our use of this term is to capture the diversity in the field including, but not limited to, mindfulness meditation, mindful listening, mindful walking, reflective journaling, reflective inquiry, dialogue, yoga, qi gong, or tai chi.

15. Kimberlé Crenshaw. "Mapping the Margins: Intersectionality, Identity Politics, and Violence Against Women of Color." *Stanford Law Review* 43 (1993): 1241–99.

16. Crenshaw. "Mapping the Margins," 1241–99.

17. Roxanne Ng. "Decolonizing Teaching and Learning Through Embodied Learning: Toward an Integrated Approach, in *Valences of Interdisciplinarity: Theory, Practice and Pedagogy*, edited by Raphael Foshay. Vancouver: University of British Columbia Press, 2012.

18. Ng. "Decolonizing Teaching and Learning Through Embodied Learning"

19. Angela Harris, Margaretta Lin, and Jeff Selbin, "From "the Art of War" to "Being Peace": Mindfulness and Community Lawyering in a Neoliberal Age." *California Law Review* 95 (2007): 2074–2131.

20. Harris, Lin, and Selbin, "From 'the Art of War' to 'Being Peace,'" 2074–2131.

21. Harris, Lin, and Selbin, "From 'the Art of War' to 'Being Peace,'" 2074–2131.

22. Harris, Lin, and Selbin, "From 'the Art of War' to 'Being Peace,'" 2074–2131.

23. bell hooks. "Buddhism and the Politics of Domination." In *Mindful Politics: A Buddhist Guide to Making the World a Better Place*, edited by Melvin McLeod. Somerville: Wisdom Publications, Inc., 2006.

24. Angela Davis. "Mindfulness and the Possibility of Freedom: Angela Davis and Jon Kabat-Zinn in Dialogue." Talk, East Bay Meditation Center, Berkeley, January 15, 2015.

25. Kay Gendron, S. Rama, *The Art of Joyful Living*, Pennsylvania: The Himalayan Institute Press, 1996, vii–ix.

26. For purpose of our chapter we adopt an understanding of praxis expressed by Paulo Freire as the intentional integration of action and reflection. To this end, praxis is not simply action based on reflection, but instead is defined as actions informed by reflections, which embody a commitment to transformation. Paulo Freire. *Pedagogy of the Oppressed*. New York, Continuum International Publishing Group, 2000.

27. Sri Swami Satchidananda. *The Yoga Sutras of Patanjali*. Virginia: Integral Yoga Publications, 2012.

28. *Asteya* or Non-Stealing refers to not obtaining personal possessions that are not freely given and also applies to not hoarding another person's time and energy. Non-stealing forms the basis for healthy boundaries within relationships and requires that practitioners honor the time and energy of others. *Brahmacharya* is frequently translated as Celibacy. While ascetics renounce sexual interaction, for modern yoga practitioners, *Brahmacharya* requires living a sexually principled life, not using sex to obtain power, leverage, or advantage over another.

29. Satchidananda. *The Yoga Sutras of Patanjali*.

30. The three leading contributors to this literature were Professors Gerald López, Lucie White, and Anthony Alfieri. They advocate a collaborative approach that respects clients' decision-making capacities, seeks allies in the pursuit of social justice, and is open to learning from clients and community partners.

31. Gerald P. López. *Rebellious Lawyering: One Chicano's Vision of Progressive Law Practice.* Boulder, CO: Westview Press, 1992.
32. Harris, Lin, and Selbin. "From "the Art of War" to "Being Peace," 2074–2131.
33. Chip Hartranft. *The Yoga Sutras of Patanjali.* Boston: Shambhala Publications, Inc., 2003.
34. angel Kyodo Williams. *Being Black: Zen and the Art of Living with Fearlessness and Grace.* New York: The Berkeley Publishing Group, 2000.
35. Anthony Alferi. "Community Education and Access to Justice in a Time of Scarcity: Notes from the West Grove Trolley Case." *Wisconsin Law Review,* 121 (2013): 121–43.
36. Hartranft. *The Yoga Sutras of Patanjali,* Boston: Shambhala Publications, Inc., 2003.
37. Michael McCann. "Law and Social Movements." In *The Blackwell Companion to Law and Society,* edited by Austin Sarat. Hoboken: Wiley-Blackwell, 2004.
38. Hartranft. *The Yoga Sutras of Patanjali.*
39. Robert F. Cochrain, Jr., John M.A. DiPippa, and Martha M. Peters. *The Counselor-at-Law: A Collaborative Approach to Client Interviewing and Counseling.* New York: Lexis Nexis, 2006.
40. *Saucha* or Purity applies to cleanliness in body, mind, and home. Additionally, *Saucha* centers on the recognition of negative thoughts, destructive patterns, and harsh self-talk to create an uplifting, calm, and pleasant mind space which also supports the meditative limbs of yoga. *Tapas* or Purification means removing intoxicants from the body or removing impurities from the mind, such as attachments and negative thought patterns to create powerful transformation and clarity. *Isvarapranidhana* translates as Celebration of the Divine. While one interpretation could be honoring God in a spiritual sense a more contemporary interpretation acknowledges the Divine as everything outside of our individual control or power. This wider notion of the Divine extends to include all of humanity, understanding that everything we think, say, and do affects not only our inner world, but also our outer world. Thus, *Isvarapranidhana* is accountability in the highest sense, on a communal and global scale.
41. Hartranft. *The Yoga Sutras of Patanjali.*
42. López, *Rebellious Lawyering*
43. Satchidananda. *The Yoga Sutras of Patanjali.*
44. Hartranft *The Yoga Sutras of Patanjali.*
45. Most of the contemplative law movement's work has addressed mindful aware ness as a tool for stress management or as a complement to traditional legal training grounded in helping individual lawyers be more attentive and effective in *their* own work.
46. Ng. "Decolonizing Teaching and Learning Through Embodied Learning."
47. Harris, Lin and Selbin. "From "the Art of War" to Being Peace," 2074–2131.
48. Rogers. "The Role of Mindfulness in the Ongoing Evolution of Legal Education," 387–412.
49. Harris, Lin, and Selbin. "From "the Art of War" to "Being Peace," 2074–2131.
50. López. "Living and Lawyering Rebelliously," 2041–54.
51. Hartranft. *The Yoga Sutras of Patanjali.*

REFERENCES

Alferi, Anthony. "Community Education and Access to Justice in a Time of Scarcity: Notes from the West Grove Trolley Case." *Wisconsin Law Review,* 121 (2013): 121–43.
Cochrain, Robert F., Jr., John M.A. DiPippa, and Martha M. Peters/ *The Counselor-at-Law: A Collaborative Approach to Client Interviewing and Counseling* (New York: Lexis Nexis, 2006).
Codiga, Doug. "Reflections on the Potential Growth of Mindfulness Meditation in Law." *Harvard Negotiation Law Review* 7 (2002): 110–24.

Crenshaw, Kimberlé. "Mapping the Margins: Intersectionality, Identity Politics, and Violence Against Women of Color." *Stanford Law Review* 43 (1993): 1241–99.

Davis, Angela. "Mindfulness and the Possibility of Freedom: Angela Davis and Jon Kabat-Zinn in Dialogue." Talk, East Bay Meditation Center, Berkeley, January 15, 2015.

Gendron, Kay. S. *Rama,The Art of Joyful Living* (Pennsylvania: The Himalayan Institute Press, 1996), vii–ix.

Freire, Paulo. *Pedagogy of the Oppressed* (New York, Continuum International Publishing Group, 2000).

Harris, Angela, Lin, Margaretta and Selbin, Jeff. "From "the Art of War" to "Being Peace": Mindfulness and Community Lawyering in a Neoliberal Age." *California Law Review* 95 (2007): 2074–2131.

Hartranft, Chip. *The Yoga Sutras of Patanjali* (Boston: Shambhala Publications, Inc., 2003).

hooks, bell. *Teaching Community: A Pedagogy of Hope* (New York: Routledge, 2003).

———. "Buddhism and the Politics of Domination," in *Mindful Politics: A Buddhist Guide to Making the World a Better Place*. Edited by Melvin McLeod (Somerville: Wisdom Publications, Inc., 2006).

Keeva, Steven. *Transforming Practices: Finding Joy and Satisfaction in the Legal Life* (IL: American Bar Association, 1999).

Kyodo Williams, angel. *Being Black: Zen and the Art of Living with Fearlessness and Grace* (New York: The Berkeley Publishing Group, 2000).

López, Gerald P. *Rebellious Lawyering: One Chicano's Vision of Progressive Law Practice* (Boulder: Westview Press, 1992).

———. "Living and Lawyering Rebelliously" *Fordham Law Review* 73 (2005): 2041-54.

Magee, Rhonda. "Contemplative Practices and Renewal of Legal Education." *New Directions for Teaching and Learning* 134 (2013): 31–40.

———. "Educating Lawyers to Meditate." *University of Missouri–Kansas City Law Review* 79 (2011): 535–94.

McCann, Michael. "Law and Social Movements," in *The Blackwell Companion to Law and Society*. Edited by Austin Sarat (Hoboken: Wiley-Blackwell, 2004).

Ng, Roxanne. "Decolonizing Teaching and Learning Through Embodied Learning: Toward an Integrated Approach," in *Valences of Interdisciplinarity: Theory, Practice and Pedagogy*. Edited by Raphael Foshay (Vancouver: University of British Columbia Press, 2012).

Rogers, Scott. "The Role of Mindfulness in the Ongoing Evolution of Legal Education." *University of Arkansas at Little Rock Law Review*, 36 (2014): 387–412.

Riskin, Leonard. "The Contemplative Lawyer: On the Potential Contributions of Mindfulness Meditation to Law Students, Lawyers, and Their Clients." *Harvard Negotiation Law Review* 7 (2002): 33–65.

Satchidananda, Sri Swami. *The Yoga Sutras of Patanjali* (VA: Integral Yoga Publications, 2012).

Zajonc, Arthur. "Contemplative Pedagogy: A Quiet Revolution in Higher Education." *New Directions in Teaching and Learning,* 134 (2013): 83–94.

THIRTEEN

Embodiment through Purusha and Prakrti

Feminist Yoga as a Revolution from Within

Punam Mehta

Indigenous scholar Kim Anderson (2000) writes in the book *A Recognition of Being: Reconstructing Native Womanhood*, "I have chosen to start this book by talking about myself because I want to practice an Aboriginal method of contextualizing knowledge. Feminist academics have challenged the objectification of knowledge, this kind of thinking is still prevalent in mainstream circles."[1] My cultural identity is rooted in the ancient religion of Jainism and I am also a Women's and Gender Studies instructor who has also spent most of my adult life working in the local indigenous (Metis and First Nations) communities in Manitoba. In addition, I formally studied Women's and Gender Studies, Midwifery, and Public Health at university and I am now an academic feminist and feminist yoga teacher. Currently, I am developing a theoretical framework for a Feminist Yoga Program (FYP) in my doctoral work.

In this chapter, I describe the introduction of a FYP in my hometown of Winnipeg, Manitoba, Canada with the purpose to serve the most marginalized populations. As an example, I provide a theoretical framework for a FYP, guided by both feminist and indigenous worldviews, that I have developed for indigenous pregnant women and new mothers abusing substances during pregnancy. This chapter draws on the doctoral thesis on which I am currently working, which identifies feminist yoga as an awakening and spiritual transformation in the reconciliation process with indigenous pregnant women and new mothers. The Truth and Reconciliation Commission of Canada has identified the way forward is for all Canadians to build a new relationship with indigenous peoples. The FYP I describe here becomes a way for indigenous women to participate in a cultural and spiritual healing program designed for addicted mothers using a harm reduction approach. Broadly, I envision the development of a FYP that fights for social justice for all marginalized and oppressed populations in my city.

Reflecting back on my 200-hour yoga teacher training and years of experience practicing yoga, I recall that my yoga teacher trainer had an idealized perfect body (white, thin, heteronormative, able-bodied, and young). I remember glancing around the room several times and noticing the lack of diversity in the yoga studio; I wanted to shout out *"yoga is definitely not accessible to everyone—that's why I want to became a yoga teacher!"* During my yoga teacher training, when we were going around in a circle sharing, I said, "well I learned about yoga as a child when my parents took me to Jain yoga camp." I was so happy to share this amazing experience that connected me to yoga as a child and now to my present day lived experiences with modern yoga. The teacher responded quite negatively by rolling her eyes and totally ignoring my experience, which made me feel awkward and uncomfortable in my own brown skin. She then proceeded to conflate her own Eurocentric existence with my own "ethnicity." She shared a story of her and her boyfriend's drug-inspired adventures throughout the country of India, as a way of maintaining her racial and heteronormative privilege. This experience was a form of cultural racism, the type which trickles into institutional racist policies and practices in educational institutions and in society.[2]

There are also other factors that have inspired me to engage in the creation of a FYP theoretical framework, such as how to incorporate feminist approaches to providing hands-on adjustments. For example, I really don't like it when yoga teachers touch my body during a class; I believe there are many who feel this way. When yoga teachers try to touch me, I want to yell, "Brown bodies are made differently than yours—so just go away!" A FYP understands that touching a student without consent may trigger further trauma as the individual is already experiencing internalized and externalized racism from just being in the white space. In fact, the exclusionary nature of many yogic spaces are why community-specific yoga classes have been created in attempts to create some safer spaces for marginalized groups. Hanson (2015) states "that obviously some people of color are happy practicing yoga in multi-racial spaces. No one is calling for all yoga to be segregated . . . queer and trans yoga classes . . . [should not be seen as an] end point. Ultimately I hope we can all practice in the same room. But for now, we need to gather the strength to have relationships and practices with folks outside of our own experience."[3] As an Indian woman in a predominantly white yoga space, I find it difficult to do the work of self-study and transformation when the space is full of cultural appropriation, even down to the pop music that is played. I also want to tell my yoga teacher that that the pop music that is playing during her yoga class is a form of cultural appropriation.

As I finished my yoga teacher training, I began to see that yoga in the Western world has been created for awakening and spiritual transformation for a small elite percentage of the population and this made me angry. It is also important for me to say from the start that while yoga is not a religion, there should be a common recognition of the yoga traditions rooted in Hinduism, Jainism, and Buddhism. I have come to believe that yoga represents a body of personal and spiritual development regardless of one's religion. However, because of my religious upbringing, I have a deeply spiritual worldview in which I believe everything that has life, a spirit, and we are all connected to that energy and must honor it. In this world, people often justifiably reject religion because it is seen as serving no purpose except to perpetuate patriarchy, oppression, and exclusion. I was born into a Jain family in Winnipeg, Manitoba. Jainism, due to its strict philosophical approaches to life, has been (*understandably so!*) left out of the modern yoga movement but its influence and contribution contain important theoretical underpinnings for the development of a FYP. The most famous application of five principals rooted in Jainism is the application of *ahimsa* (non-violence). Mahatmas Gandhi used this principal in the removal of colonial British from India to achieve independence.[4]

Besides religion, my story also includes that my parents were refugees to Canada (being expelled from Uganda by Idi Ami in 1972). My mother was also a teenage bride forced into an arranged marriage, a survivor of domestic violence, and was subsequently even more culturally stigmatized by divorce and transformation into single motherhood. All of these experiences meant she endured multiple oppressions in a Eurocentric Canadian racist heteropatriachial society. However, these are the factors that shaped my feminism and which shapes the worldview from which I choose to speak from in this article. More importantly, this is what I bring to my yoga practice. It is not only racism and cultural appropriation that is epidemic in yoga studios but also the lack of diversity in yoga teachers from the lesbian, gay, bisexual, and transgendered, queer, and two-spirited communities. This further perpetuates all forms of homophobia within society; for example, binary views of gender held by yoga teachers further perpetuates institutional homophobia and "dismisses the legitimacy of these individuals, thereby minimizing their contributions to learning [in the classroom]."[5] Furthermore, modern yoga's appeal (both in North American and increasingly in India) is to those who wish to pursue body-beautiful ideals. Yoga is now marketed through images of young, slender, flexible Euro-Canadian bodies in tight, expensive, and branded clothing. We need to change this perception through a feminist yoga approach. Furthermore, the lack of body-positive yoga teachers is also evident in the yoga world in which Bondy (2015) states that "We can change the misperception of what yoga looks like by encouraging people to become stewards of their own wellness. . . . We don't need to fit into these narrow stereotypes to practice yoga. . . . We need to develop a conscious culture committed to social justice and equality for everybody."[6]

All of these experiences have shaped my realization that I will not practice in a yoga studio run by people who lack the understanding of both traditional yoga and feminism. I am empowered in this decision when I think of my grandmother, who practiced *Bhakti* (devotional) yoga and shared with me those spiritual teachings as a young child. In my FYP, I want to create a feminist yoga space that seeks to heal, transform, and awaken the most marginalized populations in our city. I want a feminist yoga that doesn't compartmentalize yoga to *asana* (posture) alone. Finally, I want a feminist yoga practice and teachers that embraces all bodies and embraces the gender fluidity of the world I live in.

A VISION OF FEMINIST YOGA (AWAKENING AND SPIRITUAL TRANSFORMATION)

For me feminist yoga means healing, awakening, and spiritual transformation in the context of oppression, patriarchy, and injustice. This is the space I wish to create. My vision of feminist yoga is evolving as I teach more and more to the most marginalized populations in my city. Virginia Woolf wrote that a woman needs a room of her own. Today, I am saying that we need a feminist yoga space of our own. Part of the vision I have for a feminist yoga space is for inclusivity, meaning specific safe spaces for our LGBTQT community, welcoming and supportive for all body types and abilities, and accessible for our indigenous women, women of color, and/or immigrant and refugee women. These feminist spaces must be tailored for the specific needs to the population they serve and should be affordable, if not free. As an example, feminist yoga teachers are very cautious of the language they use when teaching, just as a Women's and Gender Studies instructor is during a class. For example, do not use binary language so as to not exclude others. Teachers should have a feminist vision of the yoga classroom that is committed to ending multiple oppressions and sexist patriarchy and to empowering to students, create community, and facilitate leadership.[7]

However, my vision of feminist yoga program does not end with the creation of safe spaces for *asana* (posture) practice. My vision embraces awakening and spiritual transformation that begins with LGBTQ communities, indigenous women, women of color, refugee communities, rural communities, and embraces those regardless of ability or age. This takes a special kind of teacher—it takes a feminist yoga teacher. As part of living in a commodity-image-based system, we are brainwashed into believing that outer attainment can provide us with what we want. I still remember my yoga training in which my teacher, a thirty-something, Eurocentric, heternoramtive said to me that yoga liberation in the Western world will happen through *asana* practice alone. I remember looking around and thinking *"NO WAY—my yoga is not going to happen that way."* This is because transformation and spiritual awakening won't work through individualist approaches but through systematic changes of structural oppression.

What does feminist yoga want us to realize? Does feminist yoga want us to know that that unity between the mind-body-spirit is the key to awakening and spiritual transformation? The essence of feminist yoga is that it can offer many possibilities for life in the patriarchal world. These can include transformation, awakening, spiritual growth, and personal development. Feminist yoga ". . . wants us to unite in that consciousness, so it is a very profound awakening that can take place gradually through the illumination and purification of something, which we often think is our mind."[8] Feminist yoga wants to help us to realize that spiritual liberation will come through decolonization of its philosophy to make it accessible to those who have lived through identities that are excluded from Eurocentric yoga studios.

FEMINIST YOGA AND PATANJALI'S YOGA SUTRAS

I feel it is important to consider the question posed by world renowned yoga scholar Georg Feuerstein when he writes, "Can a tradition [yoga] that originated five thousand years ago, possibly be relevant today?"[9] Yes, absolutely, and I think that feminist yoga is about an intellectual awakening though both theory and practice, which at its heart becomes both an art and an education venue. If we think of art as the intersection of craft with creativity, skill, sensitivity, and feminist pedagogy, then it ". . . is a theory about the teaching/learning process that guides our choice of classroom practices by providing criteria to evaluate specific educational strategies and techniques in terms of the desired course goals or outcomes."[10] Feminist yoga teaching is a life-long journey that will evolve and change as we continue to learn and grow. As a women's and gender studies instructor doing feminist indigenous health research and teaching feminist yoga, I wonder: How do I pursue and develop a feminist yoga that embodies and honors the classical yoga tradition and engages in the lives of the most marginalized populations in this modern yoga world? Is feminist yoga a form of modern yoga with classical elements?

Patanjali's *Yoga Sutras* offer a guide for people who seek truth and self-realization and are fundamental to a feminist yoga theoretical framework. The *sutras* are the most comprehensive and systematic theoretical framework from the Classical era of yoga. In my opinion, the *sutras* are even more important to modern yoga today because they define important elements of yoga theory and practice. The *sutras* provide a feminist yoga with an ethical blueprint for living a moral life and incorporating yoga into daily life. Yoga *sutra* 1.2 states the ". . . central definition of yoga is defined as the cessation [*nirohda*] of [the misidentification with] the modifications [*vritti*] of the mind [*citta*]." Feminist yoga might ask what kinds of *nirohda* (cessation) are we actually looking for in the modern yoga world that excludes our[11] bodies from its spaces? The *sutras* are important to broadening yoga beyond a physical exercise. A central component of a feminist yoga program will be to move toward the rich theoretical knowledge of yoga philosophy such as the sutras. Feminist yoga sees embodiment through the transformation of the mind-body-and-spirit occurring simultaneously. Therefore, a feminist yogi[ni] must equally practice *asana* and understand the rich teachings yoga has to offer. For example, a feminist yoga theoretical framework must incorporate the eight limbs (*agna*) as a feminist yoga ethic. So, for instance, we live in a society that does not value motherhood and instead considers it unpaid labor; in contrast, in a feminist yoga ethics, we could consider a mother who practices breathe control (*pranayama*) as a feminist approach to becoming a more empowered mother. This model of feminist yoga ethics can then be taught within the understanding of marginalization, oppression, and exclusion.

THE YOGA TRADITION AND DEVELOPING FEMINIST YOGA

Any authentic practice of feminist yoga begins with an undertaking of the question of "Who am I?" and while answers can only be found through direct, first hand experience, the yoga traditions offer a wealth of theoretical knowledge to engage in awakening and deepening spiritual understanding of life and the universe. Classical yoga tells that the principal branches of yoga are *Jnana*-yoga (wisdom), *Karma*-yoga (selfless action), *Bhakti*-yoga (Love-Devotion), *Mantra*-yoga (sacred sounds), and *Raja*-yoga. In the *Raja*-yoga system, ". . . one must start to understand the position of yoga in the history of Indian thought. It is this school of thought that provides the most systematic access to the practical dimensions of yoga."[12] An understanding of *Raja* yoga informs a FYP because of its rich contributions to knowledge and understanding of Indian thought. Furthermore, a feminist yoga theoretical framework must understand the important history of the yoga body in the modern world. As Mark Singleton (2000) writes,

> The practice of *asana* within transnational Anglophone yoga is not the outcome of a direct and unbroken lineage of Hatha-yoga. While it is

going too far to say that modern postural yoga has no relationship to practice within the Indian tradition, this relationship is one of radical innovation and experimentation. It is the result of adaptation to new discourses of the body that resulted from India's encounter with modernity.[13]

In the development of my FYP, the history of the yoga body, from India to the rest of the world, provides important contributions as well as critiques about the problems within modern yoga and its exclusionary practices. While the development of my vision of a FYP has/will be greatly informed by the "yoga traditions," when I teach yoga, I talk to students about introductory level concepts embedded in the yoga traditions, such as *purusha* and *prakrti*.

A FYP theoretical framework must include a deep understanding of the "yoga traditions" because it provides the path of knowledge for transformational and spiritual awakening in the populations most marginalized by the mainstream yoga community and within society. The system that yoga is based within is called *Samkhya;* every yoga system of India draws from it and is concerned with describing the principles of existence.[14] The *Samkhya* system embraces two core principles: *prakrti* and *purusha*. The ". . . *Patanjali* yoga system can be seen as a responsible engagement, in various ways, of 'spirit' (*purusha*=intrinsic identity as self, pure consciousness) and 'matter' (*prakrti*=the core psychophysical being), which includes mind, body, nature, and identity.[15] Also it is an integrated and embodied state of 'liberated selfhood' (*jivanmukti*)."[16] A FYP engages with *prakrti* through the multiple lived experiences of oppression and marginalization through homophobia, racism, ableism, and body-shaming. *Prakrti* encompasses all of nature and is controlled by the *gunas*, which regulates the play of energy in the world. In his book *The Integrity of Yoga Darsana: A Reconsideration of Classical Yoga*, Whicher writes that

> *Patanjali* appears to conceive of the *gunas* as three types of psychophysical force, "matter," or energy whose existence can be deduced from the "behaviour" patterns of *prakrti*. *Vyasa* provides us with a lucid commentary on the tripartite process where he describes the gunas in the following manner. *Sattva* tends towards luminosity; *rajas* towards action; *tamas* towards fixity. Through distinct, these *gunas* mutually affect each other. They change, they have the properties of conjunction and disjunction, and they assume forms created by their mutual co-operation. Distinct from each other, they are identifiable even when their powers are conjoined. They deploy their respective powers, whether of similar or dissimilar kind. When one is predominant, the presence (of the others) is inferred as existing within the predominant one from the very fact of its operation as a gunas. They are effective as engaged in carrying out the purpose of the purusha.[17]

The three gunas are *sattva, rajas,* and *tamas* which connects to my vision of a feminist yoga program. For example, a feminist yoga teacher can introduce the concepts of the gunas as it can engage students who are seeking spiritual healing from being marginalized or oppressed in society. For example, a feminist yoga teacher could explain that a society that harbors racism toward indigenous women could be explained through the concept of rajas. This perspective could be helpful to indigenous women in order to live with, resist, and heal from oppression. *Purusha* is pure consciousness. Harnessing the gunas in order to identify with *purusha* will continue until all human beings know their true nature makes important theoretical contributions for the development of a FYP. For example, healing from experiences of internalized homophobia could be addressed in a feminist yoga class through an understanding and discussion of *prakrti*.

INDIGENOUS PEOPLES OF CANADA

Winnipeg, Manitoba has one of the highest population of First Nations and Metis people in Canada. Manitoba is also the birthplace of the Metis Nation. This section presents some issues facing our indigenous peoples that can help situate the reader in the context in which I am developing a feminist theoretical framework for yoga. In Canada, the process of colonization over the past five hundred years by French and English "settlers," then by the Canadian government and Catholic churches, resulted in forced cultural assimilation of Aboriginal peoples. This process of "Indigenous cultural genocide resulted in the destruction of Aboriginal peoples' ways of life, including the separation of mother from child and countless experiences of physical, emotional, and sexual abuse of aboriginal children taken to live in residential school. Canada is at the forefront in the process of reconciliation of indigenous peoples from their experiences with residential schools over the past seven generations. Justice Murray Sinclair, who, is the former chair of the Indian Residential Schools Truth and Reconciliation Commission, says that reconciliation is about establishing and maintaining a mutually respectful relationship between Aboriginal and non-Aboriginal peoples in this country.[18] It is through decolonization that refers to the anticolonial process of critiquing Western worldviews (including indigenous and Eastern worldviews) in which reconciliation has and will continue to be facilitated greatly through the Truth and Reconciliation Commission in Canada.[19] For indigenous Metis scholar Emma LaRocque (2007), anti-colonial feminist approaches such as the concepts of "patriarchy," "oppression," and "sexism" are fundamental and critical to grasping current urgent issues faced by indigenous women today.[20] In fact, colonization and violence are deeply embedded in the embodied experiences of historical and contemporary indigenous communities. Andrea Smith (2005) writes, "because Indian[21] bodies are 'dirty,' they are considered sexually viable and 'rapable,' and the rape of bodies that are considered inherently impure or dirty does not count. Sexual violence has been used as a weapon of colonialism to destroy and assimilate Aboriginal peoples into a white, racist, sexist, hierarchy that cannot be separated from the feminist ideas that violence affects all women."[22] This result is present day trans-generational trauma, which is magnified within the lived experience of substance abusing pregnant women. Indigenous Maori scholar Linda Tuhiwai Smith (1999) writes that decolonizing, while ". . . once viewed as the formal process of handing over the instruments of government[,] is now recognized as a long-term process, involving bureaucratic, cultural, linguistic, and psychological diversity of colonial powers."[23]

This historical trauma also affected indigenous women's relationship to both childbirth and motherhood. Traditionally, Aboriginal midwives were central to the social, political, and cultural landscapes of their people prior to contact.[24] As Benoit, Carroll, and Eni (2009) identified, historically in aboriginal communities, the event of childbirth connected women to their foremothers and families to whole communities.[25] Aboriginal midwives were trained through an apprenticeship model in which mothers taught their daughters rituals and practices of their trade. There was a societal view that being born was a sacred event to celebrate the arrival of a new spirit. However, due to colonization, residential school experiences, and the implementation of Westernized medicine, normal pregnancy and childbirth was removed from traditional societies.[26] Reactions to pregnancy are as diverse as the range of human beings getting pregnant. We would like to believe that all individuals have some sort of similar experiences of joy coupled with profound love and kindness directed toward them but often this is not the case. The medicalization of childbirth poses a problem for society. Over the past few centuries, childbirth has become increasingly influenced by medical technology, and now medical intervention is the norm in most Western countries.

The medicalization had the greatest impact on indigenous peoples of Canada who lost their traditional midwives. Today, many in many rural parts of Canada First Nations and Metis women have to be flown out of their home community to the city to await the birth of their child. The article "The Spiritual Experience of High Risk Pregnancies" found that among the twelve participants cited in the article "women experience their spirituality as an essential part of who they are and that they do use their spiritual beliefs and practices to aid them in their search for meaning and to calm their fears and anxieties as they move through the experience of high-risk pregnancy."[27] The need for feminist yoga in these communities is urgent because of a FYP that I envision has the capacity to help heal multigenerational trauma from residential school experiences and colonization. This is because feminist yoga embodies a spiritual focus which can be used along with indigenous teachings and healing ways. Women who are street-involved and/or using drugs or alcohol are populations of women in Canadian communities who tend not seek access to prenatal care and other services due to many factors, including fear of losing their child to the welfare system apprehension of their children.[28] Accessing prenatal care is one of the most protective factors for pregnant women who are using drugs and/or alcohol.[29] Heaman et al. (2014) identified through an epidemiological case-control study several underlying psychosocial and structural barriers for accessing prenatal care among inner city women in Winnipeg.[30] These included being under stress, having family problems, feeling depressed, not thinking straight, not knowing where to get prenatal care, having a long wait to get an appointment, and having problems with childcare and transportation.[31] As a society we need to stop blaming substance abusing women in Canada as Buydens (2005) writes ". . . that my conclusion is that feminists must reach across class and race to defend all mothers and from mother blaming ideology."[32] The FYP model centers the role of spiritual health in the health and well-being of indigenous peoples; it is a critical component to the transformation and spiritual awakening for indigenous women in Winnipeg, Manitoba, Canada.

REFLECTIONS ON BEING A FEMINIST YOGA TEACHER FOR INDIGENOUS PREGNANT WOMEN AND NEW MOTHERS

This section will explore prenatal feminist yoga as a path toward embodiment for indigenous pregnant women and new mothers abusing substances in Winnipeg, Manitoba. I come to the yoga mat as a mother and a feminist yoga teacher whose dream is for social justice and deeper embodiment for the most Indigenous women in my city during pregnancy. I teach feminist yoga to indigenous pregnant women and new moms who have/are using substances but participating in a holistic cultural and spiritual teaching program. Integrating indigenous cultural and spiritual healing practices such as the seven sacred teachings, smudging, drumming, singing, elders, and medicine wheel, along with feminist yoga theoretical framework, allows for an embodied experience for pregnant women and new mothers. The feminist yoga I offer is integrated into the spiritual teaching program and often includes drumming and smudging. I have been teaching for three years and class sizes are up to ten participants. When I first started teaching indigenous women in the program, I was more focused on *asana* practice but now I teach more meditation to help the women get centered. In addition, often the women's children and (my own daughter) have joined the class and we often laugh and talk about what types of *asana* they would like to do. It is very different compared to a practicing in a formal yoga studio where people often don't talk or make eye contact with the person next to them.

A typical prenatal feminist yoga class for indigenous women includes opening with ceremony of smudging with sage and playing music that includes traditional drumming and then moves to breathing, gentle stretching, postures, cool down, and relaxation. We emphasize an aware-ness of the physical, emotional, psychological, and spiritual embodi-ments of pregnancy and new motherhood. For example, when teaching, I invite the women to be clear about bending from their hips, avoid doing poses that put pressure on their abdomen, and use props. The start of each class includes a focus on breathing with mother and baby and nur-turing that sacred connection. I am always conscious of the trauma in the lived experiences of my students and sensitive in the language I use. I foster an acceptance of a wide range of physical and emotional responses from the women within a yoga space. Women show up to practice in jeans and t-shirts and sometimes don't even feel comfortable taking off their socks. Often women are not able to sit or lay still. Many find it impossible to follow the formality of a one-hour yoga class, so women talk to each other, tell jokes, and laugh at the names of the all the poses and with each other.

The responses that I have received from women have been positive. They have expressed appreciation at being taught yoga, which is often not accessible to them. Some women have stated that learning to breathe during pregnancy was one of the best experiences of the classes. Finally, integrating feminist yoga with traditional indigenous spiritual practices of drumming and smudging were very important to the women who participated. FYP can be incorporated into the broader social and public health system for pregnant and new mothers as it strengthens the connec-tion between physical, emotional, mental, and spiritual health. This is because a feminist yoga program brings together indigenous women who have been colonized and traumatized from 500 years of coloniza-tion. FYP understands that in precolonial societies indigenous mothers were respected and valued for their roles and traditions which can be reclaimed from a feminist perspective on yoga. Furthermore, the devel-opment and integration of holistic mind-body therapy program has the potential to improve pregnancy experiences and possibly birth out-comes.[33] Within the academic literature there is growing body of evi-dence of yoga being used to bring about tremendous physical, psycho-logical, emotional, and spiritual transformations in marginalized popula-tions such as those youth in prisons or youth abusing substances.[34]

Adrienne Rich (1995) writes, "all human life on the planet is born of a woman. The one unifying incontrovertible experience shared by all wom-en and men is that months-long periods we spent unfolding inside a woman's body."[35] Pregnancy can bring about a variety of subjective ex-periences, as it is a period of time with tremendous physiological, emo-tional, psychosocial, and spiritual changes in a person's life.[36] World-renowned midwife Ina May Gaskin (2010) writes, "When we as a society begin to value mothers as the givers and supporters of life, then we will see social change in ways that matter."[37] Sunseri (2008) explains that a ". . . legacy of colonialism has destroyed the image of Indigenous mother-hood. Indigenous women (Metis, First Nations, and Inuit) are the most marginalized population within Canadian society."[38] Over the past decade indigenous mothers have been reclaiming their herstory and en-gaging upon the path of healing from colonialism. Kim Anderson (2000) writes, "When it comes to addressing issues related to Native women, this process involves understanding how gendered and intergeneration relations worked in the societies of our ancestors; about how our fore-mothers and grandmothers defined and then lived their identities, roles, and authorities and about how much of this was lost."[39] My FYP helps create a space for indigenous women to engage in first steps towards a more embodied self and their becoming a fully engaged indigenous mother, as they once were prior to European colonization of Turtle Is-land. Classical yoga teaches us that we must continue to strive toward the integrated and embodied state through the engagement of *prakrti* and toward the light of *pursha*. As I develop the FYP theoretical framework, it is clear to me that its primary purpose is to bring about awakening and spiritual transformation for indigenous women who are pregnant and/or struggling with substance abuse. My experience teaching feminist yoga to an indigenous community highlights the inequality to access to yoga. There is an urgent need to transform indigenous communities from the trauma of colonization, patriarchy, racism. Feminist yoga has the poten-tial to bring about healing, awakening, and spiritual transformation and the time to start to heal is now.

NOTES

1. Kim Anderson. *A Recognition of Being: Reconstructing Native Womanhood.* Cana-dian Scholars' Press, 2000.
2. Rebecca Powell. "Overcoming Cultural Racism: The Promise of Multicultural Education." *Multicultural Perspectives* 2, no. 3 (2000): 8.
3. Krista Hanson. When People of Colour Say They Want Their Own Yoga White People Should Listen. Retrieved from http://www.decolonizingyoga.com/when-people-of-color-say-they-want-their-own-yoga-white-people-should-listen/#sthash.alQ9wmVI.dpuf.
4. Christopher K. Chapple, *Yoga and the Luminous: Patañjali's Spiritual Path to Free-dom,* SUNY Press, 2008.
5. John P. Elia, "Homophobia in the High School: A Problem in Need of a Resolu-tion," *The High School Journal* (1993): 177–85.
6. Dianne Bondy, "Confessions of a Fat, Black Yoga Teacher," 2010. Retrieved from http://www.decolonizingyoga.com/confessions-fat-black-yoga-teacher/
7. Carolyn M. Shrewsbury, "What is Feminist Pedagogy?" *Women's Studies Quar-terly* (1993): 8-16.
8. Ian Whicher, Class Lecture, *The Yoga Traditions,* University of Manitoba, Sep-tember 2015.

9. Ian Whicher. *The Integrity of the Yoga Darsana: A Reconsideration of Classical Yoga*, SUNY Press, 1998, 154.

10. Shrewsbury. "What is Feminist Pedagogy?."

11. By "our bodies" I mean those who are excluded from ideal Western yoga bodies (white, thin, heteronormative, able-bodied, and young). "Our bodies" as I envision in a FYP theoretical program is defined by inclusiveness of gender fluidity and identity, bodies of color, body types, abilities, and ages.

12. Georg Feuerstein, *The Path of Yoga*, Shambhala Publications, 2011,25.

13. Mark Singleton, *Yoga Body: The Origins of Modern Posture Practice*, Oxford University Press, 2010, 33.

14. Whicher, Class Lecture, *The Yoga Tradition*.

15. Whicher, Class Lecture, *The Yoga Tradition*.

16. Whicher, Class Lecture, *The Yoga Tradition*, 59.

17. Whicher. *The Integrity of the Yoga Darsana*, 63.

18. Truth and Reconciliation Final Report (2015). Truth and Reconciliation Report. Retrieved from http://www.trc.ca/websites/trcinstitution/index.php?p=890.

19. Truth and Reconciliation Final Report (2015).

20. Emma LaRocque. "Métis and Feminist: Ethical Reflections on Feminism, Human Rights and Decolonization." *Making Space for Indigenous Feminism* (2007): 53–71.

21. Indian is not a word I would use because Indians are from India and it is word rooted back to Eurocentrism dating back to commencement of European colonization of Turtle Island.

22. A. Smith, "Native American Feminism, Sovereignty, and Social Change," *Feminist Studies* 31, no. 1, 116–132.

23. Linda Tuhiwai Smith, *Decolonizing Methodologies: Research and Indigenous Peoples*, Zed Books, 1999, 72.

24. Cecelia Benoit, Dena Carroll, Lisa Lawrence, and Munaza Chaudhry, *Marginalized Voices from the Downtown Eastside: Aboriginal Women Speak about Their Health Experiences*, Toronto: National Network on Environments and Women's Health, 2001.

25. Cecelia Benoit, Dena Carroll, and Rachel Eni, "To Watch and To Care—Stories of Aborginal Midwifery in Canada," *Canadian Journal of Midwifery Research and Practice-Revue Canadienne de la Recherche et de la Pratique Sage-femme* 5, no. 1 (2006).

26. Karen Lawford and Audrey R. Giles, "An Analysis of the Evacuation Policy for Pregnant First Nations Women in Canada," (2012): 329.

27. Sheri Price, Margaret Lake, Glenn Breen, Glenda Carson, Colleen Quinn, and Thomas O'Connor, "The Spiritual Experience of High-Risk Pregnancy, "*Journal of Obstetric, Gynecologic, & Neonatal Nursing* 36, no. 1 (2007): 63–70.

28. Nancy Poole and Barbara Isaac, *Apprehensions: Barriers to Treatment for Substance-using Mothers*, Vancouver: British Columbia Centre of Excellence for Women's Health, 2001.

29. Society of Obstetricians and Gynecologists of Canada, 2011

30. Maureen I. Heaman, Michael Moffatt, Lawrence Elliott, Wendy Sword, Michael E. Helewa, Heather Morris, Patricia Gregory, Lynda Tjaden, and Catherine Cook, "Barriers, Motivators and Facilitators Related to Prenatal Care Utilization among Inner-city Women in Winnipeg, Canada: A Case-control Study," *BMC Pregnancy and Childbirth* 14, no. 1 (2014): 227.

31. Heaman, Moffatt, Elliott, Sword, Helewa, Morris, Gregory, Tjaden, and Cook, "Barriers, Motivators and Facilitators," 227.

32. Norma L. Buydens "Bad Mothers as 'Brown' Mothers in Western Canadian Policy Discourse: Substance-Abusing Mothers and Sexually Exploited Girls," *Women and Children First: Feminism, Rhetoric, and Public Policiy* (SUNY Press, 2005) 159.

33. Kathryn Curtis, Aliza Weinrib, and Joel Katz, "Systematic Review of Yoga for Pregnant Women: Current Status and Future Directions." *Evidence-Based Complementary and Alternative Medicine*, (2012): 2.

34. Sam Himelstein, "Mindfulness-based Substance Abuse Treatment for Incarcerated Youth: A Mixed Method Pilot Study." *Transpersonal Studies*, 2010.

35. Adrienne Rich, *Of Woman Born: Motherhood as Experience and Institution*, Norton & Company, 1995.
36. Robbie Davis-Floyd, "The Technocratic, Humanistic, and Holistic Paradigms of Childbirth," *International Journal of Gynecology & Obstetrics* 75 (2001): S5–S23.
37. Ina May Gaskin, *Spiritual Midwifery*, Book Publishing Company, 2010, 2.
38. Lina Sunseri, "Sky Woman Lives On: Contemporary Examples of Mothering the Nation," *Canadian Woman Studies* 26, no. 3 (2008).
39. Anderson, *A Recognition of Being*.

REFERENCES

Anderson, Kim. *A Recognition of Being: Reconstructing Native Womanhood* (Canadian Scholars' Press, 2000).
Benoit, Cecilia, Dena Carroll, Lisa Lawrence, and Munaza Chaudhry. *Marginalized Voices from the Downtown Eastside: Aboriginal Women Speak about Their Health Experiences* (Toronto: National Network on Environments and Women's Health, 2001).
Benoit, Cecilia, Dena Carroll, and Rachel Eni. "To Watch, To Care" Stories of Aboriginal Midwifery in Canada." *Canadian Journal of Midwifery Research and Practice-Revue Canadienne de la Recherche et de la Pratique Sage-femme* 5, no. 1 (2006).
Bondy, Dione. "Confessions of a Fat, Black Yoga Teacher," 2010. Retrieved from http://www.decolonizingyoga.com/confessions-fat-black-yoga-teacher/
Buydens, Norma L. "Bad Mothers as 'Brown' Mothers in Western Canadian Policy Discourse: Substance-Abusing Mothers and Sexually Exploited Girls." *Women and Children First: Feminism, Rhetoric, and Public Policy* (SUNY Press, 2005).
Carroll, Dena, and Cecilia Benoit. "Aboriginal Midwifery in Canada: Merging Traditional Practices and Modern Science." *Reconceiving Midwifery* 263 (2004).
Chapple, K. Christopher. *Yoga and the Luminous: Patañjali's Spiritual Path to Freedom* (SUNY Press, 2008).
Curtis, Kathryn, Aliza Weinrib, and Joel Katz. "Systematic Review of Yoga for Pregnant Women: Current Status and Future Directions." *Evidence-Based Complementary and Alternative Medicine*, 2012.
Davis-Floyd, Robbie. "The Technocratic, Humanistic, and Holistic Paradigms of Childbirth." *International Journal of Gynecology & Obstetrics* 75 (2001): S5–S23.
De Michelis, Elizabeth. *A History of Modern Yoga: Patanjali and Western Esotericism* (A& C Black, 2005).
Elia, John P. "Homophobia in the High School: A Problem in Need of a Resolution." *The High School Journal* (1993): 177–85.
Embree, A. T., S. N. Hay, & T. De Bary, eds., *Sources of Indian Tradition: Modern India and Pakistan*, vol. 464. (Columbia University Press, 1988).
Feuerstein, Georg. *The Path of Yoga* (Shambhala Publications, 2011).
Gaskin, Ina May. *Spiritual Midwifery* (Book Publishing Company, 2010).
Green, Fiona Joy. "Feminist Mothers." *From Motherhood to Mothering: The Legacy of Adrienne Rich's 'Of Woman Born'* (2004): 125.
Green, Fiona Joy. "Feminist Mothering: Challenging Gender Inequality by Resisting the Institution of Motherhood and Raising Children to be Critical Agents of Social Change." *Socialist Studies/Études Socialistes* 1, no. 1 (2009).
Hanson, K. L. (2015). When People of Color say They Want Their Own Yoga White People Should Listen. Retrieved from http://www.decolonizingyoga.com/when-people-of-color-say-they-want-their-own-yoga-white-people-should-listen/#sthash.alQ9wmVI.dpuf.
Heaman, Maureen I., Michael Moffatt, Lawrence Elliott, Wendy Sword, Michael E. Helewa, Heather Morris, Patricia Gregory, Lynda Tjaden, and Catherine Cook. "Barriers, Motivators and Facilitators Related to Prenatal Care Utilization among Inner-city Women in Winnipeg, Canada: A Case-control Study." *BMC Pregnancy and Childbirth* 14, no. 1 (2014): 227.

Himelstein, Sam. "Mindfulness-based Substance Abuse Treatment for Incarcerated Youth: A Mixed Method Pilot Study." *Transpersonal Studies* (2010).

Johanson, Richard, Mary Newburn, and Alison Macfarlane. "Has the Medicalisation of Childbirth Gone Too Far?" *BMJ* 324, no. 7342 (2002): 892–95.

Gaskin, Ina May. *Spiritual Midwifery* (Book Publishing Company, 2010).

Izaguirre, Ainhoa and Esther Calvete. "Intimate Partner Violence During Pregnancy: Women's Narratives about Their Mothering Experiences."*Psychosocial Intervention* 23, no. 3 (2014): 209–15.

LaRocque, Emma. "Métis and Feminist: Ethical Reflections on Feminism, Human Rights and Decolonization." *Making Space for Indigenous Feminism*(2007): 53–71.

Lawford, Karen and Audrey R. Giles. "An Analysis of the Evacuation Policy for Pregnant First Nations Women in Canada." (2012): 329.

Lorde, Audre. *Sister Outsider: Essays and Speeches* (Random House LLC, 2007).

Powell, Rebecca. "Overcoming Cultural Racism: The Promise of Multicultural Education." *Multicultural Perspectives* 2, no. 3 (2000): 8-14.

Price, Sheri, Margaret Lake, Glenn Breen, Glenda Carson, Colleen Quinn, and Thomas O'Connor. "The Spiritual Experience of High-Risk Pregnancy." *Journal of Obstetric, Gynecologic, & Neonatal Nursing* 36, no. 1 (2007): 63–70.

King, Malcolm, Alexandra Smith, and Michael Gracey. "Indigenous Health Part 2: The Underlying Causes of the Health Gap." *The Lancet* 374, no. 9683 (2009): 76–85.

O'Reilly, Andrea, ed., *Maternal Theory: Essential Readings* (Demeter Press, 2007).

Rich, Adrienne. *Of Woman Born: Motherhood as Experience and Institution* (W. W. Norton & Company, 1995).

Shrewsbury, Carolyn M. "What is Feminist Pedagogy?." *Women's Studies Quarterly* (1993): 8–16.

Singleton, Mark. *Yoga Body: The Origins of Modern Posture Practice* (Oxford University Press, 2010).

Smith, Andrea. *Conquest: Sexual Violence and American Indian Genocide*, vol. 3. (Cambridge, MA: South End Press, 2005).

Smith, Linda Tuhiwai. *Decolonizing Methodologies: Research and Indigenous Peoples* (Zed Books, 1999).

Wong, S., A. Ordean, and M. Kahan. "SOGC Clinical Practice Guidelines: Substance Use in Pregnancy: no. 256, April 2011." *International Journal of Gynaecology and Obstetrics: The Official Organ of the International Federation of Gynaecology and Obstetrics* 114, no. 2 (2011): 190–202.

Sunseri, Lina. "Sky Woman Lives On: Contemporary Examples of Mothering the Nation." *Canadian Woman Studies* 26, no. 3 (2008).

Truth and Reconciliation Final Report (2015). Truth and Reconciliation Report. Retrieved from http://www.trc.ca/websites/trcinstitution/index.php?p=890

Walters, Andrew S., and David M. Hayes. "Homophobia Within Schools: Challenging the Culturally Sanctioned Dismissal of Gay Students and Colleagues." *Journal of Homosexuality* 35, no. 2 (1998): 1–23.

Whicher, Ian. *The Integrity of the Yoga Darsana: A Reconsideration of Classical Yoga* (SUNY Press, 1998).

Whicher, Ian. *The Integration of Spirit (purusha) and Matter (prakrti) in the Yoga Sutras*, 2009

Whicher, Ian. Class Lecture. *The Yoga Tradition* University of Manitoba. September 2015.

FOURTEEN
Yoga and Dis/Ability

Steffany Moonaz

The physical practice of yoga that has been widely popularized in the West and around the globe has historical roots in Indian philosophies of the mind. As yoga evolved, access to its teachings expanded, but the accessibility of its practices narrowed and then adapted. What follows is a discussion of yoga's opportunities and barriers for those with physical limitations and mobility challenges, historically and in modern times.

ANCIENT CONCEPTS OF YOGA

Some of the earliest Indian writings using the root word of yoga refer to it as a concept of unification. Though in modern day this union is conceptualized broadly and in many ways (mind-body, individual-collective, parts-whole, movement-breath), the earliest mentions are of union with Spirit or Divine. The Sankhya teachings were codified into an oral tradition around 750 B.C.E. and form the philosophical underpinnings for the yoga practices that are later outlined in Patanjali's *Yoga Sutra*.[1] However, the Sankhya contains no detail of specific tools or practices for fostering a state of unification, but speaks more to the underlying concepts and the relationship between Nature and Spirit. Likely originating in the sixth century B.C.E. is the *Taittiriya Upanishad*, which includes the first mention of yoga as a technical practice, wherein the individual aims to gain control of the senses.[2]

Sometime after the fifth century B.C.E., the *Bhagavad Gita* emerged with more clarity regarding the paths to self-realization through practice.[3] These practices, however, are not the detailed physical postures and breathing techniques described much later; rather, the path to "unification" described as yoga is suggested to be through devotion, right living, spiritual duty, withdrawal of senses, and meditation. And while postures are not described, action is certainly an aspect of the practice, specifically "Yoga is skill in action," without attachment to the results of that action.[4] Yoga was considered primarily to be a more expeditious path toward the ultimate goal of what today might be called enlightenment, or elevation to the status of divine being. The practices of yoga for many years after its emergence include seated meditation, breathwork, and other practices largely related to control of the mind. In fact, the second of Patanjali's *Yoga Sutras* declares, "Yogas chitta vritti narodhah," that to restrain the mind's modifications is yoga.[5] The *Yoga Sutras*, which are dated to around 400 C.E., contain the first mention of *asana*, described only as a "steady, comfortable posture" (Satchidananda, 2012, 152). Finding a comfortable posture assures that the body will be less of a distraction from meditation when in a state of balance and alignment.

DISABILITY AND EARLY YOGA

The teachings of yoga before the Common Era were conveyed largely through oral tradition and generally in close mentoring relationships between sage and seeker. Indeed, even in the *Bhagavad Gita*, Arjuna is instructed, "Find a wise teacher, honor him, ask him your questions, serve him; someone who has seen the truth will guide you on the path to wisdom."[6] Because yoga was primarily a practice of the mind, there would have likely been few physical barriers to yoga practice, except the access to a teacher and the willingness on the part of the teacher to confer those teachings.

As India was predominantly a Hindu country, karma prevailed as an explanation for many life circumstances, including congenital disability or the later emergence of accidents and illnesses that might confer disability. For those living with disability during this era in India, yoga may have been seen as a set of tools for transcending the karmic bonds that resulted in this lifetime of disability. However, being born with or acquiring disability was also far more likely among those of lower castes and would be seen as suggesting of karmic misfortune. Therefore, individuals with physical difference of many kinds would be less likely to encounter these teachings. Even being born as a women was considered "rotten karma" to be overcome, as it is stated in the *Bhagavad Gita*, "Those who take refuge in me, Arjuna, even if they are born in evil wombs as women or laborers or servants, also reach the supreme goal."[7]

In fact, the body as a whole was sometimes described as something foul and profane. In the *Maitrayani Upanishad*, a king beseeches a sage, asking, "Sir, what is the use of enjoyment in this body which smells badly and is a mass of bones, skins, etc., attacked by lust, anger, etc., separation from near and dear people, hunger, thirst, etc. We see that all this is decaying, like flies and mosquitoes which live and die."[8] Here, the body, even in a healthy state, is portrayed as something to be transcended and overcome, avoiding the otherwise inevitable and undesirable rebirth into another physical body. It is only with the emergence of tantra yoga in the first century C.E., that the body is described as "a dwelling place for the Divine"[9] and an opportunity to experience embodied enlightenment, that is, liberation that is attained without shedding the body, but still existing within it.

HATHA YOGA'S EMERGENCE

Over time, a focus on the physical practice of yoga, including specific postures, emerged as a more elaborate preparation for seated meditation practice. The physical postures were intended to better align and balance the body so that seated meditation could be practiced without pain, discomfort, or distraction. Still, in India, the focus of yoga practice was generally on the mental practices and breath work that would be a tool to foster stillness of the mind. Even as late as the twentieth century, Swami Satchidananda stated, "Pranayama (breathwork) alone is not a practice. Our main purpose is to calm and control the mind."[10]

The development of hatha yoga likely originated in the ninth or tenth centuries C.E., though one of preeminent historical texts documenting specific postures with detailed instruction is the *Hatha Yoga Pradipika*, written in the fifteenth century. The *Pradipika's* third chapter on *asana* suggests that the physical practice keeps the yogi strong, with supple limbs and good health. While it is stated that this will eventually help with the spiritual pursuits of raja yoga, it is suggested to first focus on "strength, health, and litheness of the body."[11] Many of these fifteen physical postures would be unattainable for modern healthy persons, let alone those with mobility challenges or disabling conditions. Nowhere in the *Pradipika* is there mention of pose modifications, or alternate postures should the pose be inaccessible as described.

As the physical practices evolved, they were said to be associated with specific benefits, though some claims were in the realm of the fantastical. These claims tended to be grandiose, and not rooted in systematically gathered or even anecdotally observed evidence. The first examples of therapeutically applied yoga from a clinical perspective were presented in the *Yoga Mimansa*, a peer-reviewed journal first published in 1924. *Yoga Mimansa* aimed to present scientific evidence on the effects of yoga practice, using "modern scientific methods." The first edition states that "nothing that has not been tested either clinically or in the laboratory will appear in the pages of this periodical."[12] It is here that we see the first mention of therapeutics in the context of yoga practice, and not merely the strengthening and suppleness of healthy bodies. In addition, the *Yoga Mimansa* presents cautions for specific health conditions, where a particular practice might be inappropriate if executed vigorously. There is also the suggestion to "err on the safe side" (45). Variations in duration of the posture, for example, are provided for those using the poses for therapeutic application. While many of the physical practices described even in the *Yoga Mimansa* might have been unavailable to those with movement limitations, for some conditions, the physical practice was now being considered as a tool in itself for addressing challenges of the physical body, not only as a preparation for achieving more subtle states of consciousness.

YOGA'S COLLISION WITH THE WEST

Swami Vivikananda attended the Parliament of the World's Religions in 1893. He made a lasting impression that is sometimes marked as the beginning of the era of modern yoga.[13] The ancient texts and/or practices of yoga (meditation, breath control, ethical lifestyle) took hold among some groups of philosophically minded Westerners, but it was not until the mid-twentieth century that yoga took hold in mainstream America. That was due partly to the peace movement, partly to the opening of several yoga schools in the United States by swamis coming from India, and partly due to the repackaging of hatha yoga as an exercise plan for fitness and agility.

While the swamis were bringing the full package of yoga and its philosophy, it was the physical practice that evolved most profoundly in the West through the last twentieth century. Students who trained with swamis from India developed their own unique styles and methods of yoga practice and training, and the status of "yoga teacher," which was once conferred by a guru after year of intensive study, was now offered through short didactic programs.

YOGA AND ATHLETICISM

Even before coming to the West, yoga *asana* was sometimes used to demonstrate physical prowess. In the late 1800s, yogis traveling in Europe demonstrated impressive yoga *asana* in performances for cash, which was both impressive and scrutinized for its potential clash with the austerity expected of spiritual seekers.[14] Tirumalai Krishnamacharya, perhaps one of the most influential yoga teachers of the early twentieth century, traveled around India giving talks and yoga demonstrations, often presenting some of the most challenging and impressive *asanas* to his audience. It was one of these demonstrations that was seen by a young Pattabhi Jois, who became his student the next day[15] and later established the style of ashtanga yoga, which took a strong hold in the West that remains today.

While the practice of *asana* was not central to early yogic philosophy or practice, yoga collided with the physical culture movement in India as well as in Europe and the United States. The small number of yoga's physical postures grew. ". . . there were firmly established exercise traditions in the West that included variants of 'hatha yoga' now popularly taught in America and Europe. As a result, the sheer number of positions and movements that could be thenceforth classified as *asana* swelled considerably and continues to do so."[16] This emphasis on the physical practice of yoga was embraced not only by the West, but by India as well. Instead of yoga being foremost a practice of the mind and a way of living, it became a specific set of practices for development of body-mind-spirit. Shri Yogendra suggests this in his writing from 1928, that yoga is "a comprehensive practical system of self-culture . . . which through interchangeable harmonious development of one's body, mind and psychic potencies ultimately leads to physical well-being, mental harmony, moral elevation and habituation to spiritual consciousness."[17]

It is the integration and even predominance of physical practice as an avenue into enhanced biopsychospiritual health that has been accepted and perpetuated for over a century in the West, and has been reclaimed by India in modern times.[18] It is perhaps because of its grounding in physical practice that the tenets of yoga have gained such widespread acceptance. In 1937, it was written that:

> Yogic physical culture is now no longer esoteric. Instead of being exclusively practiced by Yogis it has become popular among persons with no particular spiritual aims. Formerly it used to be practiced as the first step and fundamental part of spiritual life. . . . But in modern times Yogic physical culture has escaped from the cloistered boundaries of the hermitage into the larger world.[19]

While the expanding physical culture of yoga seemed most accessible to the world at large, this shift may have made yoga practice less accessible to those with physical limitations or disabilities—the very individuals who could possibly benefit most from the therapeutic effects of yoga's philosophy, teachings, and even the physical practices themselves.

Outcomes Associated with Therapeutic Yoga

In the 1980s the evaluation of yoga's therapeutic application moved westward when Dean Ornish, a student of Swami Satchidanada, published the effects of a lifestyle program including yoga on health outcomes in heart disease patients.[20] In this early work, the yoga program was referred to simply as "stress management," since most of the medical community and the general public was either unfamiliar or untrusting of yoga as a therapeutic modality. Ornish was able to demonstrate that yoga practice, combined with vegan diet, social support, and walking, was associated with reversal of heart disease morbidity—an outcome that was not possible through medical intervention. While these findings paved the way for future yoga researchers, early yoga research in the West was generally conducted with little or no funding by researchers who had a personal interest in the topic, and even then, it was not considered a serious line of scientific inquiry. As such, studies tended to have small sample sizes and to use less rigorous methodology.

With the development of the National Center of Complementary and Alternative Medicine in 1998 (now the National Center for Complementary and Integrative Health), research into the therapeutic applications of yoga could attract more serious funding and could use more rigorous scientific methods. In recent decades, the growth of therapeutic yoga research has been exponential, with increasing frequency of clinical trials, greater rigor, and more systematic reviews of cumulative evidence.[21] Decades later, thousands of research studies have been conducted on the effects of yoga practice for dozens of health conditions. It is perhaps these interdisciplinary research teams who have been some of the most proactive in developing adaptations of yoga practices for less fit, agile, or well populations. While yoga has developed as an intense and demanding physical practice in the West, it has also developed as a highly modifiable practice for persons of varying abilities. The emerging evidence that yoga can be safe and effective for those with physical limitations has also spawned expansion of yoga classes and programs for these populations.

Arthritis, the leading cause of disability in the United States, is associated with pain, inflammation, fatigue, and diminished quality of life. Numerous studies have now shown that a yoga practice adapted to the needs and abilities of each individual can have a significant impact on disease symptoms.[22] Not only can yoga be adapted for limited mobility, but it can even reduce mobility limitations by improving physical fitness for those who may be self-limiting due to pain and other symptoms.

What may be more profound than the impact of yoga practice on disease symptoms is the impact that the practice can have on the outlook and perspective of those living with the physical challenges. A comprehensive therapeutic yoga practice includes modified physical *asana* that can improve fitness, including strength and flexibility.[23] It also includes gentle breathing practices and relaxation techniques, which can engage the parasympathetic nervous system and reduce the stress-pain cycle,[24] which can otherwise exacerbate disease symptoms and common comorbidities, including mood disorders.[25] But the ancient practices of meditation and mind control are also part of many modern yoga programs. It is perhaps this "cessation of the mind modifications" from Patanjali's *Yoga*

Sutras and the underlying yoga philosophy that may serve to have the greatest impact for less mobile individuals.

While physical disease and disability may be associated with suffering, yoga states that the root cause of all suffering are the "kleshas" or afflictions of the mind. These afflictions, such as attachment and repulsion, can be addressed through meditation and the application of yogic principles such as the yamas and niyamas, the ethical principles of yoga that lay the foundation for the remaining eight limbs.[26] For those with physical symptoms and limitations, yoga practice may help to reduce discomfort associated with suffering, but the philosophy of yoga may also help individuals to reframe the experience of their condition in order to live with limitations in a different way.

A CASE EXAMPLE

Jennifer Daks is in her late twenties. She was diagnosed with juvenile rheumatoid arthritis as a toddler and experienced a long remission from ages seven through eighteen. When a flare occurred in her late teens, her rheumatologist suggested yoga as a tool for helping to manage the condition. Unfortunately, even poses such as Child's Pose (Balasana) that were suggested as relaxing and restorative were incredibly painful for Jennifer. She began to cry and question why she wasn't able to execute something so simple, that seemed to be enjoyable for other students in the class. Eventually she found therapeutic yoga practices that modified *asana* for her joint disease, using props and variations. She also found that the breathwork, meditation, and the principles in which yoga is built upon were helpful in managing daily life with disease symptoms and flares.

Many years later, when Jennifer was experiencing another flare, she found herself in a yoga class, practicing a supported Balasana with props. While she was still experiencing discomfort, she realized in that moment how far she had come in relationship to her disease. In that moment of heightened awareness, she cried again, but she was not wondering why she couldn't fully execute the pose. In fact, she was feeling gratitude for the arthritis that brought her to a deeper awareness of her body and a set of tools for living differently than she would have without the experience of the disease. Yoga's practices may have helped her manage the symptoms, but yoga's philosophy helped her to manage her life.

YOGA THERAPY AND DIS/ABILITY

Concurrent with the emergence of yoga protocols for clinical populations has been the growth of yoga therapy as a practice and profession around the world. Yoga therapy is a profession that applies the tools of yoga to help address individual health concerns and foster a shift toward greater wellness. Yoga therapy considers the whole person, their individual challenges and abilities, as well as their concerns and goals. Instead of offering the same practices to all-comers, yoga therapy tailors a plan of care, recommending specific (and often modified) yoga practices as tools for self-care. While individual yoga therapists have been practicing around the globe for many years, it is in the last decade that standards have been developed for the training and credentialing of yoga therapists.[27] As yoga therapy becomes credentialed and professionalized, there has been greater integration of yoga therapists into health care settings, such as hospitals, senior care facilities, integrative health practices, and clinics.[28] Yoga in these settings is being adapted for diverse patient populations, and is offered to patients in hospital beds and wheelchairs, from pediatrics to geriatrics.

Unfortunately, many individuals with limited mobility do not know of the distinction between yoga classes for high levels of fitness and yoga therapy for help with managing chronic conditions. While some of the research findings on yoga have been widely disseminated, the details about their highly adapted practices have not. Individuals with limited mobility sometimes seek local yoga classes, only to find that they are not accessible and may even exacerbate symptoms. One woman with arthritis was even told that yoga would not be safe by her doctor who practices yoga himself. If his exposure to yoga is vigorous and athletic, it may very well be inaccessible to his patients. However, the tools of yoga are many, and anyone with a body and a mind can bring the two into union. Anyone can work toward reducing the modifications of the mind. Anyone can work toward greater mindfulness in the moment, contentment, or nonharming.

It is the role of the yoga therapist to meet clients where they are, and to focus on the goals that are of importance to the client, while also recognizing potential areas for growth and greater balance. While the ultimate aim of yoga may be liberation from suffering, the means to that end will be different for each individual; it might be a reduction in physical pain, improved stress management, or greater acceptance of current circumstances. Often, the goals of yoga therapy change over the course of treatment, many times moving from gross to subtle. It is important to remember, however, that even to have a "goal" is not yoga. "After a while, all this struggle drops away naturally. The spiritually mature human being lets all things come and go without effort, without desire for any foreseen result. . . ."[29] For some, there is a very clear purpose to their practice of yoga, and the results are measurable, observable, tangible. In some cases, it takes working toward a goal to realize that there is no goal; and perhaps eventually the ultimate goal becomes the letting go of the goal itself.

UNDERSERVED MINORITIES

Underserved minority populations are disproportionately impacted by a variety of disabling diseases. This can be attributed to systematic oppression, including differential access to quality care and lack of resources and infrastructure to promote self-care behaviors. While arthritis affects those identifying with different racial and ethnic groups in relatively equal numbers, the severity of symptoms and disability is higher among minorities with arthritis.[30] As such, these populations stand to benefit most from non-pharmacological interventions that could help to improve symptoms and reduce disease burden. However, as with other integrative health modalities, yoga is practiced primarily by young, educated, Caucasian women.[31] This contrast is noteworthy, given that yoga was brought to the West primarily by older Indian men, but this trend is aligned with predictors of other health-seeking behaviors.[32] Interestingly, yoga is most often used to treat musculoskeletal and/or mental health conditions, for which most users felt that yoga was helpful.[33]

In research conducted at Johns Hopkins Arthritis Center into the effects of yoga for persons with rheumatoid arthritis and osteoarthritis which recruited a diverse group of participants, we found that minority race (self-identified as non-Caucasian) was the only significant predictor of attrition, even before the intervention began.[34] Due to this disparity in utilization of yoga by those most afflicted with disease symptoms, we sought to develop yoga interventions with race and language concordance.[35] Young, Caucasian, educated yoga teachers are more likely to attract students of a similar demographic, and diverse yoga researchers and interventionists are needed to study the feasibility and acceptability of yoga practice as a tool for self-care, disease management, and improved quality of life among diverse populations.

In the United States, those who self-identify as African American or Hispanic may also have strong religious ties,[36] which can present a perceived barrier to yoga practice. Due to its origins in India and close cultural ties with Hindu and Buddhist religions, yoga is sometimes seen as being in direct conflict with Christian religiosity,[37] although branches of yoga have emerged that incorporate Christian religious beliefs into the practice.[38] For example, in research conducted by the National Institutes of Health, my colleagues and I have documented a case in which a yoga research intervention took place in a local yoga studio.[39] The studio contained a statue of Patanjali, who is a historic figure from the yoga tradition. This might be considered akin to seeing a statue of a historic political figure in a government building. However, the statue was assumed to be representative of a Hindu deity and was considered "diabolical" to a religious study participant who then withdrew from the program. This raises questions about whether yoga can be practiced as a tool for self-care without involvement of the spiritual principles, and whether those spiritual principles are in conflict with major religious traditions. If yoga is to be available and accessed by diverse populations, should it be adapted, not only for different physical bodies, but also for diverse belief systems and worldviews?

GENDER AND YOGA ACCESS

In addition to the barriers that may exist for underserved minorities with regard to yoga access and utilization, there is also a gap in utilization by gender. According to a recent study, yoga practice in America is dominated by women by 83 percent.[40] Due to differences in hormones that impact ligament laxity, men[41] have less range of motion than women and may be intimidated by the agility required to execute complex *asana*. This difference in range of motion is enhanced for men who may be sedentary or have been involved in athletics that emphasize strength over flexibility—activities that would be influenced by cultural ideas about masculinity. Interestingly, the earliest yoga *asanas*, which were mostly variations on seated meditation, did not emphasize the flexibility and stretching that seems inaccessible to many men today. It may be more due to the influence of European gymnastics, which carried a socially constructed gender division between the male emphasis on strength and vigor in contrast with the female emphasis on grace and agility.[42]

In addition, it has been suggested that Americans who self-identify as men may be less comfortable with the spiritual components of yoga and the non-*asana* practices such as breathwork, chanting, and meditation.[43] Such men are less likely to seek health care,[44] but are at greater risk for some disabling pain conditions.[45] Men also seem to have higher rates of disability and depressive symptoms following musculoskeletal injuries.[46] Again, as with disabled populations and underserved minorities, those men who biologically have tighter ligaments and culturally tend to dismiss formal health care may have much to gain from the therapeutic effects of yoga, but find the practices to be less accessible and acceptable, both physically and culturally.

THERAPEUTIC YOGA VS. ACCESSIBLE YOGA

In the discussion of the therapeutic application of yoga for individuals with movement limitations, it is critical to differentiate between disease and disability. These concepts are related, often even causally, but they are not synonymous. Some common conditions lead to physical disability, including arthritis, musculoskeletal injuries, obesity, or stroke. Conversely, disability can be associated with onset of disease. Individuals with limited mobility may be less likely to engage in exercise, and may therefore be at higher risk for cardiovascular disease or diabetes. In these cases of disease *and* disability, medical care can help to manage disease states, reduce comorbidities, and optimize quality of life. In these cases, yoga therapy can serve as a safe and effective complement to medical care, and may even reduce or delay the need for some surgical or pharmacological treatments. Additionally, yoga therapy in the context of disease can help individuals to optimize quality of life regardless of disease symptom severity or limitations. However, it is possible to have the underlying biological disease state without resulting disability, and it is also possible to be disabled without the presence of disease. Both will be discussed.

The Wilson-Cleary model of health-related quality of life details a causal pathway by which biological disease affects quality of life.[47] In this model, biology leads to symptoms (i.e., pain), which impact functional status (i.e., disability), impacting general health perceptions and quality of life. Each of these relationships is moderated by characteristics of the individual and the environment. If, for example, the individual has a high pain tolerance, symptoms may not be disabling. Similarly, it is possible to have disability without poor health perceptions or reduced quality of life. As the tenets of yoga can alter individual characteristics, it is possible that yoga could interfere with the effect of disease on disability, and with the effect of disability on quality of life. Therefore, it is possible to be living with disease, but not with dis-*ease*, by accepting the limitations of the disease and finding contentment in current circumstance. The previous case of Jennifer, who found gratitude for her arthritis, is an example of disease without dis-*ease*. Even Jennifer's *disability*—the physical limitations within her knees and other joints—was not *disabling*, in that it did not interfere with Jennifer's ability, willingness, or confidence to carry out her life's activities.

There are also many individuals who may be limited in certain movements, but who are not living with disease. In these cases, adaptations to yoga *asana* may be needed for engagement in a full range of yoga practices, but the yoga is not therapeutic, because there is no intention of addressing a particular health condition or symptom. *Asana* for movement limitations is *accessible yoga*, but not *yoga therapy*. In such cases, yoga may still be practiced with the intention to relieve suffering, but it is not suffering related to any specific ailment other than the human condition itself, and the common modifications of the mind. Indeed, some suggest that impairment is only considered to be a disability if it impedes or inhibits daily activities.[48] By providing tools for activities like yoga *asana* to be available and accessible to those with physical impairments, it is possible to help diminish the extent to which impairment becomes disability, and then of course the extent to which suffering is experienced in either case.

OPPORTUNITIES FOR TRANSFORMATION

Yoga as a concept of union and unification has ancient roots in spiritual seeking, and has evolved to a set of practices and ideas that are applied across the globe to everything from physical fitness to chronic disease, and from psychological stress to existential uncertainty. The practice of yoga brings groups together in support of each other, and has been adapted to address many different goals and priorities. While the physical body has become central to modern yoga practice, there has been a split between yoga for those developing extreme fitness and yoga for those with the most extreme challenges. As yoga continues to evolve, it will ideally retain its initial goal of unification, not only of the individual with spirit, or the individual's mind and body, but in the ways that we welcome difference, physical and otherwise, into the widening tent of yoga practice.

NOTES

1. Richard Miller, *The Sankyhya Karika of Ishvara Krsna*, 1.3 ed. (Anahata Press, 2012).

2. Georg Feuerstein and Ken Wilber, *The Yoga Tradition: Its History, Literature, Philosophy and Practice*, 3rd ed. (Prescott, AZ: Hohm Press, 2001).

3. Stephen Mitchell, *The Bhagavad Gita: A New Translation* (New York: Harmony, 2002).

4. Mitchell, *The Bhagavad Gita*, 55.

5. Sri Swami Satchidananda, *The Yoga Sutras of Patanjali*, 4th ed. (Buckingham, VA: Integral Yoga Publications, 2012).

6. Mitchell, *The Bhagavad Gita: A New Translation*, 78.

7. Mitchell, *The Bhagavad Gita: A New Translation*, 78.

8. A. G. Krishna Warrier, *Maitrayani Upanishad* (Chennai: Theosophical Publishing House, 2008).

9. Feuerstein and Wilber, *The Yoga Tradition: Its History, Literature, Philosophy and Practice* .

10. Sri Swami Satchidananda, *Meditation Excerpts from Talks by Sri Swami Satchidananda* (Buckingham, VA: Integral Yoga Publications, 2011), 32 .

11. Swami Svatmarama, *Hatha-Yoga-Pradipika: Classic Text of Yoga* (United Kingdom: Thorsons, 1992).

12. S'rimat Kuvalayananda, ed., *Yoga-Mimansa* (United States: Kessinger Publishing Co., 1924).

13. David Gordon White, ed., *Yoga in Practice* (Princeton, NJ: Princeton University Press, 2011).

14. Mark Singleton, *Yoga Body: The Origins of Modern Posture Practice* (New York: Oxford University Press, 2010).

15. "Shri K. Pattabhi Jois Ashtang Yoga Institute," 2009, accessed May 13, 2016, http://kpjayi.org/biographies/k-pattabhi-jois/.

16. Singleton, *Yoga Body: The Origins of Modern Posture Practice*, 161.

17. Shri Yogendra, *Yoga Asanas Simplified* (Santa Cruz: Yoga Institute, 1988), 81.

18. Antonia Blumberg, "India Is Officially Reclaiming Yoga, and It's Complicated," *Huffington Post* (The Huffington Post), December 10, 2014, http://www.huffingtonpost.com/2014/12/10/yoga-religious-history_n_6270756.html.

19. S. Muzumdar, "'Sarvangasana'—the Greatest of Yogic Exercises. The Health Wisdom of the East Contained in One Simple Movement," *Health and Strength* (June 12, 1937).

20. Dean Ornish et al., "Effects of Stress Management Training and Dietary Changes in Treating Ischemic Heart Disease," *JAMA: The Journal of the American Medical Association* 249, no. 1 (January 7, 1983), doi:10.1001/jama.1983.03330250034024.

21. Pamela E. Jeter et al., "Yoga as a Therapeutic Intervention: A Bibliometric Analysis of Published Research Studies from 1967 to 2013," *The Journal of Alternative and Complementary Medicine* 21, no. 10 (July 21, 2015), doi:10.1089/acm.2015.0057.

22. Susan J. Bartlett et al., "Yoga in Rheumatic Diseases," *Current Rheumatology Reports* 15, no. 12 (October 31, 2013), doi:10.1007/s11926-013-0387-2.

23. Neha P. Gothe and Edward Mcauley, "Yoga Is as Good as Stretching–Strengthening Exercises in Improving Functional Fitness Outcomes: Results from a Randomized Controlled Trial," *The Journals of Gerontology Series A: Biological Sciences and Medical Sciences* 71, no. 3 (August 22, 2015), doi:10.1093/gerona/glv127.

24. M. Catherine Bushnell, Marta Čeko, and Lucie A. Low, "Cognitive and Emotional Control of Pain and Its Disruption in Chronic Pain," *Nature Reviews Neuroscience* 14, no. 7 (May 30, 2013), doi:10.1038/nrn3516.

25. Jin Qin et al., "Impact of Arthritis and Multiple Chronic Conditions on Selected Life Domains—United States, 2013," *Morbidity and Mortality Weekly Report* 64, no. 21 (June 5, 2015).

26. Satchidananda, *The Yoga Sutras of Patanjali.*

27. John Kepner, "On the Global Movement to Establish High Standards for the Training of Yoga Therapists" *Yoga Therapy Today*, (Winter 2016).

28. Nora Isaacs, "Yoga-Physical Therapy-Alternative Therapy-Pain-Rehabilitation," *New York Times*, February 8, 2015, http://www.nytimes.com/2007/05/10/fashion/10Fitness.html.

29. Mitchell, *The Bhagavad Gita: A New Translation* , 17.

30. Centers for Disease, Control, and Prevention, "Racial/Ethnic Differences in the Prevalence and Impact of Doctor-Diagnosed Arthritis—United States, 2002," *Morbidity and Mortality Weekly Report* 54, no. 5 (February 11, 2005).

31. Gurjeet S. Birdee et al., "Characteristics of Yoga Users: Results of a National Survey," *Journal of General Internal Medicine* 23, no. 10 (July 24, 2008), doi:10.1007/s11606-008-0735-5.

32. Amanda Richardson et al., "Effects of Race/Ethnicity and Socioeconomic Status on Health Information-Seeking, Confidence, and Trust," *Journal of Health Care for the Poor and Underserved* 23, no. 4 (2012), doi:10.1353/hpu.2012.0181.

33. Birdee et al., "Characteristics of Yoga Users: Results of a National Survey."

34. S. H. Moonaz et al., "Yoga in Sedentary Adults with Arthritis: Effects of a Randomized Controlled Pragmatic Trial," *The Journal of Rheumatology* 42, no. 7 (April 1, 2015), doi:10.3899/jrheum.141129.

35. Kimberly R. Middleton et al., "A Pilot Study of Yoga as Self-Care for Arthritis in Minority Communities," *Health and Quality of Life Outcomes* 11, no. 1 (2013), doi:10.1186/1477-7525-11-55.

36. G. David Johnson, Marc Matre, and Gigi Armbrecht, "Race and Religiosity: An Empirical Evaluation of a Causal Model," *Review of Religious Research* 32, no. 3 (March 1991), doi:10.2307/3511210.

37. Kremer, "Does Doing Yoga Make You a Hindu?," November 21, 2013. http://www.bbc.com/news/magazine-25006926.

38. Susan Bordenkircher, *Yoga for Christians: A Christ-Centered Approach to Physical and Spiritual Health Through Yoga* (Nashville, TN: Thomas Nelson Publishers, 2006).

39. Middleton et al., "Yoga Research and Spirituality: A Case Study Discussion."

40. "Yoga in America Study," January 13, 2016, accessed May 13, 2016, http://www.yogajournal.com/yogainamericastudy/.

41. In this sentence, the term "men" refers to the physiology of biological male sex, which is not necessarily aligned with the social construct of male gender.

42. Singleton, *Yoga Body: The Origins of Modern Posture Practice* .

43. Carolyn Gregoire, "The Real Reason Yoga Is Still Dominated by Women," *Huffington Post*, October 28, 2013, http://www.huffingtonpost.com/carolyn-gregoire/yoga-women_b_4163938.htmlfiles/61/yoga-women_b_4163938.html.

44. Kaiser Family Foundations, "Gender Differences in Health Care, Status, and Use: Spotlight on Men's Health," March 31, 2015, accessed May 13, 2016, http://kff.org/womens-health-policy/fact-sheet/gender-differences-in-health-care-status-and-use-spotlight-on-mens-health/.

45. Donald D. McGeary et al., "Gender-Related Differences in Treatment Outcomes for Patients with Musculoskeletal Disorders," *The Spine Journal* 3, no. 3 (May 2003), doi:10.1016/s1529-9430(02)00599-5.

46. McGeary et al., "Gender-Related Differences in Treatment Outcomes for Patients with Musculoskeletal Disorders."

47. I. B. Wilson and P. D. Cleary, "Linking Clinical Variables with Health-Related Quality of Life. A Conceptual Model of Patient Outcomes," *JAMA: The Journal of the American Medical Association* 273, no. 1 (January 4, 1995), doi:10.1001/jama.273.1.59.

48. Carol Thomas, "How Is Disability Understood? An Examination of Sociological Approaches," *Disability & Society* 19, no. 6 (October 2004), doi:10.1080/0968759042000252506.

REFERENCES

Bartlett, Susan J., Steffany H. Moonaz, Christopher Mill, Sasha Bernatsky, and Clifton O. Bingham. "Yoga in Rheumatic Diseases." *Current Rheumatology Reports* 15, no. 12 (2013): 387. doi:10.1007/s11926-013-0387-2.

Birdee, Gurjeet S., Anna T. Legedza, Robert B. Saper, Suzanne M. Bertisch, David M. Eisenberg, and Russell S. Phillips. 2008. "Characteristics of Yoga Users: Results of a National Survey." *Journal of General Internal Medicine* 23, no. 10 (July 24, 2008): 1653–58. doi:10.1007/s11606-008-0735-5.

Blumberg, Antonia. "India Is Officially Reclaiming Yoga, And It's Complicated." *The Huffington Post*, December 10, 2014. http://www.huffingtonpost.com/2014/12/10/yoga-religious-history_n_6270756.html.

Bordenkircher, Susan. *Yoga for Christians: A Christ-Centered Approach to Physical and Spiritual Health through Yoga*. Pap/DVD edition (Nashville, TN: Thomas Nelson. 2006).

Bushnell, M. Catherine, Marta Ceko, and Lucie A. Low. "Cognitive and Emotional Control of Pain and Its Disruption in Chronic Pain." *Nature Reviews. Neuroscience* 14, no. 7 (2013): 502–11. doi:10.1038/nrn3516.

Centers for Disease Control and Prevention (CDC). "Racial/Ethnic Differences in the Prevalence and Impact of Doctor-Diagnosed Arthritis—United States, 2002." *MMWR. Morbidity and Mortality Weekly Report* 54, no. 5 (2005): 119–23.

Feuerstein, Georg, and Ken Wilber. *The Yoga Tradition: Its History, Literature, Philosophy and Practice*. 3rd ed. (Prescott, AZ: Hohm Press. 2001).

Gothe, Neha P., and Edward McAuley. "Yoga Is as Good as Stretching-Strengthening Exercises in Improving Functional Fitness Outcomes: Results From a Randomized Controlled Trial." *The Journals of Gerontology. Series A, Biological Sciences and Medical Sciences*, August 2015.. doi:10.1093/gerona/glv127.

Gregoire, Carolyn. "The Real Reason Yoga Is Still Dominated By Women." *The Huffington Post*. October 28, 2013. http://www.huffingtonpost.com/carolyn-gregoire/yoga-women_b_4163938.html.

Isaacs, Nora. "Yoga-Physical Therapy-Alternative Therapy-Pain-Rehabilitation." *The New York Times*, May 10, 2007.. http://www.nytimes.com/2007/05/10/fashion/10Fitness.html.

Jeter, Pamela E., Jeremiah Slutsky, Nilkamal Singh, and Sat Bir S. Khalsa. "Yoga as a Therapeutic Intervention: A Bibliometric Analysis of Published Research Studies from 1967 to 2013." *Journal of Alternative and Complementary Medicine (New York, N.Y.)* 21, no. 10 (July 21, 2015): 586–92.doi:10.1089/acm.2015.0057.

Johnson, G. David, Marc Matre, and Gigi Armbrecht. "Race and Religiosity: An Empirical Evaluation of a Causal Model." *Review of Religious Research* 32, no. 3 (March 1991): 252–66. doi:10.2307/3511210.

Kaiser Family Foundation. "Gender Differences in Health Care, Status, and Use: Spotlight on Men's Health." March 31, 2015. http://kff.org/womens-health-policy/factsheet/gender-differences-in-health-care-status-and-use-spotlight-on-mens-health/.

Kepner, John. "On the Global Movement to Establish High Standards for the Training of Yoga Therapists." *Yoga Therapy Today.* 2016.

Kremer, William. "Does Doing Yoga Make You a Hindu?," November 21, 2013. http://www.bbc.com/news/magazine-25006926.

Krishna Warrier, A.G. *Maitrayani Upanishad* (Chennai: Theosophical Publishing House, 2008). http://merki.lv/vedas/Upanishadas/Maitrayani%20Upanishad%20_eng_.pdf.

Kuvalayananda, S'rimat. "Yoga Mimansa." 1924.

McGeary, Donald D., Tom G. Mayer, Robert J. Gatchel, Christopher Anagnostis, and Timothy J. Proctor. "Gender-Related Differences in Treatment Outcomes for Patients with Musculoskeletal Disorders." *The Spine Journal: Official Journal of the North American Spine Society* 3, no. 3 (May 2003): 197–203.

Middleton, Kimberly R., Regina Andrade, Steffany Haaz Moonaz, Charlene Muhammad, and Gwenyth R. Wallen. "Yoga Research and Spirituality: A Case Study Discussion." *International Journal of Yoga Therapy* 25, no. 1 (2015): 33–35. doi:10.17761/1531-2054-25.1.33.

Middleton, Kimberly R., Michael M. Ward, Steffany Haaz, Sinthujah Velummylum, Alice Fike, Ana T. Acevedo, Gladys Tataw-Ayuketah, Laura Dietz, Barbara B. Mittleman, and Gwenyth R. Wallen. "A Pilot Study of Yoga as Self-Care for Arthritis in Minority Communities." *Health and Quality of Life Outcomes* 11 (2013): 55. doi:10.1186/1477-7525-11-55.

Miller, Richard. *The Sankyhya Karika of Ishvara Krsna.* 1.3 ed. (Anahata Press, 2012).

Mitchell, Stephen. *Bhagavad Gita: A New Translation.* Reprint edition. New York: Harmony. 2002.

Moonaz, Steffany Haaz, Clifton O. Bingham, Lawrence Wissow, and Susan J. Bartlett. "Yoga in Sedentary Adults with Arthritis: Effects of a Randomized Controlled Pragmatic Trial." *The Journal of Rheumatology* 42, no. 7 (April 1, 2015): 1194–1202. doi:10.3899/jrheum.141129.

Muzumdar, S. "'Sarvangasana'—the Greatest of Yogic Exercises. The Health Wisdom of the East Contained in One Simple Movement." *Health and Strength*, June 12, 1937.

Ornish, D., L. W. Scherwitz, R. S. Doody, D. Kesten, S. M. McLanahan, S. E. Brown, E. DePuey, et al. "Effects of Stress Management Training and Dietary Changes in Treating Ischemic Heart Disease." *JAMA* 249, no. 1 (January 7, 1983): 54–59.

Qin, Jin, Kristina A. Theis, Kamil E. Barbour, Charles G. Helmick, Nancy A. Baker, Teresa J. Brady, and Centers for Disease Control and Prevention (CDC). "Impact of Arthritis and Multiple Chronic Conditions on Selected Life Domains - United States, 2013." *MMWR. Morbidity and Mortality Weekly Report* 64, no. 21 June 5, 2015): 578–82.

Richardson, Amanda, Jane Appleyard Allen, Haijun Xiao, and Donna Vallone. "Effects of Race/Ethnicity and Socioeconomic Status on Health Information-Seeking, Confidence, and Trust." *Journal of Health Care for the Poor and Underserved* 23, no. 4 (2012): 1477–93. doi:10.1353/hpu.2012.0181.

Satchidananda, Sri Swami. *Meditation Excerpts from Talks by Sri Swami Satchidananda* (Buckingham, VA: Integral Yoga Publications, 2011).

Satchidananda, Swami. *The Yoga Sutras of Patanjali.* Reprint ed. (Buckingham, VA: Integral Yoga Publications, 2012).

Shri K. Pattabhi Jois Ashtanga Yoga Institute. "K. Pattabhi Jois." 2009. http://kpjayi.org/biographies/k-pattabhi-jois/.

Singleton, Mark. *Yoga Body: The Origins of Modern Posture Practice* (Oxford ; New York: Oxford University Press, 2010).

Svatmarama, Swami. *Hatha-Yoga-Pradipika: Classic Text of Yoga* (Thorsons, 1992).

Thomas, Carol. "How Is Disability Understood? An Examination of Sociological Approaches." *Disability & Society* 19, no. 6 (2004): 569–83. doi:10.1080/09687 59042000252506.

White, David Gordon, ed., *Yoga in Practice* (Princeton, NJ: Princeton University Press, 2011).

Wilson, I. B., and P. D. Cleary. "Linking Clinical Variables with Health-Related Quality of Life. A Conceptual Model of Patient Outcomes." *JAMA* 273, no. 1 (1995): 59–65.

"Yoga In America Study." *Yoga Journal*, January 13, 2016. http://www.yog ajournal.com/yogainamericastudy/.

Yogendra, Shri. *Yoga Asanas Simplified* (Santa Cruz: Yoga Institute, 1988).

FIFTEEN

Yoga as Embodied Feminist Praxis

Trauma, Healing, and Community-Based
Responses to Violence

Beth S. Catlett and Mary Bunn

Drawing on feminist theory, trauma theory, and ashtanga yoga's philo-sophical tenets, our essay explores questions about the use of ashtanga yoga for communities affected by trauma and violence. The authors—one a clinical social worker whose work focuses on developing rehabilita-tive services for, and delivering direct mental health care to, survivors of severe violence in the United States and around the world (Mary), and the other a women's and gender studies professor whose scholarship centers on violence prevention and community activism work with urban youth (Beth)—use their own professional backgrounds and training to explore opportunities and challenges that present when bringing the tools of ashtanga yoga to diverse communities impacted by violence.

In particular, we take up questions of how an ashtanga yoga practice can promote individual healing from trauma, creating a restorative expe-rience of embodiment for violence survivors. We also look beyond the individual to a consideration of the potential that ashtanga yoga may have to animate community-engaged practices to eradicate violence and promote social justice.[1] We approach these questions with attention to the well-documented multifaceted effects of trauma.[2] Trauma is a whole body experience and individuals who have experienced violence fre-quently experience physical, psychological, and physiological symptoms as a result of their experiences.[3] Central to the practice of ashtanga yoga is a physically challenging engagement of the body, particularly in terms of the ability to "master" a specialized sequencing of postures and focused breathing techniques which in combination are believed to lead to purification and restoration of the mind and body. We interrogate the applicability of this approach for individuals and communities who are affected by violence and often live in settings of poverty and social marginalization. In this chapter, we primarily focus on two ashtanga yoga programs, one for violence-affected urban youth in New York City and another, for HIV-positive men, women, and children in post-genocide Rwanda. As part of our analysis, we consider feminist, trauma-focused, and social work approaches, questioning how they might be best integrated with the central tenets of ashtanga yoga in order to develop yoga-based programmatic initiatives that are well suited to address the challenges that face violence-affected communities.

METHODS AND ESSAY OVERVIEW

To ground this interrogation, we use two sources of data. First, as we've touched on above, our perspectives have been informed by our ongoing observation and work with two ashtanga-based programs that address violence in different contexts. Beth has spent time over the last two years working with Urban Yogis-NYC, an ashtanga yoga program for young adults from violence-affected urban communities in which participants learn the traditional ashtanga yoga method, study foundational philosophical texts, and then bring these tools to their community as a strategy to address rising levels of youth and community violence. Mary has been connected for some time to Project Air and has traveled to Kigali, Rwanda to spend time with staff and teacher trainees to understand how ashtanga yoga is being used and experienced among HIV-positive men, women, and children. Project Air uses ashtanga-informed yoga with HIV-positive individuals in Rwanda. The program began with a focus on serving women, many of who were survivors of genocidal rape during the 1994 genocide. The yoga is seen as an integrated tool to manage psychological and physiological symptoms.

This methodological approach is useful for the preliminary theoretical and analytical exploration we present in this chapter. Part of this preliminary phase of our inquiry involved rapport building with the two yoga programs that included participation and informal conversations primarily with the program staff, including teacher trainees. While the voice of program participants seems an essential ingredient, this approach seemed appropriate at this stage given the pronounced need for trust and relationship building with trauma-affected communities.

Second, we have spent the last two years having a series of structured conversations that have generated rich narratives informed by our personal practice of ashtanga yoga, our academic backgrounds and disciplines, as well as our experiences in various forms of interdisciplinary work. Our approach involves moving beyond a sole focus on reporting these conversations to an integrated analytic treatment of the thematic content embedded within this narrative discourse.[4] This process has led us to many points of notable convergence. For instance, our engagement with Project Air and Urban Yogis deepened our conviction that an ashtanga-based yoga program can be experienced as therapeutic, beneficial, and healing. Through these conversations, we also came to find some initial differences in our approaches. For example, we had distinct interpretations about the extent to which we viewed participation in yoga projects as kind of social justice activity, in and of itself, or the language that we used to describe that process. These differences do not present as incompatibilities, but rather generate rich analytic insights that help us to unpack, complicate, and develop a more nuanced understanding of the ways in which ashtanga yoga can be deployed and understood in communities impacted by trauma and violence.

We begin our analysis with a brief description of the historical context and philosophical foundations of ashtanga yoga. As part of our contextualizing, we also explore the authors' experiences as white Western feminists for whom yoga evolved from a daily individual practice to infuse their community-engaged social justice work. We then turn to a discussion of a set of thematic questions that emerged for us as we considered the various ways that intersecting systems of power, privilege, and oppression create particular opportunities, as well as limitations for this work. These thematic questions emerged through our dialogue over the last several years and include issues such as: Can ashtanga yoga serve as a unique form of intervention for diverse, trauma-impacted communities to support healing from trauma? If so, how it is experienced on an individual level? And, finally, does the work on an individual level inform community transformation and make a meaningful contribution to social justice efforts?

THE ORIGIN STORY: A BRIEF HISTORY OF ASHTANGA YOGA AND OUR PERSONAL PRACTICES

A full historical account of the development of the ashtanga yoga system is beyond the scope of this essay, but a brief description is useful to provide context for our analytic discussion. Yoga itself is traced to approximately 400 C.E. when various Sanskrit teachings were formalized and compiled into the *Yoga Sutras*, a work ascribed to Patanjali. Ashtanga yoga builds on this ancient system, was imparted to Sri. T. Krishnamacharya in the early 1900s, and later passed down to Sri K. Pattabhi Jois, commonly known as the "father" of ashtanga yoga, beginning in 1927. Jois worked tirelessly to reintroduce yoga in his own community, ultimately successful in repopularizing the practice. He also took a global focus, traveling extensively to the West and training a cadre of teachers who helped spread ashtanga yoga practice.[5]

The ashtanga yoga method is based on a specialized sequencing of physically demanding postures and focused breathing techniques. The physical poses that comprise the ashtanga yoga system include only one of the necessary eight elements that yoga philosophy describes as central to a full commitment to ashtanga yoga. Performing these physical poses in a structured sequence and with regularity is thought to foster a strengthening of the body and quieting of the mind that will prepare one for engagement with all eight aspects of yoga, which the *Yoga Sutras* characterize as limbs of a tree.[6] The ashtanga method assumes that through committed experience and the regulation of the embodied physical practice, the other seven limbs of yoga will be nourished and personal insights will begin to manifest.[7]

For purposes of this analysis, two additional features of the ashtanga yoga method are important. Regular practice of the poses is considered necessary, with students ideally practicing ashtanga six days a week, with one day set aside for rest. The traditional style of teaching/learning ashtanga is the mysore, or self-practice, method in which students work individually through a set series of increasingly challenging poses. Students are able to progress at their own pace and work to gain proficiency with poses gradually and under the guidance of a teacher. Students move forward through the sequence of poses in a highly structured way, moving to an additional pose only after achieving proficiency with the prior pose in the sequence.

Second, the relationship between student and teacher is considered central within the ashtanga method. In many ways, this relationship functions hierarchically, granting ultimate authority to the teacher in terms of regulating the student's progress through the sequence of poses in the ashtanga yoga system. But particularly in the mysore method, the teacher's role is conceptualized not only as hierarchical, but as a guide or trusted advisor for the student's own journey.[8]

We come to this work each with over a decade of dedicated ashtanga yoga practice. We both practice the traditional mysore method, and have seen first-hand the tremendous benefits ashtanga yoga has brought to our lives. What may have started primarily as a physical, exercise-focused practice soon transformed into a daily practice that sustains us physically, emotionally, spiritually, and ethically. It has been a great life support and has encouraged us to go deep, learning about ourselves—as well as the world in which we live—in many important ways. In this time, we also have observed an important relationship between our dedicated practice and commitment to service and social justice work. For instance, Mary noticed changes in her clinical work with torture survivors as her practice progressed and deepened. Initially seeing yoga as an avenue for self-care in an emotionally and spiritually demanding area of clinical social work, with time she began to see ways that yoga made her a better clinician. More settled in her own body and mind, she noticed that she could listen more deeply to clients, appreciating the depth of their suffering and strengths and able to support their healing process in a more attuned and compassionate way. And, her sense of being in service to others and commitment to anti-torture and nonviolence continued to deepen and evolve.

Beth has been particularly influenced by the way in which ashtanga yoga practice has connected her more readily to others and the world around. Indeed, yoga means union, and this translation holds great significance for Beth in her social justice work.[9] The point of practice is to awaken to the realization that we are all in this together. The sense of deepened self-knowledge and sense of connection that Beth has fostered through daily ashtanga practice has also fostered greater attention to, appreciation for, and a sense of solidarity with the needs and interests of others whose lives on the surface may appear to have no easily visible points of connection with her own. This awakening has grounded Beth firmly in a commitment to working in solidarity with others toward both individual and collective transformation. Moreover, she has developed a commitment to including yoga more prominently in her own community-based research agenda.

IMPLICATIONS OF INTERSECTIONAL FEMINIST THOUGHT FOR YOGA SERVICE

Particularly mindful of these heightened sensibilities, we approach this work with a healthy, critically focused skepticism about yoga service projects, or more specifically, about white Western feminist allies who endeavor to utilize the tools of ashtanga yoga with communities affected by violence, trauma, poverty, and marginalization. As Tema Okun discusses, there is a potent cultural conditioning within a white supremacist world to construct "others" as somehow deficient. This conditioning often results in a sort of paternalistic "wanting to help those less fortunate."[10] A similar tendency can be observed in the field of global mental health, which often centers on the assumption that war and violence result in a universally experienced phenomenon of "trauma" (and often a Western diagnosis of post-traumatic stress disorder) with little attention to how distress and suffering may be expressed differently across cultures and contexts.[11] This often leads to the implementation of interventions—most often developed and imported from the Western world—that overshadow or are in tension with indigenous healing practices and the ways in which communities may self-organize and heal.[12] While there is merit in attunement to suffering, such approaches carry a sub-

stantial risk of community-engaged work in which structures of inequality are reproduced—where pathology and deficits are located in communities of color and vulnerability and solutions lie with privileged stake-
holders.[13]

Moreover, a traditional mysore yoga practice involves an approximately two-hour daily yoga practice, six days a week, and one naturally
wonders if such a model could be possible—or relevant—among the
communities with whom we collaborate. The usefulness of ashtanga has
been a primary concern for Mary who has worked in many locations
around the world and seen firsthand many trauma-based approaches
imported to non-Western contexts only to find them of little relevance to
local communities, having exhausted dollars and resources and leaving
minimal impact. Beth has grappled for years with a sharp awareness that
her relationship to her ashtanga practice has been facilitated out of privilege. It is precisely this regular and dedicated practice that Beth believes
has had such a positive impact on her life and yet, this practice model is
accessible largely as a result of Beth's privileged social location. Sharing
her own early trepidation about the utility of yoga in Rwanda, Deirdre
Summerbell, director of Project Air, writes, "yoga takes time, yoga takes
energy, yoga takes reserves of health and wellbeing. . . . Or, more to the
point, spare time, spare energy, spare reserves of health—all of which
poverty, illness, and trauma tend to deny people."[14]

Thus, while we are interested in exploring yoga as a tool, we also are
aware of its limitations in the face of multifaceted problems resulting
from substantial poverty, social inequality, historical trauma, and structural violence. With such possibilities and limitations in mind, we turn
now to two primary questions that have emerged for us: (1) Can ashtanga
yoga foster personal healing from trauma? (2) Can ashtanga yoga animate community-based anti-violence initiatives as well as broader social
justice initiatives? We begin with an examination of how ashtanga may
foster individual healing, considering the approaches and lived experiences of participants in both Project Air and Urban Yogis.

YOGA FOR INDIVIDUAL HEALING FROM TRAUMA

The practice of ashtanga yoga is described as resulting in mental and
physical restoration.[15] While much emphasis is placed on physical poses
in ashtanga yoga, the pathway to well-being arises equally, if not primarily, from a focus on breathing. Each inhalation and exhalation is to be
synchronized with movement while maintaining a particular visual focus
point called dristi.[16] With time and attention to these three central components—breath, movement, and visual gaze—practitioners are able to
shift focus from exterior to interior processes including unhelpful physical and mental patterns, develop greater mastery of personal behaviors

and reactions, and ultimately, greater focus and presence.[17] The authors have experienced firsthand the resonance of this approach; however, we have wondered if similar benefits could be expected for Project Air participants, for example, whose experience of yoga would be complicated by multiple, severe experiences of trauma. In other words, could ashtanga yoga actually serve as a form of healing from trauma? There is a small but growing body of literature that has examined the benefits of yoga for survivors of trauma, though we are not aware of any that have focused on the ashtanga approach in particular.[18]

The women who participate in Project Air are HIV-positive, some of them were raped during the genocide, and many believe that they became infected at that time. As Cohen, d'Adesky, and Anastos discuss, "gender based violence resulted in the synchronized HIV infection of tens of thousands of women causing the current predictable AIDS epidemic in thousands of Rwanda women."[19] The Rwandan genocide was one of unimaginable loss in an incredibly condensed time period. Scaal and Elbert report that "within a period of 100 days between April and July of 1994 an estimated 800,000 to 1 million Rwandans lost their lives to genocide."[20] During this time, it is estimated that 250,000 women were raped.[21]

While HIV is a primary concern, Project Air participants have other, equally substantial vulnerabilities. Participants struggle with a wide range of symptoms including depression, anxiety, sleep problems, and bodily pain—these are the well-documented effects of systematic violence.[22] Moreover, in many cultures, women are blamed for experiences of rape and in Rwanda, one's dual status as HIV-positive and a rape survivor carries substantial risk of "severe stigmatization and marginalization."[23] And yet, despite these incredible obstacles, staff and teacher trainees describe important improvements in their well-being as a result of their participation in Project Air.

When one asks Deirdre Summerbell, director of Project Air, how women have improved, the first thing she tells you is sleep and appetite. Deirdre is a Western white woman who has spent a substantial part of her young and adult life living in Africa. She came to Rwanda nine years ago to start the ashtanga program as part of We-Actx (Women's Access to Care and Treatment), an integrated health program for persons living with HIV. When participants started practicing yoga, Deirdre noticed that it made them physically tired and hungry. Deirdre remembers an experience early into the program when a participant approached her to say that she had slept for the first time since the genocide, more than ten years after it occurred. Problems with sleep are one of the most commonly reported issues following severe trauma, and likely one of the most damaging.[24] With time, Deirdre reports, improved sleep became a trend among women participating in the program. Moreover, she also quickly realized that Project Air needed to provide a meal for participants at the end of yoga class. The physical exertion made the women hungry and yet, their poverty limited their ability to eat regularly. The increase in appetite was of course beneficial to their general health, but also particularly critical for their HIV care as antiretroviral medications needs to be taken with food.

When Project Air began, the program brought in volunteer ashtanga teachers that were willing to volunteer their time teaching yoga in Rwanda. But this approach had significant challenges. It meant that even with the minimum three-month commitment, students were seeing four different teachers in one year, not an ideal environment for learning yoga nor the optimal teacher-student relationship per the ashtanga system. Deirdre also found that many volunteers were not prepared for the impoverished conditions in Rwanda and had difficulty adapting once they arrived. Moreover, some volunteers came to their service with the potentially harmful assumption that they had more to teach than they had to learn. As a result, in the last few years Deirdre has started training some of the Project Air participants to become teachers. These teacher trainees co-teach community classes with her and participate in their own intensive training two times per week and this includes significant attention to breath work. Deirdre sees training local teachers as the solution for long-term sustainability of the program, which includes an eventual vision to turn the program over for local leadership.

Observing the two most senior teacher trainees, it would seem that this intention might be possible in the not-too-distant future. Both have very advanced physical practices and also eloquently described the more subtle and profound interior changes they have experienced as a result of ashtanga. One of the trainees shared that prior to ashtanga, she had psychological problems as a result of experiences during the genocide and was not able to organize her mind. She found that the repetitive practice of the same sequence of poses, first this pose and then the next, provided a kind of internal structure that she needed. So that with time, she began to be better able to organize her daily activities—*first I will do this and next, I will do that.* Another senior teacher trainer felt that the silence of a mysore style practice allowed for deeper, personal listening and facilitated personal change.

Similar ideas were expressed among the Urban Yogis. With a similar emphasis on personal practice and training to be teachers, they modified the traditional ashtanga six-day-a-week practice schedule to their two-day-a-week commitment and report a strong belief in the healing effects of ashtanga's system of regular and dedicated practice of a specialized sequencing of poses. For example, practitioners reported feeling grounded by the regularity and consistency of their practice and talked about the importance of the sense of discipline created by their commitment to regular practice. One Urban Yogi in particular discussed several times the ways in which, before his engagement with the Urban Yogis program, he struggled with anger and rage and often made bad choices as a result of these powerful emotions. Now, after committing to a regular embodied yoga practice, along with weekly group study, this Urban Yogi reports a sense of personal transformation that has led to a sense of peacefulness and calm, and more broadly, his commitment to a nonviolent way of life. These observations among the participants of both Project Air and Urban Yogis have deepened our confidence that a body-based approach such as ashtanga yoga can promote individual healing from the multifaceted effects of violence and trauma. We now turn to our second analytic question to consider community effects, in particular considering ashtanga yoga as a tool to animate community-based anti-violence and broader social justice initiatives.

YOGA AND SOCIAL JUSTICE WORK

Our engagement with the Urban Yogis program has inspired a confidence that a feminist-informed social justice orientation to community engagement emphasizing ethics of care, commitment, shared power, and mutual political vision is indeed possible.[25] Inherent in this approach is the recognition that meaningful anti-violence and social justice initiatives ideally originate from within the impacted communities themselves. With this ideal in mind, it is important to contextualize our analytic reflections with an understanding of the way in which Urban Yogis came to life. Urban Yogis is an integrated program of Peace Is A Lifestyle and LIFE Camp, based in South Side Jamaica, Queens, and Ashtanga Yoga New York. Led by long time anti-violence activist Erica Ford and ashtanga yoga teacher Eddie Stern (Ashtanga Yoga New York), the Urban Yogis program was inaugurated with five young adults from Queens who grew into dedicated yoga and meditation practitioners. Each of the core team members has been personally affected by tragedies due to gun and other types of violence. These young men and women have spent the past several years engaging in community activism, which has included learning the transformative tools of yoga and meditation. Inspired by their experiences, they have created an initiative to bring these tools to their community. The Urban Yogis now are all teaching yoga in the New York City public school system and inspiring other young people to choose alternative pathways toward positivity and peace.[26]

Dialogue with Eddie Stern made clear that he approaches his work with the Urban Yogis as his own civic "participation,"[27] explicitly taking the lead from community partners and grounding yoga-based programmatic initiatives in the strengths and assets of the community.[28] One moment in particular stands out as clearly illuminating this approach. When asked about his motivation to start this program, Eddie wagged his finger and replied that *he* did not found this program. Rather, as

Eddie describes the way in which Urban Yogis came to life, he talks about his deep and loving relationship with the original group of five young adults who found their way to him and their interest in exploring the ways in which yoga might enhance their lives and their ability to resist violence in their community. Moreover, Eddie talks with great pride about how each of these young people are now employed full time with the NYC public schools; connecting a commitment to yoga into full time employment, economic stability, and enhanced opportunities for community leadership are all important elements of the Urban Yogis' programmatic approach, and Stern talks passionately about this when asked about the origins, foundations, and growth of the program.

The strong, committed, and long-term relationship that the Urban Yogis team has created finds reflections in ashtanga's focus on the important relationship between teacher and student. Going into this project, Beth and Mary both had initial reservations about how well a largely hierarchical relationship between teacher and student would serve the needs of individuals and communities that are economically, politically, and socially marginalized, and whose voices are too often silenced. Indeed, the traditional teacher-student relationship appeared, on its surface, to be at odds with our approach to yoga service that emphasizes power sharing and recognition of community assets and strengths. But as Beth worked with the Urban Yogis, she was extremely touched by the genuinely loving, supportive, and committed relationship between Eddie Stern (the ashtanga yoga teacher) and the original cohort of Urban Yogis (the students). Indeed, Beth has speculated that much of the success of the Urban Yogis program is predicated on these authentic and caring relationships. At the same time, Eddie himself is somewhat of a deviation from the traditional ashtanga model of an authoritative teacher figure. He approaches his work with Urban Yogis with an evident humility, tempering his role as authoritative teacher with an embedded and vocalized awareness of, and appreciation for, his students' central role in the foundation and development of the Urban Yogis program.

Mary witnessed a similar warmth and commitment among the members of the Project Air team. Project Air now uses a very modified approach to ashtanga yoga. The yoga classes emphasize the building blocks of movement that are necessary for eventual *asana* practice such as engaging muscles, learning about and following one's pulse, and practicing balance. Observing a Project Air yoga class, therefore, looks more like a combination of dance, yoga, and tai chi than traditional ashtanga yoga. Deirdre has found this to be important for yoga students who have not had prior experience with exercise or physical education of any kind and therefore benefit from a more deconstructed approach to learning. On one particular morning, the teacher training session took place in the Project Air garden, a beautiful space situated on a hillside of Kigali and filled with fragrant flowers, grass, and tall trees. The trainees were traversing the yard, practicing the movements, laughing easily at missteps and also congratulating each other for moments of physical accomplishment. Deirdre, naturally, plays a central role in all of this. She speaks easily with the women in Kinyurwanda and expresses great warmth while also focusing them on the movements and techniques. The moment was very moving and conjured the work of a number of politically minded, relationally oriented trauma clinicians who describe survival from severe violence as an act of resistance in and of itself. It is the survivor metaphorically saying, *you set out to destroy me and look at me, I survived and not only that, I am thriving.*[29] It also crystalized the central tenets of the program which, as much as yoga, emphasize long-term commitment to individuals and groups, the centrality of relationships, and fostering of community, all of which function as powerful antidotes to the effects of systematic violence.

These examples have brought us to the belief that the tools of an ashtanga yoga-based program can be built on principles of community, anti-violence, solidarity, and social justice. Furthermore, ashtanga yoga programs appear most effective when they are situated within a multi-faceted approach in which the various needs of individuals and communities are being addressed. As expected, we see considerable differences between the Urban Yogis and Project Air in this regard. In a manner similar to the Urban Yogis program, Project Air also is training teachers as an avenue for economic opportunity and compensates them for their participation in the training program. At the same time, however, the poverty for Rwanda is entrenched and the need for structural change pressing if Project Air trainees are to realize the fullest expression of their healing. Thus, programmatic differences are not unexpected and indeed are vital since effective yoga-based interventions must account for the specificities of lived experiences and develop strategies that foster useful methods of community intervention.[30] These differences notwithstanding, we see in both programs a connection between the study of yoga and broader goals for social justice and social change in areas such as employment and economic opportunity, alleviating hunger and social isolation, creating opportunities for community leadership, among others. Moreover, these programs appear to us to embed precisely what intersectional feminist and social work perspectives require: recognizing that we are all situated within intersecting systems of inequality and developing criteria against which we measure our accountability to the communities with whom we are engaged.[31]

CONCLUSION

We see in the Urban Yogis and Project Air reflections of the work of feminists and relationally oriented clinicians and scholars in the trauma field who are steeped in a long history of intentionally bringing a healing and social justice orientation to community engagement, based in an awareness of difference and collective responsibility put to work to create social change.[32] Indeed, bringing yoga into different communities—and into a variety of political, economic, and cultural contexts—carries substantial risks about which we remain keenly aware. But a mindfulness of these risks should not be used as a justification to retreat from community-engaged yoga programs. Rather, this work should be carefully approached, and should include a process whereby white Western feminist allies critically reflect on our locations within intersecting axes of privilege and oppression, deepening our understanding of the ways in which our own personal identities and experiences, as well as our structural positionalities, are implicated in the work we do.[33] Engagement with the Urban Yogi program in NYC and Project Air in Rwanda has inspired a confidence that indeed such an approach is possible. It also illustrates that "yoga service" can be undertaken with an explicit recognition of the assets and strengths that exist in communities impacted by violence, and that we can work in solidarity with such communities to promote healing, social change, and social justice.

Our experiences over the last two years have prompted a critical reflection on the foundations of these programs' apparent strengths and successes. For instance, we are now questioning whether we believe it is really the ashtanga system per se that leads to effective individual and community outcomes. Perhaps utilizing a trauma-informed lens to address individual and community violence, and then developing participatory, mutual, community-led yoga programs is more foundational for program success. Including yoga as part of an integrated program model may be particularly beneficial in terms of addressing pressing health, social, and economic needs. Moreover, we now wonder how much of the positive impact of these programs is the fact of community building in and of itself. Perhaps what we can and should work toward in some contexts is bringing people together to nurture a sense of connection and community with others. This sense of community is indeed at the center of yoga's philosophical underpinnings.[34]

We also see the local leadership model evidenced in both Urban Yogis and Project Air as central to program success. That is, both Urban Yogis and Project Air have developed a program model in which early participants/students in the program now have developed into yoga teachers and program leaders who have central responsibility for growing and steering the directions of the programs. Furthermore, specifically with the Urban Yogis, the original five students have emerged as strong community leaders who bring the transformative tools of yoga and mindfulness to their anti-violence community activism. They are committed to the transformative potential of this approach, and to an ongoing long-term process of inspiring other young people to choose alternatives to violence that center positivity and peace.

Finally, we conclude this project with a sharpened mindfulness about the critical problems many such programs face in terms of long-term funding and sustainability. Especially in the trauma-focused work, the field is increasingly captivated by brief, protocol-based interventions. And yet, our work with Urban Yogis and Project Air only strengthens our conviction that thoughtful, trauma-informed work has to be long-term by nature, able to be flexible, and respond to local needs and local leadership. While awareness of these obstacles is important, it's equally important to not let a search for funding overshadow the community-defined objectives of these programs.[35] Moving forward it is our intention to continue our involvement with these two projects, working in partnership with local community leaders to provide the support they think will be most useful. We are committed to collaborating with, but not coopting, these projects, working over the long term in a way that brings to life our feminist grounding in shared power, community accountability, and an ethic of connection and care.

NOTES

1. Given the twin focus on breath and movement in ashtanga yoga, as well as other unique features of the practice, we were curious to explore the extent to which ashtanga yoga, in particular, may foster healing and social change.

2. Bessel A. Van Der Kolk, "The Body Keeps the Score: Memory and the Evolving Psychobiology of Posttraumatic Stress," *Harvard Review of Psychiatry* 1, no. 5 (1994): 253–65; Babette Rothschild, *The Body Remembers: The Psychophysiology of Trauma and Trauma Treatment* (New York: W. W. Norton & Company, 2000).

3. Van Der Kolk, "The Body Keeps the Score," 253–65; Babette Rothschild, *The Body Remembers*.

4. This narrative-centered methodology is modeled in Frida Kerner Furman, Elizabeth A. Kelly, and Linda Williamson Nelson. *Telling Our Lives: Conversations on Solidarity and Difference* (Lanham, MD: Rowman & Littlefield Publishers, 2005) 12.

5. Shazia Omar, "The Wisdom of Pattabhi Jois—Ashtanga Yoga Master," The Daily Star, October 18, 2015.

6. Alistair Shearer and Patañjali, *The Yoga Sutras of Patanjali* (New York: Bell Tower, 2002).

7. Seven limbs: yama: ethical restraints; niyama: personal observances; *asana*: physical postures; pranayama: breathing practice; pratyahara: sense control; dharana: concentration; dhyana: meditation; and samadhi: contemplation. Jois, K. Pattabhi. *Yoga Mala: The Original Teachings of Ashtanga Yoga Master.* 2nd ed. (New York: North Point Press, 2010).

8. Jois, K. Pattabhi, *Yoga Mala*.

9. Yoga. Dictionary.com, *Collins English Dictionary—Complete & Unabridged 10th Edition*. HarperCollins Publishers. http://dictionary.reference.com/browse/yoga.

10. Tema Okun, *The Emperor Has No Clothes: Teaching about Race and Racism to People Who Don't Want to Know* (Charlotte, NC: Information Age Pub., 2010) 54.

11. Judith K. Bass, Paul A Bolton, and Laura K Murray, "Do Not Forget Culture When Studying Mental Health," *The Lancet* 370, no. 9591 (2007): 918–19.

12. Alastair Ager, "Tensions in the Psychosocial Discourse: Implications for the Planning of Interventions with War-affected Populations," *Development in Practice 7*, no. 4 (1997): 402–7.

13. Derek Summerfield, "A Critique of Seven Assumptions Behind Psychological Trauma Programmes in War-Affected Areas," *Social Science & Medicine* 48, no. 10 (1999): 1449–462.

14. Diedre Summerbell, "The Story of Project Air," http://www.project-air.org/downloads/About_Project_Air.pdf

15. Pattabhi, *Yoga Mala*.

16. Pattabhi, *Yoga Mala*.

17. Gregor Maehle, *Ashtanga Yoga Practice and Philosophy: A Comprehensive Description of the Primary Series of Ashtanga Yoga, Following the Traditional Vinyasa Count, and an Authentic Explanation of the Yoga Sutra of Patanjali* (Novato, CA: New World Library, 2007).

18. David Emerson and E. Hopper, "Trauma-Sensitive Yoga: Principles, Practices, and Research," *International Journal of Yoga Therapy* 19 (2009): 123–28; David Emerson and Elizabeth Hopper. *Overcoming Trauma Through Yoga: Reclaiming Your Body*. Berkeley, CA: North Atlantic Books, 2011; C.c. Streeter, P.l. Gerbarg, R.b. Saper, D.a. Ciraulo, and R.p. Brown. "Effects of Yoga on the Autonomic Nervous System, Gamma-aminobutyric-acid, and Allostasis in Epliepsy, Depression and Post-traumatic Stress Disorder." *Medical Hypotheses* 78, no. 5 (2012): 571–79; Becky Thompson. *Survivors on the Yoga Mat: Stories for Those Healing from Trauma* (Berkeley, CA: North Atlantic Books, 2014); Bessel A. Van Der Kolk, Laura Stone, Jennifer West, Alison Rhodes, David Emerson, Michael Suvak, and Joseph Spinazzola. "Yoga as an Adjunctive Treatment for Posttraumatic Stress Disorder: A Randomized Controlled Trial." *Original Research* 75 (2014): E1–E7.

19. Cohen, D'Adesky, and Anastos, "Women in Rwanda," 613–15. 613.

20. Susanne Schaal and Thomas Elbert, "Ten Years After the Genocide: Trauma Confrontation and Posttraumatic Stress in Rwandan Adolescents," *Journal of Traumatic Stress* 19, no. 1 (2006): 95–105. 96.

21. Cohen, D'Adesky, and Anastos, "Women in Rwanda," 613–15. 613.

22. Judith Lewis Herman, *Trauma and Recovery* (New York: Basic Books, 1992); John P. Wilson and Boris Drozdek. *Broken Spirits: The Treatment of Traumatized Asylum Seekers, Refugees, War and Torture Victims* (New York: Brunner-Routledge, 2004); De Jong, Joop T. V. M., Ivan H. Komproe, Mark Van Ommeren, Mustafa El Masri, Mesfin Araya, Noureddine Khaled, Willem Van De Put, and Daya Somasundaram. "Lifetime Events and Posttraumatic Stress Disorder in 4 Postconflict Settings." *JAMA* 286, no. 5 (2001): 555–62; Bessel Van Der Kolk, and Alexander C. McFarlane, eds., *Traumatic Stress: The Effects of Overwhelming Experience on Mind, Body, and Society* (New York: Guilford Press, 2012).

23. Maggie Zraly, and Laetitia Nyirazinyoye, "Don't Let the Suffering Make You Fade Away: An Ethnographic Study of Resilience Among Survivors of Genocide-Rape in Southern Rwanda," *Social Science & Medicine* 70, no. 10 (2010): 1656–664. 1657.

24. Metin Başoğlu, *Torture and Its Consequences: Current Treatment Approaches* (Cambridge: Cambridge University Press, 1992).

25. Tania D Mitchell, "Critical Service-Learning as Social Justice Education: A Case Study of the Citizen Scholars Program," *Equity & Excellence in Education* 40, no. 2 (2007): 101–12.

26. For more information about the Urban Yogis, see www.urbanyogis.org.

27. Eddie Stern, "Urban Yogis: Picking Up Mats, Putting Down Guns," YouTube. November 25, 2013. https://www.youtube.com/watch?v=CHJrER2roS0.

28. John P. Kretzmann and John L. McKnight, *Building Communities from the Inside Out: A Path Toward Finding and Mobilizing Community Assets* (Chicago: ACTA Publications, 1993).

29. Ignacio Martín-Baró, *Writings for a Liberation Psychology*, Adrianne Aron and Shawn Corne, eds., (Cambridge, MA: Harvard University Press, 1994); Judith Lewis

Herman. *Trauma and Recovery* (New York: Basic Books, 1992); "Caring for Torture Survivors: The Marjorie Kovler Center," in *The New Humanitarians: Inspiration, Innovations, and Blueprints for Visionarie,* edited by Chris E. Stout, by Mary Fabri, Marianne Joyce, Mary Black, and Mario González, 157–188 (Westport, CT: Praeger, 2009) 157.

30. Evelyn Nakano Glenn, "Race & Yoga Working Group," Lecture, University of California at Berkeley.

31. Beth S. Catlett and Amira Proweller, "College Students' Negotiation of Privilege in a Community-Based Violence Prevention Project," *Michigan Journal of Community Service Learning* 18, no. 1 (2011): 34–48; Okun, Tema. *The Emperor Has No Clothes.*

32. Laura Megivern, "Political, Not Partisan: Service-Learning as Social Justice Education," *The Vermont Connection* 30 (2010): 60–71. 63.

33. Patricia Hill Collins, *Black Feminist Thought Knowledge, Consciousness, and the Politics of Empowerment* (New York: Routledge, 1990); "Mapping the Margins: Intersectionality, Identity Politics, and Violence Against Women of Color," in *The Public Nature of Private Violence: The Discovery of Domestic Abuse,* edited by Martha Fineman and Roxanne Mykitiuk, by Kimberle Crenshaw, 93–118 (New York: Routledge, 1994); Tema Okun, *The Emperor Has No Clothes;* Beth Richie, *Arrested Justice Black Women, Violence, and America's Prison Nation* (New York: New York University Press, 2012).

34. Deborah Adele, *The Yamas & Niyamas Exploring Yoga's Ethical Practice* (Chicago: On-Word Bound Books, 2009), preface.

35. INCITE! Women of Color Against Violence, ed., *The Revolution Will Not Be Funded: Beyond the Non-Profit Industrial Complex* (New York: South End Press, 2009).

REFERENCES

Adele, Deborah. *The Yamas & Niyamas Exploring Yoga's Ethical Practice* (Chicago: On-Word Bound Books, 2009), preface.

Ager, Alastair. "Tensions in the Psychosocial Discourse: Implications for the Planning of Interventions with War-affected Populations." *Development in Practice* 7, no. 4 (1997): 402–7.

Başoğlu, Metin. *Torture and Its Consequences: Current Treatment Approaches* (Cambridge: Cambridge University Press, 1992).

Bass, Judith K, Paul A Bolton, and Laura K Murray. "Do Not Forget Culture When Studying Mental Health." *The Lancet* 370, no. 9591 (2007): 918–19.

"Caring for Torture Survivors: The Marjorie Kovler Center," in *The New Humanitarians: Inspiration, Innovations, and Blueprints for Visionarie.* Edited by Chris E. Stout, Mary Fabri, Marianne Joyce, Mary Black, and Mario González (Westport, CT: Praeger, 2009),157–188, 157.

Catlett, Beth S., and Amira Proweller. "College Students' Negotiation of Privilege in a Community-Based Violence Prevention Project." *Michigan Journal of Community Service Learning* 18, no. 1 (2011): 34–48.

Cohen, Mardge H., Anne-Christine D'Adesky, and Kathryn Anastos. "Women in Rwanda: Another World Is Possible." *The Journal of the American Medical Association* 294, no. 5 (2005): 613–15, 613.

Collins, Patricia. *Black Feminist Thought Knowledge, Consciousness, and the Politics of Empowerment* (New York: Routledge, 1990).

De Jong, Joop T. V. M., Ivan H. Komproe, Mark Van Ommeren, Mustafa El Masri, Mesfin Araya, Noureddine Khaled, Willem Van De Put, and Daya Somasundaram. "Lifetime Events and Posttraumatic Stress Disorder in 4 Postconflict Settings." *JAMA* 286, no. 5 (2001): 555–62.

Emerson, D., and E. Hopper. "Trauma-Sensitive Yoga: Principles, Practices, and Research." *International Journal of Yoga Therapy* 19 (2009): 123–28.

Emerson, David, and Elizabeth Hopper. *Overcoming Trauma Through Yoga: Reclaiming Your Body* (Berkeley, CA: North Atlantic Books, 2011).

Herman, Judith Lewis. *Trauma and Recovery* (New York: Basic Books, 1992).

INCITE! Women of Color Against Violence, ed., *The Revolution Will Not Be Funded: Beyond the Non-Profit Industrial Complex* (New York: South End Press, 2009).

Jois, K. Pattabhi. *Yoga Mala: The Original Teachings of Ashtanga Yoga Master.* 2nd ed. (New York: North Point Press, 2010).

Kerner Furman, Frida, Elizabeth A. Kelly, and Linda Williamson Nelson. *Telling Our Lives: Conversations on Solidarity and Difference* (Lanham, MD: Rowman & Littlefield, 2005) 12.

Kretzmann, John P, and John L McKnight. *Building Communities from the Inside Out: A Path Toward Finding and Mobilizing a Community Assets* (Chicago: ACTA Publications, 1993).

Maehle, Gregor. *Ashtanga Yoga Practice and Philosophy : A Comprehensive Description of the Primary Series of Ashtanga Yoga, Following the Traditional Vinyasa Count, and an Authentic Explanation of the Yoga Sutra of Patanjali* (Novato, CA: New World Library, 2007).

"Mapping the Margins: Intersectionality, Identity Politics, and Violence Against Women of Color," in *The Public Nature of Private Violence: The Discovery of Domestic Abuse.* Edited by Martha Fineman and Roxanne Mykitiuk, by Kimberle Crenshaw (New York: Routledge, 1994) 93–118.

Martín-Baró, Ignacio. *Writings for a Liberation Psychology.* Edited by Adrianne Aron and Shawn Corne (Cambridge, MA: Harvard University Press, 1994).

Megivern, Laura. "Political, Not Partisan: Service-Learning as Social Justice Education." *The Vermont Connection* 30 (2010): 60–71, 63.

Mitchell, Tania D. "Critical Service-Learning as Social Justice Education: A Case Study of the Citizen Scholars Program." *Equity & Excellence in Education* 40, no. 2 (2007): 101–12.

Nakano Glenn, Evelyn. "Race & Yoga Working Group." Lecture, University of California at Berkeley.

Okun, Tema. *The Emperor Has No Clothes: Teaching about Race and Racism to People Who Don't Want to Know* (Charlotte, NC: Information Age Pub., 2010) 54.

Omar, Shazia. "The Wisdom of Pattabhi Jois—Ashtanga Yoga Master." *The Daily Star,* October 18, 2015.

Richie, Beth. *Arrested Justice Black Women, Violence, and America's Prison Nation* (New York: New York University Press, 2012).

Rothschild, Babette. *The Body Remembers: The Psychophysiology of Trauma and Trauma Treatment* (New York: W. W. Norton & Company, 2000).

Schaal, Susanne, and Thomas Elbert. "Ten Years After the Genocide: Trauma Confrontation and Posttraumatic Stress in Rwandan Adolescents." *Journal of Traumatic Stress* 19, no. 1 (2006): 95–105, 96.

Shearer, Alistair, and Patañjali. *The Yoga Sutras of Patanjali* (New York: Bell Tower, 2002).

Stern, Eddie. "Urban Yogis: Picking Up Mats, Putting Down Guns." YouTube. November 25, 2013. https://www.youtube.com/watch?v=CHJrER2roS0.

Streeter, C.c., P.l. Gerbarg, R.b. Saper, D.a. Ciraulo, and R.p. Brown. "Effects of Yoga on the Autonomic Nervous System, Gamma-aminobutyric-acid, and Allostasis in Epliepsy, Depression and Post-traumatic Stress Disorder." *Medical Hypotheses* 78, no. 5 (2012): 571–79.

Summerfield, Derek. "A Critique of Seven Assumptions Behind Psychological Trauma Programmes in War-Affected Areas." *Social Science & Medicine* 48, no. 10 (1999): 1449–462.

Summerbell, Deirdre. "The story of project air." http://www.project-air.org/downloads/About_Project_Air.pdf

Thompson, Becky. *Survivors on the Yoga Mat: Stories for Those Healing from Trauma* (Berkeley, CA: North Atlantic Books, 2014).

Van Der Kolk, Bessel A., and Alexander C. McFarlane, eds., *Traumatic Stress: The Effects of Overwhelming Experience on Mind, Body, and Society* (New York: Guilford Press, 2012).

Van Der Kolk, Bessel A., Laura Stone, Jennifer West, Alison Rhodes, David Emerson, Michael Suvak, and Joseph Spinazzola. "Yoga as an Adjunctive Treatment for Post-traumatic Stress Disorder: A Randomized Controlled Trial." *Original Research* 75 (2014): E1–E7.

Van Der Kolk, Bessel A. "The Body Keeps the Score: Memory and the Evolving Psychobiology of Posttraumatic Stress." *Harvard Review of Psychiatry* 1, no. 5 (1994): 253–65.

Wilson, John P., and Boris Drozdek. *Broken Spirits: The Treatment of Traumatized Asylum Seekers, Refugees, War and Torture Victims* (New York: Brunner-Routledge, 2004).

Yoga. Dictionary.com. *Collins English Dictionary—Complete & Unabridged.* 10th ed. HarperCollins Publishers. http://dictionary.reference.com/browse/yoga.

Zraly, Maggie, and Laetitia Nyirazinyoye. "Don't Let the Suffering Make You Fade Away: An Ethnographic Study of Resilience Among Survivors of Genocide-Rape in Southern Rwanda." *Social Science & Medicine* 70, no. 10 (2010): 1656-664. 1657.

SIXTEEN

Yoga, Postfeminism, and the Future

Ariane Balizet and Whitney Myers

This essay began with a question: *Is yoga feminist?* On the surface, yoga and feminism appear to overlap significantly in aims, method, and philosophy. Mainstream Western yoga is perceived as an overwhelmingly female domain, as women tend to outnumber men in yoga classes as well as in media representation. Yoga media regularly aligns images of women with messages of individual empowerment, freedom, independence, and well-being. Meditations on yoga concepts (such as *ahimsa* or *aparigraha*) can be imported with little effort into political philosophies centered on nonviolence and social justice. Many thriving yoga methods actively seek to provide support for individuals dealing with trauma and abuse, thereby acknowledging that such abuse is a real and significant problem. Yoga pedagogy usually focuses on body awareness and acceptance as essential to physical practice, and eschews competition, appearance, or even weight loss as a motivation for yoga. Perhaps most crucially, this last point emphasizes the importance of the body to yogic pursuits, an emphasis mirrored by intersectional feminism's sustained attempts to draw attention toward gender, race, ethnicity, age, sexuality, and (dis)ability as interconnected identity categories with political significance.

At base, however, the practices and media representation(s) of mainstream Western yoga increasingly reflect a set of priorities and aims that more closely resemble postfeminist sensibilities than feminist ones. The marketing of yoga products and services—along with the spaces and communities associated with yoga—consistently remit to messages of empowerment and satisfaction through individual achievement, entrepreneurship, and consumerism. Mainstream depictions of yoga rarely acknowledge systemic or cultural barriers to personal achievement, such as sexism, racism, homophobia, or poverty. Instead, significant emphasis is placed on a specific pathway to individual advancement: physical discipline (through *asana*, meditation, and possibly eating practices) supports mental/emotional discipline, which eliminates perceived barriers to the achievement of specific, real-world goals (such as obtaining a degree, starting a new business, or traveling abroad). This pathway is bolstered on all sides by robust markets offering means of expressing and/or publicizing one's position on the road toward empowerment through seminars, retreats, health and beauty products, nutrition supplements, apparel, and a vast array of other retail goods. Core tenets of feminist thought and practice, such as collaboration and attention to fundamental systems of injustice, have no place in the mainstream rhetoric of yoga empowerment. Individual power is construed not as a function of intersectional identity but rather as the complete disavowal of all identity categories and their political ramifications.

In this way, mainstream yoga fits neatly into postfeminist discourses that praise women's strength while dismissing gender's role in shaping identity *or* culture. Postfeminism, according to Mary G. McDonald, "does not refer to the absence of feminisms, but rather to the rising number of women (and men) who now take for granted the accomplishments and goals of second-wave feminism."[1] Postfeminism begins with the assumption that the worthy objectives of feminism—gender equality, female empowerment, women's independence—have already been achieved, rendering self-described feminists out-of-touch and feminism itself obsolete. Postfeminist rhetoric maintains, for example, that increased participation by women in typically male domains (such as business, politics, or collegiate and professional sports) demonstrates the absence of barriers to women's success in all areas of public life. As McDonald illustrates in her assessment of early marketing for the Women's National Basketball Association (WNBA), the laudable achievement of these (relatively few) exceptional athletes indicates, within a postfeminist mindset, the possibilities for excellence now available to all women. Postfeminism is not necessarily predicated on women's inferiority (as is misogyny) or rightful subordination within a naturalized gendered hierarchy (as is anti-feminism or sexism). Quite to the contrary, postfeminism is most commonly identified by its alignment of women with high achievement in areas that can be quantified according to competitive financial, athletic, and political markets. Yet postfeminism also emphatically rejects collective efforts to improve the status of all women or to address issues of racial, sexual, and class privilege among women by focusing on a select few whose success may be appreciated outside any political context. For Jess Butler, this characterizes postfeminism as "incredibly ambivalent: it simultaneously rejects feminist activism in favor of feminine consumption and celebrates the success of feminism while declaring its irrelevance."[2] Postfeminist discourses are quick to assert, however, that while gender is no longer an obstacle to women's success as individuals, it remains a significant marker of their worth—that is, women's adherence to specific standards of female beauty and attractiveness remains crucial to their positions of power within public life. Postfeminism says you can be strong *and* sexy—or rather, you can be strong *if you also remain* sexy.

By celebrating exceptionally successful women as evidence that gender inequity no longer exists, postfeminism advances two troubling arguments. The first is that women's accomplishments are manifestations of individual power and are not relative to gender, class, race, sexuality, or ability. The second is that such accomplishments must be measured by financial gain or competitive success in some other elite market. Together, these arguments comprise a neoliberal worldview, into which mainstream yoga rhetoric has similarly been adopted. For Brenda Weber,

> Neoliberalism disallows systemic injustices (like racism or sexism), arguing instead that in a free market, all players compete on a level playing field and thus rise or fall strictly on the strengths of their merit and effort (or in this case, their market value).[3]

Though far from a singular, monolithic institution, mainstream yoga nevertheless reflects this logic overall by assuming individual autonomy under all circumstances. Personal success in any field—from receiving a lucrative promotion to holding a perfectly vertical handstand—is imagined as the result of hard work and discipline, having nothing to do with cultural factors such as the gender wage gap or embodied realities such as living with a disability.

This is not to say, of course, that *all* (or even most) yoga practices fulfill and sustain a postfeminist or neoliberal worldview. Our point is that feminist analysis of mainstream representations of yoga illustrates how deftly yogic concepts and practices have been incorporated into postfeminist discourse with the effect of suppressing yoga's feminist and activist potential. In the first part of this essay, we examine postfeminist rhetoric across a variety of mainstream yoga media by focusing on three interconnected yogic paradigms: the marketing of the "yoga girl," the persistence of consumerism as an extension of yoga practice, and the message that one's emotional state is directly connected to one's physical discipline and financial success (what we term "emotional neoliberalism"). By examining these paradigms in yoga-related media (including advertising, journalism, and social media platforms), we argue that while the lived experience of practicing or studying yoga may support feminist aims, cultural representations of yoga have been largely co-opted by postfeminist and neoliberal aims. In the second part of this essay, we turn our attention to ways in which contemporary yoga practices are cultivating complex and potentially feminist communities in contrast to the competitive individualism promoted by postfeminist and neoliberal rhetoric.

We explore related yogic paradigms of celebrating diverse "yoga identities" (especially through social media), pedagogical practices that value individual consent and self-worth, and the development of real-world, identity-based yoga communities and groups that occasion a richer, more active integration of yoga and feminist action. We conclude with some thoughts on how efforts such as these might be supported through the conscious application of feminist methodologies including collaboration, critical cultural (and rhetorical) analysis, and increased attention to intersectional identity.

Briefly, however, we want to provide a bit more detail about who we are as authors, as our social location(s) clearly play a role in shaping our approach to these important questions of yoga's relationship to feminism and postfeminism. We are both tenured English professors (at separate universities) in Fort Worth, Texas. We have each completed 200-hour RYT certification and have taught yoga classes at independently owned yoga studios in Fort Worth. We are both cisgender women; one of us is white, one is biracial and Latina. We are both married to men and not yet disabled. At the time of this writing, one of us is in her third trimester of pregnancy; the other gave birth only weeks ago. We both teach literature and writing classes that focus on gender, class, race, ethnicity, sexuality, (dis)ability, age, and/or social action. Finally, we both produce scholarship that is informed by feminist aims, methods, and theory. Our perspective is therefore shaped by the presence of feminism within the academy in general and the humanities in particular; our positions within the university system allow for and reward plenty of engagement with feminist theory and practice on a regular basis. It will be little surprise, then, to see that our conclusions reflect a powerful belief in the merits of academic feminism, as our methods (collaboration and critical rhetorical analysis) as well as our theoretical position (intersectional feminism) have such purchase within the interdisciplinary field of Women's and Gender Studies. Our hope is that this essay will begin a conversation that first recognizes the utility of yoga within postfeminist campaigns and then actively mobilizes yoga to advance feminism and social justice.

YOGA AND POSTFEMINISM

In "Ruminations of a Feminist Fitness Instructor," Alisa Valdés notes wryly that her title "is enough to make most people laugh: feminist aerobics instructor. Huh? It's like being a fascist poet."[4] The perceived contradiction between self-identifying as a feminist and working within a fitness industry that reveres and promises slender female bodies is one that we (the authors) poignantly recognize. In yoga, this is largely due to the way women are represented in yoga media: paradoxically, women are depicted in ways that emphasize empowerment, discipline, and independence from the mainstream—all while conforming to nearly impossible traditional standards of beauty. We see this in the ubiquitous cultural fantasy of the "yoga girl," the idealized yoga practitioner whose body, beauty, and purchasing power mark her as the epitome of yoga aspiration. The yoga girl is both a fiction of mainstream advertising and a potent marker of self-presentation through social media. In a survey of four issues of *Yoga Journal* (May–September 2015), we observed that women were consistently represented in problematic terms that yoked abstract concepts of power and freedom to material priorities of physical beauty and consumerism. Whether demonstrating a sequence of poses to build "core strength" or modeling colorful yoga pants in advertisements for Lululemon, Onzie, and Hard Tail, the yoga girl is instantly recognizable. She is young. She is very slim but noticeably toned; her most crucial physical features are her defined arms and flat abdominals. She wears little makeup but looks beautiful, calm, and poised. She is almost always white. The yoga girl can balance on her arms or one foot with ease—usually in a sublime natural landscape, such as on a mountaintop, in a meadow, or on the beach. She may be twisted into a magnificent pretzel or sitting serenely. The viewer is invited to admire her body both for its appearance and its impressive flexibility and strength—manifest either in her ability to hold a challenging *asana* or in her demonstrated peace and stillness in meditation.

What distinguishes the yoga girl from other archetypes of female beauty found in glossy magazines is the deep ambivalence she is meant to inspire: although she herself conforms to familiar standards of women's appearance, the yoga girl also represents profound physical discipline that ostensibly dismisses superficial beauty. The clothing modeled by the yoga girl is advertised primarily in terms of its performance—style, though important, is always subordinate to freedom of movement and functionality. Perhaps most crucially, women in yoga media are depicted alongside deeply contradictory messages about the connection between physical practice and appearance. The May 2015 issue of *Yoga Journal*, for example, includes a feature that focuses on the gluteus muscles from the perspectives of anatomy and *asana* practice. On the verso side of a two-page spread, the reader sees a close-up of a woman's backside in tight black pants, over which the title of the article—"Your greatest *asset* [italics in original]"—is printed in yellow.[5] On the recto side, in slightly smaller but prominent writing: "A strong, balanced backside is key for a stable and pain-free practice."[6] On one page, the sight of a firm, round rear end seems to confirm what the article's title asserts: yoga will give practitioners the sexy body (parts) preferred by mainstream beauty standards. One the facing page, the text dismisses superficial goals, focusing entirely on promoting physical strength and avoiding injury. This is the ambivalence occasioned by the yoga girl: her yoga must not be motivated by superficial concerns, but the results of her yoga must be proximate to a thin and sexy ideal. In this way, the omnipresence of the yoga girl in mainstream advertising powerfully exemplifies postfeminist rhetoric: she exhibits impressive physical discipline without losing her attractiveness. She may be admired for feats of strength because they do not challenge the gender hierarchy that prioritizes female beauty. In short, she may be strong—very strong—because she is also very sexy.

If the yoga girl is idealized through the juxtaposition of thin, beautiful models with altruistic depictions of yoga practice, she is literalized through social media, in which individuals can post pictures of themselves, viewable publicly, indexed by the hashtag "#yogagirl." We followed this hashtag using the Instagram application for several weeks in the summer and fall of 2015 and noticed several common themes in the images selected by users for this classification. Images tagged "#yogagirl" reflected a substantially more diverse group of women than was witnessed in the pages of *Yoga Journal*, as women of varied age, body size, race, ethnicity, and perceived ability embraced the "#yogagirl" identity. Some women used the forum of social media to document their progress toward a particular pose and, seemingly, welcomed their distance from an "ideal" pose or body with laughter and self-acceptance. The majority of these images and videos, however, featured slim, beautiful, and usually white cisgender women performing extremely challenging poses and sequences (the hashtag "#yogawoman" reveals similar images, but produces only a fraction of the results). Many were staged to look like an advertisement or magazine feature: women posted images of themselves meditating on the beach, holding *natarajasana* (or Dancer's Pose) before a setting sun, or performing a backbend on top of a mountain. Indeed, the line between corporate advertisement and amateur yoga practitioner is nearly imperceptible in these images for two reasons. The first is that women adopting the yoga girl persona on social media are often deliberately attempting to replicate, to one degree or another, the professional images found in mainstream yoga media. The second is that many of these self-described yoga girls are also offering their images for advertising purposes by "tagging" or linking to companies that provide yoga products—such as the manufacturer of the clothing modeled in the image or corporate "sponsors" of periodic yoga challenges. In this way, the yoga girl's purchasing power is essential to her self-presentation; she validates her presence on social media through an association with desirable goods and provides free publicity for the company that made her leggings. Yoga is thus construed as a physical, spiritual, and consumer practice.

The deep contradiction inherent in mainstream depictions of yoga—women may be strong and independent as long as they are sexy, active participants in an economy of luxury goods—comprises a discourse that fits neatly into a postfeminist worldview. Yoga represents the "level playing field" that characterizes postfeminist rhetoric; yoga's wide accessibility as an activity makes individual success a product of hard work and discipline. Compared to other physical activities—such as professional sports or dance—yoga does not come with the assumption that some individuals are born gifted or talented in this area. One woman's development of a slender body and/or ability to perform an acrobatic yoga *asana* thus serves as evidence that such achievement is available to *all* women, if they have the commitment and discipline of the yoga girl.

This discipline extends beyond the physical body, however. Mainstream depictions of yoga also promote the notion that the practice of yoga can lead to financial gain by removing mental obstacles to individual success. Put another way: the pedagogical function of yoga media argues that the realization of personal goals is a matter of proper mindset and in no way connected to cultural factors such as race, class, gender, and ability privilege. The yoga apparel manufacturer Lululemon has published a "manifesto," for example, which features dozens of brief phrases and aphorisms that are published on the company website and reproduced on the company's advertising materials (including print ads and shopping bags distributed at its retail stores). Despite the phrase in largest print—"Friends are more important than money"—the majority of the Lululemon manifesto addresses success as a material reality.[7] "Nature wants us to be mediocre because we have a greater chance to survive and reproduce," the manifesto posits. "Mediocrity is as close to the bottom as it is to the top, and will give you a lousy life."[8] The "lousy life" Lululemon challenges us to avoid is one that fails to strive for higher levels of success, implying that only those who excel are truly fulfilling their potential. Crucially, success is directly related to the individual's ability to think positively and work independently toward a goal. Aphorisms such as "Life is full of setbacks. Success is determined by how you handle setbacks" and "The conscious brain can only hold one thought at a time. Choose a positive thought" frame qualities such as positivity or resilience as manifestations of independent choice.[9] Intersectional identity categories including race, class, or physical and mental (dis)abilities have no place in this formulation. This manifesto exemplifies what we call *emotional neoliberalism*, a term meant to capture the notion that even our emotional states are subject to the notion of the "level playing field." Emotional neoliberalism asserts that negative thoughts, emotional baggage, or history of trauma or abuse can (and must) be purged by individual will; such purging unlocks higher achievement of individual consumer and entrepreneurial goals. As long as individuals *choose* positivity and ambition—and practice the discipline necessary to cultivate those choices—neither mental health issues such as depression nor cultural ills such as racism, sexism, and homophobia have the power to hold them from "success."

The deep ambivalences of postfeminist texts such as the Lululemon manifesto and #yogagirl hashtag also reflect this emotional neoliberalism.

The manifesto suggests: "Write down two personal, two business and two health goals for the next 1, 5, and 10 years. Do this four times a year. Goal setting triggers your subconscious computer."[10] This advice—the written commitment to seventy-two separate goals per year—suggests a path toward individual achievement that begins with controlling one's "subconscious computer." By accessing this aspect of the mind, the manifesto implies, an individual may work more diligently toward personal, business, and health goals. The achievement of these goals, presumably, corresponds to a successful and therefore happy life. Next to this formula, however, the manifesto declares: "The pursuit of happiness is the source of all unhappiness."[11] If you're unhappy, this text proclaims, you aren't working hard enough to discipline your body and mind toward fulfilling your highest potential. Still unhappy? You're working too hard.

We understand that readers may bristle at our discussion of corporate entities as representational of contemporary yoga. Again, we want to stress that our analysis here is pointed at rhetoric and depictions of yoga in broadly accessible mainstream venues. We do maintain, however, that the postfeminist ideology manifest in these representations of yoga have the effect of suppressing yoga's potential for social action. By rooting success in the physical and mental discipline of the individual, postfeminist portrayals of yoga invalidate the premises of intersectional feminism as well as its aims of increasing the visibility of identity categories and working against systemic forms of social injustice. Furthermore, postfeminist rhetoric suggests that any benevolent, charitable, or social action beyond one's personal practice is "outreach"—a term that separates the individual from those impacted by efforts to identify and support disadvantaged groups. This separation thus underscores the irrelevance of intersectional identity; if neither gender, race, sexuality, ability, nor age prohibits yoga practice, then yoga practitioners need not feel as though they are personally affected by those social realities. And yoga "outreach" is often—though of course not always—performed in cooperation with corporate sponsors whose financial aims are supported by the multiplatform publicity they receive through social media. In what follows, we examine contemporary yoga practices that resist (or eschew altogether) postfeminist individualism and address the core questions of self-presentation through social media, the pedagogy of yoga rhetoric, and the relevance of intersectional identity to yoga practice through the cultivation of diverse and, often, controversial communities. As we will show, sustaining yoga's feminist potential poses a fundamental challenge to the messages of individual empowerment promised by mainstream yoga media.

YOGA FEMINISMS

As the above critique suggests, mainstream Western yoga could do well to take a page out of academic feminism and its attention to intersectionality, neoliberalism, and postfeminism. This seems to be a natural fit, as yoga, academia, and feminism have always been linked together within popular culture. Based on our own experience as students and teachers at various studios in several states, academics have a tendency to frequent yoga classes; it is not at all unusual to unroll your mat next to someone also pursuing tenure or spending time as a yoga student before returning home to a large stack of papers. It would seem that, as more people familiar with feminism practice yoga, the more urgent the conversation would be regarding how yoga could move in a more feminist, equitable direction. Yet, while the significant tensions inherent within the yoga community are easily discerned simply by picking up the most recent issue of *Yoga Journal*, it is possible that the critical eye we bring into our classroom pedagogies is almost wholly absent in our yoga spaces.

In some ways, this is an intriguing phenomenon as yoga classes, mindfulness and meditation practices, and academic studies proclaiming yoga's effect on brain stimulation or related to contemplative teaching strategies are increasingly present in higher education. This ambivalence can be characterized as reluctance to critically examine yoga because we have an intimate stake in this conversation—we *want* yoga to be feminist so we can continue our yoga practice unencumbered, simply moving through *asana*, pranayama, and meditation without wondering how we might, as yogis, support the feminist project. If we bring our feminist selves into our yoga, the challenge thus becomes that instead of assuming yoga's aim (and inherent practice) is feminist, as feminist scholars, and feminist yogis/teachers, we must bring something to the table. We cannot simply pretend the tensions do not exist. So, where is the feminist potential in our community? And how might our own pedagogical and analytical expertise offer counter-narratives to some of the more troubling postfeminist trends currently typifying mainstream Western yoga? While the culture of yoga can indeed be characterized as postfeminist, it is possible to identify within mainstream yoga culture "yoga feminisms," or strategies of inquiry, critique, analysis, and action that are answering Melanie Klein's compelling challenge to "consciously direct the culture of yoga, creating something subversive, powerful, and real." [12] There *is* movement within the yoga community that offers tangible solutions to issues of perception and representation.

One of the more commonly accepted cultural "truths" we are interested in problematizing is the misrepresentation of yoga "community" frequently invoked through mainstream depictions of what Western yoga looks like. Ironically, perhaps the most easily identifiable "yoga feminism" also is found in the creative and communal space of social media. While postfeminist and neoliberal ideologies have been relatively successful in their attempts to co-opt the yoga body online, collaborative social media platforms such as Instagram, Twitter, and Tumblr simultaneously push for a redefinition of what that body looks like. Such online activity thus challenges more popular platforms where the images only serve to reinforce/re-present strikingly similar narratives of what counts as "yoga." For example, the 2015 #ilovethisbodytribe challenge asked yogis to photograph their most criticized body part, post the picture to social media, and compassionately redefine how they spoke about the photo. The resulting visual and textual conversation collected on Eat Breathe Thrive's website included gratitude for c-section scars and saddlebags, acknowledgment for breasts and bellies, and a continuous refrain of "I am enough." While at first such rhetoric might read as lip service to body-positive movements, Chelsea Roff (founder and director of the nonprofit) would argue differently; in a 2014 interview with *Yoga Journal*, Roff makes explicit the potential connections between disordered eating and "the culture of modern yoga that attract[s] and potentially exacerbate[s] individuals struggling with disordered eating and body dissatisfaction."[13] This social media challenge (and others like it) invokes a new type of community, disrupting images of perfection in particular yoga poses in favor of difference: in yoga bodies, yoga postures, and really, in what we recognize as "strong" and "sexy."

The popular Tumblr site Black Yogis is another creative online space offering alternative narratives to mainstream yoga images. Created "to encourage more black people to practice yoga," the site is used as a communal gathering space: people post photographs of their yoga practice and poses, instructors advertise classes and workshops, and others use the site to search for yogis within their local communities.[14] Underneath the polished veneer of workshop advertisements and beautifully photographed postures are rhetorical arguments, both explicit and not, regarding identity and inclusion. For example, in October 2015 a post was made requesting suggestions for a "Yoga Justice" playlist with an explicit goal of "educat[ing] others in how to teach yoga with a sensitivity to various social identities and circumstances."[15] Music was an integral part of this mission. In August 2015, a photograph of a yogi participating in the Instagram challenge #PlanksAroundtheWorld while wearing a head wrap and surrounded by African art was "liked" and shared by many followers. A few posts later, a link to a *Washington Post* article featuring a photograph of African American high school football players prepping for the season with Bikram yoga sessions generated much interest. Another well-liked post links to the Facebook site for the Urban Yoga Foundation, a New York-based nonprofit organization that brings yoga to diverse communities and schools. Even simply paying attention to the hashtags posters use to describe their photos and the html tags the site employs for searchability offer glimpses into a wider, more diverse yoga community than commonly represented in popular social media: black-owned studios, black men yoga, ebony yoga, rasta yoga, and black yoginis are popular descriptors on the site. In essence, Black Yogis argues that identity does matter and that for many, the "community" most frequently invoked as representative of yoga is flawed, both in terms of what it looks like and what it values.

The preoccupation with yoga, image, and identity evident in popular social media platforms only serves to reinforce the powerful way in which text and image shape our realities. Thus, as feminist yoga teachers, we have an increased responsibility to pay attention to how even our visual representations and the messages they convey about "who counts" create an inclusive (or divisive) space for all students. In an article entitled "Yoga Studios: Everyone's Welcome?" Andrea Macdonald characterizes the Western yoga world as an "unsafe" and "unwelcoming" place for many people. Specifically calling studios to task for the message their websites send to potential students about appearance, income, and ability, she challenges us to cultivate what we would call a more critical rhetorical awareness, considering "what . . . these photos teach potential students and community members about who belongs in the yoga world."[16] Studios have a responsibility to acknowledge Macdonald's challenge and carefully consider what their branding, marketing, website, and teaching staff visually projects as ideal—a certain body type or color, for example. Too frequently, these artifacts simply echo that which we see in mainstream media. While studios often attempt to counter such representations by using students in their promotional materials, repeatedly the students (and their stories) offer representations echoing the tenets of emotional neoliberalism found in mainstream depictions of yoga. Online testimonials tend to link students' individual achievements outside of the studio to the discipline they have cultivated on the mat. Weight loss, professional successes, personal decisions about marriage, children, and divorce—all can be attributed to the discipline of a regular yoga practice. The combined effect of such stories thus becomes, once again, a whitewashing of individual nuance in favor of a singularly defined and represented yoga body.

Many studios appear to be recognizing this perception problem, however, and actively working to offer a counter-narrative. For example, while the "Our Teachers" page on the YogaOne website (a group of five studios in Houston, Texas) presents many teachers who, on the surface, embody a recognizable "yoga girl" stereotype, it is clear that the studio embraces diversity in its teaching staff. The staff photographs vary in gender, age, race, body type, and body language (some smile or make outrageous faces while others do not, some face the camera head on or turn to the side, and arm positioning ranges from behind the back to a "Namaste"). The teachers wear clothing neither uniform in color or design nor even recognizable as yoga wear (there is even a flannel shirt and

Houston Astros hat!). As viewers move through the website, there are plenty of photographs of white, thin, flexible, serene women framed by language encouraging viewers to "transform," "inspire," and "deliver," but these images are augmented by yoga bodies of all colors and sizes. This kind of approach and implied argument about who/what matters (the irreverence of the teaching staff, the lack of uniformity among staff photos, and even the use of bright, primary colors throughout the site) has a significantly different rhetorical impact than many other studio sites. By resisting the trend of uniform "ideal" yoga bodies as authorities, the site seems to say. And, with over 350 class offerings per week, the approach seems to be working.

The existence of identity-based yoga classes represents a more explicit (and controversial) argument speaking back to the emotional neoliberalism prevalent in mainstream yoga culture. The popularity of such classes affirms that our experiences in yoga can be (and often are) directly connected to identity categories, even if the community invoked in such classes comes at the expense of a wider, and perhaps entirely fictional concept of inclusion. While Seattle yoga studio Rainier Beach Yoga was accused in 2015 of racism for offering a monthly yoga class created specifically for people of color, such classes are not entirely unusual in the yoga community. The Yoga Center of Minneapolis offers a class called "Big A#%! Yoga," designed "especially for bigger women and men who want to begin yoga but want to do it a setting where everyone is similar in size and shape."[17] Similarly, Studio 34, a yoga space in Philadelphia, Pennsylvania, holds a weekly "Queer and Trans Yoga" class. This class is the only one out of twenty-four offerings prefaced by a quotation attributed to Audre Lorde before the class description on the studio website—"Caring for myself is not self-indulgence, it is self-preservation and that is an act of political warfare"—and the description speaks to creation of a safe space for expression and representation.[18] Further examples are easily accessed on studio websites; the simple fact is that classes created for specific people who identify in a certain way are becoming increasingly more present in yoga spaces. Just consider how popular and normalized Pre/Postnatal Yoga, Yoga for Men (more commonly referred to as "Broga"), or even Yoga for Athletes classes are among studio communities.

However, when studios offer classes for identity categories that are more overtly political in nature, highly emotional responses are not uncommon. In an article addressing the vitriolic chatter the Seattle class generated, Krista Lee Hanson passionately affirms the need for such identity-specific spaces, noting that they provide a place for "students . . . to bring their full selves more honestly and vulnerably into the practice. Even if the students never say a word about their experiences in class, just knowing that other people in the room have come to heal similar wounds or celebrate similar victories gives immense power to the practice."[19] Jacoby Ballard, co-founder of the Third-Root Community Health

Center in Brooklyn, New York (a space that currently offers Family Friendly, Queer and Trans Yoga, Yoga for Abundant Bodies, and Yoga en Español) agrees, offering a similar reading of this perceived exclusivity. He suggests that "sometimes we need to just be around our own in order to heal and not face the injustice in the world. It is not about exclusion."[20] Healing, safety, and community are values familiar to those enacting feminist pedagogies in classrooms across the country. Yes, these spaces can be politically fraught and engender passionate opinions. But the tension between feminism's commitment to speaking out against fundamental systems of injustice and mainstream yoga's embracing of neoliberal ideologies cannot be ignored. While such classes might puzzle contemporary feminists because of their ties to second-wave separatism, they enact yoga feminism by asserting and insisting upon intersectionality. As feminists, we can affirm the extraordinary value of this trend in the yoga community, recognizing that identity-based classes affirm the material and lived realities of privileging one identity category (body size, race, or sexuality) over another (gender).

Beyond considering what our studios, images, and class offerings imply about yoga and community, an increased emphasis on and attention to our pedagogical, rhetorical practices as yoga teachers is an integral component of a yoga feminism. As we moved through research for this article regarding mainstream yoga's perceived exclusivity and privilege, language has been a connecting thread binding disparate topics together. Some of the focus centers upon gendered assumptions instructors make in class. Ballard, Nick Krieger, and other LGBT writers provide multiple illustrative examples of unintentional (but no less impactful) "hurtful and invisibilizing gendered language, assumptions, and jokes" related during a yoga class.[21] These teachers urge the yoga community to think more carefully about the privilege associated with gender and how teaching scripts that make assumptions about who can and cannot carry children in pregnancy, describe what something feels like in a female vs. a male body, and even cues directing men and women in different ways can be divisive to students in class who may identify in gender nonconforming ways.

A more nuanced rhetorical awareness also asks teachers to consider how small discursive shifts carry messages about teacher/student relationships. In "Engaged Pedagogy in the Feminist Classroom and Yoga Studio," Jennifer Musial's discussion of the difference between "correcting" a student's pose vs. offering an "assist" or "enhancement" is a familiar one to feminists teaching, assessing, and evaluating in academic spaces. Such a linguistic choice, Musial argues, creates a relationship between student and teacher in which the teacher affirms the student's preexisting yoga practice and knowledge while still offering her own expertise and support.[22] Thus, the student is not characterized as or made to feel "deficient" but instead becomes an active participant in his or her own learning. Similarly, in her discussion of consent-based yoga, Mac-donald advocates for what she terms "invitational language," making the argument that such language "reduces pressure and encourages an in-quisitive rather than striving attitude."[23] She uses the examples of "if you like. . ." or "when you're ready. . ." as ways teachers might approach calling a particular sequence or pose, a rhetorical move that encourages students to consider how a yoga pose feels (i.e., self-compassion) vs. how a yoga pose looks (self-criticism).[24] The yoga practice thus becomes a more inward journey and less about reaching the apex or perfection of a shape, "connect[ing] us with our bodily experience on an internal, emo-tional, and subtle level" (ultimately, on a plane of creativity) and rejecting the static "project of mimicking an externally-defined 'yoga body.'"[25] Such pedagogical approaches affirm student difference and diversity simply for what they are—differences—not as temporary challenges call-ing for correction through discipline and mental fortitude. Critical rhetor-ical analysis of the language used in yoga pedagogy thus recognizes and reaffirms intersectionality in the yoga classroom.

CONCLUSION

Is yoga feminist? As we have endeavored to show, contemporary yoga practices and their representation(s) in popular media have the capacity to reflect sharply opposed ideologies—including emotional neoliberalism and nuanced, embodied intersectionality. We can no more fully assess yoga's feminist potential than we can singularly define "yoga" in the twenty-first century (or "feminism," for that matter). What we hope this essay illustrates, however, are the diverse ways (both aligned with and opposed to feminism) yoga may be deployed to convey influential mes-sages about gender, identity, and power. If yoga practitioners want to create more feminist spaces in yoga, we must not shrink from the often-difficult work of examining beloved media, methods, and ideologies through a critical lens. The rewards of doing so, we believe, are many— and they mark the difference between the postfeminist yoga of today and yoga's feminist future.

NOTES

1. Mary G. McDonald, "The Marketing of Women's National Basketball Associa-tion and the Making of Postfeminism," *International Review for the Sociology of Sport* 35, no. 1 (2000): 36.
2. Jess Butler, "For White Girls Only? Postfeminism and the Politics of Inclusion," *Feminist Formations* 25, no. 1 (2013): 44.
3. Brenda R. Weber, "Teaching Popular Culture through Gender Studies: Feminist Pedagogy in a Postfeminist and Neoliberal Academy?" *Feminist Teacher* 20, no. 2 (2010): 127.

4. Alisa L. Valdés, "Ruminations of a Feminist Fitness Instructor," in *Listen Up: Voices from the Next Feminist Generation*, ed. Barbara Findlen, (Seattle, WA: Seal Press, 2001) 25.

5. Kate Siber, "Your Greatest *Asset*," *Yoga Journal* (May 2015): 78.

6. Siber, *Yoga Journal*, 79.

7. "The Lululemon Manifesto," Lululemon, accessed November 30, 2015, http://www.lululemon.com/about/manifesto

8. "The Lululemon Manifesto."

9. "The Lululemon Manifesto."

10. "The Lululemon Manifesto."

11. "The Lululemon Manifesto."

12. Melanie Klein, "Yoga's 21st Century Facelift and the Myth of the Perfect Ass(ana)," *Elephant Journal*, last modified November 12, 2012, http://www.elephantjournal.com/2012/11/yogas-21st-century-facelift-the-myth-of-the-perfect-assana/.

13. YJ Editor, "Uncovering Yoga's Hidden Eating Disorder Epidemic," *Yoga Journal*, October 8, 2014, http://www.yogajournal.com/food-diet/uncovering-yogas-hidden-eating-disorder-epidemic/.

14. "About," *Black Yogis*, accessed November 30, 2015, http://blackyogis.tumblr.com/.

15. Autipacha, "Yoga Justice Playlist Questionnaire," *Black Yogis*, last modified October 4, 2015, http://blackyogis.tumblr.com/post/130517099262/yoga-justice-playlist-questionnaire

16. Macdonald, "Yoga Studios: Everyone's Welcome?" *Decolonizing Yoga*, accessed November 30, 2015, http://www.decolonizingyoga.com/yoga-studios-everyones-welcome/.

17. "Big Asana," *Yoga on High*, accessed November 30, 2015, http://yogaonhigh.com/classes/specialty-classes/big-asana#sthash.AKuAkmja.dpuf.

18. "Class Descriptions," *Studio 34: Yoga, Healing, Arts*, accessed November 30, 2015, http://studio34yoga.com/yoga-movement/class-descriptions/.

19. Krista Lee Hanson, "When People of Color Say They Want Their Own Yoga, White People Should Listen," *Decolonizing Yoga*, accessed November 30, 2015, http://www.decolonizingyoga.com/when-people-of-color-say-they-want-their-own-yoga-white-people-should-listen/#sthash.lONQpioc.j3wbj1D8.dpuf.

20. Seane Corn, "Jacoby Ballard: Personal Transformation + Healing Yoga," *Yoga Journal*, March 24, 2015, http://www.yogajournal.com/article/lifestyle/jacoby-ballard-finding-transformation-healing/.

21. Nick Krieger, "Why Queer and Trans Yoga?" *Decolonizing Yoga*, accessed November 30, 2015, http://www.decolonizingyoga.com/trans-queer-yoga/.

22. Jennifer Musial, "Engaged Pedagogy in the Feminist Classroom and Yoga Studio," *Feminist Teacher* 21, no. 2 (2011): 220.

23. Macdonald, "With Your Permission: Yoga, Consent and Authentic Embodiment," *Decolonizing Yoga*, accessed November 30, 2015, http://www.decolonizingyoga.com/with-your-permission-yoga-consent-and-authentic-embodiment/#sthash.NpTalLWQ.dpuf.

24. Macdonald, "With Your Permission."

25. Carol Horton, "Yoga and Feminism: Continuing the Conversation," *Carol Horton, Ph.D: writer, educator, activist* (blog), May 5, 2014, http://carolhortonphd.com/yoga-and-feminism/.

REFERENCES

autipacha. "Yoga Justice Playlist Questionnaire." *Black Yogis*. Last modified October 4, 2015. http://blackyogis.tumblr.com/post/130517099262/yoga-justice-playlist-questionnaire

Black Yogis. "About." Accessed November 30, 2015. http://blackyogis.tumblr.com/.

Butler, Jess. "For White Girls Only? Postfeminism and the Politics of Inclusion." *Feminist Formations* 25, no. 1 (2013): 35–58.

Corn, Seane. "Jacoby Ballard: Personal Transformation + Healing Yoga." *Yoga Journal,* March 24, 2015. http://www.yogajournal.com/article/lifestyle/jacoby-ballard-finding-transformation-healing/.

Hanson, Krista Lee. "When People of Color Say They Want Their Own Yoga, White People Should Listen." *Decolonizing Yoga.* Accessed November 30, 2015. http://www.decolonizingyoga.com/when-people-of-color-say-they-want-their-own-yoga-white-people-should-listen/#sthash.lONQpioc.j3wbj1D8.dpuf.

Horton, Carol. "Yoga and Feminism: Continuing the Conversation." *Carol Horton, Ph.D: writer, educator, activist* (blog), May 5, 2014. http://carolhortonphd.com/yoga-and-feminism/.

Klein, Melanie. "Yoga's 21st Century Facelift and the Myth of the Perfect Ass(ana)." *Elephant Journal.* Last modified November 12, 2012. http://www.elephantjournal.com/2012/11/yogas-21st-century-facelift-the-myth-of-the-perfect-assana/.

Krieger, Nick. "Why Queer and Trans Yoga?" *Decolonizing Yoga.* Accessed November 30, 2015. http://www.decolonizingyoga.com/trans-queer-yoga/.

Lululemon. "The Lululemon Manifesto." Accessed November 30, 2015. http://www.lululemon.com/about/manifesto.

Macdonald, Andrea. "Yoga Studios: Everyone's Welcome?" *Decolonizing Yoga.* Accessed November 30, 2015. http://www.decolonizingyoga.com/yoga-studios-everyones-welcome/.

———. "With Your Permission: Yoga, Consent and Authentic Embodiment." *Decolonizing Yoga.* Accessed November 30, 2015. http://www.decolonizingyoga.com/with-your-permission-yoga-consent-and-authentic-embodiment/#sthash.NpTalLWQ.dpuf.

McDonald, Mary G. "The Marketing of Women's National Basketball Association and the Making of Postfeminism." *International Review for the Sociology of Sport* 35, no. 1 (2000): 35–47.

Musial, Jennifer. "Engaged Pedagogy in the Feminist Classroom and Yoga Studio." *Feminist Teacher* 21, no. 2 (2011): 2012–228.

Sibor, Kate "Your Greatest Asset," *Yoga Journal,* May 2015, 78–85.

Studio 34: Yoga, Healing, Arts. "Class Descriptions." Accessed November 30, 2015. http://studio34yoga.com/yoga-movement/class-descriptions/.

Valdés, Alisa L. "Ruminations of a Feminist Fitness Instructor," in *Listen Up: Voices from the Next Feminist Generation.* Edited by Barbara Findlen, 25-32 (Seattle, WA: Seal Press, 2001).

Weber, Brenda R. "Teaching Popular Culture through Gender Studies: Feminist Pedagogy in a Postfeminist and Neoliberal Academy?" *Feminist Teacher* 20, no. 2 (2010): 124–138.

YJ Editor. "Uncovering Yoga's Hidden Eating Disorder Epidemic." *Yoga Journal,* October 8, 2014. http://www.yogajournal.com/food-diet/uncovering-yogas-hidden-eating-disorder-epidemic/.

Yoga on High. "Big Asana." Accessed November 30, 2015. http://yogaonhigh.com/classes/specialty-classes/big-asana#sthash.AKuAkmja.dpuf.

SEVENTEEN

Queering Yoga

An Ethic of Social Justice

Jacoby Ballard and Karishma Kripalani

Much has been written on the commoditization of yoga. In the North American context, we identify a yoga studio culture as reflecting certain privileges: offering a normative, cisgender, thin, able-bodied, secular, affluent, whitewashed expression of yoga—yoga as packaged for a particular consumer. This is a product and reflection of what bell hooks calls white supremacist capitalist patriarchy. What happens, then, if you aren't this yoga studio's target audience? What is going wrong? And how can we create the conditions for safety and conversation? In recent years, we have both observed and been part of yoga activism as creative resistance in response to globalized, neoliberal power dynamics. In this chapter, we engage with yoga as a site to explore an ethic of care grounded in a queer politic of social justice. We outline the tensions within mainstream yoga spaces for this politic through a consideration of race, gender, and sexuality, and offer strategies for when harm occurs. Questions of accountability and alliance also require us to unpack the responsibility that is implicit in our approach, as we reflect upon themes of resilience and community within our social justice imperative.

SITUATING OURSELVES, LOCATING OUR EXPERIENCES

We begin by situating ourselves within the landscape of postcolonial globalized yoga, and locating our own embodied politics of affect and social justice.

Karishma is a diasporic queer South Asian cisgendered woman, a yoga practitioner, student, and facilitator. Her own family history is one of displacement from traditional homelands; at the culmination of British colonialism in India, the creation of Hindu India and Muslim Pakistan meant her Sindhi parents and grandparents were part of the refugee exodus that crossed the border. They survived the journey, but never spoke of it. Karishma grew up across continents, carrying her mother's copy of BKS Iyengar's *Light on Yoga* between bookshelves, where it mostly collected dust.

At seventeen, she took her first yoga class at a university recreation center, led by a white man with a Sanskrit name. She dropped out when it felt unsafe to be in the space when he objectified women's bodies during an *asana* exploration. Karishma has since explored several lineages and been mentored in a Himalayan tradition of hatha yoga. Trained as a sociologist, it was yoga that offered a path of integration, healing, and mental health support as she transitioned away from academia. She completed a 200-hour YTT training in India, where, out of thirty-five trainees, she was one of four brown women, and the only (self-identified) queer. Karishma has interrogated the implications of her own relationship to settler colonialism while practicing and facilitating yoga in Aotearoa New Zealand, Australia, and across Turtle Island. She currently shares yoga and embodiment practices in Toronto, Canada, where she practices attachment- and trauma-informed craniosacral therapy. With Jacoby, Karishma is part of a collective of facilitators offering social justice in yoga trainings across Turtle Island.

Jacoby grew up in the Rocky Mountains of Colorado, in a small working-to-middle-class town, a part of the world where part of the legacy of white settler colonialism is a do-it-yourself work ethic and value of independence, which he has been striving to unlearn in the interest of honoring interdependence. He was raised by a strong single mother, who despite not identifying as feminist, raised him with strong feminist values.

In middle and high school, Jacoby was bullied daily for being seen as queer. He began meditating at this time, finding refuge, focus, and strength within himself, and distance from the harmful world around him. In college he both found yoga and came out as queer, taught by a seventy-year-old woman whose presence and slow pace was challenging, soothing, ultimately compelling. Jacoby received his 200-hour training at an ashram in Atlanta where being LGBT was the norm; within that spiritual community and within the depth of yogic teachings, he came out as trans at twenty-four.

He began to realize that queer community wasn't necessarily safe for him anymore, given the politics around trans identity at the time; it was a site of harmful curiosity and judgment, which allowed him to also acknowledge how racism, ableism, and fatphobia operated within his community which he had so cherished. Iimay Ho of the organization Resource Generation said, "For queer white folks, queerness is one of the main ways they experience oppression and marginalization, and through that they are politicized and become involved,"[1] and this is certainly true for Jacoby. When he co-founded Third Root Community Health Center, a worker-owned cooperative in Brooklyn, the mission was determined to be one of empowerment, healing, and justice, which began to lead him toward a national network and sangha of such intention, analysis, and work.

Writing together, this chapter negotiates overlapping and diverging needs that relate to each of our embodied subjectivities. For both of us, our work now sits at the intersection of social justice, trauma, and healing, both within and beyond queer communities; it is at this intersection that we meet and collaborate. We write from very different identities and lived experiences, yet what brings us together is our personal and political practice of yoga and social justice as one in the same, the internal healing work of yoga a microcosm of what we work toward in the world. Karishma describes this as reflection and relationship. Jacoby describes it as love and justice. Writing together is an expression of our shared practice of justice, accountability, healing, and alliance. We share a queer politic, which we discuss in the pages that follow, of working to uproot the seeds of violence and oppression inside of ourselves as we work to uproot its manifestation and growth in the world; loving ourselves as we work toward loving the world. We approach our writing together as allyship,[2] while allowing space for "tensions, dynamics, and unresolved questions."[3] In writing together, we acknowledge the roles that our identities play in our experience of not just privilege and oppression, but the teachings of yoga and Buddhism; we also assert that regardless of our disparate identities, our shared politic is what validates and unifies our voices and truths and enables us to write together.

In this chapter, we critique the picking and choosing of practices that have produced contemporary yoga, yet we transparently note that we are both engaged in similar practices, given the complexities of receiving teachings in the ways that they are currently offered or available, and because there is not always access to a clear, nor singular, lineage.[4] Reflecting upon and engaging with our own contradictions offers an opportunity to "see the power dynamics at work in these complexities and [. . .] learn to make informed and intentional choices about what and how [we] practice."[5] Our identities impact our access to the teachings in differing ways, sometimes granted access due to privilege, sometimes denied access in various ways as a manifestation of oppression wielded against each of us.

As yoga practitioners—and accidental yoga scholars—we write and work from our experiences of the path of yoga as one of interdependence. We present our relational ethics and its potentiality as a contextual interpretation of the Yamas and Niyamas rooted in a collective ethic of care, responsibility, relationships, and social justice (see below for explanation and interpretation of the Yamas and Niyamas as practices of justice). Sometimes the racism, homophobia, misogyny, ableism, and transphobia that may be present in a space where yoga or Buddhism are offered, we remove ourselves, as we note later in this article, but in the process miss out on the teachings. Sometimes, we are able to challenge harm, exclusion, cultural appropriation, and remain in a space safely; sometimes we must do so and then leave.

QUEER POLITIC AS SOCIAL JUSTICE

"Queer" is a different identity from LGBT; they are not interchangeable. Queer is necessarily political, and not just political around issues designated "LGBT issues," but also addresses income inequality, the expansion of the prison industrial complex, the surveillance of and brutality against communities of color by police, gentrification, reproductive rights, and immigrant justice, for these issues necessarily impact queer communities and individuals. Queer became a term used by ACTUP, Outrage!, and Queer Nation in the 1980s, an identity label that not only described one's sexuality, but also pointed toward a radical anti-assimilationist politic. David Halpern writes, "Queer is by definition whatever is at odds with the normal, the legitimate, the dominant. There is nothing in particular to what it necessarily refers. It is an identity without an essence. 'Queer' then, demarcates not a positivity but a positionality vis-à-vis the normative."[6]

Further, a queer politic exposes race, gender, and sexuality as politicized tools for social control. It explicitly names and unsettles normalized white settler colonialism and its scaffolding of sex and gender. This is a politic that critiques apolitical stances and politics that gloss over asymmetrical power relationships; one that prioritizes queers of color.[7] Going beyond the identity politics of LGBT2QI, a queer politic is an unsettling; a commitment to identifying structural inequalities and an opposition to neoliberal individualism in the contemporary North American yoga space: "A decolonial queer politic is not only antinormative, but actively engages with anticolonial, critical race and Indigenous theories and geopolitical issues such as imperialism, colonialism, globalization, migration, neoliberalism, and nationalism."[8] Queer people were involved in galvanizing U.S.-Central American solidarity movements in the 1980s and 1990s, a part of anti-Apartheid boycotts, integral to the labor movement and Communist Party, informing and infusing these movements with an understanding of and advocacy for queer people and issues. In current political work, we see queer-identified people leading within immigrant justice, #BlackLivesMatter, disability justice, domestic workers rights, prison abolition, organizing young people with wealth, and within healing justice work. Queer politic is a belief in justice for all people, and an intersectional understanding of identity.

In our engagement with contemporary, globalized yoga and a decolonial queer politic, the work of Jasbir K. Puar is instructive. She writes, "Envisioning and expanding on queer diasporas as a political and academic intervention not only speaks directly to the gaps around sexuality in ethnic studies, Asian American studies, and forms of postcolonial studies; it also points gay and lesbian studies, queer studies, and even women's studies . . . toward the need to disrupt the disciplinary regimes that continually reinvent bodies of theory cohered by singular, modernist subjects."[9] Queer diasporas form this intervention within yoga as well, acknowledging how the presence and practices of yoga in the Western world is directly impacted by colonization and pointing toward the lack of a justice politic in many yoga spaces, which then creates an unwelcoming environment to those who experience injustice every day. Puar writes of envisioning, and it is a queer imaginary that we invoke, one that commits to collective responsibility to co-create justice as an intention and intervention.

The meaning of yoga has been stretched and bent to meet the needs of its multiple audiences. While some argue that yoga is Hindu and needs to be returned to its roots,[10] others claim that yoga "is a distinctly American cultural phenomenon."[11] While a retracing of the trajectory of yoga is beyond the scope of this chapter, we accept that there isn't one authentic homogenous yoga, and that there are and have been many yogas, responding to and in relationship with sociohistorical contexts.[12] We understand contemporary Modern Postural Yoga (MPY) as a new, shifting creation born of amalgamations and reinterpretations and, after Foucault, offering a technology of the self.[13] We also identify a second, counter-cultural yoga; the yoga of safe spaces, of access, of queer and trans yoga, of yoga for people of color (POCs).

Borrowing from social geography, we locate the contemporary yoga space part of a "landscape of care." As such, we include consideration of affect and see yoga as offering "practical or emotional support,"[14] which may be understood "in terms of interdependency, reciprocity and multidirectionality."[15] As a noninstitutionalizd space of care, the engaged yoga site can be a site of "hopeful and at times transformative relations that emerge within these settings."[16]

In summary, we identify a queer politic as social justice. Following bell hooks, this is about a radical co-creating of communities founded in love; "a combination of care, commitment, knowledge, responsibility, respect, and trust."[17] It is about acting with a principle of "love in action" through discomfort.[18] Much in the same way that our yoga mat is a place of practice and process, that we step off and return to, we orient to a queer politic as a point of departure and return. In this way, we engage with the complexities of the current state of yoga as "another practice for learning about diversity, critical analysis, self-reflection, and informed choices."[19]

YOGA IS SOCIAL JUSTICE, BUT OUR STUDIOS AREN'T JUST

Yoga is malleable signifier—what one person means by "yoga" is not necessarily what another understands as yoga. A contemporary social product as well as site of personal praxis, its own history of evolution in India challenges simplistic boundaries of "authenticity."[20] It is often cited that Patanjali's *Yoga Sutras* has limited description of a physical *asana* or movement practice, and the practices that are mentioned are in fact to prepare the body for a comfortable seated meditation. However it is clear that "yoga" brings together practices from many traditions, and has changed and been reinterpreted over time, place, and audience.

Depending on where you are, a North American yoga class may be a pastiche of: the physicality of the ashtanga section of Patanjali's yoga; a vendantic approach that dismisses the physical body; a secularized version of hatha (tantric) yoga's subtle anatomy and physiology;[21] and Western scientifically legitimated "evidence" that the practice offers mind-body benefits.[22] In a culture of *Eat, Pray, Love*, and spiritual shopping, we note the construction of the yoga consumer at a sociohistorical moment where yoga meets the neoliberal subject's rejection of traditional symbols of authority, such as the Church.[23] While the occasional yoga quote from the *Yoga Sutras* might be thrown in for authenticity, the emphasis is on experiential knowledge as the way to transformation, transcendence and our "Truth."[24]

There are four paths (and many sub paths) of yoga· Jnana, Bhakti, Karma, and Raja. MPY incorporates "palatable" elements of *asana*, pranayama, and some dhyana (maybe). Counter to some interpretations of yoga as a withdrawal from the world, we understand the Yamas and Niyamas of Patanjali's raja yoga as guidelines to relationships and responsibility, to ourselves and each other. The goal of these practices is personal liberation. Our commitment is to a queer politic of interdependence: as Murri academic and activist Lilla Watson suggests, "your liberation is bound up with mine." With reference to the *Yoga Sutras*, and in opposition to MPY, which focuses on postures and breath control,[25] we discuss the relational ethics offered by the first two limbs of yoga: Yamas and Niyamas. The externally oriented Yamas offer guidance on how to live in the world "in a way that serves individual and collective liberation."[26] The Niyamas advise daily practices to sustain us and keep us on our path. The Yamas involve Ahimsa (harmlessness or kindness), Satya (truth or integrity), Asteya (non-stealing, or gratitude), Aparigraha (nongreed or generosity), and Brahmacharya (respectful and wise use of sexual energies). The Niyamas involve Saucha (purification practices), Svadyaya (self-study), Tapas (discipline or raising intensity), Santosha (contentment), and Ishvara Pranidana (surrender and devotion). We believe that to practice the Yamas and Niyamas is revolutionary, anti-capitalist, anti-racist, and challenges male supremacy and white supremacy, for they create peace within the self and therefore peace within one's relationships on both a small and a broad scale. Together, they offer guidance through intentional mindfulness practices for a life of committed justice and alliance. The Yamas and Niyamas, the concepts of samskara and vidya/avidya—these are all leading us toward truth, kindness, and harmony. In this way, we can understand the practice of yoga as the practice of social justice. Yet, many of the places where we practice yoga are not just. We may observe who is and is not present at a given studio—is there an involvement and community engagement, or a sense of separateness or exclusion? It can be noticed by what kinds of teachers are selected to teach at yoga conferences or kirtan summits. The injustice is going to be present unless we are actively working against it, resisting and undermining it—because we live in an unjust society. As LA-based teacher and Off the Mat, Into the World founder Hala Khouri says "if we are not anti-racist, then we are racist."

In our return to Patanjali's Yamas and Niyamas, it is necessary to note the prevalence in some yoga communities of the idea that yoga is for every body, and every body has equal access to freedom through technologies of the self. "In this imaginary, ancient Sanskrit texts[27] are interpreted through an ethos of universal oneness. Individuals are urged to transcend false identifications that create bounded notions of self so that markers of separate identity such as gender, ethnicity, race, class, nationality and even humanity fall away and all beings are ultimately understood as one. Freedom is then achieved by dropping societal constraints on the self that are seen to cause suffering."[28] It is important to identify this as "spiritual bypassing" that further denies difference and inequality: avoiding conversation about privilege, power, and oppression by imagining it unspiritual or spiritually insignificant. Ruth Williams remarks,

> While the neoliberal rhetoric of spiritual empowerment presents itself as revolutionary in so much as it flies in the face of a traditional patriarchal vision of submissive femininity, it adopts the notion of revolution to the most depoliticized possibilities: revolution is alive and well just as long as it's a revolution from within that stays within.[29]

Dedunu Sylvia of the Buddhist Peace Fellowship notes that there is

> a focus on East Asian practices appropriated and co-opted by White America. Countless "mindfulness" books and workshops and trainings at heavy costs. Glorified retreats for White, able-bodied, thin, cis, straight, and class-privileged peoples. Images and films focused almost exclusively on the attainment of nirvana by the White man. Histories of generational attachment to colonialism, slavery, genocide, and con-

quest, all unapologetically glossed over through exotified ventures to the "third world." All I can see is Buddhist practice—particularly "mindfulness" and "loving-kindness" ideals—used to placate resistance from marginalized populations. Upheld to weaponize model minority myths of Asian passivity in contrast to Black liberation. Exercised in the service of corporate, capitalist, and militarized agendas.[30]

Though Sylvia is writing of Western Buddhism, this could also be said of many communities of yoga. Though the specifics differ, spiritual bypass is a manifestation of racism within our spiritual communities.

Robin Rollan, who runs a blog called Black Yogis says, "That upscale white woman is the image of yoga. . . . I think a lot of us see yoga as something that's not for us, because of the lack of imagery [of people of color in yoga]. It is changing, but the image of a white, affluent, thin person is still very entrenched."[31] This has the impact that colleagues that teach yoga to black communities spend a portion of their program convincing them why it's a practice for them, too. Yoga studios often have two bathrooms or locker rooms: men and women; this presents a significant barrier to gender nonconforming and transgender people who often do not feel comfortable (or are often harmed or harassed) changing or showering even in the locker room of their identified gender. Many yoga studios are located up a single or several flights of stairs, rendering the practice inaccessible for disabled students. The prices of many yoga classes is $15 to $20, which is more than some families can budget for food in a day, or they offer "work trade" where low-income students help out at the studio to receive free or reduced rate classes. But these students likely not only do not have money, they don't have time to dedicate in this way when they could be working to earn money to pay their bills.

If we are truly practicing yoga, whose root means union, united, or unity, then how can we exclude people in this way? Are we practicing ahimsa—nonviolence or kindness—if we only allow some teachers that "fit the studio's image" the opportunity to teach and grow their offering? Are we practicing aparigraha, or nongreed or noncovetousness if we are charging $5,000 for a week-long yoga retreat? Can we practice asteya if we are not examining the impact of colonization and cultural appropriation as part of our practice? If we are practicing vidya, or seeing clearly, then how can we not speak to and respond to oppression and violence in our communities and society *as* yogis, understanding interdependence such that violence "out there" is in fact violence at our own doorstep and in our own hearts?

Safety is a key aspect of accessibility. The Coalition for Safer Space offers this definition: "A safer space is a supportive, non-threatening environment that encourages open-mindedness, respect, a willingness to learn from others, as well as physical and mental safety. It is a space that is critical of the power structures that affect our everyday lives, and where power dynamics, backgrounds, and the effects of our behavior on others are prioritized."[32] To this end, we can observe alternative spaces that are set up with an explicit agenda of safety for specific marginalized communities, many of which carry legacies of trauma, which we address below. The prioritization of safety acknowledges "that human beings need to feel safe in order to learn something new. If you are not the racial or cultural majority you may not feel safe learning yoga."[33] The emergence of yoga for specific communities—such as queer and trans yoga, or yoga for POC—is one important response to the need for safety within these spaces. Yet, as relational spaces, even these are not free of power, politics, and privilege. Just because you are gay and committed to social justice doesn't mean you are not capable of (mis)appropriation.[34]

Many yoga studios and projects claim that "yoga is for everybody," but are they truly willing to do what it takes to make their space inviting to all of these different communities? Some studios provide the excuse that doing renovations to make the space accessible to disabled, fat, and trans people is too expensive, or a white-owned studio may give up on marketing to communities of color or low-income communities after "unsuccessful" attempts. We can come up with all of the excuses of why it's difficult—and yes, combating institutional and interpersonal oppression is difficult—but if we don't put in the effort to shift who benefits from yoga, who teaches yoga, who brings yoga into their own communities, with humility and effort, then we are not in our fullest expression of yoga.

WHY RACE, GENDER, SEXUALITY MATTERS IN A YOGA CLASS

A queer politic inevitably interrogates discourses of care and responsibility. As we trace the imprints of history that shape our own lived experiences, we might ask ourselves honest questions about "the ability and desire to care for each other."[35] The legacies of colonialism and its shaping of contemporary neoliberal structures and relationships are often erased in the "one love" yoga space. Ancestral trauma lives in and through the body, and somatic practices such as yoga may allow or provoke trauma to surface; when skillfully supported, these practices can also be the site of processing and integration, of healing. But, what does it look like to acknowledge the past in a way that allows a shared politic of co-creation? Raghuram notes that "forgetting or 'disremembering' the past may lead to forms of disintegration and denial that are damaging to responsible and 'care-full' agency. However, remembering the past, and even apologising for it, may be cleansing but is not in itself a simple remedy for past injustices."[36]

Karishma's experience of being a brown body in a mainstream yoga studio on colonized lands of Aotearoa New Zealand, Australia, and Turtle Island has often been one of displacement. As a student and as a teacher, unless she is at a self-identified POC space, she is almost always a minority as a South Asian body in a yoga studio. It is striking that in Toronto, a city where over 50 percent of the population is a POC, she finds herself in a sea of white faces. She is a "temporal anachronism";[37] in the production of contemporary yoga, her Indian ancestry is produced as an absence;[38] her experience is one of erasure.[39]

As a student, this means listening to mispronunciation of words such as chakras (Shahkras), even Namaste (Nah-mas-tAY), which reflects that the person speaking, perhaps the same person who owns the studio, simply does not need to learn how to pronounce it right (and they are just repeating what they've been taught). Classes may be sequenced to a backdrop of accented kirtan chanting mantras, prompting her to wonder if the people in the room know that these are intended as medicine; that specific pronunciation produces specific sound vibrations. Conversely, as a brown body with an Indian name, she is often met with assumptions about her knowledge and experience. As a diasporic South Asian woman, she is attuned to cultural appropriation as colorful accents of "indo-chic." Exotification and tokenism of objects of worship and of her own body is a part of the cost of participation in yoga studios. At times, this means that she will self-exclude to protect herself, thus missing out on teachings.

Karishma recalls that daily experiences of casual racism and micro-aggressions were the norm in Melbourne, Australia. Yoga studio experiences were similarly alienating. It was while living here that she began sharing PWYC yoga with a group of women of color volunteer staff who worked with a refugee and asylum seeker advocacy organization. The practice was open to all, but the space was dominated by brown bodies and privileged their lived experience. Mantra, mudra, pranayama, and meditation were integral parts of the practice, which wasn't sanitized for easy consumption. For the women who participated, the anti-oppressive, accessible classes created a safe and inclusive space and opportunity to come into relationship with the impact of daily violence.

Notably, white cultural supremacy and spiritual bypassing are not only expressed by white folks. Karishma describes the challenge experienced when an Indian mentor, upon being asked about the issue of Western cultural appropriation in the context of yoga, responds with the impossibility of such a thing, because yoga is universal. There are times where we will fall short of others' expectations of us, and when we will be disappointed by our assumptions of others. At these times, sangha, or engaged, critical spiritual community can offer both safety and support, a space where we can let go, and be caught. Sanghas can be a medicine of being witnessed and acknowledged, when so often, too often, we are not seen and not heard. They can be a safe and supportive opportunity to acknowledge our own privileges and learnings as we negotiate the lived realities of our commitments. For those of us who aspire to the ideals of a queer politic, of co-creating justice, we must learn to negotiate the subtleties of what this means in practice. Perhaps where we turn is to sangha and/or perhaps we turn back to our mentors to engage in uncomfortable dialogue with conflicting philosophy and its implications. A student-teacher relationship is striated with its own lines of power, and the forms that care and justice take are deeply contextual.

WHEN HARM OCCURS

Even in practicing the entirety of the Yamas and Niyamas, harm happens—that is unavoidable, and part of the condition of being human, so we are not asking for perfection, but we are surely requesting practice. Here, we are writing about the larger, entrenched, institutional forms of oppression that have created such grooves or samskaras that can be largely invisible to those who benefit. The yoga mat is a space with boundaries, opportunities, mirror, transformation, and a meeting place of negotiating responsibility "as ethical place-making."[40] Critically, it is a space that is co-created. A space of relationality and multiplicity; a site of becomings, as we move from remembering to recreating possibility.

While we aspire to an ethic of care and interdependence, we acknowledge that these terms are not neutral. Raghuram warns against the dangers of discourses of responsibility, reminding us that: "colonialism was itself justified through tales of universalism and in defence of humanism."[41] It is necessary to be vigilant of asymmetrical power relationships that ask those historically disempowered to do the work, to necessarily do more work. "Practicing decolonial allyship [. . .] also means deepening an understanding of the way colonial narratives may be embedded within 'social justice,' 'intersectional,' or 'critical literacy' discourses and practices despite their claim to do the opposite."[42] Charitable, one-sided responsibility can ultimately be disempowering; thus it is necessary for concepts of responsibility and care to be open to being determined contextually.[43] In this engagement, we can expect challenge as part of the process. We may find that "an unanticipated set of emotions and painful imperatives flow through into both responsibility and care."[44] And there are times when we will choose to prioritize the care and love that we commit to, toward ourselves and our own well-being.

Practice has informed how to interface with harm—from microaggressions to great trauma. In Buddhism, the Dharma is depicted in the image of a dove, with one wing being the wing of compassion, and one wing being the wing of wisdom. The dove cannot fly with only one of those wings; both are necessary. Wisdom is an understanding that transcends the moment—it can mean to understand the context of racism in our country in order to be truly informed on what might be happening when a black woman does not want her head rubbed by a white teacher with essential oils in savasana. It can mean understanding that disabled people cringe when they hear disability metaphors—such as "blindness" being used to describe a lack of awareness, or "crippled" being used to describe an obstacle. Wisdom involves having a broad perspective, a great level of care for every being on the planet, and deep, engaged self-awareness. Wisdom involves understanding the thoughts, language, and actions that create harmony or healing, and those that lead to harm.

For those vulnerable in a yoga classroom, wisdom can mean discernment—to discern, when a teacher says something homophobic, "Can I stay here? Is it to the benefit of my heart to leave?" Sometimes, drawing a boundary is the most compassionate thing that we can do to stop harm from happening, or to physically remove ourselves from a situation of harm. The Buddha taught two things: suffering and the end of suffering. When a trigger is present, to remove ourselves from harm in the moment while working in deep ways to heal the trigger does end suffering. Yet, sometimes, leaving the situation does not prevent the harm from festering, resentment from building, anger from rising, and ultimately leads to a greater degree of harm. And, sometimes, to stay in the moment, to feel into the difficulty, trust in ourselves and the other person, is the quickest way to resolve harm. We must make these decisions moment-by-moment: "This complex and painful interdependence, this mutuality, poses challenges for thinking about both care and responsibility."[45]

For those with more power and privilege in a situation, it can be quite powerful to stay with the difficulty as a practice of compassion, moving toward the tension. This can be when we use the wrong pronoun for a student, when we normalize a thin body in giving alignment instructions, when we don't acknowledge the pain of a specific community that is in the news as part of our work in the yoga classroom. Yogi and activist Teo Drake said at the 2014 Yoga Service Council Conference, "When you move into discomfort, it allows me to shift out of pain."

For many, yoga is a tool to help us better negotiate the acute and chronic trauma experienced in the world. Anxiety, depression, and other PTSD symptoms, both apparent and not, are present in yoga spaces. Research has shown the impact of oppression, microaggressions, and race-based stress as trauma. Yoga is, for many, part of a therapeutic landscape and a site for healing. Yet, the terrain is always, already, shaped by dynamics of power and privilege and our experiences in these spaces may be retraumatizing. Thus, social justice work is also trauma work. It is practicing presence in the face of triggers that threaten our sense of self, our emotional safety, and even our survival in a world shaped by structural inequalities and histories of violence. In the United States, around 7.7 million adults over the age of eighteen have been diagnosed with post-traumatic stress disorder.[46] Many with PTSD probably remain undiagnosed. Nearly half of incarcerated people in the United States have children; those children make up 2.3 percent of the population under the age of eighteen.[47] Almost 14 percent of high school students have considered suicide, and 7 percent have attempted and 30 percent of students are bullies or victims of bullies.[48] Nearly nine out of ten LGBT students report verbal harassment, about 25 percent report physical harassment.[49] More than half of all adults have alcoholism in their family history.[50] In 2014, 11.3 million undocumented immigrants lived in the United States who live in fear of being reported and deported daily, a reality that prevents them from seeking public services or other forms of aid.[51] One in three women and one in seven men are survivors of sexual violence, and 64 percent of transgender people.[52] Not all of these experiences are necessarily lead to trauma, for trauma is an experience that overwhelms one's experience to cope, leaving one feeling helpless, hopeless, and out of control. The above named experiences elicit one's vulnerability, which can lead to this overwhelm. Individuals with these experiences are in our yoga classrooms, and a teacher being trauma-informed allows an experience in yoga to be healing rather than triggering or traumatizing.

This reality of trauma in our communities is especially relevant for those of us looking to offer yoga to our own communities or those not often present within the yoga classroom—veterans, disabled people, fat people, trans people, low-income people, undocumented people—as the oppression of those communities are both an expression and a result of trauma. An understanding of ancestral trauma and the ways we carry that history into everyday living can inform how we offer "service yoga projects."

Given this, we may well ask ourselves: "What are the limits to responsibility and how are these worked through in different spatial arrangements? When does acting responsibly mean refusing to be responsible? It also suggests the limits to care: who benefits from delivering care? Is care necessarily good for the carer/cared? When does caring actually become an irresponsible act?"[53] Certainly, this work is not about what is easy and comfortable. The klesha of dvesa, or the affliction of aversion to discomfort,[54] is likely to arise. For this, how can we create space for mistakes? How can we support generative conversations? How can we recognize harm when we are the perpetrators?

Compassion, Buddhist teacher Noah Levine says, is "the wise response to pain."[55] We move toward the pain with tenderness and attention, whether it is our own pain or that of another being. Compassion is not condoning that harm was caused; it is the quickest means to resolve it and create healing. It is not soft or weak, it is strong, for it is much easier to hate; it is much more difficult not to harm, not to kill living beings. We might use compassion—either compassion for ourselves or compassion for the person causing harm when we feel resourced enough to do so—perhaps in the moment, but perhaps long after the moment has passed. It is never too late or too soon to apply compassion.

Last year a teacher asked Jacoby to demonstrate a handstand, which he was capable of doing. The teacher knew him, she knew that he is trans, she knows his pronoun. Yet, while he was upside down and she was describing the alignment to other students, she called Jacoby "she" many times, perhaps eighteen or nineteen, he stopped counting. As Laverne Cox says, to not use a trans person's correct pronoun is an act of violence. Jacoby felt that violence, in his vulnerable state of being upside down, wounded by each use of "she." When the teacher was finished and instructed everyone else into their own practice, Jacoby came down to the ground, feeling shame, humiliation, fear, anger. He felt heat rising in his body, he felt shaking from deep inside. Tears welled up. He sat against the wall, and came into meditation for the remainder of the class. Jacoby offered himself, again and again, phrases of compassion: "This is a moment of suffering. Suffering is a part of life. May I turn toward this pain with compassion, and allow this unwanted situation to deepen my practice and expand my heart." When practice ended, Jacoby let himself move slowly. He decided while changing into street clothes that he could speak to the teacher, but that he would not hold her guilt or regret, that he would not take care of her in that moment, for Jacoby had his own pain to hold. When he spoke to her, she understood the harm that she had caused, and she tried to explain and apologize. Jacoby told her, "I don't need to hear the how or why or what happened for you. I just need to tell you that it hurt, incredibly." And then Jacoby left. As someone socialized as female, he has been taught to care for others' feelings before his own, yet here he had been able to take care of his own suffering.

Sometimes, in the moment, it is plenty to just feel our feelings, to grieve, to rage. And as we continue to build and refine our practice, we may gather more strength and skillfulness to meet harm in the moment with compassion and clarity more of the time, acting and speaking with ahimsa and satya. Each of us then has the capacity to literally be change agents, to only pass on kindness when we are confronted by harm. Martin Luther King Jr. was someone who ascribed to ahimsa not just as a personal commitment, but as a political tactic.[56] Indeed, compassion is refusing to engage in retaliation out of a recognition that it creates further harm and separation, and demands incredible self-care and community care to be resourced enough to show up with such wisdom. Chelsea Jackson Roberts of Atlanta likens yoga to revolution, saying, "It really is when you're taking an entire practice that is hundreds of thousands of years old and using it as a tool to resist oppression, a tool to feel liberated."[57] This is the way that our practice changes the world, by not adding to the violence, but meeting harm with care, attention, and clarity, and an intention to transform the moment.

RESPONSIBILITY/ACCOUNTABILITY/ALLIANCE

Teachers are guides; they are not ever going to achieve liberation for a student—that work is that of the student's alone. Teachers point the way, hopefully, or shine light over the land that they have already traveled. A student is also a teacher's teacher, an element of the relationship is that the student also encourages or demands that the teacher grow, expand, evolve. A teacher is also human, who makes mistakes, who is a student of life, who is working toward their own liberation.

Having a teacher, or a guide, has been an essential element of many Eastern traditions, including yoga. Jacoby has been lucky enough to find two who can skillfully hold him, in his queerness, in his transness, in his activist rage and grief about the state of the world that arises again and again, and who can also point out what a student is not aware of, what is not yet within the scope of his practice, or where his wounds remain unhealed. This balance is what Jacoby looks for in a teacher, and what he strives to be as a teacher. He is slow to trust teachers, for so many have disappointed him—either right off the bat by saying something insensitive in their classrooms, or at a critical moment where he needs them to show up with courage and compassion.

It is said within Buddhist practice that the most important practice of a teacher is that of the precepts or pañca sila—to be harmless, to be honest and truthful, to not steal, to not use intoxicants, and to not harm through sexuality. And we can see, in many spiritual traditions, the harm created by spiritual teachers or religious leaders who do not engage in these practices. Pañca sila is nearly identical to the Yamas and Niyamas (with the exception of intoxicants and nongreed), and the suggestion out of the Buddhist tradition that a teacher, mentor, leader, or authority figure need follow these as a primary practice is one that prevents great harm and instills trust. These practices are common through various religions and spiritual traditions, which communicates their value to humanity.

When Jacoby asked an elder gay Buddhist teacher of color to be his teacher in 2014, the teacher wrote a long, beautiful, profound letter outlining his experience of the dharma in the West, and asking pertinent questions for Jacoby's own path. One of his reflections that Jacoby continues to hold with compassion is that "every teacher that I have ever had has disillusioned me or disappointed me at some point." Jacoby wondered if this is just part of the spiritual path in general, or if it more pertains to people whose identities are not reflected in that of their teachers—people of color, disabled people, and queer and trans people. Thus, stepping into the role of teacher is profound, vulnerable, and courageous, a willingness to confront our own edges, our own limits of understanding, and a willingness to stay open to whomever and whatever comes, all within the public eye.

As a trans yoga teacher, Jacoby feels allegiant and accountable to his own community. This means engagement with his community—showing up to events and rituals, keeping a pulse on what is happening in queer community whenever he teaches queer and trans yoga so that the class can be respite or can be resounding, depending on what is called for. It also means manifesting community values in how he teaches and the institutions that he is a part of. Jacoby feels an importance to being out as trans so that young trans people or trans people new to yoga or just trans people in his community in general can be mirrored and understand that the practice can nourish and impact their own lives. There is a pressure in being "only one of a few," for Jacoby can never represent his entire community, yet because there are so few in that role, that is indeed the expectation. Jacoby works to show up with integrity, kindness, and vulnerability, and reach out to other trans teachers or allies when he hits a roadblock.

Sparkle Thorton, a trans yoga teacher in Oakland, recounts that, "Countless times over the years, I have been in classes where I am misgendered, avoided, or where the teacher didn't seem to know what transgender means. Although this made me uncomfortable, what I got out of the class was so useful for my healing that in a twisted way, it was worth it. There are classes out there taught by queers more and more, and my mission is to make yoga easier to access than it has been for me." [58] Many people who face daily oppression find the value of the teachings, yet are harmed by the teachers of yoga, which originates from privilege and lack of training that is carried through generations of yogis. Trans teacher Teo Drake adds, "The teachings of yoga have never failed me, but the teachers certainly have." [59]

In Karishma's work, she often comes up against the limitations of identity-based politics. She is often been approached by folks looking for "a POC yoga teacher" or "a yoga teacher who is actually brown." She understands and relates to this need, for access to lineage and teachers who reflect and share lived experience. This reflects the need for safe space as mentioned above; at the same time it assumes safety based on identity. A recent client, a politicized woman from the South Asian diaspora, described learning yoga with a South Asian man, and the room being full of primarily "thin South Asian women." However, the teacher was not trauma-informed, nor did he offer variations of forms to allow for different body shapes. Consequently, this client has found greater safety in a yoga space led by a body-positive white woman.

Karishma names her first true teacher as a white man who lived his yoga. His physically demanding *asana* classes helped to balance symptoms of anxiety, and the books he would bring in to share at the end of practice guided her to what she understands as the heart of yoga. Her first meditation teacher was a white woman, a Zen monk. When Karishma traveled to India to complete fieldwork for her MA thesis, she took the opportunity to seek out an Indian yoga teacher. She found an Indian woman who led her through exercise routines, and then an Indian man leading a very strict, alignment-focused style of yoga. She learned to open practice with prayer and to explore Sirsasan with confidence. One day, while she explored Baddha konasan, he placed his hands on her knees and, without asking permission, firmly pushed both her knees to the ground; thereby causing long-term injury. Two years later, Karishma met her mentor, an Indian yogi with whom she continues to study. His hatha philosophy means that there has always been space for queerness in his community of students; however, as with the other South Asian yogini she studies with, there are also challenges in different understandings and lived experiences of race and social justice. Karishma notes that every identity-based assumption she has ever had about what type of teacher she wanted or needed has been both met and overturned.

And yet. At the first POC meditation retreat Karishma attended, Buddhist teacher Larry Yang reflected that we need these identity-based spaces because of the safety they offer us. Because so often, too often, the dominant culture means that we are invisible, unacknowledged, or harmed. We need such safe spaces to allow us to experience and engage with practice, so that we can then go into the world as it is. So that, ultimately, we can then practice in mixed spaces. The goal of these spaces is not necessarily to always stay in these spaces. It is about engagement. As someone who has navigated mixed spaces her whole life, Karishma recalls giving a mental nod to this idea, and putting it aside. At the closing of that retreat, she describes watching herself in amazement as deep sobs rocked her body, at the recognition of deep wounding. This POC-only space for practice had allowed her to be witnessed, and to witness herself. The shared solidarity and safety of this space was something she had never experienced; something that she never knew she needed.

What is needed to fulfill the role of teacher is community. Luckily, we have both found that in many other colleagues who are "the only one" in other ways, as well as dedicated allies who hold both practice and justice as significant commitments in their lives. What comes up around the vulnerability of being "one of a handful" is that we too need to be held. We need sangha. We need teachers. We need folks we can fall apart with. In ayurveda, the practitioner must be nourished and grounded within themselves if they are to work with another in a healing manner. We are each a better teacher if we are nourished and connected to community.

We must also live with our own humanity if we are to have the honor of sitting in the seat of "teacher" or "instructor" or "facilitator." We will make mistakes, we will say the wrong things, we will be unaware of some realities of people we are trying to work with. We will be humbled again and again. So the role of teacher demands self-compassion, or as Maddy Klyne offers, "a balance of vulnerability and nobility."[60]

LIMITATIONS OF 200-HOUR TRAININGS AND
AREAS FOR GROWTH

These discussions inevitably highlight the limitations of the YTT model, where two hundred hours of training qualifies someone to be a teacher of yoga. They also point to the dangers of considering the practice of yoga lightly, as exercise (with perhaps some mind-body add-on benefits of stress relief). We note the shift from a traditional gurukul model for yogic teachings in India, to an apprenticeship model, to the more recent "digestible" package of the 200-hour training (with the notable exceptions of the iyengar and ashtanga paths). At the time of writing, this does not include a nuanced or politicized understanding of Yamas and Niyamas as social justice. It does not include trauma-informed training. It does not include the development of facilitation skills that can honor as well as negotiate human difference and structural oppression.

The work of a yoga teacher can include the realms of anatomy instructor, choreographer, DJ, philosopher, therapist, spiritual guide, leadership development, social justice organizer, fundraising, business manager — quite a lot to pack into two hundred hours! The teachers of such Yoga Teacher Trainings cannot possibly include all of the philosophy, anatomy, eight spokes of practice within two hundred hours, and the business of yoga, let alone include teachings around social justice, trauma, or discussion of fat, trans, disabled bodies and how to adapt practice or the history of yoga and how that was impacted by colonization. The 200-hour model sets teachers up for potential disaster, not having the skills to do what needs doing in various situations that they will encounter. Most teachers do not necessarily have mentors once they've graduated from this 200-hour training, so there is a lack of guidance in correcting when something goes wrong or when the understanding of someone certified to teach yoga is inadequate.

In various trainings it has been said that the retreat center, the training, or the practice itself is a place to "escape from the world out there," but many of us can never "escape," for the realities "out there" are the very realities present in the yoga classroom: racism, colonialism, economic disparity, heterosexism, ableism, ageism, transphobia; these differences arise in everything from how fellow students are dressed to how the body and alignment is talked about by the teacher to the pronunciation of Sanskrit or understanding of the philosophy. If yoga is a practice of union, then isn't it implicit within that understanding that the racism in the world exists within our own hearts, the judgment based on ability, age, or gender, also is present within us? Or that the racism in the world exists because there is racism within our own individual hearts and minds? Within each of us are wholesome and unwholesome seeds, and the practice is to water that which creates harmony and healing, and not to water that which creates harm to us individually, or to anyone else.

Two hundred-hour trainings largely do not discuss trauma, yet, as we have discussed above, a vast portion of our society has undergone trauma. An understanding of the impact of trauma in childhood, the rates at which it occurs, and the impact on one's short-term and long-term health and how that intersects with addiction, incarceration, abuse makes an understanding of Yoga for 12-Step Recovery, the Lineage Project, or Trauma-Sensitive Yoga not just an area for further study, but a great necessity in becoming a skillful yoga teacher.

Furthermore, we must look at who is teaching these Yoga Teacher Trainings, and how much they cost. There is a need for established yoga teacher training to actively employ people of color as trainers, "rather than just have black people sit on their boards, and participate in workshops and retreats."[61] says Jana Long of the Black Yoga Teachers Alliance. Green Tree Yoga in south Los Angeles is offering their teacher training to their members for just $500, when it usually costs $3,500 or more, which means a greater array of people will become qualified to teach, and likely will bring their communities into the classroom or take yoga out to their own communities. Creating equality and justice within yoga involves a deep examination from the internal landscape of each of us involved (uprooting the seeds of violence within each of us), to our relationships (who is your yoga community?), how the teachings are offered and to whom, with what kind of languaging, and the institutions that offer and market yoga.

THE ROLE AND POSSIBILITIES OF ALLIANCE AND ACCOUNTABILITY AS STUDENTS AND TEACHERS OF YOGA

Yoga provides a profound opportunity to reflect on ourselves, and how we are living, if what we invest our time and money in are truly bringing us happiness, and if we are creating the compartments or separations within our own souls that we see in society. As the first line of Patanjali's *Yoga Sutras* offers, "And now begins the practice of yoga," we have the opportunity to begin again, again, and again, to continue to refine ourselves and how we contribute to the world around us. Our conscious and unconscious behavior and habitual patterns are part of this place making: "Most of us contribute to a greater or lesser degree to the production and reproduction of structural injustice precisely because we follow the accepted and expected rules and conventions of the communities in which we live. Usually we enact standard practices in a habitual way, without explicit reflection on what we are doing, having in the foreground of our consciousness and intention our immediate goals and the particular people we need to interact with to achieve them."[62]

Alliance is compassion, courage, and integrity practiced across lines of difference, where one in the more privileged position utilizes their position to the advantage of those without or with less power. Mindful engagement with the Yamas and Niyamas is a practice of allyship. The Yamas of nonviolence, truth, nonstealing, nonattachment, and modification of our energy guide us away from repeating cycles of aggression, lies, stealing, greed, and displacement of energy that pervade the world around us. The attention and reflection of the Niyamas of purity, contentment, nonattachment, discipline, devotion, and surrender guide us, in our personal behavior and thought process, away from being attached, unclear, discontent, undisciplined, and eager to control our lives and the world around us.[63]

Hip-hop yoga teacher David Jason Williams says, "When we acknowledge the differences, and that there is suffering, we are essentially practicing being present and mindful."[64] Alliance demands an understanding of the oppression of other communities outside one's own experience and leveraging one's own power to the benefit of others. This practice involves understanding the circumstances of other communities—that people are being harmed, people are dying, families are being torn apart, people are being pathologized and institutionalized, at the same time that communities also have answers to their own problems, they have incredible skills, gifts, and knowledge, they have teachings of wisdom and compassion within their own spiritual practices to benefit all of humanity. Alliance is essential for liberation, as it illuminates the shadows within ourselves and within society, and only by examining and confronting the shadow can the light break in.

Those with power need to ask themselves, how am I going to keep (queer people, fat people, people of color, disabled people) alive? Do you interrupt painful jokes about a specific community? Do you read the books, listen to the music, know the names of the leaders cherished by other communities? Do you give your time or money to organizations run by other communities? How are you willing to change your thinking, to speak and act in a way that benefits those with less power than you? Alliance is a practice that is never complete, where one will make mistakes again and again, where we will be humbled, and where our hearts will break and be put back together. Kate Johnson writes, "there is wisdom here, too, if we are willing to listen—even when we think we know what 'better' looks like, and are in a rush to get there. This Body wants to get better, I can tell. May we patiently tend to every hurt, and heal from the inside out."[65]

The practice of ahimsa and satya for straight folks is to use their position of privilege and the protection that comes with it to confront homophobia and transphobia, again and again, potently, and with love rather than shame or blame, to create more space for us in the world, and in the yoga classroom. To hold up to others that there is another way to be, a way of love for all expressions of humanity. The more straight folks do this work, the more space there is, and the less we have to exhaust ourselves fighting. The practice for white people is to learn to see racism in all of its micro and macro forms, internal and institutional, and to challenge it, use the entitlement that comes with privilege to challenge the incorrect pronunciation of Sanskrit, the lack of teachers of color in a given studio, the assumption that the yoga classroom is an escape from "the world out there." The practice for able-bodied people or thinner people is to challenge the normalizing of thin bodies and hyper-able bodies in alignment and physiology instruction, postures considered "relaxing," and in the pace of a class.

Alliance in the yoga classroom and studio can take many shapes and forms. It can be playing music that is liberating, nourishing, or comforting to other communities. It can be ensuring that teachers of various identities are given classes, lifted up, provided with leadership development. It can mean understanding and being ready to explain the meaning of Hindu gods or goddesses in the space, the words of bhajans, or the correct pronunciation of Sanskrit. It can mean only inhabiting a space that is accessible to a disabled person—whether they be blind, have chronic pain, move with crutches, or have chemical sensitivities. It can mean having gender-neutral changing rooms, or a studio providing an anti-oppression training for their entire teaching staff, so that the leaders of the space can together study practices for collective liberation. If we do not do this work, we are compliant with the injustice present in the world. If we do this work, we open ourselves toward liberation, where possibilities and relationships are revealed before us.

And, we remind ourselves that the imperative of allyship is itself not neutral. Spivak advises caution;[66] Jessica Danforth similarly asks us to be wary of imposing "good intentions" in the engagement with "consensual allyship": "solidarity and allyship are great in theory but when imposed they replicate the same oppression we're resisting."[67] White settler history reminds us of the importance of self-reflection, and of community accountability it is clear as we call into question the impacts of the best of intentions "which have allowed settlers to overlook the potentially harmful outcomes of their well-intentioned actions. These 'good intentions' can also be enacted within and across our closest relationships, as we try to 'protect' our loved ones from the violence of racist, transphobic, or homophobic systems and interactions."[68]

THE VALUE OF OUR OWN SPACE TO PRACTICE

Jacoby began teaching Yoga for All Genders in 2006 at the New York City LGBT Center. The class ran for eight years, steadily building in number and intimacy. By the end, the regulars were good friends, familiar with each others' physical capacities and spiritual journeys. What they all had in common was that they never would have entered a yoga studio to begin their practice, for they felt alienated, out of place, stared at, they weren't wearing the "right" clothes. In Yoga for All Genders, there were older gay men and women, young genderqueers, femmes, butches, trans-women who passed, transmen who did not pass. It was a beautiful cross-section of the community. When Jacoby started his own studio in Brook-lyn in 2008, they began queer and trans yoga; since then, Jacoby has taught it as a workshop and retreat all over the country.

What has occurred as a result of queer and trans yoga is beautiful-Jacoby's former students began a committed yoga practice, they started attending other classes of his, and eventually the classes of other teachers, their confidence ignited. Some queer and trans yoga students are now teachers. Queer and trans yoga is a regular weekly or monthly class in over twelve cities around the country. Now, more queer and trans people are practicing yoga, bringing yoga skills and understanding back to our own communities, and changing the mainstream yoga practice just by being there and being queer. Those leading these classes receive emails from queer folks across the country, who are inspired to practice, or see the value that yoga could bring to their lives as they encounter bullying, harassment, suicides of loved ones or suicidal thoughts themselves, ad-diction and recovery, difficulties with body image. Yoga is a tool belt among many other tool belts, and its impact in queer community is be-coming noticed.

Many times in specialized classes for specific communities (fat yoga, yoga for people of color, queer and trans yoga), a backlash we face from yogis outside of our own communities is that the space itself is "exclu-sionary" or antithetical to the teaching of yoga, as oneness and unity. In fact, a class for people of color in Seattle was discontinued in 2015 out of threat of a legal case. These classes are not the goal in and of themselves, but to teach yoga in an environment where the history and reality of harm is recognized and held. These spaces are important in the current moment to provide healing and eventually the resources necessary for integration. For those within the class, the experience is healing, and the space provides a refuge not otherwise experienced. Calia Marshall, who teaches Brown Sugar yoga for people of color in New York, says, "To have a space where you can come and have other people look like you takes some of the pressure off." She offers to those outside of a given community, "It's important to listen to people, to value them saying 'there's a need for this space' means that there's a need for this space."[69] This is the work of alliance, to vocalize and show support for any com-munity's or individual's expressed need, without judgment or personal-ization. For some people to access the teaching of yoga, they can be in an integrated space at once, for others, they need the shelter healing with and of their own community. If we want to provide access to the teach-ings, shouldn't we support the varied and creative ways that that access is attained?

CONCLUSION

Queer people are a significant component of current work being done on the connection of yoga and social justice, and are in some ways leading the movement alongside others who are directly impacted by oppression. There is a long history of coalition politics, anti-racism, and anti-capitalism within queer communities, and so we bring that history of collaboration and cooperation to yoga/justice work. Thus we see queer people engaged with and leading many of the organizations doing more prominent yoga and justice work currently: South Asian American Practitioners of Yoga in America, the Black Yoga Teacher's Conference, the Yoga and Race Conference, Fat Yoga, the Samarya Center, the Center for Transformative Change, the Yoga Service Council, Yoga International, the Yoga Service Council, Off the Mat, Into the World, the Accessible Yoga Conference. And yet, work within these organizations is imperfect, complicated, challenging, evokes or creates wounds, repeats dynamics of oppression we want to disrupt.

The Yamas and Niyamas offer a path and invitation to relationship and dialogue of the politics of possibility. We draw on the embodied ethics of the Yamas and Niyamas to invoke a queer politic of social justice that emphasizes our interconnectedness. This is no simple task. The Yamas and Niyamas are not prescriptive in their application. They require exploration and ongoing dialogue, so that we can develop shared as well as individual skillful means as we co-create spaces of practice. Through this, we approach the complexities of socially engaged yoga that calls for shared ownership, without reproducing the dynamics that allow the burden of responsibility and change to fall upon these who are already burdened. This engagement requires an acknowledgment, and further, a leveraging of privilege to support communities and individuals in our solidarity and visioning.

May we use the practices of yoga to liberate our own selves from internalized violence and value all aspects of ourselves as reflections of the divine. May we show up in alliance for all of humanity as essential to the practice of yoga. May we live into the invitation and aspiration of liberation daily, individually, and collectively.

NOTES

1. Lyons, "How This Rich Kid Plans to End Income Inequality for Everyone."
2. Hunt and Holmes, "Everyday Decolonization: Living a Decolonizing Queer Politics," 167.
3. Hunt and Holmes, "Everyday Decolonization," 167.
4. Karishma notes that her own training and mentorship in India has been in an integrative approach to yoga that intentionally weaves together the richness of various lineages of yoga teachings and philosophy.

316 *Jacoby Ballard and Karishma Kripalani*

5. Berila, *Integrating Mindfulness Into Anti-oppression Pedagogy: Social Justice in Higher Education*.
6. Halpern, *Saint Foucault: Towards a Gay Hagiography*, 62.
7. Hunt and Holmes, "Everyday Decolonization."
8. Hunt and Holmes, "Everyday Decolonization," 156–57.
9. Puar, *Queer in Asian America*.
10. Hindu American Foundation, "Yoga Beyond Asana: Hindu Thought in Practice."
11. Yoga in school not same as teaching religion, California judge rules. Marty Graham. July 1, 2013. http://www.reuters.com/article/us-usa-yoga-california-idUS-BRE96016Y20130702.
12. We include here the dynamic historical relationship between Buddhism and yoga.
13. This, in turn, has spawned multiple yoga subcultures. See "Who Owns Yoga?" Bhanu Bhatnagar.
14. Milligan and Wiles, "Landscapes of Care," 737.
15. Milligan and Wiles, "Landscapes of Care," 737.
16. Conradson 2001 cited in Milligan and Wiles, "Landscapes of Care," 748.
17. Musial, "Engaged Pedagogy in the Feminist Classroom and Yoga Studio," *Feminist Teacher* 21, no. 3 (2011): 212–28.
18. bell hooks, cited in Musial, "Engaged Pedagogy in the Feminist Classroom and Yoga Studio."
19. Berila, *Integrating Mindfulness Into Anti-oppression Pedagogy: Social Justice in Higher Education*.
20. See Singleton, "Salvation through Relaxation: Proprioceptive Therapy and its Relationship to Yoga."
21. Lalonde, "Embodying Asana in All New Places: Transformational Ethics, Yoga Tourism and Sensual Awakenings."
22. See the mainstreaming of "yoga and meditation for well being" (e.g., mbsr "validated" by Western science).
23. Lalonde, "Embodying Asana in All New Places."
24. Singleton, "Salvation through Relaxation: Proprioceptive Therapy and its Relationship to Yoga".
25. De Michelis, *A History of Modern Yoga: Patanjali and Western Esotericism*.
26. Ballard, "The Yamas and Niyamas As a Practice of Justice."
27. Singleton, "Salvation through Relaxation."
28. Lalonde, "Embodying Asana in All New Places."
29. Williams, "Eat, Pray, Love: Producing the Female Neoliberal Spiritual Subject."
30. Sylvia, "Five Responses to the Awkwardly Titled 'New Face of Buddhism.'"
31. Murphie, "Why Your Yoga Class is So White."
32. Coalition for Safer Space. "What Are, and Why Support, 'Safer Spaces'".
33. Avery, "Radical Diversity: Setting a Yoga Standard for Equality".
34. Allen Ginsberg may have chanted OM for seven hours during the 1968 Chicago riots in an effort "to calm everyone down" but his pronounciation nevertheless elicited a response from "an Indian gentleman who had passed him a note telling him his pronunciation was all wrong," (Baker, 2008: 214–15).
35. Raghuram et al., "Rethinking Responsibility and Care for a Postcolonial World," 25.
36. Raghuram et al., "Rethinking Responsibility and Care for a Postcolonial World," 12.
37. Hindess, 2007, in Raghuram et al., "Rethinking Responsibility and Care for a Postcolonial World," 19.
38. Sousa, 2003, in Raghuram et al., "Rethinking Responsibility and Care for a Postcolonial World," 19.
39. The denial of the mutual relationship between coloniser and colonised in the postcolonial context produce the global South in discourses of absence (of resources,

knowledge, etc). Sousa, 2003, in Raghuram et al., "Rethinking Responsibility and Care for a Postcolonial World," 19) identifies five moncultures responsible for this identification "monocultures of knowledge, linear time, classification, the universal/global, and the criteria of capitalist productivity and efficiency. These monocultures shape the imaginaries of both the global North and the South, so that some people and places are treated as temporal anachronisms (Hindess, 2007). This denial of coevalness (related to the discourse of linear time) has meant that the shared presence and shared relationship of the North with other places has not been acknowledged, and it is this temporality that postcolonial theory critiques most consistently" (Raghuram et al., "Rethinking Responsibility and Care for a Postcolonial World," 19).

40. Raghuram et al., "Rethinking Responsibility and Care for a Postcolonial World," 11–12.

41. Lester, 2002, in Raghuram et al., "Rethinking Responsibility and Care for a Postcolonial World," 23.

42. Hunt and Holmes, "Everyday Decolonization: Living a Decolonizing Queer Politics," 165.

43. Beasley and Bacchi, 2007, cited in Raghuram et al., "Rethinking Responsibility and Care for a Postcolonial World," 286.

44. Raghuram et al, "Rethinking Responsibility and Care for a Postcolonial World," 27

45. Raghuramet et al., "Rethinking Responsibility and Care for a Postcolonial World," 17.

46. National Institute of Mental Health, "The Numbers Count: Mental Disorders in America."

47. Glaze and Marushack, "Parents In Prison and Their Minor Children."

48. Bullying and Suicide. www.bullyingstatistics.org.

49. http://www.makebeatsnotbeatdowns.org/.

50. "Bullying Fact Sheet," accessed February 18, 2016. http://www.makebeatsnotbeatdowns.org/facts_new.html.

51. Krogstad, et al. "Five Facts About Illegal Immigration in the U.S."

52. Krogstad et al. "Five Facts About Illegal Immigration in the U.S." Pew Research Center. November 19, 2015.

53. Raghuram et al., "Rethinking Responsibility and Care for a Postcolonial World," 18.

54. Musial, "Engaged Pedagogy in the Feminist Classroom and Yoga Studio."

55. Levine, *Heart of the Revolution: The Buddha's Radical Teachings on Forgiveness, Compassion, and Kindness.*

56. In his Christmas Speech in 1967, Martin Luther King, Jr. illustrated the strength and impact of ahimsa: Somehow we must be able to stand up against our most bitter opponents and say: 'We shall match your capacity to inflict suffering by our capacity to endure suffering. We will meet your physical force with soul force. Do to us what you will and we will still love you. . . . But be assured that we'll wear you down by our capacity to suffer, and one day we will win our freedom. We will not only win freedom for ourselves; we will appeal to your heart and conscience that we will win you in the process, and our victory will be a double victory."

57. Rodulfo, "Do We Need Yoga Classes Dedicated to Women of Color?"

58. Ewan Duarte,. "Sparkle Thorton is a Trans Yogi."

59. Teo Drake, Yoga Service Council Conference talk, "Beyond Duality".

60. Madeline Klyne, Forgiveness Retreat, Insight Meditation Center.

61. Rosalie Murphy, "Why Your Yoga Class is So White."

62. Rosalie Murphy, "Why Your Yoga Class Is So White," *The Atlantic*, July 8, 2014.

63. Jacoby Ballard, "Using the Yamas and Niyamas Toward Real Peace."

64. Helen Avery, "Radical Diversity: Setting a Yoga Standard for Equality."

65. Kate Johnson, "Five Responses to the Awkwardly Titled 'New Face of Buddhism.'"

66. "I wrote 'unlearn your privilege' before I set foot in the activist sphere. You must use your privilege . . . and turn it around against itself. Indeed, you cannot unlearn your privilege, and if you keep too focussed on trying, you are engaged in a kind of narcissism. If using your privilege is feudal, within a feudality without feudalism, history has left us no other choice. Proceed with caution, develop some rage against a history that does not allow you a choice." Raghuramet et al., "Rethinking Responsibility and Care for a Postcolonial World," 18.
67. Jessica Danforth, 2011, in Hunt and Holmes, "Everyday Decolonization: Living a Decolonizing Queer Politics," 167.
68. Hunt and Holmes, "Everyday Decolonization: Living a Decolonizing Queer Politics," 167.
69. Christina Rodulfo, "Do We Need Yoga Classes Dedicated to Women of Color?"

REFERENCES

Avery, Helen. "Radical Diversity: Setting a Yoga Standard for Equality." *Wanderlust Journal* (February 2016).
Baker, Deborah. *A Blue Hand: The Beats in India* (Penguin Press, 2008).
Ballard, Jacoby. "The Yamas and Niyamas As a Practice of Justice." *Elephant Journal* (August 6, 2014).
Berila, Beth. *Integrating Mindfulness Into Anti-oppression Pedagogy: Social Justice in Higher Education* (Routledge, 2015).
Coalition for Safer Space. "What Are, and Why Support, 'Safer Spaces'".
De Michelis, Elizabeth. *A History of Modern Yoga: Patanjali and Western Esotericism* (Bloomsbury, 2004).
Drake, Teo. Yoga Service Council Conference talk, "Beyond Duality." 2014.
Duarte, Ewan. "Sparkle Thorton is a Trans Yogi." *Original Plumbing Magazine* (February 2014).
Glaze, Lauren E. and Marushack, Lauren M. "Parents In Prison and Their Minor Children." Bureau of Justice Statistics (August 2008).
Graham, Marty. "Yoga in School not Same as Teaching Religion, California Judge Rules." July 1, 2013. http://www.reuters.com/article/us-usa-yoga-california-idUS-BRE96016Y20130702.
Halpern, David. *Saint Foucault: Towards a Gay Hagiography* (Oxford University Press, 1997) 62.
Hindu American Foundation, "Yoga Beyond Asana: Hindu Thought in Practice."
Hunt, Sarah and Cindy Holmes "Everyday Decolonization: Living a Decolonizing Queer Politics" *Journal of Lesbian Studies* 19, no. 2, (2015): 154–72, doi: 10.1080/10894160.2015.970975
Johnson, Kate. "Five Responses to the Awkwardly Titled 'New Face of Buddhism.'" *Buddhist Peace Fellowship Website*. January 27, 2016.
King Jr., Martin Luther and Washington, James. *A Testament of Hope: The Essential Writing and Speeches of Martin Luther King, Jr.* (Harper One, 2003).
Klyne, Madeline. Forgiveness Retreat, Insight Meditation Center. 2014.
Krogstad, Jens Manuel and Passel, Jeffrey S. "Five Facts About Illegal Immigration in the U.S." Pew Research Center. November 19, 2015.
Lalonde, Angelique Maria Gabrielle. "Embodying Asana in All New Places: Transformational Ethics, Yoga Tourism and Sensual Awakenings." PhD dissertation, 2012.
Levine, Noah. *Heart of the Revolution: The Buddha's Radical Teachings on Forgiveness, Compassion, and Kindness* (Harper One, 2011).
Lyons, Gila. "How This Rich Kid Plans to End Income Inequality for Everyone". *Good: The Local Globalists* (September 2015).
Milligan, Christine, and Janine Wiles. "Landscapes of Care." *Progress in Human Geography* 34, no. 6 (2010): 736–54.
Murphie, Rosalie. "Why Your Yoga Class is So White." *The Atlantic* (June 8, 2014).

Musial, Jennifer. "Engaged Pedagogy in the Feminist Classroom and Yoga Studio." *Feminist Teacher* 21, no. 3. (2011): 212–28.

National Institute of Mental Health, "The Numbers Count: Mental Disorders in America."

Puar, Jasbir K. *Queer in Asian America.* Edited by David L. Eng and Alice Y. Hom. (Temple University Press, 1998).

Rabin, Roni Caryn. "Nearly 1 in 5 Women in U.S. Survey Say They Have Been Sexually Assaulted." *New York Times.* December 14, 2011.

Raghuram, P., Madge, C., Noxolo, P. "Rethinking Responsibility and Care for a Postcolonial World." *Geoforum* 40, no. 1 (2009): 5–13.

Rodulfo, Christina. "Do We Need Yoga Classes Dedicated to Women of Color?" *Elle Magazine.* October 12, 2015.

Singleton, M. "Salvation through Relaxation: Proprioceptive Therapy and its Relationship to Yoga." *Journal of Contemporary Religion* 20, no. 3 (2005): 289–304.

Spivak, Gayatri Chakravorty. *Readings* (London: Seagull, 2014).

Sylvia, Deduna. "Five Responses to the Awkwardly Titled 'New Face of Buddhism.'" *Buddhist Peace Fellowship Website.* January 27, 2016.

Williams, Ruth. "Eat, Pray, Love: Producing the Female Neoliberal Spiritual Subject." *The Journal of Popular Culture* 47, no. 3 (2014): 613–33.

Conclusion

(Un)learning Oppression through Yoga: The Way Forward

Chelsea Jackson Roberts and Melanie Klein

Despite a growing number of critical voices challenging contemporary yoga culture, as yoga continues to grow in popularity and find a central cultural position in communities across the world, capitalistic consumer culture leaves its inevitable mark. In spite of a budding backlash against this mark, yoga continues to thrive as a multi-billion dollar industry and shows no signs of slowing down. As a result of yoga's absorption into mainstream Western culture, many of the dominant cultural values, norms, characteristics, and attributes have woven their way into yoga, thereby drastically altering the nature and context of the practice as well as the culture that envelopes it.

Yoga as a practice of mindfulness is akin to feminist consciousness-raising. Feminists in the 1960s and 1970s created consciousness-raising groups as a way for women to identify and combat internalized oppression and agitate for social change. This powerful and necessary tool was inspired by the practice of "Speaking Truth to Power" in the Civil Rights Movement and reminiscent of the Old Left's focus on catalyzing workers by making them aware of their own oppression.[1] In this way, yoga, as an embodied practice that develops and heightens awareness, has the ability to heal, transform, and create change not only in individuals but in communities and the larger culture.

Unfortunately, one of the most troubling consequences of yoga's filtration through the dominant systems and structures in place is that it contributes to systems of oppression that silence many and privilege a chosen few. As a result, there is a critical need for bodies of both theory and practice that offer insight into the ways in which yoga can be used as a tool to resist oppression and offer a framework for social change that is mindful, embodied, and viable.

The intention behind this book is to contribute to and deepen the conversations focused on how yoga can be used as a tool to confront, interrogate, and resist oppression. This anthology brings to the forefront voices and perspectives that are often silenced and not considered when it comes to understanding power, privilege, and oppression. Utilizing an intersectional feminist framework, this book seeks to demonstrate not only the multiple forms of power and oppression that exist but the countless ways in which these forms of structured inequality intersect and overlap. Throughout the various sections, the authors make the intersectional nature of these power structures clear and demonstrate the complexities and contradictions that characterize contemporary yoga as it is situated in this context. This work contributes to humanizing ways of understanding[2] oppression by utilizing yoga as a framework for critiquing systems as well as resisting exclusionary practices within and across yoga communities.

Through this collection, we have opened a conversation, one that we hope continues to grow and deepen, focused on how the (un)learning of oppression takes both individual and collective effort and when partnered with research, understandings, and experiences grounded in yoga, has the potential to dismantle systems of oppression in holistic ways in which we liberate the whole self, not just the intellect. Valuing the body as a critical site that experiences both trauma and resilience, this collection illuminates the multiple ways yoga has been used as a tool to reinscribe the social injustices that pervade society and also offers evidence for how embodied empowerment can exist for those who have experienced marginalization when liberatory practices like yoga are applied.

YOGA AS A PRACTICE OF FREEDOM

The authors within this collection argue in many ways that a critical perspective of yoga is one that resists hegemony and inequality. Similar to the ways yoga awakens different parts of the physical body and aspects of the subtle body, this collection posits how our ways of knowing begin to shift into an embodied empowerment that resists marginalization and challenges stereotypes when a critical and intersectional perspective of yoga is applied.

This collection encourages a reimagining of pedagogical practices in ways that value and reclaim the body, lived experiences, and the counternarratives[3] that are often silenced by dominant and exclusionary practices. Serving as a springboard for conversations relating to mindfulness and unlearning oppression, this anthology values the body as a site that experiences myriad power dynamics while navigating the world. More specifically, the authors of this collection value the body as the site that experiences, interprets, confronts, and even resists oppression, thus, positioning and understanding the body as valuable text that can receive and convey information. Viewing the body as text acknowledges the significant role critical inner literacy[4] plays when resisting internalized oppression and how practices and theories grounded in yoga strengthen ways of knowing.

Critical literacy[5] theorists believe that literacy is a social practice and inherently political, especially when an understanding of text is used to interpret, name, and challenge oppression. As a result, pedagogies anchored in an understanding for critical inner literacy, like this anthology, argue for more expansive ways of understanding the complexities and contradictions that exist across communities and practices of yoga. Consequently, the practice of yoga can have a socially transformative impact when space is created for practitioners to be active participants and not passive consumers. Yoga is not inherently transformative, instead it can be significantly influenced by the values placed on it by dominant narratives that have the potential to reinforce systems of domination. Therefore, it is critical to approach embodied practices like yoga with an intersectional and critical lens that lends itself to liberation and freedom.

YOGA AS PRAXIS

This collection illuminates the ways in which structural, hegemonic, and ideological forms of oppression impact the lives of individuals across multiple communities. Through a feminist and intersectional lens, the authors of this collection have illustrated not just the effects of oppression, but have offered deliberate responses to and anti-oppressive examples for how yoga can be applied to real-world experiences and used as a tool for transformation. Through both theory and practice, this collection serves as a steppingstone toward learning how yoga can be used in liberatory ways during the twenty-first century.

As the multi-billion dollar industry of yoga continues to grow, so will the number of yoga studios, community outreach, and teachers. Certification courses across the globe will either resist oppression by applying lenses similar to the ones used within this collection, or reinforce deeply embedded societal oppressions by choices made in marketing, outreach, and teaching pedagogy. Looking toward yoga as praxis encourages yoga theorists, teachers, and students to think critically about the ways in which yoga is shared, especially when it comes to undergirding societal norms that are either being challenged or accepted through pedagogy. Anti-oppression theorist Paulo Freire asserts,

> The role of critical pedagogy is to lead students to recognize various tensions and enable them to deal effectively with them. Trying to deny these tensions ends up negating the very role of subjectivity. The negation of tension amounts to the illusion of overcoming these tensions when they are really just hidden.[6]

Similar to the consequences of neglected tension or injury in the physical body, ignoring and denying the pain that comes with systemic and internalized oppression does not make the discomfort disappear. In fact, it's very likely that it will deepen and spread over time. Yoga practice offers an opportunity to excavate the pain, discomfort, and stress in the body-mind.

But social oppression does not conveniently come to a halt once a practitioner enters their local yoga studio. As we've pointed out in this collection, the fact is that studios may (and often do) reinforce exclusionary spaces and further contribute to the marginalization of subordinate groups. Not only may the cost of individual classes or a studio membership bar people from access, the space itself may be unwelcoming in a variety of ways and reinforce the notion that yoga practice is reserved only for able-bodied, cisgender, white populations with the time and money to practice. Furthermore, too often those who need and may benefit from yoga the most never make it to the studio in the first place because of the "yoga body" stereotypes that proliferate not only contemporary yoga media but images representing "yoga" and "yogis" in the dominant cultural discourse. Representation matters and when the dominant impression of yoga is one involving elaborate feats of human strength and flexibility not unlike gymnastics performed by young, lithe, bendy, thin, and toned bodies in exotic locales, and perfect lighting with hair and make-up artists as well as stylists at the ready, it often becomes difficult to see oneself in the practice (not to mention intimidating and off-putting).

This book seeks to challenge these deeply entrenched and intersecting social biases and prejudices that are too often reflected in contemporary yoga culture, placing yoga in a wider context, a context that extends far beyond studio culture and reaches individuals and communities across race, class, gender identity, sexual orientation, age, and ability. This included redefining yoga above and beyond the one-dimensional stereotypes that dominate the cultural landscape. It's our hope and intention that this book will break new ground by not only engaging in a critical examination of yoga but offering these new ways of envisioning the practice and culture that has such tremendous potential in raising consciousness and prompting both individual transformation as well as social and political change.

NOTES

1. Alice Echols, *Daring to Be Bad: Radical Feminism in America 1967–1975*. (Minneapolis, MN: University of Minnesota Press, 1989).

2. Django Paris and Maisha Winn, eds, *Humanizing Research: Decolonizing Qualitative Inquiry with Youth and Communities*(Los Angeles: SAGE Publications, Inc., 2014).

3. Daniel Solórzano and Tara Yosso, "Critical Race Methodology: Counter-Storytelling as an Analytical Framework for Education Research," *Qualitative Inquiry* 8 (February 2002): 23–44.
4. Chelsea Jackson, "Developing Critical Inner Literacy: Reading the Body, the Word, and the World," PhD dissertation, Emory University, 2014.
5. Paulo Freire, *Pedagogy of the Oppressed* (New York: Herder and Herder, 1970).
6. Freire, *Pedagogy of the Oppressed*, 49.

REFERENCES

Echols, Alice. *Daring to Be Bad: Radical feminism in America 1967–1975* (Minneapolis, MN: University of Minnesota Press. 1989).

Freire, Paulo. *Pedagogy of the Oppressed* (New York: Herder and Herder, 1970).

Jackson, Chelsea. "Developing Critical Inner Literacy: Reading the Body, the Word, and the World," PhD dissertation, Emory University, 2014.

Paris, Django and Maisha Winn, eds. *Humanizing Research: Decolonizing Qualitative Inquiry with Youth and Communities*. (Los Angeles: SAGE Publications, Inc., 2014).

Solórzano, Daniel and Tara Yosso, "Critical Race Methodology: Counter-Storytelling as an Analytical Framework for Education Research," *Qualitative Inquiry* 8 (February 2002): 23–44.

Index

ableism, 31
Abry, Alexandra W., 144
Absolute Oneness (*Samadhi*), 214, 221–222
academic feminism, 280, 285
accessibility, 38, 119, 228, 247; gender and, 252; safety and, 300–301; therapeutic yoga vs., 252–253
accountability, 307–309, 311–313
activism: community and, 100; digital, 176; embodied, 14, 29–38; scholarly, 14; understandings of, 98–99; yoga culture and, 91–104
activist, sustaining, 101–103
advertisements: Aflac, 136–137; Carl's Jr., 130–132; female body controlled in, 129–132; gender binary in, 135; Hyatt Hotels, 134–136; Kerasal, 137–138; liberation and, 132; sexism in, 130–132, 132, 135; spirituality and, 130; transcendence in, 132–134, 135, 136, 137; Victoria's Secret, 132–134; yoga in, 126, 129–138, 138n1–139n2, 282; *Yoga Journal*, 138n1; yogis as corporate shills and, 137–138
affirmations, 199
afflictions of the mind (kleshas), 249, 305
Aflac, 136–137
Agniel, Marguerite, 159–160
ahimsa (nonviolence), 23, 27, 95, 198, 312; in Jainism, 229; King practicing, 306, 317n56; as *Yama*, 22, 210, 214–215
alcohol abuse, 235–236
Alferi, Anthony, 215
alienation, 37
alliance, 307–309, 311–313
Alter, Joseph S., 157

American Academy of Physical Education, 116
Anderson, Kim, 227, 238
angels, 133
anorexia, 144, 145
Aparigraha (Non-Grasping), 214, 216, 217, 300
apartheid, 102–103
appearance, experience and, 203
appropriation. *See* cultural appropriation
arthritis, 248, 249, 251
artifact, body as, 193–194, 196
asana (postures): athleticism and, 246–249; in eight limbs of yoga, 213, 218–220; emphasis on, 3; first mention of, 244; flexibility in, 252; modern, 113; sexualization of, 155–158, 162, 164–170; translation of, 95
ascetic yogis, 45–49
ashtanga yoga, 112, 247; healing from trauma through, 259–260, 260, 260–263, 263–271, 271n1; history of, 261–262; mysore method, 262, 264, 266; personal practices of, 262–263; teachers, 262, 266, 268
Asteya (Non-Stealing), 214, 223n28
athleticism, 246–249
authenticity, 71
autoethnography, 143
Avery, Bylle Y., 179
Awakened Qualities. *See Yama*
awakening, in feminist yoga, 230–231

Ballard, Jacoby, 288–289
Baptiste, Baron, 147–148
barriers: class, 42, 52, 54–58; to meditation, 55; race, 50, 52–53, 54–55, 58; to yoga, 41–58

327

About the Contributors

Ariane Balizet is associate professor of English and faculty affiliate of the women and gender studies program at Texas Christian University and a registered yoga teacher (RYT 200). She is the author of *Blood and Home in Early Modern Drama: Domestic Identity on the Renaissance Stage* (Routledge). Her research focuses on blood, bodies, and gender in the literature of the English Renaissance as well as Shakespeare and contemporary girlhood. Recent publications include articles on domesticity and violence on the Renaissance stage, representations of Jews in early modern poetry and drama, and film/TV adaptations of Shakespeare. She is currently working on a book project entitled *Shakespeare and Girl Culture*.

Jacoby Ballard, E-RYT 500, has been teaching yoga and doing justice work since 1999. In 2008, he co-founded Third Root Community Health Center in Brooklyn to connect holistic healing and social justice, and he is grateful to be part of a growing and supportive national network committed to this work. Jacoby teaches locally and nationally, find more at jacobyballard.com.

Beth Berila, PhD, 500-RYT, is director of the women's studies program and a full professor in the ethnic and women's studies department at St. Cloud State University. She is also a 500-hour registered yoga teacher and an ayurvedic yoga specialist. Her book, *Integrating Mindfulness into Anti-Oppression Pedagogy: Social Justice in Higher Education*, was published in 2015 by Routlege. She serves on the leadership team of the Yoga and Body Image Coalition. Her work focuses on gender and popular culture and on feminism, yoga, and mindfulness as embodied modes for unlearning oppression and relearning more empowering ways of being. Learn more about her work at http://www.bethberila.com.

Diana York Blaine is professor of writing and gender studies at the University of Southern California and teaches rhetoric, feminist theory, and literature. Her work focuses on representations of the body in American culture, examining the ways in which gendered and raced narratives produce normative subjectivity in the United States. She has published on the ideology of the body in William Faulkner, Thomas Pynchon, the Jon Benet Ramsey murder case, the Dr. Phil show, the Mummies of the

World Exhibit, and Michael Jackson's memorial service. Her current project examines discourses of fitness in mainstream American culture.

Mary Bunn, MA, LCSW, has extensive experience developing and delivering rehabilitative services for survivors of torture, war, human rights violations, and political violence. Previously associate director of Heartland Alliance Marjorie Kovler Center and International Programs, Mary now works as a consultant to national and international organizations with a focus on mental health programming for migrating and post-conflict communities. Her work has taken her to Iraq, Cambodia, Jordan, the DRC, and Thailand. She is an adjunct instructor in the master's program at the University of Chicago, School of Social Service Administration where she is also a doctoral student. Mary is a dedicated ashtanga yoga student, practicing the traditional mysore style for nearly ten years.

Beth S. Catlett, PhD, is associate professor and chair of the Department of Women's and Gender Studies at DePaul University. She is the cofounder and director of the Beck Research Initiative for Women, Gender, and Community which specializes in community-based programs and research involving gendered violence and social movements to create community change. Her areas of scholarly interest include community-based research, violence in intimate relationships, and the uses of contemplative practices to inspire social justice. Beth has been a dedicated practitioner of ashtanga yoga for over a decade, practicing the traditional mysore method.

Kimberly Dark is a writer, storyteller, and speaker who helps audiences discover that we are creating the world, even as it creates us. She has been invited to present her unique presentations and workshops at hundreds of universities, conferences, and other venues around the English-speaking world during the past twenty years. She lectures in a graduate program in sociological practice at California State University, San Marcos and has been teaching yoga since 1999. Learn more at www.kimberlydark.com.

Lauren Eckstrom is a 500-hour E-RYT Yoga Alliance certified instructor and meditation teacher. She leads workshops, retreats, and teacher trainings both locally and internationally. She regularly partners with licensed therapists, community leaders, and studios to help facilitate workshops and conversations that advocate yoga as a healing practice. The programs focus on topics such as reclaiming body image and making yoga inclusive for practitioners of all abilities, body types, and backgrounds. In 2012, Lauren associate produced and was heavily featured in the DVD series "The Ultimate Yogi," and, in 2015, co-authored and published *Holistic Yoga Flow: The Path of Practice*.

Jillian Ford, PhD, is associate professor of social justice at Kennesaw State University in Kennesaw, Georgia. Her teaching, research, and community involvement centers onsocial justice education, womanist studies, and decolonial studies. Her out-of-work passions include reading, yoga, utilizing snail mail, laughing, and engaging in warm-weather outdoor activities.

Thalia González is activist, writer, and associate professor and chair of the politics department at Occidental College and visiting scholar at the UCLA School of Law. She teaches and writes in the fields of civil and human rights, restorative justice, juvenile justice, race and law, and public interest and community legal practice. For more than a decade, she has integrated contemplative practices into her teaching as a critical pedagogy. Thalia is a member of the leadership team for the Yoga and Body Image Coalition and serves as lead facilitator for the "Conversation with Modern Yogis" Series.

Marcelle M. Haddix is a Dean's associate professor and chair of the reading and language arts department in the Syracuse University School of Education. Her scholarly interests center on the experiences of students of color in literacy and English teaching and teacher education and the importance of centering blackness in educational practices and spaces. She directs two literacy programs for adolescent youth: the *Writing Our Lives* project, a program geared toward supporting the writing practices of urban middle and high school students within and beyond school contexts, and the *Dark Girls* afterschool program for black middle school girls aimed at celebrating black girl literacies. Known as The ZenG, she is a 200-hour certified registered yoga instructor who specializes in yoga for underrepresented groups and for community-based organizations. She also practices veganism and healthy, soulful living.

Carol Horton, PhD, is author of *Yoga Ph.D.: Integrating the Life of the Mind and the Wisdom of the Body*, and co-editor of *21st Century Yoga: Culture, Politics, and Practice*. Currently, she is editing *Best Practices for Yoga for Veterans*, and writing a book on the Encinitas "yoga in schools" case. She serves on the board of the Yoga Service Council, and teaches yoga at Chaturanga Holistic Fitness and the Gary Comer Youth Center in Chicago. An ex-political science professor, Carol holds a doctorate from the University of Chicago and is author of *Race and the Making of American Liberalism*. Learn more at http://carolhortonphd.com.

Chelsea Jackson Roberts, PhD, is educator, activist, and founder of Yoga, Literature, and Art Camp for Teen Girls at Spelman College Museum of Fine Art. Her activism and research are grounded firmly in understanding communities that practice yoga and the ways in which embodied practices are used to understand trauma and participate in healing and resistance. Chelsea's ethnographic research and community work are sustained by the Atlanta-based nonprofit, Red Clay Yoga (redclayyoga.org) and Chelsea serves as a community partner to the Yoga and Body Image Coalition and contributor to *Yoga and Body Image: 25 Personal Stories About Beauty, Bravery, and Loving Your Body*. Chelsea is also the founder and facilitator of chelsealovesyoga.com, a blog focused on sharing the lived experiences of yoga practitioners across multiple communities.

Kerrie Kauer received her PhD in sport studies with a concentration in women's studies at the University of Tennessee, Knoxville in 2007. Her research, teaching, and activism focus on issues of gender inequality, social justice, and antioppression embodiment. She is also a 200 RYT and completed the Leadership Intensive with Off The Mat, Into the World in 2010 and was part of OTM's Global Seva Challenge–India in 2012. You can also find her teaching yoga at various studios and groups in the Pittsburgh area.

Roopa Kaushik-Brown is in the justice and social inquiry PhD program at the School of Social Transformation (ASU). Her research areas include critical race theory, and racial mobilities in law, hip hop, and the contemplative practices, specifically yoga. Birth and reproductive justice matters are central to Roopa, who is a mother, an experienced doula, and a certified prenatal yoga instructor. In 2013, Roopa launched SAAPYA, South Asian Arts and Perspectives on Yoga and America. She has a JD from UC Berkeley School of Law (Boalt Hall), and a Master's in cinema studies from Tisch School of the Arts (NYU).

Melanie Klein, MA, is professor of sociology and women's studies. She is committed to communal collaboration, raising consciousness, media literacy education, and promoting positive body relationships. She is the co-editor of *Yoga and Body Image: 25 Personal Stories About Beauty, Bravery and Loving Your Body* (Llewellyn, 2014) with Anna Guest-Jelley, a contributor in *21st Century Yoga: Culture, Politics and Practice* (Horton & Harvey, 2012), is featured in *Conversations with Modern Yogis* (Shroff, 2014), and a featured writer in Llewellyn's *Complete Book of Mindful Living* (Llwellyn, 2016). Klein is the co-founder of the Yoga and Body Image Coalition, the Los Angeles chapter lead for Women, Action & the Media and actively works with Global Girl Media and Proud2Bme.

Karishma Kripalani, MA., RCST®, is a trauma-informed craniosacral therapist and yoga facilitator. Drawing on a background in public health research and ongoing study in the field of early childhood attachment,

Karishma works to empower folks to both self-regulate and co-regulate through embodiment and somatic practices. She has offered yoga in various communities; working with queer youth, teenage mothers, children, elders, and those with chronic pain and anxiety.

Punam Mehta is a feminist yoga teacher completing her doctorate on "The Meaning of Feminist Yoga for Indigenous Mothers using Substances during Pregnancy." She has worked for the past fifteen years with First Nations and Metis communities in her home province of Manitoba. Punam is also an instructor in the Department of Women's and Gender Studies at the University of Manitoba where she designed and teaches a course on "Feminist Approaches to Addictions."

Steffany Moonaz is associate academic director of integrative health sciences and chair of the institutional review board at the Maryland University of Integrative Health. Her scholarship focuses on the evaluation of yoga interventions for individuals living with rheumatic disease. She earned her PhD from the Johns Hopkins Bloomberg School of Public Health.

Jennifer Musial is assistant professor in the women's and gender studies program at New Jersey City University. Dr. Musial is working on her monograph *Pregnant Pause: Reproduction, Death, and Media Culture*, which looks at racialized grievability in cases of fatal violence against pregnant women. Certified as a yoga teacher in 2010, she has taught in studios, prisons, jails, and drop-in spaces. She is deepening her interest in trauma-informed, antioppressive yoga teaching.

Whitney Myers is associate professor of English at Texas Wesleyan University and a registered yoga teacher (RYT 200). Her research focuses on mindfulness, pedagogy, and the writing classroom as well as rhetorical histories in off-reservation boarding schools. Recent publications include "In, Through, and About the Archive: What Digitization (Dis)Allows," a co-authored chapter appearing in *Rhetoric and the Digital Humanities* (University of Chicago) and "Raise Your Right Arm/And Pull on your Tongue!": Reading Silence(s) at the Albuquerque Indian School" in *Histories of High School and Normal School Writing Instruction, 1839-1969* (forthcoming; Southern Illinois University Press).

Enoch H. Page is a researcher and published anthropologist who earned his BA and MA from Washington University in St Louis, Missouri and his PhD from Northwestern University in Evanston, Illinois. He recently retired from the University of Massachusetts–Amherst where he taught for twenty years as a tenured faculty member of the Department of Anthropology. His interests include the anthropology of colonial and postcolonial racial formations in the African diaspora, urban anthropology, and the anthropology of consciousness. In addition to his current research on consensual silences in the climate change discourse, he also enjoys writing, reading, editing, gardening, and volunteering.

Sarah Schrank is professor of history at California State University, Long Beach. She received her PhD from the University of California, San Diego and has held research fellowships from the Haynes Foundation, The Huntington Library, Princeton University, and The Wolfsonian. She is the author of *Art and the City: Civic Imagination and Cultural Authority in Los Angeles*, as well as numerous essays and articles on public art, urban history, and American body culture. She has two forthcoming books, *Free and Natural: Naked Living and the American Cult of the Body*, and *Healing Spaces, Modern Architecture and the Body*, a co-edited collection.

Maria Velazquez recently completed her dissertation on black women, wellness, and online community at University of Maryland, College Park. She is presently the Griot Institute's Postdoctoral Fellow in Africana Studies at Bucknell University.